CW01668769

How to access your on-line resources

Kaplan Financial students will have a MyKaplan account and these extra resources will be available to you online. You do not need to register again, as this process was completed when you enrolled. If you are having problems accessing online materials, please ask your course administrator.

If you are not studying with Kaplan and did not purchase your book via a Kaplan website, to unlock your extra online resources please go to www.en-gage.co.uk (even if you have set up an account and registered books previously). You will then need to enter the ISBN number (on the title page and back cover) and the unique pass key number contained in the scratch panel below to gain access.

You will also be required to enter additional information during this process to set up or confirm your account details.

If you purchased through the Kaplan Publishing website you will automatically receive an e-mail invitation to register your details and gain access to your content. If you do not receive the e-mail or book content, please contact Kaplan Publishing.

Your code and information

This code can only be used once for the registration of one book online. This registration and your online content will expire when the final sittings for the examinations covered by this book have taken place. Please allow one hour from the time you submit your book details for us to process your request.

Please scratch the film to access your unique code.

Please be aware that this code is case-sensitive and you will need to include the dashes within the passcode, but not when entering the ISBN.

KAPLAN PUBLISHING

CIMA

Subject BA3

Fundamentals of Financial Accounting

Study Text

CIMA Certificate in Business Accounting

Published by: Kaplan Publishing UK

Unit 2 The Business Centre, Molly Millars Lane, Wokingham, Berkshire. RG41 2QZ

Notice

The text in this material and any others made available by any Kaplan Group company does not amount to advice on a particular matter and should not be taken as such. No reliance should be placed on the content as the basis for any investment or other decision or in connection with any advice given to third parties. Please consult your appropriate professional adviser as necessary. Kaplan Publishing Limited, all other Kaplan group companies, the International Accounting Standards Board, and the IFRS Foundation expressly disclaim all liability to any person in respect of any losses or other claims, whether direct, indirect, incidental, consequential or otherwise arising in relation to the use of such materials. Printed and bound in Great Britain.

Kaplan is not responsible for the content of external websites. The inclusion of a link to a third party website in the text should not be taken as an endorsement.

Kaplan Publishing's learning materials are designed to help students succeed in their examinations. In certain circumstances, CIMA can make post-exam adjustment to a student's mark or grade to reflect adverse circumstances which may have disadvantaged a student's ability to take an exam or demonstrate their normal level of attainment (see CIMA's Special Consideration policy). However, it should be noted that students will not be eligible for special consideration by CIMA if preparation for or performance in a CIMA exam is affected by any failure by their tuition provider to prepare them properly for the exam for any reason including, but not limited to, staff shortages, building work or a lack of facilities etc.

Similarly, CIMA will not accept applications for special consideration on any of the following grounds:

- failure by a tuition provider to cover the whole syllabus
- failure by the student to cover the whole syllabus, for instance as a result of joining a course part way through
- failure by the student to prepare adequately for the exam, or to use the correct pre-seen material
- errors in the Kaplan Official Study Text, including sample (practice) questions or any other Kaplan content or
- errors in any other study materials (from any other tuition provider or publisher).

Acknowledgements

Questions from past live assessments have been included by kind permission of CIMA.

We are grateful to the CIMA for permission to reproduce past examination questions. The answers to CIMA Exams have been prepared by Kaplan Publishing, except in the case of the CIMA November 2010 and subsequent CIMA Exam answers where the official CIMA answers have been reproduced. Questions from past live assessments have been included by kind permission of CIMA

British Library Cataloguing-in-Publication Data

A catalogue record for this book is available from the British Library.

ISBN: 978-1-78740-690-2

Contents

Introduction

This document references IFRS® Standards and IAS® Standards, which are authored by the International Accounting Standards Board (the Board), and published in the 2020 IFRS Standards Red Book.

How to Use the Materials

These Kaplan Publishing learning materials have been carefully designed to make your learning experience as easy as possible and to give you the best chances of success in your CIMA Cert BA Objective Test Examination.

The product range contains a number of features to help you in the study process. They include:

- a detailed explanation of all syllabus areas
- extensive 'practical' materials
- generous question practice, together with full solutions.

This Study Text has been designed with the needs of home-study and distance-learning candidates in mind. Such students require very full coverage of the syllabus topics, and also the facility to undertake extensive question practice. However, the Study Text is also ideal for fully taught courses.

The main body of the text is divided into a number of chapters, each of which is organised on the following pattern:

- **Detailed learning outcomes.** These describe the knowledge expected after your studies of the chapter are complete. You should assimilate these before beginning detailed work on the chapter, so that you can appreciate where your studies are leading.
- **Step-by-step topic coverage.** This is the heart of each chapter, containing detailed explanatory text supported where appropriate by worked examples and exercises. You should work carefully through this section, ensuring that you understand the material being explained and can tackle the examples and exercises successfully. Remember that in many cases knowledge is cumulative: if you fail to digest earlier material thoroughly, you may struggle to understand later chapters.
- **Activities.** Some chapters are illustrated by more practical elements, such as comments and questions designed to stimulate discussion.
- **Question practice.** The text contains exam-style objective test questions (OTQs).
- **Solutions.** Avoid the temptation merely to 'audit' the solutions provided. It is an illusion to think that this provides the same benefits as you would gain from a serious attempt of your own. However, if you are struggling to get started on a question you should read the introductory guidance provided at the beginning of the solution, where provided, and then make your own attempt before referring back to the full solution.

If you work conscientiously through this Official CIMA Study Text according to the guidelines above you will be giving yourself an excellent chance of success in your Objective Text Examination. Good luck with your studies!

Quality and accuracy are of the utmost importance to us so if you spot an error in any of our products, please send an email to mykaplanreporting@kaplan.com with full details, or follow the link to the feedback form in MyKaplan.

Our Quality Coordinator will work with our technical team to verify the error and take action to ensure it is corrected in future editions.

Icon explanations

Definition – These sections explain important areas of knowledge which must be understood and reproduced in an assessment environment.

Key point – Identifies topics which are key to success and are often examined.

Supplementary reading – These sections will help to provide a deeper understanding of core areas. The supplementary reading is **NOT** optional reading. It is vital to provide you with the breadth of knowledge you will need to address the wide range of topics within your syllabus that could feature in an assessment question. **Reference to this text is vital when self-studying.**

Test your understanding – Following key points and definitions are exercises which give the opportunity to assess the understanding of these core areas. Note that not all questions are exam style, some are for understanding only.

Illustration – To help develop an understanding of particular topics. The illustrative examples are useful in preparing for the Test your understanding exercises.

Exclamation mark – This symbol signifies a topic which can be more difficult to understand. When reviewing these areas, care should be taken.

New – Identifies topics that are brand new in subjects that build on, and therefore also contain, learning covered in earlier subjects.

Study technique

In this section we briefly outline some tips for effective study during the earlier stages of your approach to the Objective Test Examination. We also mention some techniques that you will find useful at the revision stage. Use of effective study and revision techniques can improve your chances of success in the CIMA Cert BA and CIMA Professional Qualification examinations.

Planning

To begin with, formal planning is essential to get the best return from the time you spend studying. Estimate how much time in total you are going to need for each subject you are studying. Remember that you need to allow time for revision as well as for initial study of the material.

With your study material before you, decide which chapters you are going to study in each week, and which weeks you will devote to revision and final question practice.

Prepare a written schedule summarising the above and stick to it!

It is essential to know your syllabus. As your studies progress you will become more familiar with how long it takes to cover topics in sufficient depth. Your timetable may need to be adapted to allocate enough time for the whole syllabus.

Students are advised to refer to the CIMA website, www.cimaglobal.com, to ensure they are up-to-date.

Students are advised to consult the syllabus when allocating their study time. The percentage weighting shown against each syllabus topic is intended as a guide to the proportion of study time each topic requires.

Tips for effective studying

(1) Aim to find a quiet and undisturbed location for your study and plan as far as possible to use the same period of time each day. Getting into a routine helps to avoid wasting time. Make sure that you have all the materials you need before you begin so as to minimise interruptions.

(2) Store all your materials in one place, so that you do not waste time searching for items every time you want to begin studying. If you have to pack everything away after each study period, keep your study materials in a box, or even a suitcase, which will not be disturbed until the next time.

(3) Limit distractions. To make the most effective use of your study periods you should be able to apply total concentration, so turn off all entertainment equipment, set your phones to silent mode, and put up your 'do not disturb' sign.

(4) Your timetable will tell you which topic to study. However, before diving in and becoming engrossed in the finer points, make sure you have an overall picture of all the areas that need to be covered by the end of that session. After an hour, allow yourself a short break and move away from your Study Text. With experience, you will learn to assess the pace you need to work at. Each study session should focus on component learning outcomes – the basis for all questions.

(5) Work carefully through a chapter, making notes as you go. When you have covered a suitable amount of material, vary the pattern by attempting a practice question. When you have finished your attempt, make notes of any mistakes you made, or any areas that you failed to cover or covered more briefly. Be aware that all component learning outcomes are examinable.

(6) Make notes as you study, and discover the techniques that work best for you. Your notes may be in the form of lists, bullet points, diagrams, summaries, 'mind maps' or the written word, but remember that you will need to refer back to them at a later date, so they must be intelligible. If you are on a taught course, make sure you highlight any issues you would like to follow up with your lecturer.

(7) Organise your notes. Make sure that all your notes, calculations etc. can be effectively filed and easily retrieved later.

Progression

There are two elements of progression that we can measure: how quickly students move through individual topics within a subject; and how quickly they move from one course to the next. We know that there is an optimum for both, but it can vary from subject to subject and from student to student. However, using data and our experience of student performance over many years, we can make some generalisations.

A fixed period of study set out at the start of a course with key milestones is important. This can be within a subject, for example 'I will finish this topic by 30 June', or for overall achievement, such as 'I want to be qualified by the end of next year'.

Your qualification is cumulative, as earlier papers provide a foundation for your subsequent studies, so do not allow there to be too big a gap between one subject and another. For example, E1 *Managing finance in a digital world* builds on your knowledge of the finance function from certificate level and lays the foundations for E2 *Managing performance* and all strategic papers particularly E3 *Strategic management* and P3 *Risk management*.

We know that exams encourage techniques that lead to some degree of short term retention, the result being that you will simply forget much of what you have already learned unless it is refreshed (look up Ebbinghaus Forgetting Curve for more details on this). This makes it more difficult as you move from one subject to another: not only will you have to learn the new subject, you will also have to relearn all the underpinning knowledge as well. This is very inefficient and slows down your overall progression which makes it more likely you may not succeed at all.

In addition, delaying your studies slows your path to qualification which can have negative impacts on your career, postponing the opportunity to apply for higher level positions and therefore higher pay.

You can use the following diagram showing the whole structure of your qualification to help you keep track of your progress. Make sure you seek appropriate advice if you are unsure about your progression through the qualification.

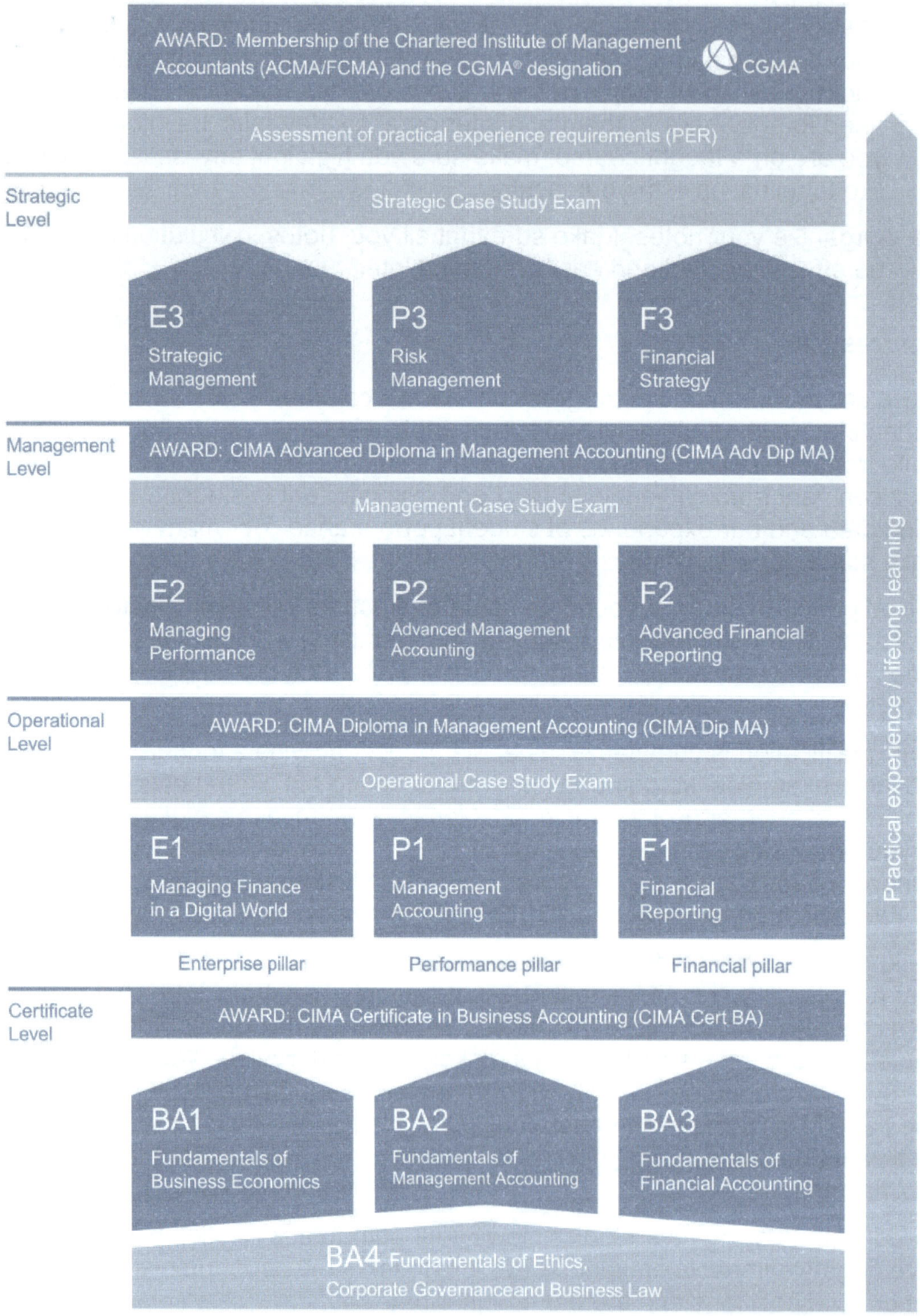

Reproduced with permission from CIMA

Objective Test

Objective Test questions require you to choose or provide a response to a question whose correct answer is predetermined.

The most common types of Objective Test question you will see are:

- multiple choice, where you have to choose the correct answer(s) from a list of possible answers – this could either be numbers or text
- multiple response with more choices and answers, for example, choosing two correct answers from a list of five available answers – this could be either numbers or text
- number entry, where you give your numeric answer to one or more parts of a question, for example, gross profit is $25,000 and the accrual for heat and light charges is $750.
- drag and drop, where you match one or more items with others from the list available, for example, matching several accounting terms with the appropriate definition
- drop down, where you choose the correct answer from those available in a drop down menu, for example, choosing the correct calculation of an accounting ratio, or stating whether an individual statement is true or false
- hot spot, where, for example, you use your computer cursor or mouse to identify the point of profit maximisation on a graph
- other types could be matching text with graphs and labelling/indicating areas on graphs or diagrams.

CIMA has provided the following guidance relating to the format of questions and their marking:

- questions which require narrative responses to be typed will not be used
- for number entry questions, a small range of answers will be accepted. Clear guidance will usually be given about the format in which the answer is required e.g. 'to the nearest $' or 'to two decimal places'
- item set questions provide a scenario which then forms the basis of more than one question (usually 2–4 questions). These sets of questions would appear together in the test and are most likely to appear in BA2 and BA3
- all questions are independent so that, where questions are based on a common item set scenario, each question will be distinct and the answer to a later question will not be dependent upon answering an earlier question correctly
- all items are equally weighted and, where a question consists of more than one element, all elements must be answered correctly for the question to be marked correct.

Throughout this Study Text we have introduced these types of questions, but obviously we have had to label answers A, B, C etc. rather than using click boxes. For convenience we have retained quite a few questions where an initial scenario leads to a number of sub-questions. There will be questions of this type in the Objective Test Examination but they will rarely have more than three sub-questions.

Guidance re CIMA on-screen calculator

As part of the CIMA Objective Test software, candidates are provided with a calculator. This calculator is on-screen and is available for the duration of the assessment. The calculator is available in Objective Test Examinations for BA1, BA2 and BA3 (it is not required for BA4).

Guidance regarding calculator use in the Objective Test Examinations is available online at: https://connect.cimaglobal.com/

CIMA Cert BA Objective Tests

The Objective Tests are a two-hour assessment comprising compulsory questions, each with one or more parts. There will be no choice and all questions should be attempted. The numbers of questions in each assessment are as follows:

BA1 Fundamentals of Business Economics – 60 questions

BA2 Fundamentals of Management Accounting – 60 questions

BA3 Fundamentals of Financial Accounting – 60 questions

BA4 Fundamentals of Ethics, Corporate Governance and Business Law – 85 questions

All questions are equally weighted. All parts of a question must be answered correctly for the question to be marked correct. Where questions are based upon a common scenario, each question will be independent, and answers to later questions will not be dependent upon answering earlier questions correctly.

Structure of subjects and learning outcomes

Each subject within the syllabus is divided into a number of broad syllabus topics. The topics contain one or more lead learning outcomes, related component learning outcomes and indicative syllabus content.

A learning outcome has two main purposes:

(a) to define the skill or ability that a well prepared candidate should be able to exhibit in the examination

(b) to demonstrate the approach likely to be taken in examination questions.

The learning outcomes are part of a hierarchy of learning objectives. The verbs used at the beginning of each learning outcome relate to a specific learning objective e.g.

Calculate the break-even point, profit target, margin of safety and profit/volume ratio for a single product or service.

The verb **'calculate'** indicates a level three learning objective. The following table lists the learning objectives and the verbs that appear in the CIMA Cert BA syllabus learning outcomes.

CIMA VERB HIERARCHY

CIMA place great importance on the definition of verbs in structuring objective tests. It is therefore crucial that you understand the verbs in order to appreciate the depth and breadth of a topic and the level of skill required. The objective tests will focus on levels one, two and three of the CIMA hierarchy of verbs. However, they will also test levels four and five, especially at the management and strategic levels.

Skill level	Verbs used	Definition
Level 3 Application How you are expected to apply your knowledge	Apply	Put to practical use
	Calculate	Ascertain or reckon mathematically
	Conduct	Organise and carry out
	Demonstrate	Prove with certainty or exhibit by practical means
	Prepare	Make or get ready for use
	Reconcile	Make or prove consistent/compatible
Level 2 Comprehension What you are expected to understand	Describe	Communicate the key features of
	Distinguish	Highlight the differences between
	Explain	Make clear or intelligible/state the meaning or purpose of
	Identify	Recognise, establish or select after consideration
	Illustrate	Use an example to describe or explain something
Level 1 Knowledge What you are expected to know	List	Make a list of
	State	Express, fully or clearly, the details/facts of
	Define	Give the exact meaning of
	Outline	Give a summary of

CIMA Cert BA resources

Access to CIMA Cert BA resources including syllabus information is available online at www.cimaglobal.com.

Additional resources

This Study Text is designed to be comprehensive and therefore sufficient to meet the needs of students studying this subject. However, CIMA recognises that many students also want to read around particular topic(s), either to extend their knowledge and understanding, or because it is particularly relevant to their work environment.

CIMA has therefore produced a related reading list for those students who wish to extend their knowledge and understanding, whether for personal interest or to help support work activities as follows:

BA1 – Fundamentals of Business Economics

Principles of Economics 3rd ed.	McDowell & Thom
Applied Economics 12th ed.	Griffiths & Wall
Mathematics for Economists: An Introductory Textbook 4th ed.	Pemberton & Rau

BA2 – Fundamentals of Management Accounting

Management and Cost Accounting	Colin Drury
Management Accounting	Catherine Gowthorpe

BA3 – Fundamentals of Financial Accounting

Financial Accounting – An Introduction	Pauline Weetman
Frank Wood's Business Accounting 1 & 2	Frank Wood & Alan Sangster

BA4 – Fundamentals of Ethics, Corporate Governance and Business Law

Students can find out about the specific law and regulation in their jurisdiction by referring to appropriate texts and publications for their country.

Managing Responsible Business	CGMA Report 2015
Global Management Accounting Principles	CIMA 2015
Embedded Ethical Values: A guide for CIMA Partners	CIMA Report 2014
Business Ethics for SMEs: A Guide for CIMA Partners	CIMA Report 2014
Ethics: Ethical Checklist	CIMA 2014
Ethics Support Guide	CIMA 2014
Acting under Pressure: How management accountants manage ethical issues	CIMA 2012

SYLLABUS GRIDS

BA3: Fundamentals of Financial Accounting

Syllabus overview

The main objective of this subject is to obtain a practical understanding of financial accounting and the process behind the preparation of financial statements for single entities.

These statements are prepared within a conceptual and regulatory framework requiring an understanding of the role of legislation and of accounting standards. The need to understand and apply necessary controls for accounting systems, and the nature of errors is also covered. There is an introduction to measuring financial performance with the calculation of basic ratios.

Note: Students are required to be aware of the format and content of published accounts but are not required to prepare them. No detailed knowledge of any specific accounting treatment contained in the International Financial Reporting Standards (IFRSs) – including the International Accounting Standards (IASs) – is necessary, except in terms IAS 2 and the treatment of inventory, IAS 16 and IAS 38 for basic non-current asset transactions.

IAS 1 and IAS 7 formats will form the basis of the financial statements. The terminology used for all entities will be that of International Financial Reporting Standards. This will enable students to use a consistent set of accounting terms throughout their studies.

Assessment strategy

There will be a two hour computer based assessment, comprising 60 compulsory objective test questions. Short scenarios may be given to which one or more objective test questions relate.

Syllabus structure

The syllabus comprises the following topics and weightings:

Content area		Weighting
A	Accounting principles, concepts and regulations	10%
B	Recording accounting transactions	50%
C	Preparation of accounts for single entities	30%
D	Analysis of financial statements	10%
		100%

BA3A: Accounting principles, concepts and regulations (10%)

Learning outcomes

On completion of their studies, students should be able to:

Lead	Component	Level	Indicative syllabus content	Study text chapter
1. Explain the principles and concepts of financial accounting.	a. Explain the need for accounting records. b. Identify the needs of different user groups. c. Distinguish between the purposes of financial and management accounts. d. Explain capital and revenue, cash and profit, income and expenditure, assets and liabilities. e. Explain the underlying assumptions, policies and accounting estimates. f. Identify the need for and information to be included in an integrated report. g. Describe the accounting equation. h. Explain the need for accounting codes.	2 2 2 2 2 2 2 2	• Accounting records to be kept and their uses; concept of stewardship. • Users of accounts and their information needs. • Functions of financial and management accounts; purpose of accounting statements. • Capital and revenue; cash and profit; income, expenditure, assets and liabilities. • Underlying assumptions, policies, accounting estimates; historical cost convention; qualitative characteristics of the Framework, elements of financial statements. • The principles and elements of the Framework for integrated reporting. • The accounting equation formula. • Use of coding in record keeping.	1
2. Explain the impact of the regulatory framework on financial accounting.	a. Explain the influence of legislation and accounting standards on published accounting information.	2	• Regulatory influence of company law; role of accounting standards; IASs and IFRSs; formats for published accounts.	2

BA3B: Recording accounting transactions (50%)

Learning outcomes

On completion of their studies, students should be able to:

Lead	Component	Level	Indicative syllabus content	Study text chapter
1. Prepare accounting records.	a. Prepare the books of prime entry. b. Apply the principles of double- entry bookkeeping. c. Prepare nominal ledger accounts. d. Prepare the trial balance. e. Explain the nature of accounting errors. f. Prepare accounting entries for the correction of errors. g. Prepare accounting entries for non-current assets. h. Prepare a non-current asset register.	3 3 3 3 2 3 3 3	• Record sales, purchase, income and expense transactions in the sales day book, purchase day book, cash book, returns books, and sales/purchase ledger. • The accounting equation; double-entry bookkeeping rules; journal entries. • Record all types of business transactions in nominal ledger accounts. • Completing the trial balance from given ledger account balances. • Errors including those of principle, omission, and commission. • Journal entries and suspense accounts. • In accordance with IAS 16 – acquisition, depreciation (straight line, reducing balance), revaluation, impairment and disposal of tangibles. • In accordance with IAS 38 – intangibles and amortisation. • Information to be recorded in a non-current asset register.	3, 4, 5, 11, 12, 15
2. Prepare accounting reconciliatio ns.	a. Prepare bank reconciliation statements. b. Prepare petty cash statements under an imprest system. c. Prepare sales and purchase ledger control account reconciliations.	3 3 3	• Reconciliation of the cashbook to the bank statement. • Using the imprest system for petty cash. • Reconciliation of sales and purchase ledger control accounts to sales and purchase ledgers.	13
3. Prepare accounting entries for specific transactions.	a. Calculate sales tax. b. Prepare accounting entries for sales tax. c. Prepare accounting entries for payroll. d. Prepare accounting entries for the issue of shares.	3 3 3 3	• Calculation of sales tax on all business transactions. • Accounting entries for sales tax. **Note:** No knowledge of any specific tax systems/rules/rates will be required. • Accounting entries for basic payroll information. **Note:** No knowledge of any specific income tax rules will be required. • Issue at full market price, rights issue and bonus issue.	5, 7, 8

BA3C: Preparation of accounts for single entities (30%)

Learning outcomes

On completion of their studies, students should be able to:

Lead	Component	Level	Indicative syllabus content	Study text chapter
1. Prepare accounting adjustments.	a. Prepare accounting entries for accruals and prepayments. b. Prepare accounting entries for irrecoverable debts and allowances for receivables. c. Prepare accounting entries for inventories.	3 3 3	• Calculations and journals for accruals and prepayments (income and expenses). • Prepare journals for irrecoverable debts and allowances for receivables from given information. • In accordance with IAS 2 – calculation of the figure for closing inventory for inclusion in the financial statements (FIFO, LIFO and average cost) and the journal entry to record it.	6, 9, 10
2. Prepare manufacturing accounts.	a. Prepare basic manufacturing accounts.	3	• Manufacturing accounts produced from given information. **Note:** No calculation of overheads and inventory balances is required.	17
3. Prepare financial statements for a single entity.	a. Prepare financial statements from a trial balance. b. Prepare financial statements from incomplete records. c. Prepare a statement of cash flows.	3 3 3	• In accordance with IAS 1 – Statement of profit or loss and other comprehensive income; statement of financial position; statement of changes in equity. • Calculate missing numbers using the accounting equation, profit margins and mark-ups, receivables and payables ledgers, and cash and bank ledgers. • In accordance with IAS 7 – operating, investing and financing sections.	14, 16, 18

BA3D: Analysis of financial statements (10%)

Learning outcomes

On completion of their studies, students should be able to:

Lead	Component	Level	Indicative syllabus content	
1. Identify information provided by accounting ratios.	a. Identify the information provided by the calculation of accounting ratios. b. Identify reasons for the changes in accounting ratios.	2 2	• Information provided by accounting ratios. • Reasons for the changes in accounting ratios.	19
2. Calculate basic accounting ratios.	a. Calculation of profitability ratios. b. Calculation of liquidity ratios. c. Calculation of risk ratios.	3 3 3	• Ratios: return on capital employed; gross, operating and net profit margins; non-current asset turnover. • Trade receivables collection period and trade payables payment period; current and quick ratios; inventory turnover. • Gearing and interest cover.	19

Information concerning formulae and tables will be provided via the CIMA website, www.cimaglobal.com.

Chapter

1

The accounting environment

Chapter learning objectives

When you have completed this chapter, you should be able to:

- explain the principles and concepts of financial accounting
- apply the accounting equation to record the effect of transactions

1 Introduction

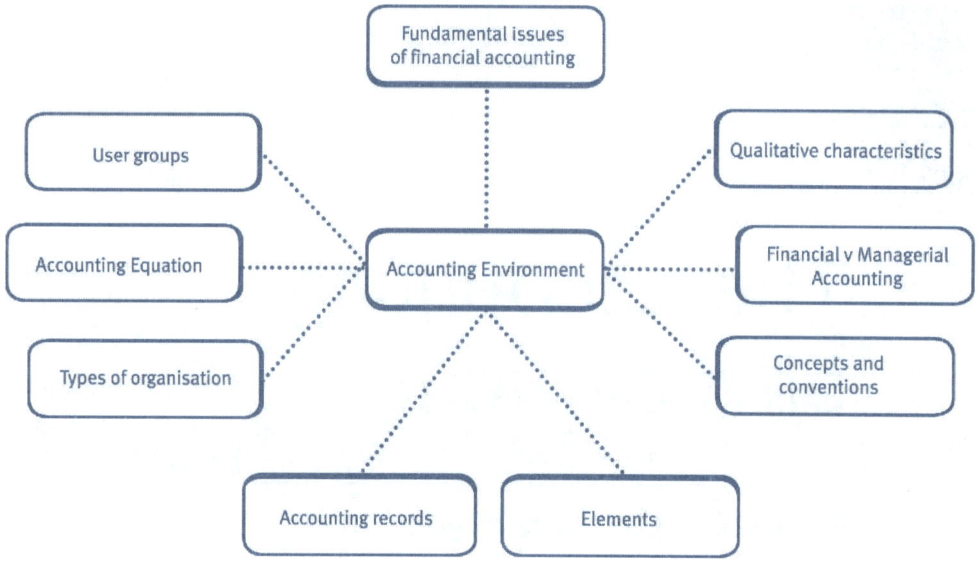

This chapter provides:

- an introduction to the accounting environment and
- an introduction to the fundamental issues associated with financial accounting.

Much of the chapter relates to the first syllabus area 'accounting principles, concepts, and regulations'.

This chapter covers:

- the different types of business entity
- the need for accounting records and which accounting records are maintained
- the concept of stewardship
- the user groups of financial accounting information
- the definition of accounting, including use of coding in record keeping
- the differences between financial and management accounting
- the elements of the financial statements
- the accounting equation, including classification of transactions
- the qualitative characteristics of financial information
- the historical cost convention and other valuation bases
- the explanation of accounting concepts and fundamental terms, and
- a glossary of accounting terms.

2 What is a business entity?

A business is an **entity that regularly enters into transactions that are expected to provide a reward measurable in monetary terms**. It is thus obvious from everyday life that many business entities exist. What is less obvious is that their organisational (legal) structure and therefore their accounting requirements may differ.

There are two main reasons for the different organisational structures that exist – **the nature of their activities and their size.**

Note that information relating to the different types of entity organisational structure is provided for information and awareness only to provide context and understanding for your financial accounting studies. Many accounting transactions will be common to all types of business entity, such as cash receipts and payments and, therefore, the same accounting principles will apply irrespective of the nature of the business entity.

However, note that you will not be examined on specialised transactions relating to partnerships, local or national government or non-profit making entities. The focus of your studies for this subject is accounting principles and transactions relating to sole traders and companies.

For convenience, and to be consistent with CIMA terminology, reference will usually be made to an 'entity', rather than a 'business' or an 'organisation' or 'company'.

Profit-making entities

Some entities are formed with the intent of making profits from their activities for their owners:

(a) **Sole traders (sole proprietors)**

Who are they?

These are entities that are **owned by one person**. They tend to be small because they are constrained by the limited financial resources of their owner. The sole trader will also have unlimited personal liability for debts incurred by the business.

(b) **Partnerships**

Who are they?

These are entities **owned by two or more persons** working in common with a view to making a profit. The greater number of owners compared with a sole trader increases the availability of finance and this is often the reason for forming such a structure. As with a sole trader, each of the partners in the business has unlimited personal liability for debts incurred by the business.

(c) **Limited liability companies ('companies')**

Who are they?

These are entities **recognised in law as 'persons' in their own right.** Thus a company may own assets and incur liabilities in its own name. There is a separation in law between ownership of the company by shareholders and its management by directors.

The crucial distinction between a company and either a sole trader or a partnership is that the shareholders of a company have only limited liability for debts incurred by the business, whereas sole traders and partners have unlimited personal liability for debts incurred by the business.

The accounting requirements of companies must meet certain minimum obligations imposed by legislation, for example, via company law and other regulations. Some of these requirements also constitute recommended accounting practice for other types of business entity.

Two types of company can be identified: **private limited companies** and **public limited companies.**

Who are they?

Public limited companies are **'listed' on a stock exchange**. Listed companies may have many thousands of owners (shareholders) who are even further removed from the running of the business.

In private limited companies the **owners are usually also actively involved in running the business**. In this way they are similar to sole traders and partnerships. This is rarely true of public companies, where the owners are unlikely to be involved in the day-to-day activities of the business. Instead, the shareholders will elect a board of directors to manage the company on a day-to-day basis on their behalf. These distinctions can be important when considering the accounting requirements, which are more onerous for public companies.

The accounting requirements relating to the financial statements of companies are considered in more detail in subsequent chapters of this publication.

Non-profit-making entities

Other entities are formed with the objective of providing services, without intending to be profitable in the long term:

(a) **Clubs and societies**

Who are they?

These entities exist to provide facilities and entertainments for their members. They are often sports and/or social clubs and most of their revenue is derived from the members who benefit from the club's facilities and activities. They may carry out some activities that are regarded as 'trading' activities, in which profits are made, but these are not seen as the main purpose of the entity. For example, a tennis club may hold a summer barbeque to raise funds for the club.

(b) **Charities**

Who are they?

These exist to provide services to particular groups, for example people with special needs and to protect the environment. Although they are regarded as non-profit-making, they often carry out trading activities, such as running shops to raise income.

(c) **Local and central government**

Who are they?

Government departments are financed by members of society (including businesses). Their finances are used to provide the infrastructure in which we live, and to redistribute wealth to other members of society. The accounting requirements of local and central government are not within the syllabus and learning objectives of this subject.

3 The need for accounting records

Accounting records are used to record transactions entered into by an entity, whatever form it may take (e.g. sole trader, partnership, company etc.). This information can then be used to meet a range of needs or requirements as follows:

- they help an entity to record, summarise and classify transactions in a logical and systematic manner
- they help managers to easily locate information required, such as details relating to an individual sales or purchase transaction
- they help managers to easily keep track of amounts owing to the entity from customers and amounts owed to suppliers
- they help managers and owners to meet legal obligations relating to the maintenance of accounting records

- they form the basis of preparation of management accounting information used by managers for control and decision-making purposes
- they form the basis of financial accounting information used to prepare annual accounts for business owners and other interested parties, such as tax authorities.

What accounting records are maintained?

In most entities, the principal transactions that take place include sales, purchases (of goods and of services) and payroll-related transactions. Other transactions include incurring costs for rent, heat and light, fuel and power and office expenses such as telephone, postage and stationery. All of these transactions (and any others entered into by an entity) must be adequately captured by the accounting system to form the basis of preparation of financial accounting and management accounting information.

With most transactions a supporting document will be created to confirm that the transaction has taken place, when the transaction took place and the associated value of the transaction. This documentation is vital to the financial accountant, who uses the information on the documents as a data source to initiate the measurement and recording of the transactions.

The table below summarises the main types of business documentation and sources of data for an accounting system, together with their content and purpose.

	Contents	**Purpose**
Quotation	Quantity/description/details of goods required.	To establish cost from various suppliers and cross refer to purchase order.
Purchase order	Details of supplier, e.g. name, address. Quantity/ description/details of goods required and price. Terms and conditions of delivery, payment, etc.	Sent to supplier as request for supply. To check to the quotation and delivery note.
Sales order	Quantity/description/details of goods required and price.	Cross checked with the order placed by customer. Sent to the stores/ warehouse department for processing of the order.
Despatch note (goods despatched note – GDN)	Details of supplier, e.g. name and address. Quantity and description of goods	Provided by supplier. Checked with goods received and purchase order
Goods received	Quantity and description of	Produced by the business receiving the goods as

	Contents	Purpose
note (GRN)	goods.	proof of receipt. Matched with despatch note from supplier and purchase order.
Invoice	Name and address of supplier and customer; details of goods, e.g. quantity, price, value, sales tax, terms of credit, etc.	Issued by supplier of goods as a request for payment. For the supplier selling the goods/services this will be treated as a sales invoice. For the customer this will be treated as a purchase invoice.
Statement	Details of supplier, e.g. name and address. Includes details of date, invoice numbers and values, payments made, refunds, amount owing.	Issued by the supplier. Checked with other documents to ensure that the amount owing is correct.
Credit note	Details of supplier, e.g. name and address. Contains details of goods returned, e.g. quantity, price, value, sales tax, terms of credit, etc.	Issued by the supplier. Checked with documents regarding goods returned.
Debit note	Details of the supplier. Contains details of goods returned, e.g. quantity, price, value, sales tax, terms of credit, etc.	Issued by the business receiving the goods. Cross referred to the credit note issued by the supplier.
Remittance advice	Method of payment, invoice number, account number, date, etc.	Sent to supplier with, or as notification of, payment.
Receipt	Details of payment received.	Issued by the selling business indicating the payment received.

4 The concept of stewardship

Stewardship is a relationship of accountability by one person or group for their management of resources and decision-making on behalf of another person or group (sometimes referred to as a principal). In a financial accounting context, employees (whether managers or directors) are ultimately accountable to the owners of that business (such as shareholders in a corporate entity) for the use of resources under their control and for the outcome of decisions they make in the use of those resources.

Accountability or stewardship is therefore exercised by managers and directors periodically providing financial accounting information to their principal or business owner, normally in the form of annual financial statements.

As such, the steward is placed in a position of trust to manage and account for the resources placed under their control by the principal. Accordingly, they should uphold fundamental ethical principles as follows:

- Integrity
- Objectivity
- Professional competence and due care
- Confidentiality
- Professional behaviour.

Ethical issues are considered in more detail in BA4 *Fundamentals of Ethics, Corporate Governance and Business Law.*

The stewardship role of management

In a sole trader business or a partnership the owners of the business entity are answerable only to themselves. They own the business entity and they are responsible for its day-to-day operations. In a corporate entity this is not necessarily the case. With the exception of owner-managed companies, it is likely that shareholders do not have any involvement in the day-to-day activities of the running and decision-making of the business entity. They provide the capital and they appoint directors to manage the business entity on their behalf.

In return the directors will receive remuneration in the form of salary and other benefits. The profit generated by the entity, however, belongs to the shareholders. It is the responsibility of the directors/management to ensure that the assets of the entity are safeguarded. This may involve ensuring that:

- all assets are recorded correctly, they exist, and are properly maintained and insured
- procedures are in place to prevent misappropriation or misuse of assets
- the accounting system is efficient and effective

- no expenditure is undertaken, or liability incurred, without proper procedures for its authorisation and control
- the financial statements are prepared in accordance with current legislation and accounting standards.

The term often given to these responsibilities is 'the stewardship function'. Management acts as stewards on behalf of shareholders, members and other beneficiaries, and may be answerable if they fail in this duty. That is not to say that it is their responsibility to make as much profit as possible, or even that they are to blame if losses are made, but that they must take appropriate steps to manage the risks, within the confines of the business world.

5 Who uses financial information?

Accounting information is used by many discrete groups, both individuals and entities. To develop an understanding of how financial statements may be used, it is useful to **classify these users into groups**, and to consider the reasons why they use financial statements and what benefit or understanding they hope to gain from doing so.

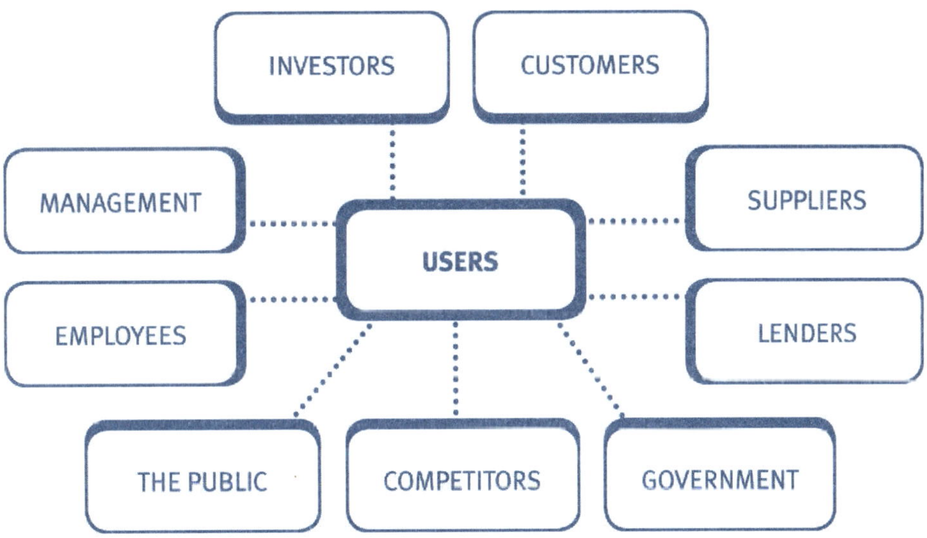

Any classification of this sort is somewhat arbitrary, and many users fall into more than one classification. However, the following groups are commonly recognised as having particular needs for accounting information.

(a) **The investor group**

Owners are better able to make decisions regarding their investment (e.g. should they sell shares or retain shares or buy more shares?) if they have relevant information. They are also able to make decisions regarding how the business entity is managed and controlled (e.g. vote to appoint or remove directors).

What do they require?

This group includes **both existing and potential owners** of shares in corporate entities. They require information concerning the performance of the corporate entity measured in terms of its profitability and the extent to which those profits are to be distributed to shareholders. They are also interested in the social/economic policies of the corporate entity so that they may decide if they wish to be associated with such an entity. For example, does the corporate entity adhere to sound ethical principles and environmental practices?

(b) **The lender group**

What do they require?

This group includes both **existing and potential providers** of secured or unsecured, long or short-term loan finance. They require information relating to the ability of the entity to repay the interest on such loans as they fall due. Additionally, they are also interested in the longer-term growth and stability of the entity to ensure that it is capable of repaying loans at the due date. In addition, if the loan is secured, the value of the assets used as security is important as a means of recovering the amount due if the entity defaults on repayment.

(c) **The employee group**

What do they require?

This group includes **current, potential and past employees**. They require information relating to the ability of the entity to pay wages and pensions on a continuing basis. In addition, they are interested in the future prospects of the entity because these issues will affect job security and employment prospects within the entity.

(d) **The analyst/adviser group**

What do they require?

This group includes a range of **advisers to investors, employees and the general public.** The needs of these users will be similar to those of their clients. The difference is, perhaps, that in some instances, the members of this group will be more technically qualified and experienced to understand and evaluate financial accounting reports.

(e) **The business contact group**

What do they require?

This group includes **customers and suppliers** of the entity. Customers will be concerned to ensure that the entity has the ability to provide the goods/services requested and to continue to provide similar services in the future. Suppliers will wish to ensure that the entity will be capable of paying for the goods/services supplied when payment becomes due.

(f) **The government**

What do they require?

This group includes **taxation authorities, plus other local and national government agencies and departments**. The taxation authorities will calculate the entity's taxation liability based upon the accounting reports and information submitted. Other government agencies will collect economic and financial data to measure and evaluate national and regional economic performance, such as employment rates and production or output levels.

(g) **The public**

What do they require?

This group includes **taxpayers, consumers and other community and special interest groups**. They require information relating to the policies and practices of the entity and how those policies and practices affect the community. For example, the general public has become increasingly aware of, and interested in, the environmental impact a business entity has as a result of its trading activities, and what may be done to minimise any adverse impact. Similarly, the general public has also developed an interest in whether an entity takes advantage of exploitative working and employment practices to minimise operating costs. When an entity is perceived to be operating in a way which is not socially responsible, it may affect the reputation of that entity and also its profitability if, for example, there is a consumer boycott of its products.

(h) **Internal users**

What do they require?

The **management of the entity** requires information to assist it in the performance of its duties. Three different levels of management can be identified:

- **Strategic** – this is the most senior level of management within an entity. In a commercial entity it is referred to as the board of directors. This level of management requires information to assist it with major decisions affecting the long-term future of the entity.
- **Tactical** – this is often referred to as middle management. This level of management requires information to support it with monitoring performance and to make decisions to enable the entity to achieve its short- to medium-term targets.
- **Operational** – this is the level of management responsible for decisions which control and manage the day-to-day activities of the entity. It is common for information to be provided to this level of management in non-financial terms, such as hours worked, quantity of components produced, and so on.

Having considered what a business entity is, and who the principal users of financial information are, it is now appropriate to consider what accounting is, how accounting information is recorded and how it is summarised.

6 An overview: what is accounting?

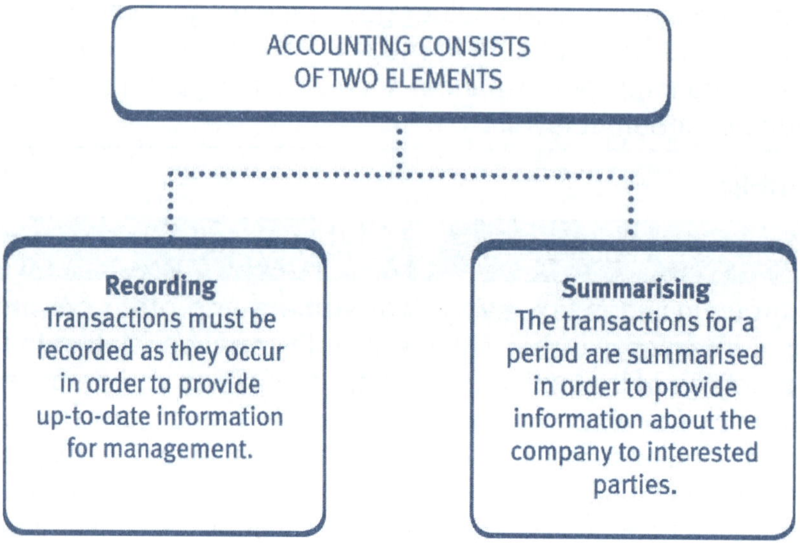

What is the objective of recording and summarising accounting transactions and how is that information then used?

The objective of recording and summarising transactions is to provide useful and relevant financial information to the managers, owners and other parties interested in an entity. In the context of financial accounting, this is achieved by the preparation of financial statements.

A significant proportion of the syllabus for this subject deals with the recording, summarising and classifying of accounting transactions to prepare financial statements.

How are accounting transactions recorded and summarised?

Transactions are initially recorded (i.e. listed) in books of prime entry. These books are simply a record of similar transactions recorded in sequential order (e.g. sales made on credit), which are periodically totalled, with the totals posted into the double-entry accounting system. This enables an individual transaction to be captured or recorded in a book of prime entry, whilst minimising the number of entries made in the double-entry accounting system.

This principle will apply regardless of the method used to record accounting transactions. Small entities with relatively few transactions may maintain a manual set of accounting records. Larger entities may enter into hundreds of thousands of transactions each year and they may use computerised accounting records to manage the volume of transactions effectively. Whichever method of maintaining accounting records is used, it will be based upon the same bookkeeping principles.

As each transaction is recorded in a book of prime entry, it will also have a code applied. One common feature of most accounting systems is the use of coding systems that are logical, comprehensive and also flexible enough to enable summarisation and further analysis to be made.

Books of prime entry are considered in further detail later in this publication.

Further detail on accounting

Accounting can be described as being concerned with **measurement and management**. Measurement is largely concerned with the recording of past data, and management with the use of that data in order to make decisions that will benefit the entity.

The measurement process is not always easy. One of the most common problems is that of when to recognise or record a transaction. For example, if we obtain goods from a supplier with payment due 60 days after the goods have been received, when should that transaction be recorded?

The following possibilities may be considered:

- when the order was placed
- when the goods were received
- when the invoice was received from the supplier; or
- when the supplier was paid.

Accounting, therefore, involves the exercise of judgement by the person responsible for converting data into meaningful information. It is this feature that distinguishes accounting from bookkeeping.

Accounting may be defined as:

- the **classification and recording** of monetary transactions
- the **presentation and interpretation** of the results of those transactions in order to assess financial performance for an accounting period and the financial position at the end of that accounting period
- the **monetary projection** of future activities arising from the alternative planned courses of action.

Note the three aspects considered in this definition: **recording, reporting and forecasting:**

1 Accounting is partly a matter of record-keeping. The monetary transactions entered into by a business entity need to be controlled and monitored, and for this a permanent record is essential. For an efficient system of record-keeping, the transactions must first be classified into categories appropriate to the enterprise concerned.

2 At appropriate intervals, the individual transactions must be summarised as a basis for preparation of statements of financial performance and position of a business entity.

3 Finally, accounting information can be the basis for planning and decision-making.

An alternative explanation is that accounting is part of the management information system (MIS) of an entity. In this context, the accounting element is referred to as an accounting information system (AIS).

Accounting can thus be said to be a method of providing information to management (and other users) relating to the activities of an entity. In order to do this it relies on the accurate collection of data from sources both internal and external to the entity. The recording of this data is often referred to as bookkeeping.

7 Use of accounting information

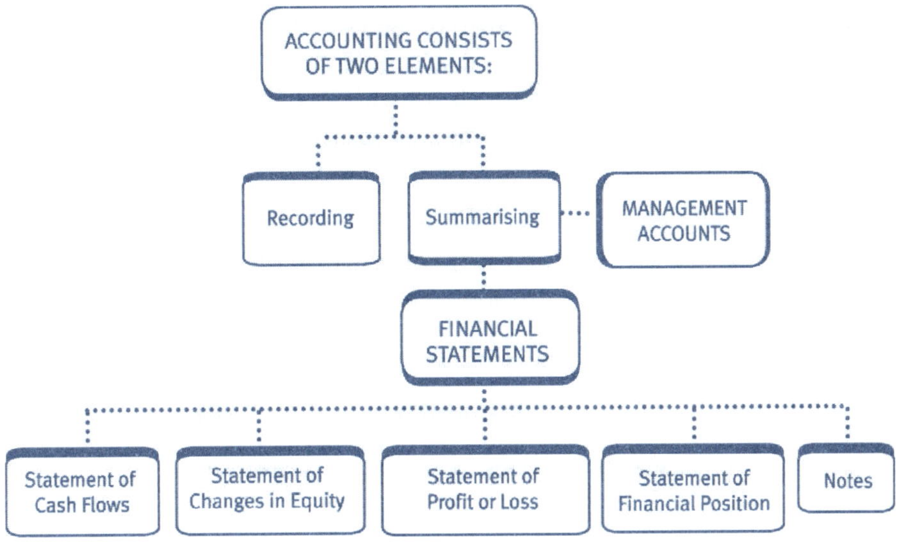

The accounting system of a business entity **records and summarises** accounting transactions so that useful information can be prepared for managers and others. Managers need accounting information to help them to manage and control the entity (management accounting) and to prepare financial statements for external users (financial accounting). Normally financial accounting consists of preparing financial statements for external users which comprise the following:

- statement of profit or loss and other comprehensive income – comprises a summary of income and expenses for an accounting period
- statement of financial position – comprises a summary of assets and liabilities and capital at a specific date
- statement of changes in equity – comprises a summary of the movement in capital or equity (i.e. ownership interest) for an accounting period
- statement of cash flows, and
- notes to the financial statements.

This information is crucial to various stakeholders of the business entity, who will analyse that information to make significant economic decisions. It is of vital importance that stakeholders have good quality information to be able to make their decisions.

As you progress through your studies for this subject, you will learn how to record accounting transactions and how to prepare financial statements. Subject BA2 Fundamentals of Management Accounting deals with the use of accounting information for management and control purposes.

8 Financial accounting and management accounting

Financial accounts are produced primarily for owners of business entities and external users. International Accounting Standards (IAS® Standards) and International Financial Reporting Standards (IFRS® Standards) help to reduce the differences in the way that companies draw up their financial statements in different countries.

Management accounts are prepared for managers and others who control the business entity. The key distinctions between financial accounting and management accounting are summarised in the following diagram.

ACCOUNTING

Financial accounting	Management accounting
• Production of summary financial statements for external users.	• Production of detailed accounts, used by management to control the business and plan for the future.
• Prepared annually (six-monthly or quarterly in some countries).	• Normally prepared monthly, often on a rolling basis.
• Generally required by law.	• Not mandatory.
• Reflects past performance and current position.	• Includes budgets and forecasts of future activities, as well as reflecting past performance.
• Information calculated and presented in accordance with international accounting standards.	• Information computed and presented in order to be relevant to managers.

Financial accounting

Financial accounting can be described as the classification and recording of monetary transactions of an entity in accordance with established concepts, principles, accounting standards and legal requirements, and their presentation, by means of various financial statements, during and at the end of an accounting period.

Further detail on financial accounting

Two points in particular are worth noting about this description:

1 Financial statements **must comply with accounting rules** published by the various regulatory bodies. In other words, an entity does not have a completely free hand as to how it prepares and presents financial statements. The reason for this is that the financial statements are primarily intended for the use of people outside of the entity. Without access to the more detailed information available to insiders, these interested parties may be misled unless financial statements are prepared based upon uniform principles and standards.

2 Financial accounting is **partly concerned with summarising the transactions of an accounting period and classifying and presenting the summary in a coherent form**. This is because financial statements are intended for use by external third parties. These outsiders have a need for, and a right to receive, specified financial accounting information at defined intervals, and not be subject to the discretion and choice of management.

Management accounting

Management accounting can be described as the process of identification, measurement, accumulation, analysis, preparation, interpretation and communication of information used by management to plan, evaluate and control within an entity and to assure appropriate use of and accountability for its resources

Further detail on management accounting

Management accounting also comprises the preparation of financial reports for non-management groups such as shareholders, lenders, regulatory agencies and tax authorities.

Although the needs of external users of accounts are addressed in this definition, the emphasis of management accounting is upon providing **information to help managers to control and direct the business entity.** The nature and extent of information produced, and the way in which it is presented, is at the discretion of the managers concerned: they will request whatever information, in whatever format, they believe to be appropriate to meet their needs.

Internal and external information

Just as distinctions can be made between financial accounting and management accounting, distinctions can also be made between the nature and extent of information available within a business entity for management and control purposes, and informaticn available to external third parties as follows:

		Internal information	External information
1	Availability	This is confidential and retained within the entity	This is available to anyone who can access it – usually from a public registry
2	Frequency	As and when required by the entity e.g. weekly, monthly etc.	Usually annually – as required by law and regulation
3	Content and format	No standard content or format required – as required to meet business needs. It may be very detailed and may contain budgeted and forecast information, along with financial and non-financial information	Standard format and content set by legislation and technical accounting standards. Typically it is highly summarised with focus upon historical financial information
4	External audit requirement to provide credibility to information	No external audit requirement	Most companies are required to have an external audit
5	Compliance with technical accounting standards	There is no requirement for this, although may be desirable to do so	Annual financial statements must comply with technical accounting standards

The remainder of this publication will focus upon financial accounting, and the preparation of financial statements. As a basis for doing this, a number of important accounting terms, principles and concepts need to be defined and explained.

9 Elements of the financial statements

The IASB® Conceptual Framework for Financial Reporting ('Framework') identifies five **'elements of the financial statements'** as follows:

Assets	) These elements are
Liabilities	) used to form the basis of
Capital	) the statement of financial position
Income	) These elements are used to form the basis of
Expenses	) the statement of profit or loss

Each of the elements will now be defined and explained before going on to consider the accounting equation and financial statements in more detail.

The Framework was updated in 2018, and this study text includes updated definitions of the elements of the financial statements.

Asset

The IASB Framework defines an asset **'a present economic resource controlled by the entity as a result of past events.**

An economic resource is a right that has the potential to produce economic benefits' (Framework, para 4.4).

This usually means that an asset has been purchased and is owned by the entity. However, be aware that it is possible to have control or use of an asset without owning it, for example, when leasing or hiring an asset

Further detail on assets

Examples of assets are land, buildings, plant and machinery, motor vehicles, inventories of goods, receivables, bank balances and cash. Assets may be described as **tangible or intangible**. Tangible assets are those that have physical substance and can be seen or touched (e.g. land, buildings, equipment, inventories, etc.). Intangible assets do not have physical substance and cannot be seen or touched (e.g. owning a licence or a brand). Usually intangible assets have some form of legally-based rights or entitlement, such as a patent or registered trademark. You will learn more about intangible assets in Chapters 7 and 8 of this publication.

Liability

The IASB Framework defines a liability as **'a present obligation of the entity to transfer an economic resource as a result of past events'** (Framework, para 4.26).

Further detail on liabilities

Thus a liability can be described as an amount owed by a business entity to an individual or other business entity. Examples of liabilities are payables, loans received and bank overdrafts.

Capital (also known as equity)

The Framework defines equity as **'the residual interest in the assets of the entity after deducting all its liabilities'** (Framework, para 4.63).

In this context, capital or equity is not easy to define, but it can be regarded as a special kind of liability that exists between a business entity and its owner(s). In effect, it shows the net amount invested in the business entity by the owner(s) and would be due to them if business activities were terminated.

The above elements can then be arranged into the accounting equation as follows:

Assets = Liabilities + Capital, or

Capital = Assets – Liabilities, or

Liabilities = Assets – Capital

The accounting equation will be studied in more depth towards the end of this chapter.

Further detail on capital

To return to the accounting equation, you can perhaps see that the assets of an entity have been provided, or 'financed', by liabilities due to either outsiders or to the owners. This emphasises the importance of the separate entity concept described previously. As we regard the owners as being separate from the business entity itself, we can regard the amount owed by the business entity to its owners as a kind of liability. Effectively, we can restate the accounting equation in an even simpler form:

Assets of the business entity = Liabilities of the business entity

This statement is always true no matter what transactions the business entity undertakes. Any transaction that increases or decreases the assets of the business entity must increase or decrease its liabilities by an identical amount.

You may be wondering exactly what is meant by saying that capital is an amount 'owed' by the business entity to its owners. How can the business entity 'owe' anything in this way? How has it incurred a debt?

The answer is that when a business entity commences, it is common for the owners to 'invest' some of their private or personal resources into the business. As the business entity operates it generates its own resources in the form of profits, which technically belongs to the owners.

Some of the profit may remain in the business entity, whilst some profit may be withdrawn by the owners in the form of goods or cash. This withdrawal of profits in simple entity structures such as sole traders is known as 'drawings'.

Income

The Framework defines income as **'increases in assets or decreases in liabilities that result in increases in equity, other than those relating to contributions from holders of equity claims'** (Framework, para 4.68).

In simple terms, for most business entities this will be sales revenue earned on the sale of goods or provision of services to customers. It could also include other items such as bank interest received.

Expense

The Framework defines expenses as **'decreases in assets or increases in liabilities that result in decreases in equity, other than those relating to distributions to holders of equity claims'**(Framework, para 4.69).

This may occur, for example, when purchasing goods for resale or by incurring operating and other costs such as wages, heat and light charges or repairs to factory machinery.

Capital and revenue transactions

Since the accounting equation makes use of three of the elements of the financial statements as follows:

Assets – Liabilities = Capital

or, it can be re-stated as:

Assets = Capital + Liabilities

It therefore demonstrates the relationships that exist within any business entity. The equation is the basis of one of the most common accounting statements prepared – **the statement of financial position.**

This equation will form the basis of much of your studies for this subject to record accounting transactions. It will be considered in further detail later in this publication. Consequently, it is important that you understand the following distinctions:

- between capital and revenue transactions, and
- between cash and profit.

Capital transactions

Capital transactions relate to costs incurred that will affect the entity in the long term, i.e. more than a year.

For the purpose of your studies for this subject we will assume this relates to purchases of non-current assets such as buildings, plant and machinery etc.

Capital costs or capital expenses will **NOT** be included as an expense in the statement of profit or loss but as a non-current asset in the statement of financial position.

Revenue transactions

Revenue transactions relate to expenses that will only affect the entity in the current accounting period, for example wages, rent payable and vehicle running costs.

Revenue expenses will be included as expenses in the statement of profit or loss and **NOT** in the statement of financial position.

Capital transactions = statement of financial position

Revenue transactions = statement of profit or loss

Capital and revenue transactions – further information

Capital transactions

The word 'capital' means different things in different contexts. You have already seen how the word is used to identify the investment by an owner in the business entity. Capital transactions are those that affect the business entity in the long term, as well as in the current period. Capital expenditure is expenditure on non-current assets, and capital receipts would result from the disposal of those assets. Other transactions that are regarded as capital transactions are the obtaining of, and repayment of, non-current finance. Capital transactions initially affect the statement of financial position. Of course, non-current assets are used up over a number of years, and so eventually they will be consumed. We account for this by including depreciation in the statement of profit or loss. You will consider this is more detail as you progress through your studies for this subject.

Revenue transactions

Revenue transactions are those that affect the entity in the current accounting period. Revenue receipts come from sales, and sometimes in the form of income from investments. Revenue expenditure is expenditure on items that are consumed in the current accounting period, for example the running expenses of the entity, cost of sales and so on. Revenue transactions affect the figures in the statement of profit or loss.

Cash and profit

A key point to understand is the difference between cash and profit.

Cash may be regarded as the value of notes and coins (including bank balances) an entity has access to at any point in time. Consequently, cash transactions are accounted for based upon the date of receipt and payment of cash.

Profit is the difference between sales revenue less expenses incurred during an accounting period, which is accounted for on an accruals basis. In effect, this means that transactions are accounted for on the date that they are entered into, which may not be the same as the date of receipt or payment of cash. It is explained further elsewhere in this chapter.

The profit or loss for an accounting period will not be matched by an equal increase or decrease in the cash and bank balances of an entity for several reasons. This may be demonstrated by two relatively simple examples as follows:

- consider the situation of a business entity that sells goods on credit for $100. When the sale is made, sales revenue of $100 can be recorded in the accounting records. However, there will not be an equivalent increase in the cash and bank balances until the customer actually pays for the goods at some later date.
- consider the situation of a business entity that purchases new office equipment at a cost of $500, paying cash immediately. This represents the purchase of a non-current asset, and the reduction in the value of another asset (cash and bank balances) by $500. Therefore, this transaction affects only the statement of financial position and does not immediately affect the profit or loss for that accounting period.

As you progress through your studies for this subject, you will come across further examples of transactions which do not have an equal impact upon profit and cash. Some of those transactions are noted below for reference:

- some accounting transactions do not affect the profit or loss for an accounting period, but do affect cash and bank balances, such as:
  - capital introduced into the business entity by the proprietor
  - cash drawings from the business entity by the proprietor
  - purchase of non-current assets, such as property plant and equipment.
- some accounting transactions do affect the profit or loss for an accounting period, but do not affect cash and bank balances, such as:
  - accounting for accruals and prepayments
  - accounting for depreciation
  - accounting for irrecoverable debts and allowances for receivables.

10 The qualitative characteristics of financial information

So far, we have considered who the users of financial information are, and for what purpose they may require financial information. All of the user groups identified, both internal and external to the entity, require that financial information provided should be useful. In this context, information should:

- enable its recipient to make effective decisions
- be adequate for taking effective action to control the entity or provide valuable details relating to its environment
- be compatible with the responsibilities and needs of its recipient
- be produced at optimum cost
- be easily understood by its recipient
- be timely, and
- be sufficiently accurate and precise for the purpose of its provision.

The Framework requires that financial information should have certain qualitative characteristics to ensure that it meets the needs of users.

The Framework identifies two fundamental qualitative characteristics and four enhancing qualitative characteristics as follows:

(i) **Fundamental qualitative characteristics**

   – **Relevance**

   – **Faithful representation.**

(ii) **Enhancing qualitative characteristics**

   – **Comparability**

   – **Verifiability**

   – **Timeliness**

   – **Understandability.**

Note that the content relating to the qualitative characteristics of useful financial information is relevant in subject F1 Financial Reporting in the CIMA Professional Qualification.

Further detail on qualitative characteristics

For decisions to be made, the information must be relevant to the decision and be clearly presented, stating any assumptions upon which the information is based, so that the user may exercise judgement as appropriate.

Often, better information may be provided at additional cost or after an additional time delay. The adequacy of information is important, and factors such as the cost of the information and the speed with which it is available may be more important than it being 100 per cent accurate.

The information provided must be communicated to the person responsible for taking any action in respect of the information provided. In this regard it is better to distinguish information between that which relates to controllable aspects of business activities and that which relates to non-controllable aspects. The controllable aspects may then be further divided into those that are significant and an exception reporting approach applied.

Fundamental qualitative characteristics

(i) **Relevance** – Is guided as per the Framework in terms of information becoming relevant when it influences the economic decisions of users by helping them evaluate past, present or future events or confirming or correcting their past evaluations.

The relevance of information can be affected by its nature and materiality. Some items may be relevant to users simply because of their nature whereas some items may only become relevant once they are material. Hence, materiality is a threshold quality of information rather than a primary characteristic.

According to the Framework, information is material if its omission or misstatement could influence the decisions of users.

Materiality – As per the Framework materiality is an entity- specific aspect of relevance and depends on the size of the item or error judged in the particular circumstances of its omission or misstatement.

Information is material if its omission or misstatement could influence the economic decisions of users taken on the basis of the financial statements i.e. would an inappropriate decision or judgement be made if information was not available or if it had been misstated?

(ii) **Faithful representation**

In accordance with the Framework is information is to represent faithfully the transactions and other events that it purports to represent, they must be accounted for and presented in accordance with their substance and economic reality and not merely their legal form.

Financial information should possess the following characteristics if it is to faithfully represent the performance and position of a business entity:

Completeness

To be understandable information must contain all the necessary descriptions and explanations.

Neutrality

Information must be neutral, i.e. free from bias. Financial statements are not neutral if, by the selection or presentation of information, they influence the making of a decision or judgement in order to achieve a predetermined result or outcome.

Free from error

Information must be free from error within the bounds of materiality. A material error or an omission can cause the financial statements to be false or misleading and thus unreliable and deficient in terms of their relevance.

Free from error does not mean perfectly accurate in all respects. For example, where an estimate has been used the amount must be described clearly and accurately as being an estimate.

Enhancing qualitative characteristics

The Framework identified that the following items are required as enhancing characteristics of useful financial information:

Comparability

Users must be able to compare financial statements over a period of time in order to identify trends in financial position and performance. Users must also be able to compare financial statements of different entities to be able to assess their relative financial position and performance.

In order to achieve comparability, similar items should be treated in a consistent manner from one accounting period to the next and from one entity to another. However, it is not appropriate for an entity to continue accounting for transactions in a certain manner if alternative treatments exist that would be more relevant and reliable.

Disclosure of accounting policies should also be made so that users can identify any changes in these policies or differences between the accounting policies of different entities.

Verifiability

Verification can be direct or indirect. Direct verification means verifying an amount or other representation through direct observation i.e. counting cash at a specific date. Indirect verification means checking the inputs to a model, formula or other technique and recalculating the outputs using the same methodology i.e. recalculating inventory amounts using the same cost-flow assumption such as first-in, first-out method.

Timeliness

Timeliness means having information available to decision makers in time to be capable of influencing their decisions. Generally, the older the information is the less useful it becomes.

Understandability

Information needs to be readily understandable by users. Information that may be relevant to decision making should not be excluded on the grounds that it may be too difficult for certain users to understand.

Understandability depends on:

- the way in which information is presented, and
- the capabilities of users.

It is assumed that users:

- have a reasonable knowledge of business and economic activities, and
- are willing to study the information provided with reasonable diligence.

For information to be understandable users need to be able to perceive its significance.

11 The historical cost convention

At what value should transactions be recorded?

Normally, transactions are recorded at historical cost. This is the agreed monetary value of a transaction at the time it takes place. For example, the cost of raw materials purchased from a supplier, or the cost of a machine purchased for use in the business entity. It also applies to sales transactions – they will be recorded at the agreed monetary value when the transaction takes place.

The advantages of using historical cost include:

- it is easily understood by most people
- it is usually easy to reliably identify or determine e.g. by reference to a purchase invoice
- it is an objective basis of measurement, whereas other valuation bases such as fair value or market value are subjective

The disadvantages of using historical cost include:

- it may not be relevant to the needs of some users of financial information who require information based upon current costs and prices
- it may become out of date, particularly when considering the impact of inflation on costs over a period of time
- it presumes that historical cost is based upon a stable unit of currency which enables comparison over time; this is probably not the case.

As you progress through your studies for this subject, you will learn that there are other bases of measuring financial transactions for inclusion in the financial statements, but historical cost is the most comprehensive and commonly used basis of measurement.

Further detail on historical cost

Traditionally, financial statements have been prepared using the historical cost concept and, to a large extent, still are. This is a system of accounting in which all values are based on the costs incurred or revenue receivable at the date of the transaction.

This means that all of the assets, liabilities, expenses and revenue are recorded using the costs and prices ruling at the date of the transaction as the basis of any accounting entries. This method is objective as each value can be supported by the amount paid to the third party at the date of the transaction.

However, it is accepted that this concept has many shortcomings, and over the years many attempts have been made by accountants to develop alternative valuation or measurement methods. The main difficulty with the concept is that in times of changing price levels, it has the effect of overstating profits and understating asset values.

Consider the purchase of two plots of land: one was purchased 3 years ago for $5,000 and the second plot, identical in terms of size and function, was purchased in the current year for $9,000. If you told an external user that you have two plots of land; one valued at $5,000 and one at $9,000 they would assume that the second plot was either larger or more valuable to the business entity. This, however, is not the case as they are identical. They were simply purchased in different economic circumstances. In this situation, the historical cost concept has painted a misleading picture of the assets of a business entity.

Consider a second example: you purchase a plot of land today for $10,000. You do absolutely nothing to it, leaving it to grow wild. Alternatively, also for $10,000, you could have purchased 100,000 units of your entity's core raw material. Two years later you sell that land, completely untended, for $12,000. With that $12,000 you could now purchase 100,000 units of your entity's core raw material, which has also inflated in value. In the financial statements you record a $2,000 profit upon disposal of the land.

However, ask yourself: has your business entity actually received any increased benefit from owning this land? No: your purchasing power is the same as it was two years previously. So have you really made a profit and is it misleading to the users of the financial statements to suggest as such?

Why is this a problem? Well consider a further example: You set up a business entity and you acquire 10,000 widgets from a supplier at a cost of $10 each, giving a total cost of $100,000. You sell the widgets for $10.50 each, earning revenue of $105,000. You have just made a profit of $5,000; you can pat yourself on the back for some business well done. Or can you?

In the interim period the purchase cost of your widgets has increased to $11. So how many replacement items can you now purchase for your business entity with $105,000? Only 9,545: your business has just shrunk because you have not earned enough revenue to replace your inventory. Ideally, you should have priced your product at $11.50 or more so that you could have replaced all 10,000 items and retained some profit for yourself. It can be seen that the use of the historical cost concept thereby overstates profits and understates statement of financial position asset values. Application of this concept reduces the usefulness of financial statements produced.

The theory of capital maintenance

As seen in the example above; during inflationary times, the profit may only be sufficient to replace inventory, assets and pay for expenses, if the same level of activity is to be maintained. In that case, it is not really a 'profit' at all, as we think of profits as being an improvement. Indeed, the profit may not even be sufficient to maintain that level of activity, and – even worse – if some or all of the profits are paid out to the owners of the business entity, the level of activity may have to be reduced. In this case, the business entity has failed to maintain sufficient capital to support the same level of business activity.

Capital maintenance is therefore important as it implies profit is only earned if the value of the entity's net assets or operating capacity has increased during the accounting period. The Framework makes reference to:

- financial capital maintenance – profit is made only if the financial or monetary amount of net assets at the end of the reporting period exceeds the amount at the start of the period, after excluding transactions with owners
- physical capital maintenance – profit is made only if the physical productive capacity of the entity exceeds the physical productive capacity at the start of the period, after excluding transactions with owners.

Whilst historical cost is the most commonly adopted basis for recording transactions, some transactions may be recorded using alternative bases, such as:

- fair value – this may be considered to be the market value of an item i.e. at what price could it be sold?
- net realisable value – this is the estimated selling price of an item, less any further costs that must be incurred in order to make the sale.

These bases, along with the accounting requirements relevant to their application, will be explained in subsequent chapters of this publication as you progress with your studies for this subject.

12 The accounting equation in action

The accounting equation is a simple expression of the fact that at any point in time the assets of the entity should be equal to the equity plus the liabilities.

For every transaction that an entity enters into their will be a dual effect.

The dual effect principle states that every transaction has two financial effects.

(a) If, for example, you spend $2,000 on a car and pay for it by cheque, you will have $2,000 less money in the bank, but you will have acquired an asset worth $2,000.

(b) Again, if you owe a payable $100 and sent them a cheque for that amount, you will owe $100 less than before, but you will have $100 less money in the bank.

To see the accounting equation in action, study the following worked example.

Worked Example 1.A

On 31 March, Ahmed's employment with GSL came to an end and on 1 April, Ahmed set up in business as a sole trader trading as 'Ahmed's Matches', to sell boxes of matches from a tray on a street corner.

Ahmed deposited $100 into a bank account opened in the name of Ahmed's Matches. He persuaded a supplier of matches to let him have an initial inventory of 400 boxes, costing 5¢ each, and promised to pay for them one week later.

During his first day of trading he sold 150 boxes at 12¢ each – generating $18 in cash. Feeling pleased, he took $5 from the cash tin and treated himself to supper at the local café.

He also wrote a cheque for $5 to his supplier in part payment for the initial inventory of boxes.

Required:

Illustrate the effect of each of these transactions upon the accounting equation.

Solution:

To begin with, the only asset of the business entity was $100 in the business bank account. Capital invested by Ahmed also amounted to $100 and the accounting equation would then be as follows:

Assets		=	**Liabilities**	+	**Capital**	
Bank	$100.00	=	0	+	Capital	$100.00

The business entity then acquired matches worth $20 with a corresponding liability due to the supplier. The accounting equation now looks like this:

Assets		=	**Liabilities**		+	**Capital**	
Bank	$100.00		Payables	$20.00		Capital	$100.00
Inventory	$20.00						
	$120.00	=		$20.00	+		$100.00

When Ahmed sold 150 boxes, he made a profit of (150 × 7¢) = $10.50. His remaining inventory was reduced to 250 boxes at 5¢ each ($12.50). He also acquired a further asset in the process: cash in hand of $18. The accounting equation now looks like this:

Assets		=	**Liabilities**		+	**Capital**	
Bank	$100.00		Payables	$20.00		Original capital	$100.00
Cash in hand	$18.00					Profit	$10.50
Inventory (20 – 7.50)	$12.50						
	$130.50	=		$20.00	+		$110.50

Don't forget that when Ahmed sold the inventory we must remove the cost of items sold from the inventory balance, i.e. 150 boxes × 5¢ = $7.50. We can see that the sale had three effects on the accounting equation – inventory was reduced by the cost of the goods sold, i.e. $7.50, cash increased by the amount the goods were sold for, i.e. $18 and the capital balance increased by the profit on the sale amounting to $10.50.

Then Ahmed withdrew $5 from the business entity for his private use. This amount (referred to as drawings) reduced the sum owed to him by the business entity. The accounting equation now looks like this:

Assets		=	**Liabilities**		+	**Capital**	
Bank	$100.00		Payables	$20.00		Original capital	$100.00
Cash in hand (18 – 5)	$13.00					Profit earned	$10.50
Inventory	$12.50					Less: drawings	($5.00)
	$125.50	=		$20.00	+		$105.50

Finally, Ahmed made a payment to his supplier, reducing the funds in the business bank account, and also reducing the amount of the liability due to the supplier. The accounting equation now looks like this:

Assets		=	**Liabilities**		+	**Capital**	
Bank (100 – 5)	$95.00		Payables (20 – 5)	$15.00		Original capital	$100.00
Cash in hand	$13.50					Profit earned	$10.50
Inventory	$12.50					Less: drawings	($5.00)
	$120.50	=		$15.00	+		$105.50

Test your understanding 1

J Jones commenced business on 31 January 20X1, transferring $5,000 from her personal bank account into a business bank account. During the first week of February 20X1 the following transactions occurred:

1 Feb Bought motor van costing $800 paying by cheque

2 Feb Bought goods on credit:

P Smith $400

E Holmes $250

3 Feb Sold goods for cash $600 (cost $400)

4 Feb Banked cash $600

Paid P Smith $400 by cheque

5 Feb Sold goods on credit (cost $200)

J Amos $200

A Turner $300

Required:

Show the accounting equation at the end of each day's transactions.

Accounting coding systems

As a method of summarising and classifying transactions in an organised manner, business entities usually make use of coding systems as part of their record-keeping. Such coding systems enable managers to access relevant information, whether it is an individual transaction, or a group of similar transactions.

By now you will realise that a busy entity will have a large number of ledger accounts and subsidiary records within and outside the accounting system. Using the titles of accounts to locate and cross-reference transactions could be difficult in such situations. Imagine the tax authorities maintaining all the records of individual taxpayers according to their name. There will be hundreds of thousands of taxpayers with the surname Smith, or Khan or Jones – and thousands called John Smith or Helen Jones. Each needs a unique code to identify them from the others. The same applies to accounting systems. The ledger accounts require unique codes, as do inventory items, employees on the payroll and so on.

We could simply number them 1, 2, 3 and so on, but that would not be particularly helpful in locating an individual item. Some kind of coding system is needed. This is particularly important in computerised systems, which use codes to transfer data throughout the system.

Entities could perhaps start with the five main categories of ledger accounts, for example

- Assets Code 1 (e.g. machinery and inventory)
- Liabilities Code 2 (e.g. bank loans)
- Capital Code 3 (e.g. ownership interest in the entity)
- Expenses Code 4 (e.g. wages and heat and light)
- Revenues Code 5 (e.g. sales revenue).

The five categories noted above are referred to as 'the elements of the financial statements' and are defined and explained in this chapter.

This could then be subdivided into more specific categories, for example:

- Non-current assets Code 12 (e.g. machinery)
- Current assets Code 13 (e.g. inventory of goods for sale).

Non-current assets could be further divided into types, for example, plant (1), motor vehicles (2), office equipment (3) and so on.

Codes could be included to identify the location of such items within the entity, e.g. sales department, purchasing department, wages department and factory locations for example. This would enable depreciation to be charged to the department that utilises a particular non-current asset.

The following structure illustrates how a coding system may be used for a nominal ledger in a large entity.

A six-digit code is used: the first digit represents the functional analysis; digits 2 and 3 represent the cost centre (i.e. the department); and digits 4–6 represent the type of expense involved.

Function		**Cost centre (within production)**		**Nominal ledger expense analysis**	
1	Production	10	Machining	100	Raw material X
2	Sales	11	Assembly	101	Raw material Y
3	Administration	12	Finishing	201	Skilled-labour wages
				202	Unskilled-labour wages
				203	Salaries
				301	Rent
				601	Postage
				602	Stationery

An example code could be 110202, which represents unskilled-labour wage cost incurred in the machining cost centre of the production function.

It is generally accepted that codes should be:

(a) **Unique.** In order to avoid ambiguity, each item must have only one possible code.

(b) **Useful.** There is no point in using a code if there is to be no benefit from its use. The code will need to be logical and understood by those who use and apply it.

(c) **Compact.** It is generally accepted that the shorter the code the easier it is to learn and therefore the likelihood of mistakes and confusion is reduced. Thus, a code should be as short and compact as possible.

(d) **Meaningful.** If the code can be made meaningful by the characters of the code being connected in some way to the item that the code represents, the code will be more easily remembered and understood.

(e) **Self-checking.** The biggest problem with the use of codes is that users of the codes often remember them incorrectly. To ensure that the information provided by the system is of value, each of the codes used must be validated. If a numeric code is used it can be designed in such a way as to be self-checking – this will help in identifying coding mistakes and avoid the processing and production of incorrect information.

(f) **Expandable.** When designing a coding system it is important to consider the requirements of the entity in the future. The design of accounting systems often involves a large amount of time and this is then followed by a period when the users are learning the system. If the code is not expandable, then it is likely that the system will have to be changed sooner rather than later. This will be costly in design time and will cause difficulties because the users of the system will have to learn the new system.

(g) **Standard size.** If codes are of varying size, then different users may write the same code differently. For example, if a part of a coding system comprises up to four characters, then the three-digit code AB1 could be written in a number of ways, with spaces and dashes in different places. Using AB01 would prevent this.

Use of accounting coding systems therefore helps an entity to classify, arrange and summarise its accounting transactions.

13 Accounting concepts

This introduction to the accounting environment would not be complete without explanation of some key accounting concepts which you will encounter throughout your accountancy studies. As you consider these concepts, bear in mind that they often require the exercise of judgement and estimation to arrive at reasonable or acceptable monetary values to include in the accounting records when absolute precision may be impossible or very time-consuming to achieve.

The need for concepts reflects the fact that accounting is not a precise science – it requires understanding rather than rote or mechanical learning of techniques. These concepts could form the basis of questions in the examination – either being able to define a concept or to apply it based upon information provided.

Note that accounting concepts may also be referred to a 'accounting principles' or 'accounting conventions'.

Separate entity concept

During the discussion of user groups earlier in this chapter, reference was made to the principle that the law recognises **a corporate entity as a 'person' in its own right, distinct from the personalities of its owners** (known as shareholders). This represents application of the 'separate entity' concept, whereby the owners of the business entity are regarded as separate from those who manage and control the activities of the entity.

This concept is applied when recording accounting transactions for any business entity, irrespective of whether there is a legally-recognised separation of ownership and control of that business entity. For example, a sole trader both owns and manages the business entity, but the accounting records are maintained as if the business entity was separate or distinct from its owner. The consequence of applying this concept is that the financial statements prepared for a business entity will present only the financial performance and position of the business entity itself. Any transactions between the owner(s) of the business entity and the entity itself will be reflected within the capital or equity section of the statement of financial position.

For larger entities, this concept also helps to illustrate application of the stewardship relationship between the entity managers/directors who prepare the financial statements for the benefit of the entity owners (shareholders).

Further detail – separate entity concept

Consider the situation of a corporate entity that incurs debts in its own name and then has difficulty in paying them. Its suppliers may be entitled to seize the assets owned by the corporate entity. However, they have no claim against the personal assets owned by the shareholders (the business owners): it is the corporate entity that owes money, not its owners. In law, this distinction does not exist with other forms of business entity, such as the sole proprietor. If Bill Smith is in business as a plumber, trading under the name of 'Smith & Co. Plumbing Services', the law recognises no distinction between the business and the individual. If there are debts outstanding for plumbing supplies, and the business assets of Smith & Co. are insufficient to pay them, the suppliers can demand payment from Bill Smith the individual, who may be forced to sell his personal assets – home, car, and so on. In this respect the accounting concept does not correspond with the strict legal form of the business entity. It is an absolutely crucial concept in accounting that, regardless of the legal form of a business entity – corporate entity, sole trader, partnership or whatever – the business entity is treated as a separate entity from its owner(s). For accounting purposes, Bill Smith the individual is not the same as Smith Plumbing Services.

This reflects the fact that accounting information relates only to business transactions. What Bill Smith does as an individual is of no concern to the accountant, and his private transactions must be kept quite separate from the business transactions of Smith & Co. Students sometimes find this concept hard to grasp, particularly when they notice that, as a consequence of it, Bill Smith the individual can actually have business dealings with Smith & Co. For example, Bill may take some copper piping from the inventory held by Smith & Co. in order to repair the heating system in his own home. From the accounting point of view, a business transaction has occurred: Smith & Co. has supplied an individual called Bill Smith with some piping, and its value must be accounted for.

Despite its apparent artificiality, the significance of this concept will become apparent as you progress through your studies for BA3 and apply the principles of the accounting equation.

Accruals or matching concept

This concept refers to the basis upon which income and expenses are recognised in the statement of profit or loss. Income recognised in the statement of profit or loss should be matched with the expenses incurred in earning or generating that inflow of economic benefits to determine the profit or loss for an accounting period. Income is recognised when it has been earned, not when the cash is received from the customer. Expenses are recognised when they are incurred, not when the cash is paid to the supplier. For example, it may be necessary to estimate how many years a machine is likely to be used in the business, so that its cost or usage can be spread over that time period.

This concept will be considered and applied in subsequent chapters of this publication.

Prudence concept

This concept refers to the basis upon which items are measured or valued for inclusion in the financial statements. In the statement of financial position, assets should not be overvalued and liabilities should not be undervalued. In the statement of profit or loss, income should be recognised only when it is probable that it will be received, and expenses are recognised as soon as they are incurred. In effect, when there is doubt regarding the precise value of an item for inclusion in the financial statements, caution should be exercised, so that assets and income are not overstated and liabilities and expenses are not understated. For example, it may be necessary to form a judgement on whether any amounts due from credit customers may not be received, and to recognise such amounts as an expense. This concept will be visited throughout subsequent chapters of this publication.

Accounting policies and estimation techniques

Accounting policies are the principles, conventions, rules etc. applied by a business entity when determining the value at which assets and liabilities, revenue and expenses, will appear in the financial statements. Management should use those policies which it believes will be most useful to those who rely on the financial statements. These users will include, for example, shareholders and lenders, as discussed earlier in this chapter. Management can assess which policies will be most useful by considering the characteristics of useful information, as discussed earlier, including, for example, relevance and reliability.

The implementation of accounting policies requires certain items to be estimated. We can appreciate that the preparation of financial statements relies on judgement and that not all values used can be regarded as definitive or precise. Accountants have developed a number of techniques to arrive at figures which have to be estimated. For example, we will see as we progress through our studies for this subject that a business entity may calculate an allowance for receivables, but this is only an estimate as to which trade receivables may not pay. This allowance is normally calculated based upon assessment of knowledge relating to each specific receivable or customer as appropriate. This is a technique to estimate future irrecoverable debts based upon the information available at that time.

Another example we will encounter in our studies for this subject is depreciation, where the straight-line method and the reducing-balance method are two techniques used to estimate the consumption of a non-current asset in a specific accounting period, over its expected useful life to the business.

Going concern concept

This concept assumes that a business entity will continue to operate for the foreseeable future, which is normally interpreted as being for twelve months following the accounting year end. Application of this concept enables financial statements to be prepared without the need to account for realisable or break-up values of assets and liabilities, which would result in the preparation of financial statements with limited value to users.

The Framework states that this is an underlying assumption when preparing financial statements. If this is not an appropriate assumption, there should be disclosure in the financial statements to explain the basis on which the financial statements have been prepared.

As you progress through your studies for this subject, you will realise that many accounting treatments are based upon application of this concept. For example, when accounting for a non-current asset, an entity will estimate how many years of use that asset will provide so that its cost can be spread over that useful life. This is known as depreciation and will be explained in more detail in the chapters dealing with non-current assets. When accounting for depreciation of non-current assets, it is assumed that there will be future years against which the cost of the non-current asset can be allocated. When calculating accruals and prepayments, it is assumed that the business entity will still be operating in the following accounting period.

Stable monetary unit concept

Accounting information is prepared using monetary measurement, such as dollars or yen. There is a presumption that the monetary value of a currency is stable from one accounting period to the next, which means that financial information can be combined (e.g. to prepare financial statements for an accounting period), or can be compared (e.g. comparison of profitability of a business entity from one accounting period to the next). However, this is not usually the case in the real world as most economies experience inflation (and some experience deflation). Consequently, comparing the statement of profit or loss of a business entity for two consecutive years may mean that any changes are partly due to inflation and not changes in the level of business activity.

Money measurement concept

Application of this concept requires that items are included in the financial statements only if and when they can be reliably measured in monetary terms. For example, many business entities refer to their employees as one of their greatest assets. However, the monetary value of employees to the business entity (as distinct from their payroll costs) cannot be reliably determined, and therefore are not included as assets in the statement of financial position.

Monetary measurements are used because if all the items covered by an accounting statement are stated as an amount of money, then the cost of the items can be identified and their aggregate cost determined. Therefore, there is a unity of meaning that makes financial statements readily understood and provides a common denominator for financial analysis.

Materiality concept

Materiality is a concept applied to the preparation of annual financial statements for investors and other external interested parties. Information is regarded as material if its omission or misstatement will change the view presented by the financial statements: in other words, it may lead users of financial statements to make inappropriate judgements or decisions based upon that financial information. Materiality is also a threshold quality such that only material items and values are presented in the financial statements, with immaterial or insignificant information summarised, aggregated or omitted from being reported in the financial statements. This allows users to focus upon the material or significant information that is relevant to them.

For example, consider the situation of a business entity that had an inventory valuation of $917,148 at the end of the accounting year. Would this valuation be materially or significantly misstated if it was included in the annual accounts at a rounded amount of, say, $917,000, or expressed in another way as $0.9m? Hopefully, you can form a judgement that some degree of approximation or rounding does not materially or significantly change the inventory valuation reported in the annual accounts and can still be regarded as reliable information for users of financial statements.

Thus the materiality concept should make the financial statements relevant to users. The distinction between what is significant and what is not varies depending on the size of the entity, and is a matter of judgement. Determining at what point an item becomes material depends partly on value, partly on the nature of the item concerned and partly on its effect on the results that will be reported.

The consistency concept

The consistency concept states that the accounting treatment of like items should be accounted for in the same way, within an accounting period and from one accounting period to the next. The usefulness of financial accounting lies to a considerable extent in the conclusions that may be drawn from the comparison of the financial statements of one year with those of a preceding year, or of one entity with another.

Much of the information thus derived would be meaningless if the choice of accounting methods were not applied consistently year by year. An example of an accounting issue where consistency is important is the method of valuation of inventory which is stated at the lower of cost and net realisable value.

The objectivity concept

Financial statements should not be influenced by the personal bias of the person preparing them. Thus, figures used in financial statements should be objective. Ideally, this should mean that any two accountants would produce the same figure, for example, for profit. In practice, there is always some judgement when preparing financial statements but when exercising that judgement the accountant should be neutral and not try to produce, for example, a larger, or smaller, profit to benefit his/her own purposes. Financial statements which are objective should be reliable.

The dual aspect concept

This concept is the basis of double-entry bookkeeping and it means that every transaction entered into has a dual effect on the position of the entity as recorded in the ledger accounts at the time of that transaction.

The realisation concept

This concept states that we recognise sales revenue as having been earned at the time when goods or services have been supplied, i.e. when the contractual obligation has been satisfied. In basic terms, sales are realised when the right to receive revenue has been earned by the reporting entity. If income has been earned but not yet received we should also recognise a matching asset as well as the sales revenue. The asset represents the right to receive benefit (usually cash), from the customer.

Although not within the BA3 syllabus, the following illustration demonstrates this concept well. Consider the situation of goods sold on a 'sale-or-return' basis. The goods are not strictly 'sold' until they have been accepted by the buyer or the deadline for their return has passed. Strictly speaking the sale of these goods should only be recognised by a business entity when it is virtually certain that the goods will not be returned and the sale transaction is therefore regarded as complete.

The periodicity concept

It can be argued that the only correct measurement of an entity's profitability is that which is made at the end of the entity's life. However, there is a need to assess the financial position (i.e. statement of financial position) and performance (i.e. statement of profit or loss) of an entity during its life by producing periodic financial statements. This concept enables comparisons to be made between one accounting period and another.

14 Glossary of terminology

CIMA is an international qualification. Consequently, it is important that the terminology used in the examination is standardised to ensure understanding and to avoid confusion.

The majority of this terminology is sourced from IAS 1 *Presentation of Financial Statements* and IAS 7 *Statement of Cash Flows*. However, there are some terms in other areas of the syllabus which may have more than one meaning in different countries.

The table below summarises some of the official terminology used by CIMA, along with examples of alternative terms which may be use in countries around the world to aid student understanding.

CIMA Terminology	Examples of alternative terminology
Concept	Convention
Separate entity concept	Business entity concept
Dual effect concept	Dual aspect concept
Not-for-profit organisation/entity	Non-trading organisation/entity
Nominal ledger	General ledger
Cashbook	Bank/Cash account
Sales tax	Value added tax, central sales tax, service tax, goods and services tax
Social security tax	National insurance
Income tax	Corporation tax (entities), Pay as You Earn (PAYE) (individuals)
Inventory	Stock
Irrecoverable debts	Bad debts
Allowance for receivables	Provision for doubtful debts
Accumulated depreciation	Provision for depreciation
Loan notes	Loan stock, debentures
Sales ledger	Debtors' ledger, receivables' ledger
Purchase ledger	Creditors' ledger, payables' ledger
Returns inwards	Sales returns
Returns outwards	Purchase returns
Sales ledger control account	Debtors' ledger control account, receivables' ledger control account
Purchase ledger control account	Creditors' ledger control account, payables' ledger control account

15 Chapter summary

In this chapter you have studied:

- the need for accounting records to meet the information needs of different user groups
- the different types of business entity
- the qualitative characteristics of useful financial information
- the historical cost convention and alternative bases of valuation
- some fundamental terms associated with financial accounting.

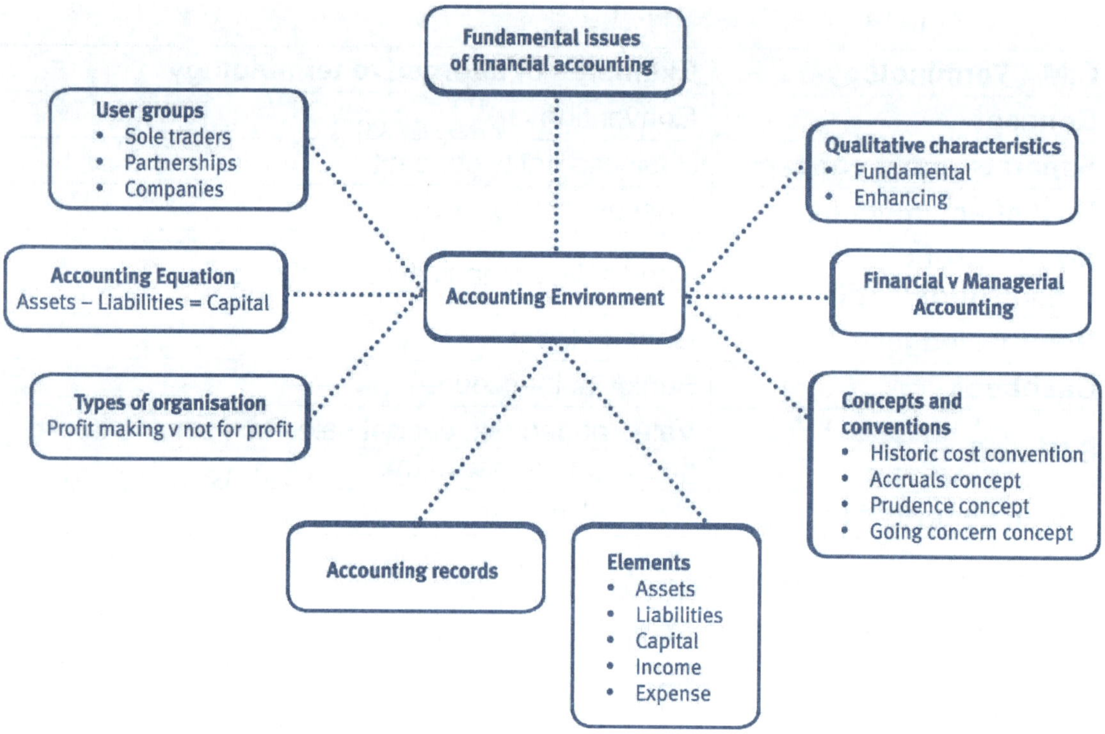

Test your understanding questions

Test your understanding 2

The main aim of accounting is to:

A maintain ledger accounts for every transaction

B provide financial information to users of such information

C produce a trial balance

D record every financial transaction individually

Test your understanding 3

The main aim of financial accounting is to:

A record all transactions in the books of account

B provide management with detailed analyses of costs

C present the financial results of the entity by means of recognised statements

D calculate profit

Test your understanding 4

Financial statements differ from management accounts in that they:

A are prepared monthly for internal control purposes

B contain details of costs incurred in manufacturing

C are summarised and prepared mainly for external users of accounting information

D provide information to enable the trial balance to be prepared

Test your understanding 5

Which of the following does NOT apply to the preparation of financial statements?

A They are prepared annually

B They provide a summary of the outcome of financial transactions

C They are prepared mainly for external users of accounting information

D They are prepared to show the detailed costs of manufacturing and trading

Test your understanding 6

Which of the following sentences does NOT explain the distinction between financial statements and management accounts?

A Financial statements are primarily for external users and management accounts are primarily for internal users

B Financial statements are normally produced annually, and management accounts are normally produced monthly

C Financial statements are more accurate than management accounts

D Financial statements are required by law and management accounts are not

Test your understanding 7

Match the following users with their information requirements.

1	Investors	A	Firm's ability to provide goods now and in future and pay debts
2	Lenders	B	Performance, profitability and dividends
3	Employees	C	Profit levels, tax liability and statistics
4	Business contacts	D	Firm's ability to pay interest and repay loans, the value of secured assets
5	Government departments	E	Firm's ability to pay wages, cash resources, future prospects, pay pensions

Test your understanding 8

Which of the following is a non-profit making entity?

A Sole trader

B Tennis club

C Partnership

D Corporate entity

Test your understanding 9	
Which of the following statements is incorrect?	
A	A corporate entity may have thousands of owners known as shareholders
B	It is possible for a person to be both a shareholder in a corporate entity and a director of that entity
C	A partnership must be two or more persons working in common with a view to making a profit
D	The shareholders in a corporate entity must be involved with its day-to-day activities and management

Test your understanding 10	
The 'accounting equation' can be rewritten as:	
A	assets plus profit less drawings less liabilities equals capital at the end of the accounting period
B	assets less liabilities less drawings equals capital at the start of the accounting period plus profit
C	assets less liabilities less capital at the start of the accounting period plus drawings equals profit
D	capital at the start of the accounting period plus profit less drawings less liabilities equals assets

Test your understanding 11	
An increase in inventory of $250, a decrease in the bank balance of $400 and an increase in payables of $1,200 results in:	
A	a decrease in working capital of $1,350
B	an increase in working capital of $1,350
C	a decrease in working capital of $1,050
D	an increase in working capital of $1,050

Test your understanding 12

A sole trader had opening capital of $10,000 and closing capital of $4,500. During the accounting period, the owner introduced capital of $4,000 and withdrew $8,000 for her own use.

Required:

What was her profit or loss for the accounting period (give your answer in $)?

$.......

Test your understanding 13

At 1 April 20X3, a business entity had assets of $28,000 and liabilities of $12,500. During April 20X3, the entity purchased a non-current asset for $6,000, paying by cheque, a profit of $7,000 was made, and payables of $5,500 were paid by cheque.

Required:

What was the capital account balance at 30 April 20X3 (give your answer in $)?

$.......

Test your understanding 14

The accounting equation states that Assets = Liabilities + Capital and this can change as a result of certain transactions.

Which one of the following transactions would not affect the accounting equation?

A Selling goods for more than their cost

B Purchasing a non-current asset on credit

C The owner withdrawing cash

D Receivables paying their accounts in full, in cash

Test your understanding 15

The profit of a business entity may be calculated by using which one of the following formulae?

A Opening capital + drawings + capital introduced – closing capital

B Closing capital + drawings – capital introduced – opening capital

C Opening capital + drawings – capital introduced – closing capital

D Closing capital – drawings + capital introduced – opening capital

Test your understanding answers

Test your understanding 1

Assets	=	Liabilities	+	Capital	
31 Jan					
Bank	$5,000		Nil		$5,000
1 Feb					
Bank	$4,200				
Van	$800				
	$5,000		Nil		$5,000
2 Feb					
Bank	$4,200	P Smith	$400		
Van	$800	E Holmes	$250		
Inventory	$650				
	$5,650		$650		$5,000
3 Feb					
Bank	$4,200	P Smith	$400	Original capital	$5,000
Van	$800	E Holmes	$250	Profit earned	$200
Inventory	£250				
Cash	$600				
	$5,850		$650		$5,200
4 Feb					
Bank	$4,400			Original capital	$5,000
Van	$800			Profit earned	$200
Inventory	$250	E Holmes	$250		
	$5,450		$250		$5,200

5 Feb

Bank	$4,400	E Holmes	$250	Original capital	$5,000
Van	$800			Profit earned (200 + (200 + 300 – 200)	$500
Receivable – J Amos	£200				
Receivable – A Turner	$300				
Inventory (250 – 200)	$50				
	$5,750		$250		$5,500

Test your understanding 2

B

Maintaining ledger accounts, producing a trial balance and recording transactions are all part of the bookkeeping system.

Test your understanding 3

C

Recording transactions is part of the bookkeeping function. This should be capable of providing management with internal information, but this is part of the management accounting function. The calculation of profit also results from the bookkeeping system and contributes towards the presentation of the financial results.

Test your understanding 4

C

Management accounts are prepared monthly (or more frequently) for internal control purposes; they also contain detailed information such as costing figures. The trial balance is prepared from the bookkeeping system and is used as a basis for the preparation of financial statements.

Test your understanding 5

D

Management accounts would provide detailed costs and other information regarding manufacturing and trading

Test your understanding 6

C

Test your understanding 7

1 Answer: **B**

2 Answer: **D**

3 Answer: **E**

4 Answer: **A**

5 Answer: **C**

Test your understanding 8

B

Test your understanding 9

D

A corporate entity may have many shareholders. For corporate entities listed on a stock exchange, there may be millions of shares in issue, and therefore millions of shareholders. It is possible, although not compulsory, for a shareholder to also be a director of that corporate entity. The definition of a partnership as stated in the question is correct. The position of a shareholder in a corporate entity is quite distinct from those of an employee or director. The final statement is incorrect. There is no requirement for a corporate entity shareholder to be involved in its day-to-day activities – the board of directors are elected to manage the corporate entity on behalf of its shareholders.

Test your understanding 10

C

The 'standard' accounting equation is:

Assets = Liabilities + Capital

Capital equals opening capital plus profits less drawings. The only rearrangement of this equation that maintains the integrity of the accounting equation is C.

Test your understanding 11

A

The effect on working capital is calculated as:

	$
Increase in inventory = increase in working capital	250
Decrease in bank = decrease in working capital	(400)
Increase in payables = decrease in working capital	(1,200)
Overall decrease in working capital	(1,350)

Test your understanding 12

	$
Opening capital	10,000
Introduced	4,000
Drawings	(8,000)
Loss – balancing figure	(1,500)
Closing capital	4,500

Test your understanding 13

Only the profit affects the capital at the end of the month. The capital at the start was $15,500 ($28,000 assets less $12,500 liabilities), so a profit of $7,000 increases this to $22,500. The purchase by cheque of a non-current asset affects only assets, and the payment of payables by cheque affects assets and liabilities, but neither affects capital.

Test your understanding 14

D

The accounting equation changes when one or more of assets, liabilities or capital changes. Selling goods at a profit would change capital; purchasing a non-current asset on credit would change assets and liabilities; the owner withdrawing cash would change assets and capital; receivables paying their accounts in cash would not affect any of these.

Test your understanding 15

B

Chapter

2

The Regulatory Framework of Financial Reporting

Chapter learning objectives

When you have completed this chapter, you should be able to:

- explain the influence of legislation and accounting standards on published accounting information
- explain the principles which underpin the form and content of statement of financial position and the statement of profit or loss
- classify assets and liabilities as either current or non-current
- explain and calculate gross and net profit
- identify the need for and information to be included in the integrated report.

1 Introduction

In this chapter we develop an understanding of:

- the need for, and elements of, regulation
- international financial reporting standards
- format of financial statements
- the accounting equation and statement of financial position
- the statement of profit or loss.

This chapter covers:

- the legal and regulatory framework
- application of the accounting equation
- the content and format of financial statements.

2 Why do we need regulation?

Regulation is needed because:

- it ensures the financial statements can be relied upon by a variety of users when making decisions and
- it promotes consistency and comparability of accounting information to help users interpret the financial statements.

Different countries will be subject to variety of economic, social and political factors. As a result, the way in which published financial accounts are regulated will vary from country to country. However, it may be said that there are common themes to this regulation, even if the detail may vary between countries.

IAS 1 *Presentation of Financial Statements* provides guidelines on the presentation of the financial statements which will be explored in further detail throughout this chapter.

3 Elements of regulation

A regulatory framework may consist of any or all of the following elements:

- local or national corporate law
- local or national accounting standards published by an appropriately authorised body
- international accounting standards published by the International Accounting Standards Board ('IASB')
- a theoretical or conceptual framework
- requirements of international bodies, i.e. EU.

Note that international accounting standards ('IAS') are also referred to as international financial reporting standards ('IFRS') and the terms are often used interchangeably. Strictly, however, IAS (the older standards) were issued up to 2000; since that date, following a reorganisation of the regulatory structure, IFRS (the more recently issued standards)have been issued, although both are of equal status. In many cases, reference is simply made to 'IFRS Standards' to include all relevant IAS and IFRS.

Within the CIMA Professional Qualification, the syllabus content of papers F1 Financial Reporting and F2 Advanced Financial Reporting, include the study of IFRS Standards in greater detail.

Corporate law

Many countries have legislation applying to corporate entities and this is generally known as 'company or corporate law'. The extent of detail in corporate law will vary between countries but in general they cover broad issues rather than detailed aspects of accounting. Examples of issues that may be covered by corporate law in a particular jurisdiction include the following:

- the format of financial statements and information disclosures required (sometimes more detailed than accounting standards)
- which companies are required to have their financial statements audited by a professionally qualified and appropriately registered auditor
- which individuals are excluded from appointment as a corporate entity director.

Some of these issues will be covered in CIMA Cert BA4 Fundamentals of Ethics, Corporate Governance and Business Law.

National accounting standards

Since the 1960s many countries have developed their own accounting standards as a means of regulating the reliability and content of annual financial statements. In some countries, this has been achieved by adopting a law-based approach, whilst in other countries, the accountancy profession has been at the forefront to develop generally accepted accounting practices applied by those who prepare financial statements. In the latter case, the professional accounting bodies normally have some form of recognition as a supervisory or regulatory body with appropriate authorisation to issue new or revised accounting standards, and to apply sanctions when accounting standards have not been properly applied. In more recent years, the procedure to develop a new or updated accounting standard has become a more formalised and rigorous process to ensure that they are relevant to the needs of preparers and users of financial information.

As a related issue, there has also been a move towards convergence or harmonisation of accounting standards on an international basis. This increases the consistency and comparability of accounting information and is a direct consequence of the development of multi-national business entities and international capital markets.

The accountancy profession

Many countries have their own professional accountancy qualification. In the USA for example, professional accountants are known as Certified Public Accountants ('CPA'). Some countries do not have their own professional accountancy qualification in which case trainee accountants study to achieve the professional qualification of another country or of an international accountancy body. This will also apply if students in one country believe that the accountancy qualification in another country is more prestigious than their own domestic qualification. Some professional accountancy bodies which were originally domestic qualifications in the UK have expanded their membership to become internationally recognised qualifications. Two examples in the UK are:

- The Chartered Institute of Management Accountants (CIMA)
- The Association of Chartered Certified Accountants (ACCA).

These bodies insist on their members being properly qualified, not only by passing examinations but also by obtaining appropriate practical experience, updating their skills and knowledge on a regular basis, and maintaining certain professional standards based on an ethical code.

The IASB Conceptual Framework for Financial Reporting (the 'Framework')

Accounting is a social science not a natural science, like physics and chemistry. Whereas physics and chemistry have natural laws, accounting had to develop its own 'laws' or principles. It is important that IFRS Standards published by the IASB are consistent with the conventions and that the accounting standards are consistent with each other. In order to help ensure that this occurs a framework was developed within which all standards are developed and published. This document underpins all accounting standards and provides the platform from which all future standards will be developed. This document is the 'Framework', previously referred to in Chapter 1 (dealing with elements of financial statements and the qualitative characteristics of useful financial information), and which has implicitly been the basis for much of the discussion in this publication. The Framework deals with the fundamental issues in financial reporting and a brief list of its chapters is given below.

- The objective of general purpose financial reporting – to provide financial information about the reporting entity that is useful to existing and potential investors, lenders and other creditors.
- Qualitative characteristics of useful financial information – there are two fundamental characteristics (relevance and faithful representation) and four enhancing characteristics (comparability, verifiability, timeliness and understandability).
- Financial statements and the reporting entity – objective of financial statements is to provide financial information about the reporting entity's assets, liabilities, equity, income and expenses. The reporting period covered by the financial statements should be specified. The reporting entity may be an individual entity, or a group.
- The elements of financial statements – there are five elements to the financial statements: income and expenses (used to compile the statement of profit or loss), along with assets, liabilities and equity (used to compile the statement of financial position).
- Recognition and derecognition – the Framework provides criteria to clarify when elements of the financial statements should be recognised and derecognised.
- Measurement – the Framework identifies two measurement bases: historical cost and current value. Current value could be fair value, value in use or current cost. Examples of current cost are current purchasing power ('CPP') and current cost accounting ('CCA'). Note that CPP and CCA are not included in the syllabus for this subject.
- Presentation and disclosure – entities should produce information which is relevant to users, in such a way that it faithfully represents the elements of the financial statements and which aids comparability over time and between different entities.

- Concepts of capital and capital maintenance – capital maintenance may be based upon financial capital or physical capital, with the measurement of profit based upon the increase in capital over a period of time.

Financial accounting information is vital to shareholders when making investment decisions. This is reflected in the successful operation of world stock markets, where every day billions of dollars are traded in acquiring and selling shares in companies. Each stock market usually contains the largest companies in that economy and the values of those companies are reflected by their share prices.

Given the significance of this mechanism to the health of national economies most countries have legislation to identify the form and content of financial statements. This ensures that users of the information (primarily the stock market) have good quality, relevant information to enable them to continue making investment decisions.

Note that content relating to the Framework is relevant in subject F1 Financial Reporting in the CIMA Professional Qualification.

A note on legislation

The Companies Act 2006 is the primary source of corporate law in the UK. It provides comprehensive guidance with regard to matters such as: corporate governance, entity formation and communications with shareholders, auditor liability, preparation and submission of financial statements, and administration (such as the need for a formal constitution). All corporate entities formed in the UK must comply with this legislation.

There are presently no European Union-wide corporate laws as such. However a number of minimum standards or directives exist for member states of the European Union. To date, perhaps the most significant EU directive issued has been the requirement since 2005 for all corporate entities in the EU with a stock exchange listing to adopt and apply IFRS as the basis for preparation of their annual financial statements.

International accounting standards

The syllabus for Subject BA3, Fundamentals of Financial Accounting, states that no detailed knowledge of any specific accounting treatment contained in IFRS Standards is necessary. The only exceptions to this statement are in relation to IAS 2 *Inventories*, IAS 16 *Property, Plant and Equipment* and IAS 38 *Intangible Assets* and IFRS 15 *Revenue from contracts with customers* which are included within this publication as required. The influence of IFRS Standards on this publication has three main effects:

1 **Terminology.** This text uses the words, phrases, definitions and so on used in IFRS Standards.

2 **Presentation.** The presentation of the financial statements follows IAS 1, *Presentation of Financial Statements (Revised)* and the statement of cash flows follows IAS 7 *Statement of Cash Flows*. Both IFRS Standards should be applied when preparing corporate entity financial statements.

3 **Technical.** The technical requirements of the IFRS Standards have been followed.

Note that content relating to IFRS Standards is relevant in subject F1 Financial Reporting in the CIMA Professional Qualification.

4 International Financial Reporting Standards (IFRS Standards)

Due to the increasingly global nature of investment and business operations there has been a move towards the 'internationalisation' of financial reporting. This 'harmonisation' was considered necessary to provide consistent and comparable information to an increasingly global audience.

If companies use different methods of accounting then before any decisions can be made about different entities the accounts would have to be re-stated so that the accounting concepts and principles applied are the same; only then can relevant comparisons be made.

IFRS Standards are very important and a brief description of how they are developed and published is given below.

There are four separate but related bodies which control the setting of IFRS Standards as illustrated below.

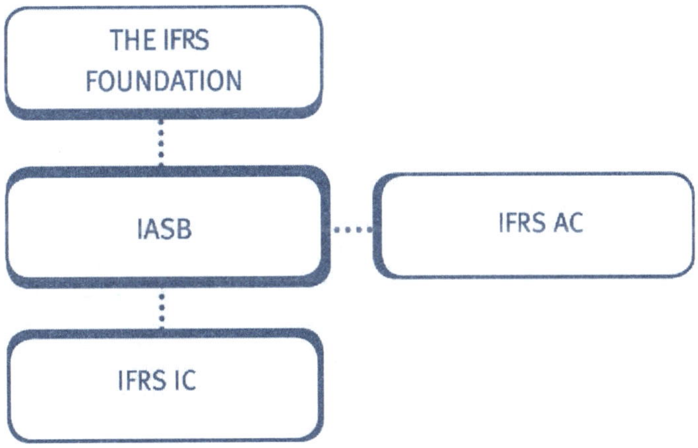

International Financial Reporting Standards Foundation

The IFRS Foundation® is the supervisory body for the IASB and is responsible, amongst other things, for the promotion and rigorous application of high-quality financial reporting standards.

International Accounting Standards Board (The Board)

The IASB is the independent standard setting body of the IFRS Foundation. Its members are responsible for the development, approval and publication of IFRS Standards and interpretations developed by the IFRS IC® (see below). Upon its creation the IASB also adopted all existing IAS, the forerunner to IFRS. All of the most important national standard setters are represented on the IASB and their views are taken into account so that a consensus can be reached.

The IFRS Interpretations Committee (IFRS IC)

The IFRS IC reviews widespread accounting issues (in the context of IFRS Standards) on a timely basis and provides authoritative guidance on these issues, abbreviated as (IFRICs) e.g. following publication of a new or revised IFRS Standard. Their meetings are open to the public and, similar to the IASB, they work closely with national standard setters.

The IFRS Advisory Council (IFRS AC®)

The IFRS AC is the formal advisory body to the IASB and the IFRS Foundation. It is comprised of a wide range of members who are affected by the IASB's work.

5 Basic format of financial statements

Having considered the regulatory environment, we can now turn our attention to developing our knowledge and understanding of the accounting equation. This builds upon our knowledge of the elements of the financial statements which were defined and explained in the previous chapter.

Remember that the accounting equation is normally stated as follows:

Assets = Liabilities + Capital.

Or, like any equation, it may also be rearranged and presented as follows:

Assets – Liabilities = Capital

What is the consequence of the various elements of regulation upon financial statements?

They provide standard formats for the financial statements which should be adopted as best practice when financial statements are prepared.

The statement of financial position is s statement of assets and liabilities of a business entity as at a specific date as follows:

Statement of financial position as at 31 December 20XX

Assets	$		**Capital + Liabilities**	$
Non-current assets			Capital	X
Land	X			
Buildings	X		Non-current liabilities	
Machinery	X		Bank loan	X
Vehicles	X			
	X			X
Current assets				
Inventories	X		Current liabilities	
Receivables	X		Payables	X
Bank balance	X		Bank overdraft	X
Cash in hand	X			
		X		
		X		X

The statement of profit or loss is a summary of the income and expenses of the business entity for a period of time (e.g. a year).

Statement of profit or loss for the year ended 31 December 20XX

	$	$
Sales revenue		X
Less: Cost of goods sold		(X)
Gross profit		X
Less expenses:		
Rent	X	
Van running costs	X	
Staff wages	X	
Other expenses	X	
		(X)
Net profit for the year		X

Note that the term 'sales revenue' may also be referred to as 'revenue' or 'sales'.

The nature and classification of both financial statements is explained and illustrated in the remaining part of this chapter and is developed further throughout this publication. In addition, there is related content in the BA4 Fundamentals of Ethics, Corporate Governance and Business Law syllabus which deals with corporate governance and corporate entity administration issues.

6 The accounting equation and the statement of financial position

The statement of financial position is simply a **statement of the assets, liabilities and capital** of a business entity at a specific date.

It is therefore nothing more than a detailed representation of the accounting equation.

The contents of a statement of financial position

In its simplest form the statement of financial position is presented horizontally with assets shown on the left-hand side and liabilities and capital on the right-hand side.

Consequently, the total of each side of the statement of financial position will be the equal – hence the statement of financial position will agree and balance.

When a statement of financial position is prepared, assets and liabilities are divided into two categories: **non-current and current.**

Non-current assets

Any asset held by an entity for more than one accounting period (i.e. at least twelve months) for use in the production or supply of goods or services, for rental to others, or for administrative purposes, and therefore not for sale in the normal course of trading. For example, an item of plant and equipment will normally be used by an entity for several years to support the manufacture of goods which are then sold to earn sales revenue.

Further detail on non-current assets

Non-current assets can be tangible, (in simple terms we can physically see and touch them), or intangible (we cannot physically see and touch them). Examples of tangible non-current assets include land, buildings, motor vehicles, machinery and equipment. Examples of intangible non-current assets include patents, development costs and goodwill. All of these assets will be discussed in more detail in later chapters.

Current assets

Cash or other assets – for example inventory, receivables and short-term investments – held for conversion into cash in the normal course of trading.

Receivables are amounts due or owing to a business entity from another person or business entity following the sale of goods or services.

Further detail on current assets

In other words, a current asset is one that is either already cash, or will be converted into cash within a short period of time.

Receivables are assets to the business entity because they are eventually converted into cash, which is a resource that can then be used by the business entity.

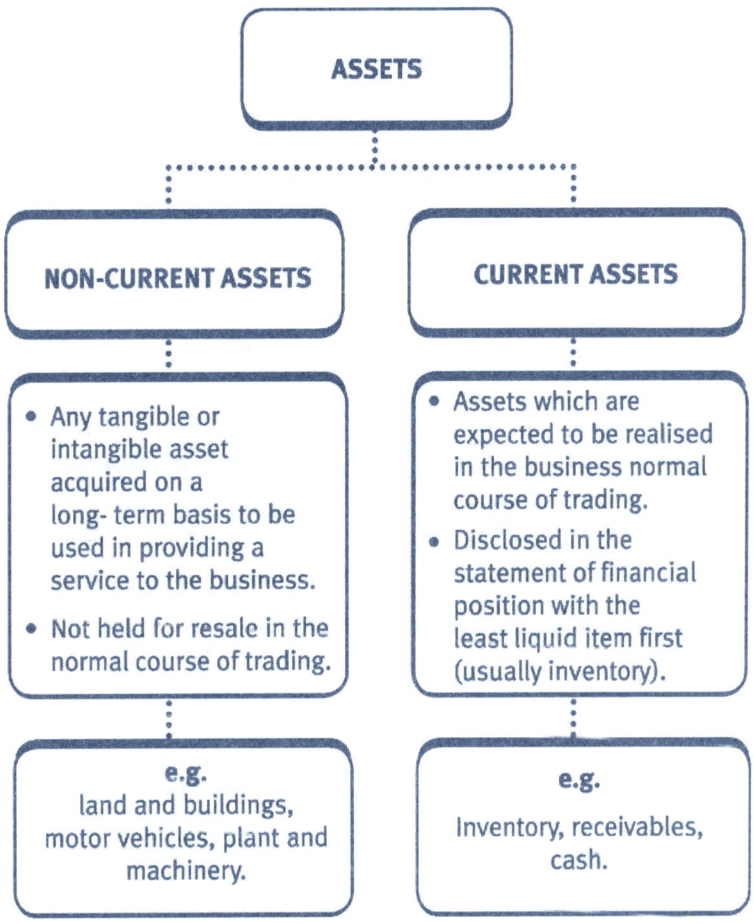

Liabilities are similarly divided into two categories, reflecting the time between the statement of financial position date and the date by which the liability is expected to be settled. These categories are referred to as current liabilities and non-current liabilities.

Current liabilities

Liabilities that fall due for payment within twelve months of the statement of financial position date (often referred to as the year-end or reporting date). They include that part of non-current loans due for repayment within 1 year and payables.

Payables are a person or another business entity to whom the entity owes money as a consequence of the receipt of goods or services in advance of payment, i.e. on credit.

Non-current liabilities

Liabilities that are due for repayment more than one year after the statement of financial position date.

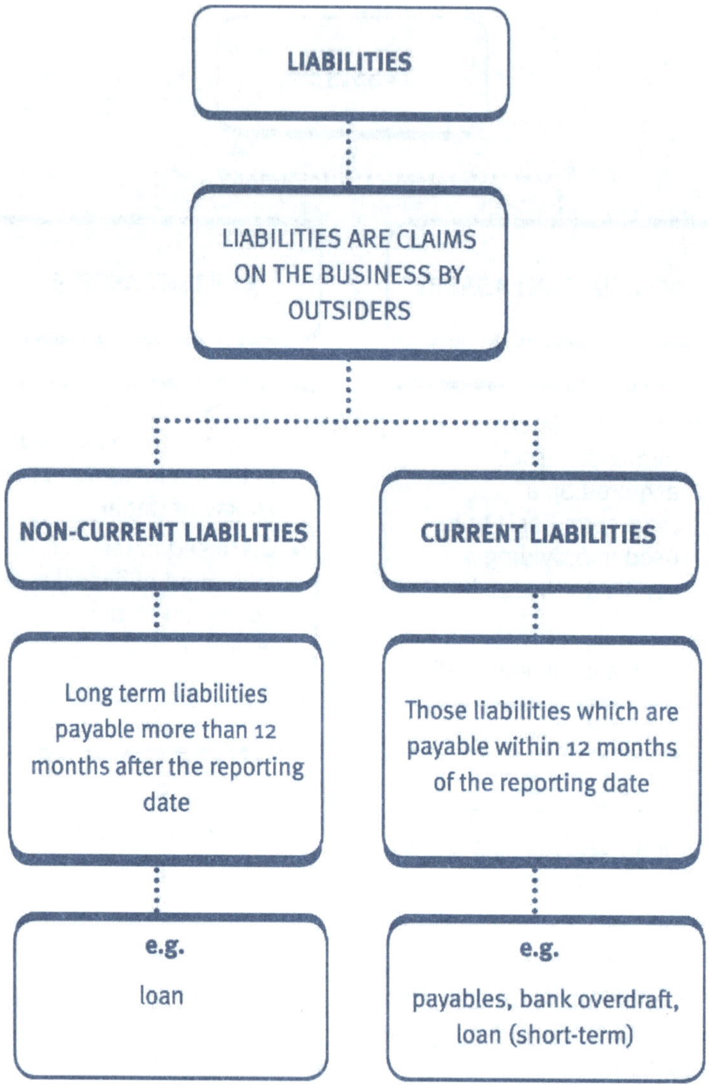

Further detail on payables

These are the financial obligations or liabilities of a business entity, and will remain so until they are paid or settled by the entity.

Worked Example 2.A

Nadim had the following assets and liabilities on 1 January:

	$
Land	200,000
Buildings	60,000
Inventories	10,000
Receivables	15,000
Bank balance	32,000
Cash in hand	5,000
	322,000
Payables	17,000
Bank loan	240,000
	257,000

Required:

What was the balance on Nadim's capital account at 1 January?

Solution

The total value of Nadim's assets on 1 January was $322,000; his liabilities totalled $257,000. Therefore his capital must be $65,000, calculated as follows

Assets	=	Liabilities	+	Capital
$322,000		$257,000		$65,000

We can now prepare Nadim's statement of financial position.

Statement of financial position of Nadim as at 1 January

Assets	$000	$000	**Capital + Liabilities**	$000
Non-current assets			Capital	65
Land	200			
Buildings	60		Non-current liabilities	
		260	Bank loan	240
Current assets				
Inventories	10		Current liabilities	
Receivables	15		Payables	17
Bank balance	32			
Cash in hand	5			
		62		
		322		322

We can see from the above that the statement of financial position could be used to calculate the value of capital. We have the value of all of the assets and liabilities – the only missing (or balancing) item is the capital balance. If this method was used the capital value would be the figure required to make the statement of financial position balance.

You should also note the order in which the current assets are listed. This is referred to as the order of liquidity. **Liquidity is the measure of how easily or quickly current assets can be converted into cash**, and it is usual for current assets to be listed from the least liquid to the most liquid (as above).

Returning to our worked example, if we assume that Nadim had the following transactions during the first week of January:

1 Bought office equipment at a cost of $7,000, and paid a $2,000 deposit by cheque, the balance to be paid at the end of March.

2 Returned some of the above office equipment to his supplier because it was faulty. Nadim had originally been charged $3,000 the items returned.

3 Received $8,000 from his receivables. They all paid him by cheque.

We can now see how these transactions affected his accounting equation.

1 Assets (office equipment) increase by $7,000 Assets (bank balance) decrease by $2,000 Liabilities (payables) increase by $5,000

Nadim's accounting equation is amended to

Assets	=	Liabilities	+	Capital
$327,000		$262,000		$65,000

2 Assets (office equipment) decrease by $3,000 Liabilities (payables) decrease by $3,000. Nadim's accounting equation becomes

Assets	=	Liabilities	+	Capital
$324,000		$259,000		$65,000

3 Assets (receivables) decrease by $8,000

Assets (bank balance) increase by $8,000

This has no net effect on Nadim's accounting equation, which will remain unchanged.

Required:

Compile Nadim's statement of financial position after the transactions have been accounted for.

Solution

Nadim's statement of financial position after these three transactions would be as follows:

Statement of financial position of Nadim as at 1 January

Assets	$000	$000	**Capital + Liabilities**	$000
Non-current assets			Capital	65
Land	200			
Buildings	60		Non-current liabilities	
Office equipment (7 – 3)	4		Bank loan	240
		264		305
Current assets				
Inventory	10		Current liabilities	
Receivables (15 – 8)	7		Payables (17 + 5 – 3)	19
Bank balance (32 – 2 + 8)	38			
Cash in hand	5			
		60		
		324		324

Vertical presentation of a statement of financial position

The statement of financial position presentation used so far is known as the horizontal format. It may be thought of as representing a set of scales, whereby the amount on each side of the centre is equal. In this way it can be said to balance.

In practice, a vertical presentation is used more often and an example using the same information is given below.

Statement of financial position: vertical format

Assets	$000	$000
Non-current asset		
Land	200	
Buildings	60	
Office equipment	4	
		264

Current assets		
Inventory	10	
Receivables	7	
Bank balance	38	
Cash in hand	5	
		60
		324
Capital + liabilities		
Capital		65
Non-current liabilities		
Bank loan		24
Current liabilities		
Payables		19
		324

Note that, whichever method of presentation is used, the assets, liabilities and capital balances are exactly the same.

The difference between the current assets and the current liabilities is known as the net current assets, if positive, or net current liabilities, if negative. It is also known as the **working capital** of the business.

Key headings

In later studies you will learn that working capital is an important measure of the short-term liquidity of an entity. In Nadim's statement of financial position above, the net current assets (working capital) is $41,000 ($60,000 – $19,000). In order to prepare the above statement you should recognise that individual assets, capital and liabilities are grouped under five main headings as follows:

1. non-current assets
2. current assets
3. capital
4. non-current liabilities, and
5. current liabilities.

7 The statement of profit or loss

The statement of profit or loss is a summary of **income generated and expenses incurred** to generate the profit over a period of time, usually a year.

Income less expenses = profit or loss for the period.

It makes use of the two elements of the financial statements not used in the preparation of the statement of financial position.

The statement of profit or loss may also be called income statement but for the purpose of the BA3 exam it should always be referred to as the statement of profit or loss.

Income

Income is the inflow of economic benefits to an entity over a period of time. This will consist of sales revenue generated from goods and services sold to customers, but may also include other items such as interest received or dividends received.

Expenses

Expenses are the outflow of economic benefits from an entity over a period of time. This may include the using of resources such as heat and light, wages and salaries or office expenses. Expenses are incurred by a business entity to help it generate economic benefits such as sales revenue

If this is related to the example of Nadim's business entity, he will try to generate sales revenue by selling his goods to customers. To sell goods, Nadim first has to buy those goods (or manufacture them – but we shall assume that Nadim is a retailer rather than a manufacturer). Obviously, there is a cost involved when buying of the goods for resale.

Running costs

He must pay rental charges and buy fuel for his delivery van. He probably pays rent for the warehouse or shop premises in which he stores his goods. If he employs anyone to help him he will have to pay wages. All of these costs will charged against the gross profit earned from the sale of the goods.

Gross profit

This is calculated by deducting the cost of goods sold from the sales revenue generated.

Cost of goods sold

These are the direct costs attributable to the production of the goods sold by a company. This is also referred to as 'cost of sales'.

Net profit

This is calculated by deducting any other running costs of the business entity from the gross profit.

Where does profit go?

What happens to this net profit when it has been earned?

- As a private individual, Nadim has living expenses like everyone else. He will need to withdraw some of the net profit from the business entity to pay for his living expenses. Such a withdrawal for personal use from the business entity is referred to as 'drawings'.
- Any profit that Nadim does not need to withdraw simply remains in the business entity, increasing its capital.

In Worked Example 1.A in chapter 1, you saw that Ahmed, trading as Ahmed's Matches, made a profit of $10.50, and withdrew $5 for himself, leaving the remaining $5.50 in the business entity to increase its capital.

In Worked Example 2.A in this chapter, you saw that a statement of financial position could be compiled for Nadim from a summary of assets and liabilities at a specific point in time. By using the accounting equation, it was possible to derive the capital balance as a balancing or missing figure as everything else was known.

This example will now be developed to deal with preparation of the statement of profit or loss.

Worked Example 2.B

During the following month, Nadim sold goods on credit to his customers for $6,000. He already had some inventory, which cost $10,000, so he used $1,000 of that inventory, and purchased further inventory at a cost of $3,000, all of which was used to fulfil the order. He has not yet paid for this extra inventory.

His rent bill for the month was $500 and his van hire and running costs were $300.

He withdrew $200 from the business entity for his private use.

Required:

Present a statement of profit or loss for Nadim for the month, and a statement of financial position at the end of the month.

Solution

Statement of profit or loss for the month

	$	$
Sales		6,000
Less: Cost of goods sold (1,000 + 3,000)		(4,000)
Gross profit		2,000
Less expenses		
Rent	500	
Van hire and running costs	300	
		(800)
Net profit earned		1,200

Notes:

1 The cost of goods sold figure can be calculated as $1,000 from existing inventory, plus $3,000 bought specially. See later in the chapter for another approach to calculate the cost of goods sold.

2 Nadim's drawings are not business expenses, but are deducted from his capital in the statement of financial position below.

The part of the statement of profit or loss which calculates gross profit is known as the trading account. The trading account is a sub-section of the statement of profit or loss although this titles does not appear within the statement of profit or loss. Nevertheless, it is a very important part of the statement of profit or loss and you may be asked to prepare a trading account in your exam.

Statement of financial position at the end of the month

Assets	$000	$000
Non-current asset		
As before		264,000
Current assets		
Inventory (10,000 – 1,000)	9,000	
Receivables (7,000 + 6,000)	13,000	
Bank balance	38,000	
Cash in hand (5,000 – 500 – 300 – 200)	4,000	
		64,000
		328,000

Capital and liabilities	
Capital	66,000
Long-term liabilities	
Bank loan	240,000
Current liabilities	
Payables (19,000 + 3,000)	22,000
	328,000

Notice that the capital of the business entity has increased by $1,000 – the amount of net profit retained in the entity. It is possible to prepare a statement of changes in capital, showing exactly how the figure of $65,000 has risen to $66,000

Statement of changes in capital

	$	$
Capital at start of the month		65,000
Net profit earned in period	1,200	
Less: profit withdrawn by Nadim	(200)	
Net profit retained in the business entity		1,000
Capital at end of month		66,000

You should see clearly from this statement how the statement of profit or loss links up with the statement of financial position: the net profit earned, shown in the statement of profit or loss, becomes an addition to capital in the statement of financial position, and Nadim's drawings from the business are deducted from this.

In later chapters we will learn more about the statement of profit or loss and how it may be part of a statement of comprehensive income. However, until then, we will simply refer to the statement of profit or loss.

The cost of goods sold

The calculation of the cost of goods sold is an important figure.

The cost of goods sold will be deducted from sales revenue when calculating the gross profit or loss in the statement of profit or loss.

When calculating the cost of goods sold we can use the following formula:

	$
Cost of opening inventory at the start of the period	X
Cost of purchases during the period	X
	X
Less: Cost of closing inventory at the end of the period	(X)
Cost of goods sold	X

Note that the cost of goods sold may also be referred to as the cost of sales.

Cost of goods sold

The statement of profit or loss will be reviewed in more detail later in this publication, but at this stage it is worth noting one general point, which will be illustrated by the particular example of the cost of goods sold.

In computing the profit earned in a period the accountant's tasks are:

- to establish the sales revenue earned in the period, and
- to establish the costs incurred by the business entity to earn or generate that revenue.

The second point is not as simple as it might appear. For example, it would not be true to say that the costs incurred in an accounting period are equal to the sums of money expended in the period. This could be illustrated by many examples, some of which will be encountered later in the text. For now, the focus is on one particular cost: **the cost of goods sold**.

A trader may continually buy goods and sell them on to customers. At the point he prepares his financial statements it is likely that he has items of inventory that were purchased during the accounting period but not yet sold. It would be wrong to include the cost of this closing inventory as part of the cost of goods sold, for the simple reason that these goods have not yet been sold.

Looking back to the beginning of the accounting period, it is likely that there was opening inventory which had been purchased during the previous accounting period. These items were presumably sold during the current accounting period and their cost must form part of the cost of goods sold, even though they were purchased in an earlier accounting period.

This illustrates that the cost of goods sold in an accounting period is not the same as the cost of goods purchased in the period. In fact, to calculate the cost of goods sold the following calculation is needed (presented here using the figures from Nadim's business above):

	$
Cost of opening inventory at the start of the period	10,000
Cost of purchases during the period	3,000
	13,000
Less: Cost of closing inventory at the end of the period	(9,000)
Cost of goods sold	4,000

It is the figure of $4,000 – not the purchases of $3,000 – that is matched with the sales revenue for the period in order to derive the figure of gross profit.

Test your understanding 1

Explain briefly what is meant by each of the following terms and provide at least one example of each:

- assets
- liabilities
- capital
- income
- expenses.

Test your understanding 2

On 1 June 20X1, J Brown started business as a gardener with a capital of $2,000 in cash. A list of figures extracted from his records on 31 May 20X2 was as follows:

	$
Cash purchases of seeds, plants, etc.	700
New motor van	1,100
Mowing machine	70
Hedge trimmer	250
Motor van expenses	300
Rent of garage	200
Paid to wife for clerical work	500
Insurance	200
Private expenses paid from bank	1,500
Cash at bank and in hand	180
Cash sales made to customers	3,000
Capital at the start of the year	2,000
Inventory of seeds, plants, etc. at the end of the year	100

Required:

(a) Prepare the statement of profit or loss for the year ended 31 May 20X2.

(b) Prepare the statement of financial position as at 31 May 20X2.

Profit and cash – a reminder

Note that in Worked Example 2.B, Nadlm's business entity made a profit of $1,200. But his bank balance remained unchanged and his cash holdings actually fell. This was because somc of the transactions that affected profit did not affect cash at the same time. For example, his customers did not pay Nadim, and nor did Nadim pay his suppliers, until after the end of the month. Also, there was a transaction that affected cash, but not profit – Nadim took $200 cash in drawings, which reduced his capital but not his profit. There are lots of other reasons why profit does not always result in an equal change in bank and cash balances. You will consider these throughout your studies for this subject.

8 The framework for integrated reporting

The International Integrated Reporting Council (IIRC) is a coalition of regulators, investors, companies, standard setters, the accountancy professional and NOn-Governmental Organisations (NGOs). Its mission is to establish integrated reporting within mainstream business practice.

Whilst the IIRC is not part of the IFRS Foundation, there is a Memorandum of Understanding between the IIRC and the IASB that recognises both bodies have a common interest in developing and promoting the quality and consistency of global corporate reporting.

One of the weaknesses of historical cost reporting is that it reports transactions and events that have already occurred. Whilst this information is useful, users of financial statements are often more interested in what may happen in the future. Consequently, the need for some form of integrated report which includes elements of historical cost reporting along with some prospective or forward-looking information to meet the needs of users has developed.

The principle behind integrated reporting is that such reports provide information on a range of financial and non-financial capitals to explain to providers of financial capital how value is created over time.

An integrated report is **'a concise communication about how an organisation's strategy, governance, performance and prospects, in the context of its external environment, lead to the creation of value in the short, medium and long term'** (IIRC®).

The six capitals identified in the IR Framework are:

- Financial – how monetary capital has changed during an accounting period.
- Manufactured – this relates to production capacity – has it increased or decreased?
- Intellectual – this will include intellectual property, patents etc.
- Human – not only the numbers employed, but also its skills, training and expertise.
- Social and relationship – the relationship between the reporting entity and its local environment
- Natural – access to resources, such as raw materials.

Note that entities are not obliged to prepare an integrated report, but, when they choose to do so, it is best practice to apply IIRC guidance.

The content of an integrated report

An integrated report should include all of the following content elements:

- Entity overview and external environment – 'What does the entity do and what are the circumstances under which it operates?'
- Governance – 'How does the entity's governance structure support its ability to create value in the short, medium and long-term?'
- Business model – 'What is the entity's business model and to what extent is it resilient to commercial pressures?'
- Opportunities and risks – 'What are the specific opportunities and risks that affect the entity's ability to create value over the short, medium and long term, and how is the entity dealing with them?'
- Performance – 'To what extent has the entity achieved its strategic objectives and what are its outcomes in terms of effects on the capitals?'
- Future outlook – 'What challenges and uncertainties is the entity likely to encounter in pursuing its strategy, and what are the potential implications for its business model and future performance?'
- Basis of presentation – 'How does the entity determine what matters to include in the integrated report, and how are such matters quantified or evaluated?'

Including this content should help entities to shift the focus of their reporting from historical financial performance to longer-term value creation. It also improves the quality of information available to interested parties.

9 Chapter summary

In this chapter you have studied:

- the regulatory environment that underpins the preparation of accounting information
- how to apply the accounting equation to record transactions
- the format and classification of the statement of financial position and statement of profit or loss
- the need for, and information in, an integrated report.

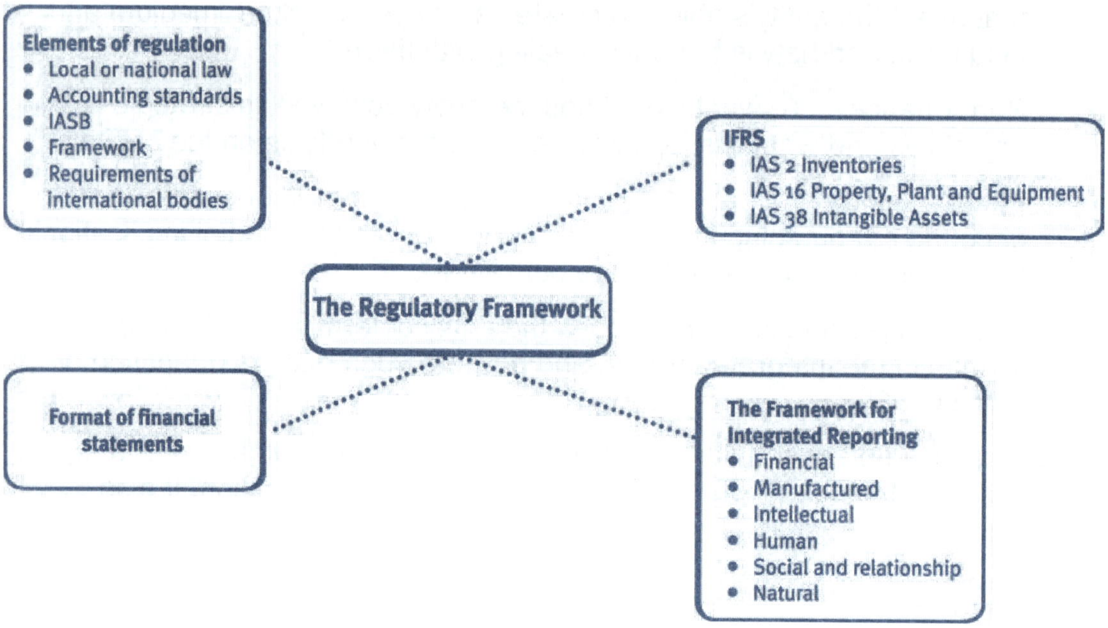

Test your understanding questions

Test your understanding 3

Gross profit for 20X1 can be calculated from:

A purchases for 20X1, plus inventory at 31 December 20X1, less inventory at 1 January 20X1

B purchases for 20X1, less inventory at 31 December 20X1, plus inventory at 1 January 20X1

C cost of goods sold during 20X1, plus sales during 20X1

D net profit for 20X1, plus expenses for 20X1

Test your understanding 4

The capital of a sole trader would change as a result of:

A a payable being paid into his account by cheque

B raw materials being purchased on credit

C non-current assets being purchased on credit

D wages being paid in cash

Test your understanding 5

You have been given the following information relating to a business entity for the month of May 20X1.

	$
Sales of goods for cash	17,000
Sales of goods on credit	28,000
Purchases of inventory on credit	19,500
Wages paid in cash	2,000
Non-current assets bought on credit	12,000
Cash withdrawn by the owner	1,600
Inventory of goods at 1 May	5,000
Inventory of goods at 31 May	6,250

Required:

What was the profit or loss for May 20X1?

	$	$	$
Sales	.............+	...............=	....
Less: Cost of sales			
Inventory at 1 May 20X1		....	
Purchases		....	
		....	
		....	
Inventory at 31 May 20X1		....	
Cost of goods sold			....
Gross profit			....
Less: Expenses – wages			....
Net profit			....

Test your understanding 6

In addition to the information in Question TYU 5, you have been provided with the following information relating to assets and liabilities at 1 May 20X1:

	$
Non-current assets	37,000
Receivables	7,000
Bank and cash	12,000
Payables	7,300

Required:

Insert the missing figures below to prepare a statement of financial position at 1 May to calculate capital at that date. This information can then be used to help prepare the statement of financial position at 31 May.

	$
Non-current assets	....
Inventory	....
Receivables	....
Bank and cash	....
Total assets	....
Less: Payables	....
Capital (i.e. Assets – Liabilities)	....

Statement of financial position: vertical format

Assets	$	$
Non-current assets		....
Current assets		
Inventory	....	
Receivables	....	
Bank and cash	....	
Subtotal		....
Capital and liabilities		
Capital at 1 May 20X1 (as per above)		....
Net profit (as per TYU 5)		....
Subtotal		....
Less: Drawings		....
Capital at 31 May 20X1		....
Current liabilities: Payables		....

Test your understanding answers

Test your understanding 1

- **Assets.** Items controlled by an entity, which may be used to generate income in the future. It includes non-current assets (land, buildings, machinery, etc.) and current assets (inventories, receivables, cash, etc.).
- **Liabilities.** Financial obligations or amounts owed by an entity to third parties. It includes loans, overdrafts and payables.
- **Capital.** The amount of investment made by the owner(s) in the entity, and not yet withdrawn. The amount includes initial and subsequent amounts introduced by the owner(s), plus any profits earned, les any drawings by the owner(s) have been retained in the business.
- **Income.** Amounts earned from the activities of the entity, which eventually result in receiving money. This includes sales revenue, interest and dividends received. Income increases profit.
- **Expenses.** Costs used up in the activities of the entity, which Includes heat, light, local business tax, inventories consumed, wages and distribution expenses. Expenses reduce profit.

Test your understanding 2

Statement of profit or loss of J Brown for the year ended 31 May 20X2

Sales	$	$
Purchases of seeds, plants		3,000
Less: Closing inventory of seeds, plants	700	
	(100)	
Cost of goods sold	——	600
Gross profit		2,400
Less: Motor van expenses	300	
Rent of garage	200	
Wife's wages	500	
Insurance	200	
		1,200
Net profit		
		1,200

Statement of financial position of J Brown as at 31 May 20X2

	$	$
Assets		
Non-current assets		
Motor van		1,100
Mowing machine		70
Hedge trimmer		250
		1,420
Currents assets		
Inventory of seeds and plants	100	
Cash at bank and in hand	180	
		280
		1,700
Capital		
Capital introduced		2,000
Add: Net profit for the year		1,200
		3,200
Less: Drawings		(1,500)
Capital at the end of the period		1,700

Test your understanding 3

D

Working backwards often confuses candidates. Try drawing up a short example of a statement of profit or loss using simple figures of your own, to prove or disprove the options given.

For example:

	$	$
Sales		20,000
Inventory at 31.12.20X0	2,000	
Purchases during 20X1	8,000	
	10,000	
Less: Inventory at 31.12.20X1	(1,000)	
Cost of goods sold		9,000
Gross profit		11,000
Less: Expenses		(4,000)
Net profit		7,000

Make all the figures different or you will make mistakes.

You can now see that options A, B and C will not give the correct answer.

Test your understanding 4

D

Transactions that affect only assets and liabilities do not affect capital.

Therefore, options A, B and C are irrelevant.

Test your understanding 5

May 20X1	$	$
Sales ($17,000 + 28,000)		45,000
Less: Cost of sales		
Inventory at 1 May 20X1	5,000	
Purchases	19,500	
	24,500	
Inventory at 31 May 20X1	(6,250)	
Cost of goods sold		(18,250)
Gross profit		26,750
Less: Expenses – wages		(2,000)
Net profit		24,750

Test your understanding 6

First of all calculate the capital at the start of the period (not forgetting the inventory balance given in TYU 5), then adjust the opening assets and liabilities for the changes given in TYU 5. Finally, add the profit to the opening capital, and deduct drawings.

	$
Non-current assets	37,000
Inventory	5,000
Receivables	7,000
Bank and cash	12,000
	61,000
Less: Payables	(7,300)
Capital	53,700

Statement of financial position as at 31.5.X1

Assets	$	$
Non-current assets (37,000 + 12,000)		49,000
Current assets		
Inventory	6,250	
Receivables (7,000 + 28,000)	35,000	
Bank and cash (12,000 + 17,000 – 2,000 – 1,600)	25,400	
		66,650
		115,650
Capital and liabilities		
Capital at the start of the period (as per above)		53,700
Net profit (as per TYU 5)		24,750
		78,450
Less: Drawings		(1,600)
Capital at the end of the period		76,850
Current liabilities:		
Payables (7,300 + 19,500 + 12,000)		38,800
		115,650

Chapter

3

Ledger accounting and double-entry bookkeeping

Chapter learning objectives

When you have completed this chapter, you should be able to:

- apply and explain the principles of double-entry bookkeeping
- prepare nominal ledger accounts
- prepare bookkeeping entries for income and expenditure
- prepare bookkeeping entries for assets, liabilities and capital.

1 Introduction

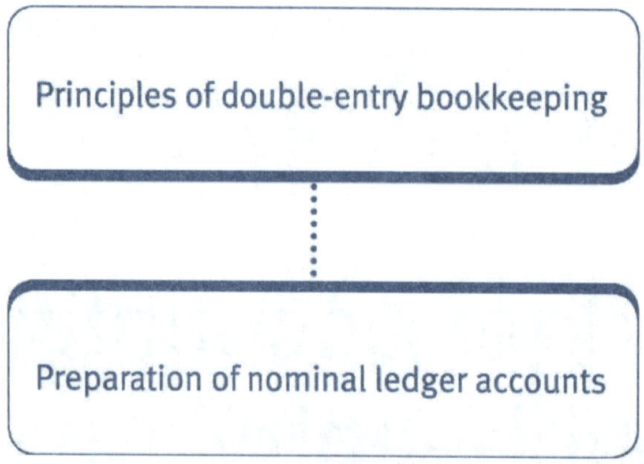

In this chapter we develop an understanding of:

- the principles of double-entry bookkeeping
- the preparation of nominal ledger accounts.

2 Duality, double-entry and the accounting equation

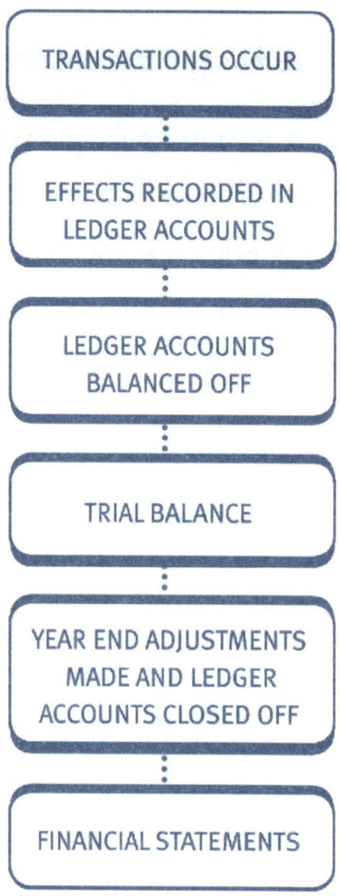

Duality concept

Each transaction that an entity enters into affects the financial statements in two ways.

For example, an entity may buy a vehicle, paying cash. The two effects on the entity are:

1 it has increased the vehicle assets it has at its disposal for generating income, and

2 there is a decrease in cash available to the entity.

To follow the rules of double entry bookkeeping, each time a transaction is recorded, both effects must be taken into account. These two effects are equal and opposite and, as such, the accounting equation will always be maintained.

The business entity concept

The business entity concept states that transactions associated with an entity must be separately recorded from those of its owner. Doing so requires the use of separate accounting records for the entity that completely excludes the assets and liabilities of the owner. This is an important concept to keep in mind when working through the accounting entries for an entity.

The accounting equation

ASSETS = EQUITY + LIABILITIES

ASSETS - LIABILITIES = EQUITY

Note that the image above used the term 'equity' which is an alternative term to 'capital' when dealing with the accounting equation.

The statement of financial position shows the position of an entity at one point in time. A statement of financial position will always satisfy the accounting equation as shown above.

The accounting equation is a simple expression of the fact that at any point in time the assets of the entity will be equal to its liabilities plus its equity.

Illustration 1 – The accounting equation

The transactions of a new business entity during its first five days were as follows:

Day 1	AVO commenced business introducing $1,000 cash.
Day 2	Bought a motor car for $400 cash.
Day 3	Obtained a $1,000 loan.
Day 4	Purchased goods for $300 cash.
Day 5	Sold goods for $400 on credit.

Required:

Use the accounting equation to illustrate the position of the entity at the end of each day (Ignore inventory for this example).

Solution

Day 1: AVO commenced business introducing $1,000 cash

The dual effect of this transaction is:

(a) the entity has $1,000 of cash

(b) the entity owes the owner $1,000 – this is capital/equity

Assets	=	Equity	+	Liabilities
1,000		1,000		0

Day 2: Bought a motor car for $400 cash

The dual effect of this transaction is:

(a) the entity has an asset (a motor car) of $400

(b) the entity has spent $400 in cash

This transaction changes the form in which the assets are held.

Assets	=	Equity	+	Liabilities
1,000		1,000		0
400 – 400		0		0
1,000		1,000		0

Note that acquiring an asset must lead to one of the following:

- reducing another asset by a corresponding amount (as above)
- incurring a corresponding liability
- increasing the equity of the owner (either capital invested or profits made and owed to the owners)

Day 3: Obtained a $1,000 loan from the bank

The dual effect of this transaction is:

(a) the entity has $1,000 cash

(b) the entity owes $1,000 to the bank

Assets	=	Equity	+	Liabilities
1,000		1,000		0
1,000		0		1,000
2,000		1,000		1,000

Day 4: Purchased goods for $300 cash

The purchase represents a cost (or an expense) to the entity. This cost will reduce the profits of the entity, which will in turn reduce equity.

The dual effect of is:

(a) The entity has an expense of $300 (expenses reduce the amount due to the owners, i.e. they reduce equity)

(b) The entity has reduced cash by $300

Assets	=	Equity	+	Liabilities
2.000		1,000		1,000
(300)		(300)		0
1,700		700		1,000

Day 5: Sold goods for $400 on credit

The dual effect of this transaction is:

(a) The entity has earned sales revenue of $400

(b) The entity has a new asset to receive of $400 from its customer

Sales revenue will increase profits and will therefore increase equity in the business entity.

Assets	=	Equity	+	Liabilities
1,700		700		1,000
400		400		0
2,100		1,100		1,000

3 Ledger accounts, debits and credits

An **account** is a record of the transactions involving a particular item.

A ledger account may be thought of as a record kept as a page in a book. The book contains many pages – many accounts – and is referred to as a ledger.

In this chapter we are concerned with the **nominal or general ledger,** which is the ledger containing all of the accounts necessary to summarise an entity's transactions and prepare a statement of financial position and statement of profit or loss.

Each account comprises two sides: the left-hand side is referred to as the **debit** side, and the right-hand side is referred to as the **credit** side. The format is shown below:

Debit (Dr)					**Credit (Cr)**
Date	Details	$	Date	Details	$

Summary of steps to record a transaction

Summary of steps to record a transaction:

1 Identify the items that are affected.

2 Consider whether they are being increased or decreased.

3 Decide whether each account should be debited or credited.

4 Check that a debit entry and a credit entry have been made and they are both for the same amount.

Additional guidance:

- transactions and events are eventually recorded in the relevant ledger accounts using a double-entry to reflect the duality concept explained previously. There is a ledger account for each asset, liability, equity, income and expense item
- traditionally each account was drawn as an enlarged 'T' that has two sides – a debit and a credit side as illustrated
- the duality concept means that each transaction will affect at least two ledger accounts
- one account will be debited and the other credited.
- whether an entry is to the debit or credit side of an account depends on the type of account and the transaction:

Debit	Credit
Increase in:	Increase in:
Purchases	**R**evenues
Expenses	**L**iabilities
Assets	**S**hareholder's equity

You can use the mnemonic 'PEARLS' to help you remember this vitally important double entry rule.

It is important to note that the opposite is also true; for example, a reduction in assets would constitute a credit entry into the appropriate ledger account.

Ledger accounts – a definition

In simple terms the ledger accounts are where the double-entry records of all transactions and events are recorded. They are the principal books or files for recording and totalling monetary transactions by account. An entity's financial statements are generated from summary totals in the ledgers.

4 What is double-entry bookkeeping?

According to the **CIMA Official Terminology**:

Double-entry bookkeeping: The most commonly used system of bookkeeping based on the principle that every financial transaction involves the simultaneous receiving and giving of value, and is therefore recorded twice.

Duality concept

Earlier in this text we saw how some transactions affected the accounting equation and the statement of financial position. We saw that each transaction had two effects: this is referred to as the **dual aspect** or **duality** concept. For example, receiving payment from a receivable increases the asset 'cash', whilst also reducing the asset 'receivables'; paying a supplier reduces the asset 'cash' whilst also reducing the liability 'payables'; In both cases, the accounting equation remains intact. The fact that every transaction has two effects – equal and opposite – means that each transaction must be recorded in two ledger accounts. This is double-entry bookkeeping.

Bookkeeping is the technique of recording financial transactions as they occur so that summaries may be made of the transactions and presented as a report to the users of accounts. The double-entry bookkeeping technique applies to the recording of transactions in ledger accounts.

Test your understanding 1

Explain what is meant by the term 'double-entry bookkeeping'.

In the earlier chapters, the following terms were introduced:

- assets
- liabilities
- capital/equity
- income, and
- expenses.

These **five items** can be put into **two categories**, according to whether they appear in the **statement of financial position** or in the **statement of profit or loss.**

- Assets, liabilities and capital appear in the statement of financial position.
- Expenses and revenue appear in the statement of profit or loss.

If you compare these pairs you will see that they are, in effect, two pairs of opposites.

Each type of asset, liability, capital, expense or income is recorded separately. This is achieved by using **separate ledger** accounts for each of them.

5 Bookkeeping entries for the financial statements

Transactions are recorded on either the debit or the credit side of a ledger account according to the following table:

Debit (Dr)	**Credit (Cr)**
Increases in assets	Decreases in assets
Decreases in liabilities	Increases liabilities
Decreases in capital	Increases in capital/equity
Increases in expenses	Decreases in expenses
Decreases in income	Increases in income

Entering transactions in ledger accounts is also called **posting** the transactions.

An expense is a cost connected with the day-to-day activities of the entity. Examples of expenses include rent, local business tax, light and heat, wages and salaries, postage and telephone i.e. costs of operating the business entity, along with the cost of items bought for resale.

Income is the term used to describe the activities that will eventually lead to the entity receiving cash. The most common source of income is that derived from the sale of its goods or services, but others include the receipt of interest on bank deposits.

Examples of debit and credit entries – assets and liabilities

Examples of debit entries:

- Increase in assets, e.g. purchase of inventory, non-current assets, increase in cash/bank
- Decreases in liabilities, e.g. payment of suppliers/loans
- Decreases in capital, e.g. drawings.

Examples of credit entries:

- Decrease in assets, e.g. sale of non-current assets, payment of receivables, decreases in cash/bank
- Increases in liabilities, e.g. purchase of goods on credit, new loans obtained
- Increase in capital, e.g. introduce new capital into the entity.

Now that you have a good grasp of the double-entry requirements for basic transactions lets apply those rules to Illustration 1 from earlier in the chapter.

The transactions from illustration its first five days were as follows: (**Note:** For simplicity all bank and cash transactions are posted to the cash account.)

Day 1 AVO commenced business introducing $1,000 cash.

Debit – cash to increase assets.

Credit – capital to increase shareholder equity/capital.

Day 2 Bought a motor car for $400 cash.

Debit – motor vehicles to increase assets.

Credit – cash to decrease assets.

Day 3 Obtained a $1,000 loan.

Debit – cash to increase assets.

Credit – loans to increase liabilities.

Day 4 Purchased goods for $300 cash.

Debit – purchases to increase purchases.

Credit – cash to decrease assets.

Day 5 Sold goods for $400 on credit.

Debit – receivables to increase assets.

Credit – sales to increase revenue.

Cash

Dr		$	Cr		$
Day 1	Capital	1,000	Day 2	Motor vehicles	400
Day 2	Loan	1,000	Day 4	Purchases	300

Capital

Dr		$	Cr		$
			Day 1	Cash	1,000

Motor vehicles

Dr		$	Cr		$
Day 2	Cash	400			

Loan

Dr		$	Cr		$
			Day 3	Cash	1,000

Purchases

Dr		$	Cr		$
Day 4	Cash	300			

Receivables

Dr		$	Cr		$
Day 5	Sales	400			

Sales

Dr		$	Cr		$
			Day 5	Receivables	400

Examples of debit and credit entries – income and expenses

Examples of debit entries:

- Increases in expenses, e.g. purchase of materials, rent, wages, electricity costs
- Decreases in income, e.g. sales returns.

Examples of credit entries:

- Decreases in expenses, e.g. purchase returns
- Increases in income, e.g. sales of goods for cash or credit.

Journal entries

In a bookkeeping system involving the recording of only day-to-day transactions, it is inevitable that there will be further year-end entries or adjustments or errors that need to be corrected outside of the normal double-entry system. In order to complete the system, a journal entry may be required. 'The journal' will be covered in more detail later in this publication but for the moment it is important to be aware that some transactions may need to be manually recorded as a journal at the year-end outside of the day-to-day transactions. Transactions recorded by journal include:

- depreciation
- the write-off of irrecoverable debts
- allowances for receivables
- accruals and prepayments.

Each of these entries will be covered later in more detail. A basic journal entry however is simply a manual debit and credit entry posted into the system in the same way as above.

Bookkeeping entries for purchases and sales

Separate ledger accounts are used to record the different types of inventory movement. Purchases and sales of inventory must always be kept in separate accounts, because one records the cost of purchase, whilst the other records sales at selling price. You might have difficulty in determining how to classify purchases and sales. You could regard purchases as being assets, or you could regard them as being expenses. It all depends on whether they are consumed during the period, and that will be unknown at the time they are bought. Similarly, sales could be regarded as decreases in inventory or as revenues. The fact is that it does not matter how you regard them. Both will result in the correct entry being made. For example, if you regard the purchase of inventory as an increase in an asset, you will make a debit entry; if you regard it as an increase in an expense, you will still make a debit entry. The same applies to sales – a decrease in inventory results in a credit entry, as does an increase in revenue. So, you will choose the right side for the entry, whichever way you classify these. The most important thing is to use the correct account – and never use the inventory account for purchases and/or sales as the inventory account is used only at the beginning and end of the accounting period.

Also note that you should **never** use either the purchases account or the sales account for anything other than the goods in which the business entity trades. Purchases of non-current assets, stationery and so on should all be recorded in their own ledger accounts.

Test your understanding 2

Tick the correct box for each of the following:

		Debit	**Credit**
1	Increases in assets	....	....
2	Increases in liabilities	....	....
3	Increases in income	....	....
4	Decreases in liabilities	....	....
5	Increases in expenses	....	....
6	Decreases in assets	....	....
7	Increases in capital	....	....
8	Decreases in income	....	....

e.g

Illustration 2

BR started a business on 1 May and, during the first month, entered into the following transactions:

1st	BR starts business as a sole proprietor with $20,000 in cash
2nd	Pays $15,000 cash into a business bank account
4th	Purchases goods on credit from JM for $2,000
6th	Purchases goods from ERD on credit for $3,000
7th	Pays wages in cash $60
10th	Pays rent by cheque $80
12th	Sells goods for cash $210
16th	Buys furniture for $1,500 paying by cheque
19th	Sells goods on credit to SP for $580
22nd	Buys goods for cash $3,900
24th	Buys fittings for cash $600
24th	Pays carriage outwards costs by cheque $25
25th	Pays wages by cash $110
25th	Sells goods for cash $430
27th	Receives part payment from SP of $330 by cheque
27th	Pays carriage inwards costs by cheque $20
28th	Pays advertising by cheque $25
28th	Sells goods for cash $890
29th	Sells goods on credit to KM for $8,090
30th	Withdraws $100 cash for his personal use

Required:

Prepare ledger account entries to record the transactions.

Note: When you draw up your accounts, you may want to leave extra lines after the bank account (approx. 10), and after all other ledger accounts (approx. 4 per account) – this exercise is continued in Chapter 4.

Note: It might help you to determine the correct ledger entries by completing a table before you start, like this (the first item is done for you):

Date	Names of accounts involved	Type of accounts	Increase/decrease	Debit/credit
1 May	Cash	Asset	Increase	Debit
	Capital	Capital	Increase	Credit

Solution:

Capital

Dr		$	Cr		$
			1 May		20,000
		20,000			20,000
balance c/f		20000	balance b/f		20,000

Cash

Dr		$	Cr		$
1 May	Capital	20,000	2 May	Bank	15,000
12 May	Sales	210	7 May	Wages	60
25 May	Sales	430	22 May	Purchases	3,900
28 May	Sales	890	24 May	Fittings	600
		21530	25 May	Wages	110
			30 May	Drawings	100
					21530
balance b/f		1760	balance c/f		1760

Bank

Dr		$	Cr		$
2 May	Cash	15,000	10 May	Rent	80
27 May	SP	330	16 May	Furniture	1,500
			24 May	Carriage out	25
			27 May	Carriage in	20
			28 May	Advertising	25

Purchases

Dr		$	Cr		$
4 May	JM	2,000			
6 May	ERD	3,000			
22 May	Cash	3,900			

JM

Dr		$	Cr		$
			4 May	Purchases	2,000

ERD

Dr		$	Cr		$
			6 May	Purchases	3,000

Wages

Dr		$	Cr		$
7 May	Cash	60			
25 May	Cash	110			

Rent

Dr		$	Cr		$
10 May	Bank	80			

Sales

Dr		$	Cr		$
			12 May	Cash	210
			19 May	SP	580
			25 May	Cash	430
			28 May	Cash	890
			29 May	KM	8,090

Furniture

Dr		$	Cr		$
16 May	Bank	1,500			

SP

Dr		$	Cr		$
19 May	Sales	580	27 May	Bank	330

Fittings

Dr		$	Cr		$
24 May	Cash	600			

Advertising

Dr		$	Cr		$
28 May	Bank	25			

KM

Dr		$	Cr		$
29 May	Sales	8,090			

Drawings

Dr		$	Cr		$
30 May	Cash	100			

Carriage outwards

Dr		$	Cr		$
24 May	Bank	25			

Carriage inwards

Dr		$	Cr		$
27 May	Bank	20			

Test your understanding 3

ATH commenced business on 1 February 20X1, paying $500 into a business bank account. (**Note:** This TYU is continued in Illustration 1 – Chapter 4)

During February the following transactions took place. All payments are made by cheque and all receipts are banked.

		$
1st	Bought goods for resale	150
5th	Paid rent	50
10th	Sales receipts	290
22nd	Paid for advertising	25
26th	ATH's drawings	100
27th	Sales receipts	240

Required:

(a) write up the bank account

(b) write up all the other accounts.

Note: When you draw up your accounts, leave ten extra lines after the bank account, and four extra lines after all other ledger accounts – this exercise is continued in Chapter 5.

Nominal ledger accounts

At this stage in your studies, all your ledger accounts are kept in a single 'book'. In later chapters you will see how the ledger accounts can be divided into several books. The main book used is called the **nominal or general ledger.**

6 Chapter summary

In this chapter you have studied:

- how financial transactions are recorded in ledger accounts, using double-entry principles.

Double-entry is the cornerstone of the entire accounting process. You will not get far in your studies of this subject unless you have a thorough grasp of its principles. Make sure you can follow the steps involved in the examples given in this chapter, and memorise the table.

It is important that you fully understand the double-entry system, as it will enable you to understand how to record more complex transactions in your subsequent studies.

Try not to analyse the reason for the 'left and right' system for recording transactions. It is simply a rule that, if everyone abides by it, leads to a common system. It can be likened to the rule for driving a car. If the rule in a country is to drive on the left, then the system works as long as everyone abides by the rule.

Practise the examples in the chapter several times until you feel competent in them.

Principles of double-entry bookkeeping

Debit	Credit
Increases in assets	Decreases in assets
Decreases in liabilities	Increases in liabilities
Decreases in capital	Increases in capital
Increases in expenses	Decreases in expenses
Decreases in revenue	Increases in revenue

Preparation of nominal ledger accounts

Test your understanding questions

Test your understanding 4

SMA commenced in business as a decorator on 1 January.

1st	Commenced business by paying $1,000 into a business bank account.
3rd	Bought a motor van on credit from ABG for $3,000.
4th	Bought decorating tools and equipment on credit from BAP for $650.
8th	Bought paint for $250, paying by cheque.
10th	Received $400 cash from a customer for work done.
12th	Bought paint for $150, paying in cash.
14th	Issued an invoice to a customer, KOR, for $750 for work done.
18th	Returned some of the decorating tools, cost $80, to BAP.
23rd	Took $50 cash to buy a birthday present for his son.
28th	KOR paid $250 by cheque towards his bill.

Required:

Write up the transactions in each account for the month of January, by completing the ledger accounts provided below:

Capital

	$		$

Bank

	$		$

Motor van

$	$

ABG

$	$

Tools and equipment

$	$

BAP

$	$

Purchases

$	$

Sales

$	$

Cash

$	$

KOR

	$		$

Drawings

	$		$

Test your understanding 5

BBA commenced in business as a market gardener on 1 March. The following transactions occurred during March:

1st	Paid $70 rent for land for the month of March, from his own funds.
3rd	Bought equipment on credit for $400 from JKL.
4th	Bought plants for $2,000, paying from his own funds.
8th	Received $100 cash for a talk to the local horticultural society.
10th	Sold plants for $1,200, being paid by cheque. A business bank account was opened with this amount.
12th	Paid wages of $50 in cash
14th	Bought plants for $800 on credit from BHH.
18th	Sold Plants for $500 on credit to PB.
23rd	Paid $100 local business tax by cheque.
28th	Paid wages of $20 in cash.
31st	Sold plants for $240, being paid in cash.

Required:

Record the above transactions in the ledger accounts provided below.

Rent expense

$	$

Capital

$	$

JKL

$	$

Equipment

$	$

Purchases

$	$

Sales

$	$

Cash

	$		$

Bank

	$		$

Wages

	$		$

BHH

	$		$

PB

	$		$

Local business tax

	$		$

Test your understanding 6

On 1 January, P Roberts started a business with $2,500 in the bank and $500 cash. The following transactions occurred during January:

2nd	He bought raw materials on credit for $700 from J Martin.
3rd	He sold goods for $300 on credit to G Goddard.
7th	He sold goods for $1,100 to K Lemon on credit.
12th	He bought equipment for $3,000, paying by cheque.
18th	He paid wages of $50 by cheque.
20th	He bought raw materials for $350, paying by cheque. He took $80 from the cash box for himself.
28th	He paid J Martin $250 by cheque.
30th	He transferred $200 cash into the bank from his cash box.

Required:

Record the above transactions in the ledger accounts provided below.

Capital

		$			$
			1 Jan	Bank	
				Cash	

Bank

		$			$
1 Jan	Capital		12 Jan	Equipment	
30 Jan	Cash		18 Jan	Wages	
			20 Jan	Purchases	
			28 Jan	J Martin	

Cash

		$			$
1 Jan	Capital		20 Jan	Drawings	
			30 Jan	Bank	

Purchases

		$			$
2 Jan	J Martin				
20 Jan	Bank				

J Martin

		$			$
28 Jan	Bank		2 Jan	Purchases	

Sales

		$			$
			3 Jan	G Goddard	
			7 Jan	K Lemon	

G Goddard

		$			$
3 Jan	Sales				

K Lemon

		$			$
7 Jan	Sales				

Equipment

		$			$
12 Jan	Bank				

Wages

		$			$
18 Jan	Bank				

Drawings			
	$		$
20 Jan Cash			

Test your understanding 7

The double-entry system of bookkeeping normally results in which of the following balances in the ledger accounts?

	Debit	Credit
A	Assets and income	Liabilities, capital and expenses
B	Income, capital and liabilities	Assets and expenses
C	Assets and expenses	Liabilities, capital and income
D	Assets, expenses and capital	Liabilities and income

Test your understanding 8

Which one of the following statements is correct?

A Assets and liabilities have credit balances

B Liabilities and revenues have debit balances

C Assets and revenues have credit balances

D Assets and expenses have debit balances

Test your understanding 9

ALCO had the following assets and liabilities at 1 January:

	$
Inventory	350
Payables	700
Receivables	400
Bank overdraft	125
Motor vehicles	880

Required:

What was the capital account balance at 1 January?

$ 805

Assets = Capital + liabilities

Capital = liabilities - assets

Test your understanding 10

The correct entries needed to record the return of office equipment that had been bought on credit from PYO, and not yet paid for, are:

	Debit	Credit
A	Office equipment	Sales
B	Office equipment	PYO
C	PYO	Office equipment
D	Cash	Office equipment

Test your understanding 11

A receives goods from B on credit terms and A subsequently pays by cheque. A then discovers that the goods are faulty and cancels the cheque before it is cashed by B.

How should A record the cancellation of the cheque in his books.

	Debit	Credit
A	Payables	Returns outwards
B	Payables	Bank
C	Bank	Payables
D	Returns outwards	Payables

Test your understanding 12

The table below shows a selection of financial transactions. Complete the columns to identify the accounts and the debit/credit entries to be made in the ledger to record each of the transactions.

	Transaction description	Account to be debited	Account to be credited
1	Sold goods on credit to BAS	BAS	Sales
2	Bought goods for sale on credit from PWA	Purchases	PWA
3	Returned goods to PWA	PWA	Purchases
4	Bought office machinery on credit from WPR	office equip	WPR
5	Returned office machinery to WPR	WPR	office
6	Received cash from PWR	Cash	PWR
7	Received payment from TWI by cheque	Bank	TWI
8	Owner's private car brought into the business	Car	Capital
9	Cheque received from PWR dishonoured	PWR	Bank

Test your understanding answers

Test your understanding 1

Double-entry bookkeeping is a system of keeping records of transactions in ledger accounts such that every transaction requires debit and credit entries of equal value. For example, there might be a debit entry of $100 equalled by two credit entries of $90 and $10, respectively. The result of this method is that the total of debit balances on ledger accounts equals the total of credit balances.

Test your understanding 2

The order of boxes should be debit; credit; credit; debit; debit; credit; credit; debit.

Test your understanding 3

Bank

20X1		$	20X1		$
1 Feb	Capital	500	1 Feb	Purchases	150
10 Feb	Sales	290	5 Feb	Rent	50
27 Feb	Sales	240	22 Feb	Advertising	25
			26 Feb	Drawings	100

Capital

		$	20X1		$
			1 Feb	Bank	500

Purchases

20X1		$			
1 Feb	Bank	150			

Rent

20X1		$			
5 Feb	Bank	50			

Advertising

20X1		$			
22 Feb	Bank	25			

Drawings

20X1		$			
26 Feb	Bank	100			

Sales

			20X1		$
			10 Feb		290
			27 Feb		240

Test your understanding 4

Capital

		$			$
			1 Jan	Bank	1,000

Bank

		$			$
1 Jan	Capital	1,000	8 Jan	Purchases	250
28 Jan	KOR	250			

Motor van

		$			
3 Jan	ABG	3,000			

ABG

		$			$
			3 Jan	Motor van	3,000

Tools and equipment

		$			$
4 Jan	BAP	650	18 Jan	BAP	80

BAP

		$			$
18 Jan	Tools	80	4 Jan	Tools	650

Purchases

		$			$
8 Jan	Bank	250			
12 Jan	Cash	150			

Sales

		$			$
			10 Jan	Cash	400
			14 Jan	KOR	750

Cash

		$			$
10 Jan	Sales	400	12 Jan	Purchases	150
			23 Jan	Drawings	50

KOR

		$			$
14 Jan	Sales	750	28 Jan	Bank	250

Drawings

		$			$
23 Jan	Cash	50			

Test your understanding 5

Rent Expenses

		$			$
1 Mar	Capital	70			

Capital

		$			$
			1 Mar	Rent	70
			4 Mar	Purchases	2,000

JKL

		$			$
			3 Mar	Equipment	400

Equipment

		$			$
3 Mar	JKL	400			

Purchases

		$			$
4 Mar	Capital	2,000			
14 Mar	BHH	800			

Sales

		$			$
			9 Mar	Cash	100
			10 Mar	Bank	1,200
			18 Mar	PB	500
			31 Mar	Cash	240

Cash

		$			$
8 Mar	Sales	100	12 Mar	Wages	50
31 Mar	Sales	240	28 Mar	Wages	20

Bank

		$			$
10 Mar	Sales	1,200	23 Mar	Local business tax	100

Wages

		$			$
12 Mar	Cash	50			
28 Mar	Cash	20			

BHH

		$			$
			14 Mar	Purchases	800

PB

		$			$
18 Mar	Sales	500			

Local business tax

		$			$
23 Mar	Bank	100			

Test your understanding 6

Capital

		$			$
			1 Jan	Bank	2,500
				Cash	500

Bank

		$			$
1 Jan	Capital	2,500	12 Jan	Equipment	3,000
30 Jan	Cash	200	18 Jan	Wages	50
			20 Jan	Purchases	350
			28 Jan	J Martin	250

Cash

		$			$
1 Jan	Capital	500	20 Jan	Drawings	80
			30 Jan	Bank	200

Purchases

		$			$
2 Jan	J Martin	700			
20 Jan	Bank	350			

J Martin

		$			$
28 Jan	Bank	250	2 Jan	Purchases	700

Sales

		$			$
			3 Jan	G Goddard	300
			7 Jan	K Lemon	1,100

G Goddard

		$			$
3 Jan	Sales	300			

K Lemon

		$			$
7 Jan	Sales	1,100			

Equipment

		$		$
12 Jan	Bank	3,000		

Wages

		$		$
18 Jan	Bank	50		

Drawings

		$		$
20 Jan	Cash	80		

Test your understanding 7

C

Test your understanding 8

D

Test your understanding 9

Capital	= Assets	– Liabilities
	= ($350 + $400 + $880)	– ($700 + $125)
	= $805	

Test your understanding 10

C

Test your understanding 11

C

Test your understanding 12

	Account to be debited	Account to be credited
1	BAS	Sales
2	Purchases	PWA
3	PWA	Returns outwards
4	Office machinery	WPR
5	WPR	Office machinery
6	Cash	PWR
7	Bank	TWI
8	Car	Capital
9	PWR	Bank

Chapter

4

From trial balance to financial statements

Chapter learning objectives

When you have completed this chapter, you should be able to:

- prepare and balance off ledger accounts
- prepare a trial balance
- prepare the entries to be made in the statement of profit or loss and statement of financial position
- close-off ledger accounts.

1 Introduction

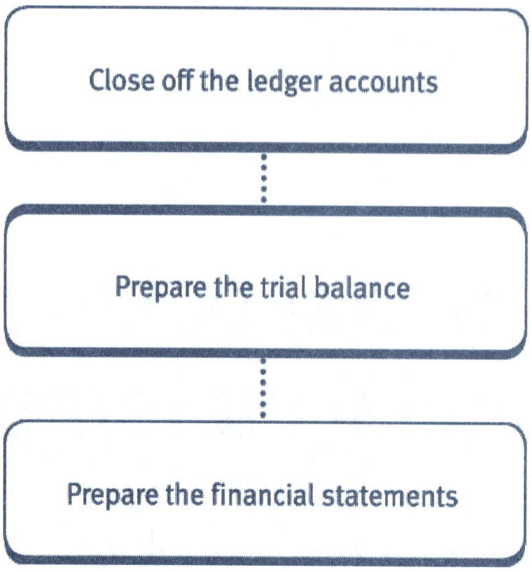

In this chapter, you will learn how to:

- balance off the ledger accounts
- prepare a trial balance
- prepare the financial statements from the trial balance and
- close off the ledger accounts.

2 Balancing the accounts

From time to time it is necessary to determine the end result of the transactions recorded in each ledger account during an accounting period. For example, the cash account will contain a number of debit and credit entries, but no clear indication of how much cash is remaining. The same applies to other ledger accounts: receivables and payables accounts will have a number of debit and credit entries, but no indication of what is currently owed to, and owed by, the business entity, as a result of those entries.

Calculating the balance on the account

When the transactions for an accounting period have been recorded, it will be necessary to find the balance on each ledger account as follows:

1. Total both sides of the T account and identify the larger total.
2. Put the larger total in **the total boxes** on the debit **and** credit side.
3. Insert a balancing figure to the side of the T account which does not currently add up to the amount in the total box. Call this balancing figure 'balance c/f' (carried forward) or 'balance c/d' (carried down).
4. Carry the balance down diagonally and call it 'balance b/f' (brought forward) or 'balance b/d' (brought down).

As an example, look at the cash account that was produced in Chapter 3, Illustration 2, BR:

Cash

Dr		$	Cr		$
1 May	Capital	20,000	2 May	Bank	15,000
12 May	Sales	210	7 May	Wages	60
25 May	Sales	430	22 May	Purchases	3,900
28 May	Sales	890	24 May	Fittings	600
			25 May	Wages	110
			30 May	Drawings	100

1 Add both sides of the ledger and enter the highest balance in the total for both the debit and credit side. In this example the debit side totals $21,530 (meaning that $21,530 was received) and the credit side totals $19,770 (meaning that amount has been paid out).

2 We should therefore take the higher figure of $21,530 and enter it into **both** totals.

3 Now find the difference required to make the lower side of the ledger agree with the total. In this example the credit side totalled to $19,770 and will therefore need an entry of $1,760 to make it agree with the account total of $21,530. This entry is called the balance carried down.

4 Finally enter the amount called the balance carried down on the diagonally opposite side of the ledger below the total and reference it as the balance bought down. This represents the opening amount on the account for the following accounting period. In this example we will have a balance bought down on the debit side of $1,760 which represents an asset.

The ledger will now look like this:

Cash

Dr		$	**Cr**		$
1 May	Capital	20,000	2 May	Bank	15,000
12 May	Sales	210	7 May	Wages	60
25 May	Sales	430	22 May	Purchases	3,900
28 May	Sales	890	24 May	Fittings	600
			25 May	Wages	110
			30 May	Drawings	100
			31 May	Balance c/d	1,760
		21,530			21,530
1 June	Balance b/d	1,760			

Note that this ledger account also illustrates that, for a ledger account balance which will be included in the statement of financial position, the closing balance at the end of one accounting period is carried down to be the opening balance at the start of the next accounting period.

If the procedure is followed in relation to the sales account, the result will be:

Sales

Dr	$	**Cr**		$
		12 May	Cash	210
		19 May	SP	580
		25 May	Cash	430
		28 May	Cash	890
		29 May	KM	8,090
				10,200

Note that, for a ledger account that will be closed-off to the statement of profit or loss, the account balance is simply totalled so that the ledger account balance can be included in the trial balance.

We will see, as the chapter progresses, that when the trial balance has been prepared and is in agreement, all income and expense accounts will be closed-off to the statement of profit or loss.

Test your understanding 1

Having balanced-off the cash account and sales account from Chapter 3 Illustration 2, BR, now balance-off the remaining ledger accounts from that illustration.

Test your understanding 2

Balance-off the ledger accounts from Chapter 3, TYU 3, ATH.

3 Preparing the trial balance

One way of checking the accuracy of the ledger entries is by listing the balances on each account, and totalling them. Because of the 'double-entry' principles applied when recording transactions, **the total of all the accounts with debit balances should equal the total of all the accounts with credit balances.** This list is known as a trial balance.

Using the information from TYU 1, the trial balance for BR at 31 May would appear as follows:

Trial balance

	Debit – $	**Credit** – $
Capital		20,000
Cash	1,760	
Bank	13,680	
Purchases	8,900	
JM		2,000
ERD		3,000
Wages	170	
Rent	80	
Sales		10,200
Furniture	1,500	
SP	250	
Fittings	600	
Advertising	25	
KM	8,090	
Drawings	100	
Carriage outwards	25	
Carriage inwards	20	
	35,200	35,200

The trial balance: A list of account balances in a double-entry accounting system. The sum of the debit balances will equal the sum of the credit balances.

Note that the accounts with **debit balances are either assets or expenses**, whilst the accounts with **credit balances are liabilities, capital or income** accounts. The only exception to this is drawings which represent a reduction in capital.

Note that, even if the totals of the trial balance agree, this does not mean that the ledger account entries and balances are free from error. For example, a transaction may be omitted completely from the ledgers or a transaction may be duplicated in the ledgers.

Neither of these situations would be identified by compilation of a trial balance. Accounting errors are considered in more detail later in this study text.

What if it doesn't balance?

If the totals of the debit and credit balances entered on the trial balance are not equal, then an error or errors have been made either:

1 in the posting of the transactions to the ledger accounts; and/or

2 in the balancing of the accounts; and/or

3 in the transferring of the balances from the ledger accounts to the trial balance.

This will be considered in more detail in a separate chapter.

Test your understanding 3

Prepare a trial balance from the ledger accounts prepared for Chapter 3 TYU 3, ATH, and which were balanced off in Chapter 4, TYU 2.

4 Closing off accounts

At the end of an accounting period (e.g. month, year etc.), the ledger accounts must be closed off to begin the preparation of the financial statements for that accounting period and the subsequent recording of transactions in the next accounting period.

The preparation of financial statements is relevant in subject F1 Financial Reporting in the CIMA Professional Qualification.

Statement of profit or loss

When the trial balance has been completed we can progress to preparation of the statement of profit or loss.

There are two parts to this statement: the trading account used to calculate gross profit and the profit or loss account used to calculate net profit for the accounting period. They are not separately labelled, and are often referred to as the statement of profit or loss.

This will contain any balances relating to **income** (mainly sales revenue) or **expense** accounts and is dealt with as follows:

- at the end of an accounting period any individual income and expense account balances that relate to the current accounting period are transferred from that account and into another ledger account called the statement of profit or loss
- this is done by closing the account relevant income or expense account
- do not show a balance c/f or balance b/f but instead put the balancing figure on the smallest side and label it 'statement of profit or loss'.

If the procedure is followed for BR's sales account, the result will be:

Sales

Dr		$	**Cr**		$
			12 May	Cash	210
			19 May	SP	580
			25 May	Cash	430
			28 May	Cash	890
31 May	Statement of profit or loss	10,200	29 May	KM	8,090
		10,200			10,200

Note that there is no longer an account balance on this ledger account and the procedure can be repeated for the following accounting period.

When the trial balance has been produced all items belonging to the statement of profit or loss will be transferred from their individual ledger accounts to the statement of profit or loss account. This is used to summarise the profit or loss for the accounting period. It is important to remember that any statement of profit or loss ledgers **MUST NOT** have any balances on them at the end of the accounting period.

Accounting for carriage inwards and carriage outwards

Business entities may pay for carriage and delivery charges on items that they buy and/or sell. Such charges are normally accounted for as an expense in the statement of profit or loss, subject to the following points:

- any carriage costs incurred on the delivery of non-current assets purchased for use by the entity are regarded as part of the cost of the asset and added to the cost of the asset, rather than charged as an expense
- any carriage costs inwards on the purchase of goods for resale or materials used for manufacturing are part of cost of sales and accounted for in arriving at gross profit
- any carriage costs outwards incurred on delivery of goods to customers are accounted for as an expense after gross profit has been calculated.

Accounting for purchase returns and sales returns

Goods purchased which have been returned to the supplier are known as either 'purchase returns' or 'returns outwards'. Goods returned by a customer are known either as 'sales returns' or 'returns inwards'.

When the statement of profit or loss is prepared, any returns inwards must be offset against sales income and any returns outwards must be offset against purchases in arriving at gross profit.

Accounting for inventory at the end of the accounting period

In earlier chapters, it was noted that the inventory account was used to record only the value of inventory at the beginning and end of the accounting period. It is not used to record the purchase, sale or return of inventory during an accounting period.

If an entity has been trading for more than one accounting period, there will be a balance on the inventory account at the start of the accounting period, which will be a debit balance (representing an asset at that date). Using information from BR, as this was its first accounting period, there will be a nil balance on the inventory account as follows:

Inventory

		$			$
1 May	Balance b/d	Nil			

At the end of the accounting period, the value of inventory at the start of the accounting period is transferred into the statement of profit or loss. This is achieved by crediting the inventory account and debiting the statement of profit or loss. The inventory account will then have a nil balance as follows:

Inventory

		$			$
1 May	Balance b/d	Nil	31 May	Statement of profit or loss	Nil

As the preparation of the statement of profit or loss continues, it will be necessary to determine the value of inventory at the end of the accounting period. This is often done by referring to a separate inventory control system, which is maintained outside the bookkeeping system (you will learn more about the valuation of inventory later in this study text).

If BR had inventory at 31 May with a value of $1,200, it is recorded in the nominal ledger as follows:

Debit Inventory $1,200, and Credit Statement of profit or loss $1,200

The inventory account will then be as follows:

Inventory

		$			$
1 May	Balance b/d	Nil	31 May	Statement of profit or loss	Nil
31 May	Statement of profit or loss	1,200			

In effect, the inventory account now has a debit (asset) balance to include in the statement of financial position as at 31 May.

If BR's ledger account balances for purchases, sales and carriage inwards costs are also closed off and transferred into the statement of profit or loss, it can now be balanced off to determine the gross profit for the accounting period as a balancing figure as follows:

Statement of profit or loss

20X1		$	20X1		$
			31 May	Inventory at 31 May	1,200
1 May	Balance b/d	Nil	31 May	Sales	10,200
31 May	Purchases	8,900			
31 May	Carriage inwards	20			
31 May	Gross profit c/d	2,480			
		11,400			11,400

Remember that this section of the statement of profit or loss is also known as the trading account i.e. that part of the statement of profit or loss used to determine the gross profit for the accounting period.

Having completed the first section of the statement of profit or loss for BR for the month of May, we can now complete the statement to determine the net profit or loss for the accounting period. Use the trial balance for BR to identify any income or expense accounts that have not been used to calculate gross profit. The net profit or loss for the accounting period can then be identified as a balancing figure, which can then be transferred to the capital account.

For clarity, the complete statement of profit or loss for BR for May is presented below.

Statement of profit or loss account

		$			$
31 May	Inventory at 1 May	Nil	31 May	Inventory at 31 May	1,200
31 May	Purchases	8,900	31 May	Sales	10,200
31 May	Carriage inwards	20			
31 May	Gross profit c/d	2,480			
		11,400			11,400
31 May	Expenses		31 May	Gross profit b/d	2,480
	Wages	170			
	Rent	80			
	Advertising	25			
	Carriage onwards	25			
	Net profit to Capital a/c	2,180			
		2,480			2,480

The statement of profit or loss can then be rearranged and presented in standard format as follows:

BR – Statement of profit or loss for the month of May

	$	$
Sales		10,200
Less: Sales returns		(Nil)
		10,200
Opening inventory	Nil	
Purchases	8,900	
Less: Purchases returns	(Nil)	
Carriage inwards	20	
Less: Closing inventory	8,920	
	(1,200)	
		7,720
Gross profit		2,480
Less expenses:		
Wages	170	
Rent	80	
Advertising	25	
Carriage outwards	25	
		300
Net profit transferred to capital account		2,180

e.g. Illustration 1

Prepare the trading account for Chapter 3, TYU 3, ATH, given that closing inventory was $50. You can use information from your answers to TYU 2 and TYU 3 in this chapter relating to ATH.

Solution

ATH – Trading account for the month ended 28 February 20X1

	$	$
Sales		530
Opening inventory	–	
Purchases	150	
	150	
Less: closing inventory	(50)	
		100
Gross profit		430

Remember that the trading account is the first section of the statement of profit or loss that determines the gross profit for the accounting period.

The statement of financial position

Chapter 2 provided an introduction to the basic format and content of a statement of financial position and you may want to refer again to that content.

Having completed the statement of profit or loss, the next stage is to prepare the statement of financial position. The statement of financial position shows the **assets, liabilities and capital** that exist as at the date at which it is prepared. It will include **ALL** ledger accounts that still have balances on them, subject to the following points:

- assets/liabilities at the end of an accounting period = Assets/liabilities at start of the next accounting period, e.g. the cash at bank at the end of one day will be the cash at bank at the start of the following day
- balancing the account will result in: a balance c/f (being the asset/liability at the end of the accounting period) and a balance b/f (being the asset/liability at the start of the next accounting period)
- the net profit or loss for the year is transferred from the statement of profit or loss to the capital account
- if there is a drawings account, it is closed off and transferred to the capital account.

The statement of financial position

It should be noted that the statement of financial position is not an 'account' and it is not part of the double-entry bookkeeping system. The statement of financial position is a list of all the balances in the ledger accounts at a specific date in time.

The ledger accounts for income and expenses will have no balance remaining, as they have been transferred to the statement of profit or loss. The inventory account will have a new balance, and the capital account will have the net profit or net loss for the accounting period transferred from the statement of profit or loss. Any balance on the drawings account will also be transferred to the capital account. The balances on the other assets and liabilities will be those as used to prepare the trial balance before the financial statements were prepared.

Net profit for the year and drawings

The balance on the statement of profit or loss

The balance on the statement of profit or loss represents the owner's profit, which has the effect of increasing his investment in the entity. At the end of the year this is transferred to the owner's capital account, by debiting the statement of profit or loss and crediting the capital account. If the balance on the statement of profit or loss is a debit balance, this represents a net loss, and the entries are reversed.

Using information from Chapter 3, Illustration 2, BR, the capital account would now appear as follows:

Capital

		$			$
			1 May	Bank	20,000
			31 May	Statement of profit or loss	2,180

Dealing with drawings

The balance on the capital account is increased by the net profit (or decreased by a net loss). The balance on the capital account is also affected by any drawings that have occurred, and that have been debited to a separate drawings account. The balance on this account now needs to be transferred to the capital account, by means of the following entries:

- Debit: Capital account
- Credit: Drawings account.

Using Chapter 3, Illustration 2, BR, the drawings and capital account would now look like this:

Capital

		$			$
31 May	Drawings account	100	1 May	Bank	20,000
			31 May	Statement of profit or loss	2,180

Drawings

		$			$
30 May	Cash	100	31 May	Capital	100

Test your understanding 4

Continuing with information from Chapter 3 Illustration 2, BR, use the remaining account balances to prepare the statement of financial position as at 31 May.

Note – Closing inventory has been valued at $1,200.

BR – Statement of financial position as at 31 May

Assets

	$	$
Non-current assets		
Furniture		
Fittings		______
Current assets		
Inventory		
Receivables		
Bank balance		
Cash in hand		
	______	______
		______
Capital and liabilities		
Capital		
Net profit for the month		______
Less: Drawings		______
Current liabilities		
Payables		______
		______

Test your understanding 5

ORE set up a business on 1st January. During the first two weeks of trading ORE had the following transactions:

January

1st	Introduced $15,000 into a business bank account by cash.
2nd	Bought goods for resale at a cost of $5,000 and paid by cheque.
2nd	Paid rent of $400 by cheque.
3rd	Bought a delivery van for $2,000 and paid by cheque.
6th	Bought $1,000 of goods for resale on credit.
8th	Sold goods for $1,500 and received a cheque for that amount.
10th	Sold all of his remaining goods for $8,000 on credit.
12th	Paid $800 to his supplier by cheque.
14th	Withdrew $500 for personal living expenses from the business bank account.

Note: On 10th January ORE sold his remaining goods so there was no closing inventory at 14th January.

Required:

(a) Complete the relevant ledger accounts for the above transactions.

(b) Extract a trial balance at 14th January.

(c) Prepare the statement of profit or loss for the first two weeks of trading.

(d) Prepare the statement of financial position as at 14th January.

5 Chapter summary

In this chapter you have studied:

- the balancing-off the ledger accounts at the end of the period
- the preparation of the trial balance
- the form and content of the statement of profit or loss
- the ledger account entries needed to prepare a statement of profit or loss
- the ledger account entries needed to record profit and drawings in the capital account
- the preparation of the statement of financial position.

This chapter is one of the most 'technical' chapters you will study. Do practise the techniques you have learned here to ensure that you have a thorough understanding of them.

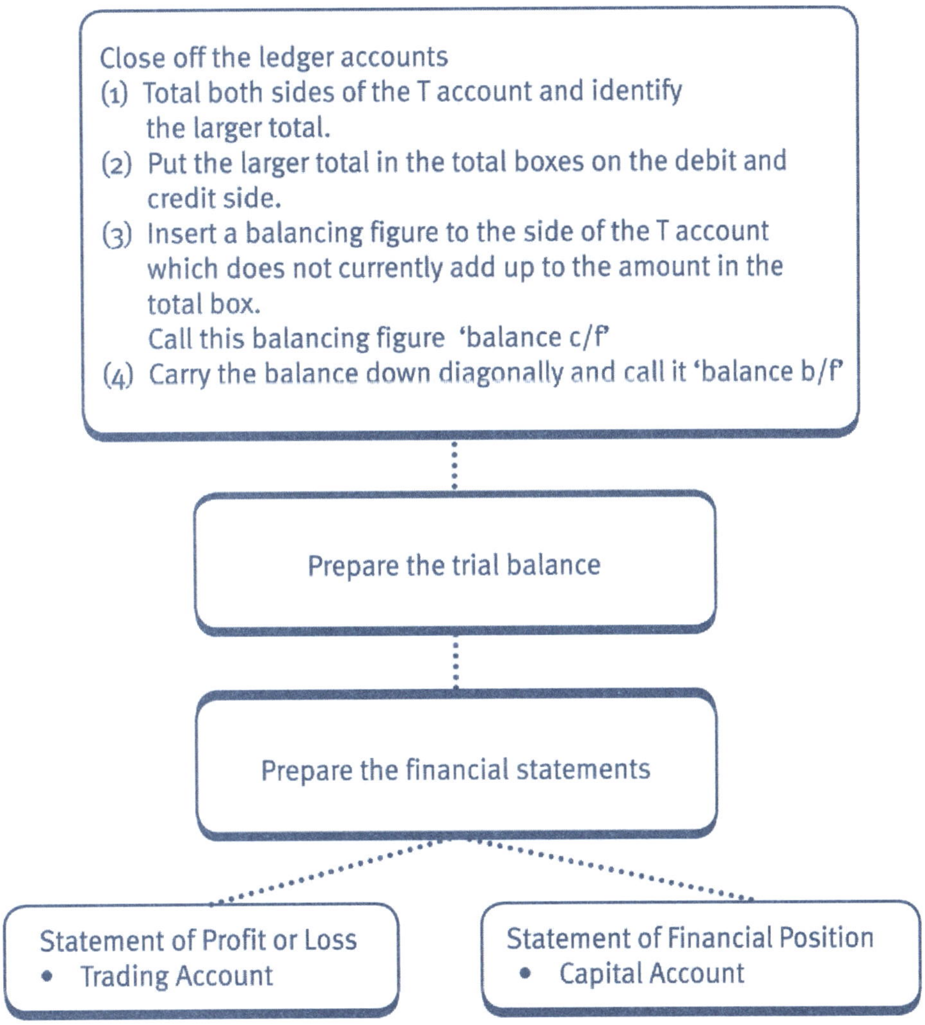

Test your understanding questions

Test your understanding 6

XLD has an account in its nominal ledger for YLT which as a credit balance of $917.

Drag and drop words from the list available to complete the following statements:

________ owes________ $917. In the ledgers of YLT this would represent ________ balance.

Available words:

XLD/YLT/an asset/liability

Test your understanding 7

On 1 January, ABC had a customer, JKL, who owed $400. During January, JKL bought goods for $700 from ABC and returned goods valued at $250. JKL also paid $320 cash to ABC.

Drag and drop words from the list available to complete the following statements:

At 31 January ABC's ledger accounts included a ________ balance for JKL of $________. This represents ________to ABC.

Available words:

debit/credit/an asset/a liability/230/530/1170

Test your understanding 8

Drag and drop words from the available list to complete the following statement:

A ________ balance arises when the total of debit entries is less than the total of credit entries. A debit balance on a ledger account can represent either ________ or ________.

Available words:

debit/credit/income/an expense/an asset/a liability

Test your understanding 9

BBA commenced in business as a market gardener on 1 March. Record the following transactions in the ledger accounts for March:

1st	Paid $70 rent for land for the month of March, from his own funds.
3rd	Bought equipment on credit for $400 from JKL
4th	Bought plants for $2,000, paying from his own funds.
8th	Received $100 cash for a talk to the local horticultural society.
10th	Sold plants for $1,200, being paid by cheque. BBA opened a business bank account with this amount.
12th	Paid wages of $50 in cash.
14th	Bought plants for $800 on credit from BHH
18th	Sold Plants for $500 on Credit to PB.
23rd	Paid $100 local business tax by cheque.
28rd	Paid wages of $20 in cash.
31st	Sold plants for $240, being paid in cash.

At 31 March, BBA had a closing inventory of plants which cost $1,400.

Required:

(a) Record the above transactions in the ledger accounts provided below and calculate the balance on each account as at 31 March.

Rent expense

	$		$

Capital

	$		$

JKL

	$		$

Equipment

	$		$

Purchases

$	$

Sales

$	$

Cash

$	$

Bank

$	$

Wages

$	$

BHH

$	$

PB

$	$

Local business tax

$	$

(b) Prepare the trial balance at 31 March:

	Debit – $	Credit – $
Rent expense		
Capital		
Equipment		
JKL		
Purchases		
Sales		
Cash		
Bank		
Wages		
BHH		
PB		
Local business tax		

(c) Prepare the statement of profit or loss for March, given that the closing inventory of plants was $1,400.

Statement of profit or loss of BBA for the month ended 31 March

	$	$
Sales		
Less: Cost of goods sold		
Purchases		
Less: Closing inventory		
Cost of goods sold		
Gross profit		
Less expenses:		
Rent		
Wages		
Business tax		
Net profit		

(d) Prepare the statement of financial position at 31 March.

Statement of financial position of BBA as at 31 March

	$	$
Assets		
Non-current assets		
Equipment		
Current assets		
Inventory		
Receivables		
Bank		
Cash		
	______	
		______
		______
Capital and liabilities:		
Opening capital		
Add: Net profit		
		______
Current liabilities		
Payables		
		______
		______

Test your understanding answers

Test your understanding 1

	$	
Capital	20,000	credit
Cash	1,760	debit
Bank	13,680	debit
Purchases	8,900	debit
JM	2,000	credit
ERD	3,000	credit
Wages	170	debit
Rent	80	debit
Sales	10,200	credit
Furniture	1,500	debit
SP	250	debit
Fittings	600	debit
Advertising	25	debit
KM	8,090	debit
Drawings	100	debit
Carriage outwards	25	debit
Carriage inwards	20	debit

Capital

		$			$
			1 May	Cash	20,000

Cash

		$			$
1 May	Capital	20,000	2 May	Cash	15,000
12 May	Sales	210	7 May	Wages	60
25 May	Sales	430	22 May	Purchases	3,900
28 May	Sales	890	24 May	Fittings	600
			25 May	Wages	110
			30 May	Drawings	100
			31 May	Balance c/d	1,760
		21,530			21,530
1 Jun	Balance b/d	1,760			

Bank

		$			$
2 May	Cash	15,000	10 May	Rent	80
27 May	SP	330	16 May	Furniture	1,500
			24 May	Carriage out	25
			27 May	Carriage in	20
			28 May	Advertising	25
			31 May	Balance c/d	13,680
		15,330			15,330
1 Jun	Balance b/d	13,680			

JM

		$			$
			4 May	Purchases	2,000

ERD

		$			$
			6 May	Purchases	3,000

Furniture

		$			$
16 May	Bank	1,500			

SP

		$			$
19 May	Sales	580	27 May	Bank	330
			31 May	Balance b/d	250
		580			580
1 Jun	Balance b/d	250			

Fittings

		$			$
24 May	Cash	600			

You should notice that the accounts that only have one entry have not been balanced-off; this is because the balance on the account can easily be seen without balancing it. However, it is a good practice to balance-off in the standard way at least once a year, to confirm that the account has been considered and included in the appropriate financial statement.

For example, the fittings account above would appear as follows:

Fittings

		$			$
24 May	Cash	600	31 May	Balance c/d	600
		600			600
1 Jun	Balance b/d	600			

The balances brought down then become the first entries in each account for the following accounting period.

Advertising

		$			$
28 May	Bank	25			

KM

		$			$
29 May	Sales	8,090			

Rent

		$			$
10 May	Bank	80			

Purchases

		$			$
4 May	JM	2,000			
6 May	ERD	3,000			
22 May	Cash	3,900			
		8,900			

Wages

		$			$
7 May	Cash	60			
25 May	Cash	110			
		170			

Carriage inwards

		$			$
28 May	Bank	20			

Carriage outwards

		$		$
29 May	Bank	25		

Drawings

		$		$
30 May	Cash	100		

Test your understanding 2

	$	
Bank	705	debit
Capital	500	credit
Purchases	150	debit
Rent	50	debit
Advertising	25	debit
Drawings	100	debit
Sales	530	credit

Test your understanding 3

	$	
Bank	705	debit
Capital	500	credit
Purchases	150	debit
Rent	50	debit
Advertising	25	debit
Drawings	100	debit
Sales	530	credit

Trial balance of ATH as at 28 February 20X1

	Debit – $	**Credit – $**
Bank	705	
Capital		500
Purchases	150	
Rent	50	
Advertising	25	
Drawings	100	
Sales		
Bank		530
	1,030	1,030

Test your understanding 4

BR – Statement of financial position as at 31 May

Assets	$	$
Non-current assets		
Furniture		1,500
Fittings		600
		2,100
Current assets		
Inventory	1,200	
Receivables	8,340	
Bank balance	13,680	
Cash in hand	1,760	
		24,980
		27,080
Capital and liabilities		
Capital		20,000
Net profit for the month		2,180
		22,180
Less: Drawings		(100)
		22,080
Current liabilities		
Payables		5,000
		27,080

Test your understanding 5

(a) **Note:** Where appropriate, ledger account balances have been transferred to the statement of profit or loss after the trial balance was extracted. Ledger account balances which are included in the statement of financial position are brought down and dated 15 Jan i.e. the start of the new accounting period.

Bank

		$			$
1 Jan	Capital	15,000	2 Jan	Rent	400
8 Jan	Sales	1,500	2 Jan	Purchases	5,000
			3 Jan	Van	2,000
			12 Jan	Payables	800
			14 Jan	Drawings	500
			14 Jan	Balance c/d	7,800
		16,500			16,500
15 Jan	Balance b/d	7,800			

Capital

		$			$
14 Jan	Balance c/d	15,000	1 Jan	Bank	15,000
		15,000			15,000
			15 Jan	Balance b/d	15,000

Rent

		$			$
2 Jan	Bank	400	14 Jan	To P&L a/c	400

Purchases

		$			$
2 Jan	Bank	5,000			
6 Jan	Payables	1,000	14 Jan	To P&L a/c	6,000
		6,000			6,000

Van

		$			$
3 Jan	Bank	2,000	14 Jan	Balance c/d	2,000
		2,000			2,000
15 Jan	Balance b/d	2,000			

Payables

		$			$
12 Jan	Bank	800	6 Jan	Purchases	1,000
14 Jan	Balance c/d	200			
		1,000			1,000
			15 Jan	Balance b/d	200

Sales

		$			$
			8 Jan	Bank	1,500
14 Jan	To P&L a/c	9,500	10 Jan	Receivables	8,000
		9,500			9,500

Receivables

		$			$
10 Jan	Sales	8,000	14 Jan	Balance c/d	8,000
		8,000			8,000
15 Jan	Balance b/d	8,000			

Drawings

		$			$
14 Jan	Bank	500	14 Jan	To Capital a/c	500
		500			500

(b) **Trial balance of ORE at 14 January**

	Debit – $	*Credit – $*
Bank	7,800	
Capital		15,000
Rent	400	
Purchases	6,000	
Van	2,000	
Payables		200
Sales		9,500
Receivables	8,000	
Drawings	500	
	24,700	24,700

(c) **ORE – Statement of profit or loss for the two weeks ended 14th January**

	$	$
Sales		9,500
Opening inventory	–	
Rent	6,000	
	6,000	
Less: Closing inventory	–	
		(6,000)
Gross profit		3,500
Expenses: Rent		(400)
Net profit		3,100

(d) **ORE – Statement of financial position as at 14 January**

Assets	$	$
Non-current assets		2,000
Van		
Current assets		
Inventory		
Receivables	8,000	
Bank balance	7,800	
		15,800
		17,800
Capital and liabilities		
Capital		15,000
Add: Net profit for the period		3,100
Less: Drawings		(500)
		17,600
Current liabilities		
Payables		200
		17,800

Test your understanding 6

XLD owes **YTL** $917. In the ledgers of YLT this would represent **an asset** balance.

Note that the wording of the statement initially refers to a ledger account balance in XLD's nominal ledger. The second sentence that requires you to think about this information from the perspective of YLT.

Test your understanding 7

At 31 January ABC's ledger accounts included a **debit** balance for JKL of **$530**. This represents an **asset** to ABC.

The ledger account would be as follows:

JKI

		$			$
1 Jan	Balance b/d	400	Jan	Refund goods	250
Jan	Sales	700	Jan	Cash	320
			31 Jan	Balance c/d	530
		1,100			1,100
1 Feb	Balance b/d	530			

Test your understanding 8

A **credit** balance arises when the total of debit entries is less than the total of credit entries. A debit balance on a ledger account can represent either **an asset** or **an expense**.

Test your understanding 9

(a) **Note:** Where appropriate, ledger account balances have been transferred to the statement of profit or loss after the trial balance was extracted. Ledger account balances which are included in the statement of financial position are brought down and dated 1 April i.e. the start of the new accounting period. For convenience, if there is only one entry in the ledger account and it relates to the statement of financial position, that ledger account balance has not been closed off and carried forward.

Rent expense

		$			$
1 Mar	Capital	70	31 Mar	To P&L a/c	70
		70			70

Capital

		$			$
			1 Mar	Rent	70
31 Mar	Balance c/d	2,070	4 Mar	Purchases	2,000
		2,070			2,070
			1 Apr	Balance b/d	2,070

JKL

		$			$
			3 Mar	Equipment	400

Equipment

		$			$
3 Mar	JKL	400			

Purchases

		$			$
4 Mar	Capital	2,000			
14 Mar	BHH	800	31 Mar	To P&L a/c	2,800
		2,800			2,800

Sales

		$			$
			8 Mar	Cash	100
			10 Mar	Bank	1,200
			18 Mar	PB	500
31 Mar	To P&L a/c	2,040	31 Mar	Cash	240
		2,040			2,040

Cash

		$			$
8 Mar	Sales	100	12 Mar	Wages	50
31 Mar	Sales	240	28 Mar	Wages	20
			31 Mar	Balance c/d	270
		340			340
1 Apr	Balance b/d	270			

Bank

		$			$
10 Mar	Sales	1,200	23 Mar	Local business tax	100
			31 Mar	Balance c/d	1,100
		1,200			1,200
1 Apr	Balance b/d	1,100			

Wages

		$			$
12 Mar	Cash	50			
28 Mar	Cash	20	31 Mar	To P&L a/c	70
		70			70

BHH

		$			$
			14 Mar	Purchases	800

PR

		$			$
8 Mar	Sales	500			

Local business tax

		$			$
23 Mar	Bank	100	31 Mar	To P&L a/c	100
		100			100

(b) The trial balance at 31 March was as follows:

	Debit – $	*Credit – $*
Rent expense	70	
Capital		2,070
Equipment	400	
JKL		400
Purchases	2,800	
Sales		2,040
Cash	270	
Bank	1,100	
Wages	70	
BHH		800
PB	500	
Local business tax	100	
	5,310	5,310

(c) Prepare the statement of profit or loss for March, given that the closing inventory of plants was $1,400.

Statement of profit or loss BBA for the month ended 31 March

	$	$
Sales		
Less: Cost of goods sold		2,040
Purchases	2,800	
Less: Closing inventory	(1,400)	
Cost of goods sold		1,400
Gross profit		640
Less expenses:		
Rent	70	
Wages	70	
Business tax	100	
		240
		400

(d) Prepare the statement of financial position at 31 March.

Statement of financial position of BBA as at 31 March

	$	$
Assets:		
Non-current assets		
Equipment		400
Current assets		
Inventory	1,400	
Receivables – PB	500	
Bank	1,100	
Cash	270	
		3,270
		3,670
Capital and liabilities:		
Capital introduced in March		2,070
Add: Net profit		400
Current liabilities		2,470
Payables (JKL & BHH)		1,200
		3,670

Chapter

5

Sales tax, discounts and the books of prime entry

Chapter learning objectives

Upon completion of this chapter you should be able to:

- account for sales tax and discounts
- prepare entries for the books of prime entry, comprising:
  - day books
  - the cash book
  - the journal
- understand that the books of prime entry are not part of the double-entry accounting system.

1 Introduction

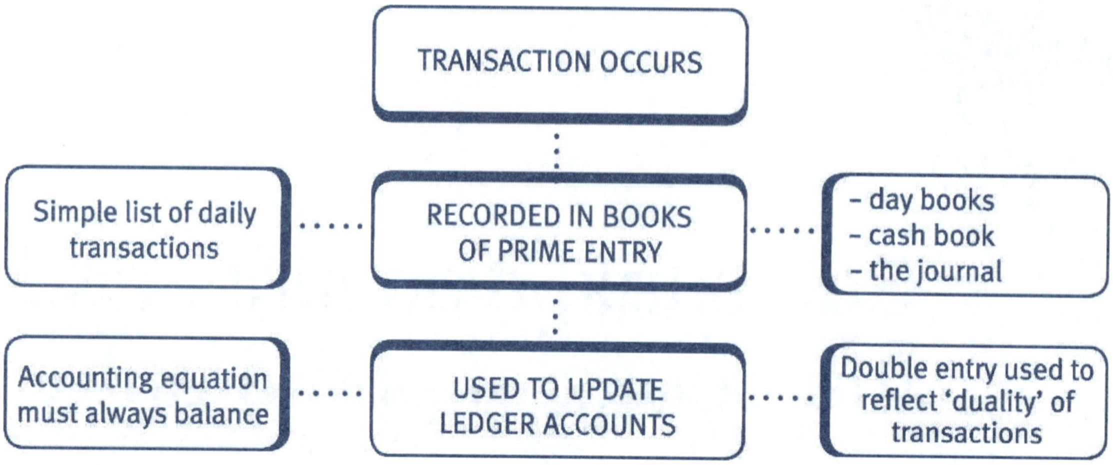

In this chapter we develop an understanding of:

- how individual transactions are recorded, classified and summarised for inclusion in the nominal or general ledger
- how to prepare accounting entries for sales tax
- how to account for discounts
- the purpose of books of prime entry.

2 Accounting records

When the relevant document/data source has been received by the financial accountant a record of it needs to be made in an appropriate place in the accounting system. However, transactions cannot simply be entered directly into the financial statements for the shareholders: there is a systematic accounting and recording process that needs to take place before the ledger account balances for the accounting period can be summarised and classified as a basis for preparing the financial statements.

The accounting system is also used to help monitor the effectiveness of the entity and to help conclude relevant transactions. For example, many goods/services are sold on credit, giving the customer a period of time to settle the amount due. Employees responsible for credit control require information from the accounting system relating to who has or has not settled their debt and, for that reason, who needs to be followed up to ensure that payment is received.

The flow of information from the initial transaction to the financial statements can be illustrated as follows:

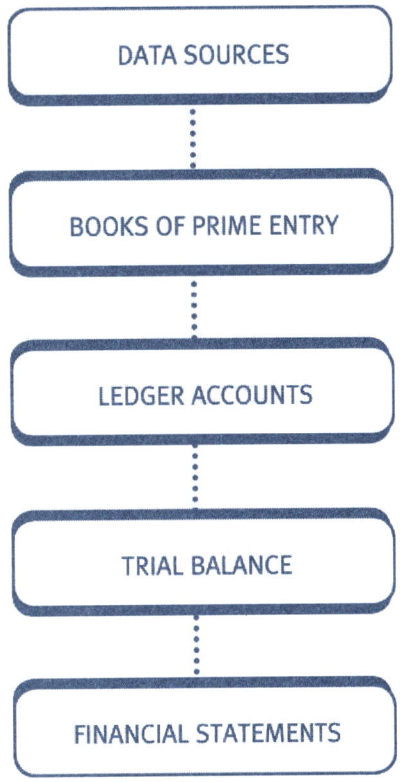

This flow of information will be considered in more detail as the chapter progresses.

3 Introduction to sales tax

Sales tax

In many countries certain business entities are required to charge a sales tax. Sales taxes are sometimes referred to as 'indirect taxes' as they are not deducted directly from income. Usually, this requires a business entity to register with the relevant tax authority if it meets specified criteria and then to administer and account for the sales tax based upon the legal requirements. In the UK this is value added tax (VAT), in France 'TVA', and 'GST' (goods and services tax) in New Zealand and other countries.

In this publication we will consistently use the generic reference 'sales tax'.

Non-registered entities

Some entities may not be required to register to account for sales tax. This may be because of their small size or because of the nature of the goods/services they supply. Such entities are referred to as 'non-registered' for sales tax purposes. In this case, they are not allowed to add sales tax to their sales, and nor can they reclaim the sales tax on their purchases.

For example, if a non-registered entity made a purchase of goods at a cost of $100, plus sales tax at 20 per cent, the accounting entries required would be as follows:

Debit:	Purchases account	$120 (gross amount)
Credit:	Payables/bank account	$120

Therefore, always read questions carefully to identify whether an entity is, or is not, required to account for sales tax to ensure that you answer the question correctly.

The key points associated with accounting for sales tax are as follows:

- a registered entity will charge its customers for goods and services supplied with the addition of sales tax – this is known as output tax, and is a liability payable to the tax authorities
- a registered entity will also incur sales tax on goods and services that it buys from other registered entities – this is known as input tax, and is recoverable, either by offsetting against the amount of output tax payable to the tax authority or as a refund from the tax authority
- for a registered entity, sales tax paid to suppliers (input tax) can normally be reclaimed and offset against output tax collected from customers, so that the net amount of output tax collected is paid to the tax authority
- even though the entity has to pay the supplier the gross amount (purchase cost plus sales tax), if the sales tax is reclaimable then it does not affect the net purchase cost of the goods and services purchased
- note that if an entity paid more input tax to its suppliers than output tax collected from its customers, it will receive a refund from the tax authority of the net amount of input tax paid.

Sales tax

The rate of sales tax varies between countries and it will also depend upon the nature of the goods and services supplied. Many countries operate a sales tax system with more than one rate of tax, but the principles of how the tax is administered remain the same.

4 Double-entry bookkeeping with sales tax

The double-entry bookkeeping records need to show the sales tax values separately so that the purchases, expenses and sales are posted net (i.e. without the addition of sales tax) and the sales tax amounts are posted to a separate sales tax account.

When making a sale the double-entry will be:

Debit:	Receivables/cash account	Gross amount (including sales tax)
Credit:	Sales tax account	Sales tax amount
Credit:	Sales account	Net amount (excluding sales tax)

When making a purchase the double-entry will be:

Debit:	Purchases account	Net amount (excluding sales tax)
Debit:	Sales tax account	Sales tax amount
Credit:	Payables/cash account	Gross amount (including sales tax)

Sales tax on non-current assets and expenses

Input sales tax is also suffered on the purchase of non-current assets and expenses, and can be reclaimed in the normal way. There are, however, generally some items on which input sales tax cannot be reclaimed, although the detail will vary between countries. Examples in the UK are:

- sales tax on passenger cars
- sales tax on entertainment expenses.

In both of the above cases, the sales tax cannot be reclaimed. Therefore, any sales tax charged by the supplier must be added to the cost of the item.

Basic tax rules for non-current assets, expenses and zero rated supplies are relevant for the exam and all relevant information will be provided. Detailed rules will not be examined.

Input and output sales tax in separate ledger accounts

When completing the sales tax return, it is necessary to provide separate totals of input and output sales tax. Therefore, some entities may keep separate ledger accounts for input tax and output tax respectively.

Zero rated and exempt supplies

Supplies of some goods and services are classed as zero-rated, which means that although they are taxable, the sales tax rate applied is zero. Common examples in the UK include basic foodstuffs and children's clothing.

Business entities that make such supplies add zero sales tax to their outputs, but are still able to reclaim the sales tax on inputs. In practical terms, this normally results with such entities receiving regular refunds of input sales tax from the tax authorities.

Other goods and services are classed as **exempt** from sales tax. Business entities supplying such goods are outside of the sales tax system. They cannot register to account for sales tax – sales tax cannot be added to outputs, and nor can input tax be claimed on inputs

5 Trade discounts

A discount is a reduction in the amount paid for goods and services. Discounts may be received from suppliers (a form of income) or allowed to customers (a reduction in revenue). There are two types of discount: trade discounts will be considered first, before moving on to consider cash or settlement discounts.

Trade discounts are offered by an entity to its customers to increase the volume of sales made.

By reducing the unit selling price, buying items in bulk then becomes more attractive. If you are able to source your products cheaper, the buyer can then sell them on cheaper to the consumer, or retain the same selling price but earn a greater profit. For example, if the buyer purchased over 1,000 items or units of a product, the seller may drop the unit selling price of those items by, say, 5%.

Trade discounts should be deducted from the quoted or list price at the point of sale and is **NOT** accounted for in the accounting records of either the seller or the purchaser i.e. only the net amount is recorded.

Therefore, trade discounts have no impact upon the amount of sales tax that may be payable or recoverable by an entity.

Trade discounts

A trade discount may be offered to customers who are also traders, which is where the term 'trade discount' originates. However, it may be offered in a range of other situations, such as to existing customers, new customers or customers buying in bulk to encourage customers to purchase goods, or increase the quantity they purchase. When the discount has been applied at the point of sale, it cannot subsequently be reversed, so it simply means that a lower price per unit is charged by the seller.

Worked Example 5.A

On 1 January, AB purchased goods for resale on credit from XY, with a list price of $250, subject to a trade discount of 20 per cent.

Required:

What was the amount of the trade discount and what are the accounting entries required by AB to record this purchase of goods?

Solution:

The trade discount on this transaction is $50 (20% × $250), and therefore the net amount payable is $200. The accounting entries required by AB to record this purchase are as follows:

		$
Debit:	Purchases	200
Credit:	Payables	200

Test your understanding 1

Oliver sold goods with a list price of $1,000 to Sam on a cash basis and allowed her a trade discount of 10%.

Required:

Show how the above should be recorded in the books of Oliver and Sam respectively.

Test your understanding 2

The following transactions relate to PTL during December 20X1.

2nd	Bought goods on credit from R Williams, list price $350, trade discount 20 per cent
8th	Bought goods on credit from Samuel, list price $750, trade discount 30 per cent
10th	Sold goods on credit to Mary Smythe for $400, no trade discount, payment terms 30 days
18th	Bought goods on credit from Amir, list price $1,000, trade discount 25 per cent
26th	Sold goods on credit John Blair, $800, no trade discount.

All transactions are subject to sales tax at 20 per cent.

Required:

Prepare the entries in the ledger accounts of PTL to record these transactions.

6 Cash or settlement discounts

This type of discount encourages credit customers to pay for purchases earlier than previously agreed.

For example, a seller may agree terms with a customer that payment is due one month following delivery of goods. The seller may also offer an early settlement discount of, say, 5% of the invoice price for payment of the amount due within seven days of delivery of the goods.

Such discounts are often referred to as 'settlement discounts' or 'prompt payment discounts'. Note that a seller cannot force a customer to pay for goods earlier than they have previously agreed.

Whilst offering this discount may encourage customer to make earlier payment, there is a related cost or expense to the seller. The seller is effectively 'giving away' part of the total amount due to them in exchange for earlier receipt of a smaller sum of cash. The amount 'given away' is a **settlement or prompt payment discount - discount allowed.** Rather than accounting for this as an expense, it is accounted for as an adjustment against revenue.

Note that, in this situation, the customer has received a benefit as they have paid a reduced amount in settlement of the total amount due. **The customer therefore needs to account for the benefit they have received as a form of income – discount received**.

Note that if goods are sold subject to a trade discount, as well as the offer of a settlement discount, the trade discount must be applied first before settlement discount is considered.

7 Accounting for cash or settlement discounts

An entity may receive a cash or settlement discount from its suppliers – known as **discounts received.** This is normally classified as other income in the statement of profit or loss.

An entity may give its customers a cash or settlement discount – often referred to as **discounts allowed**. This is accounted for as a reduction in revenue, rather than as an expense.

A settlement discount is different in nature to a trade discount. A trade discount is a definite reduction to the transaction price. Therefore, both the seller and buyer will account for the transaction based upon the price after trade discount has been deducted. A settlement discount is a reduction in the overall invoice price that is offered to the customer in exchange for earlier payment. It is for the customer to decide whether to accept the offer of the early settlement discount and pay the reduced amount within the required timescale, or to pay the full invoice amount at a later date.

In practical terms, if a settlement discount is offered to a credit customer, there is no way of knowing at the point of sale whether or not the customer will take advantage of the discount terms offered and pay the reduced amount.

This is known as 'variable consideration' as the seller does not know at the time when sales revenue is recorded whether the business will receive the full invoice amount, or the discounted amount.

Variable consideration is part of the '5-step approach' to revenue recognition outlined in IFRS 15 *Revenue from contracts with customers* (IFRS 15). Although IFRS 15 is not part of the CIMA Cert BA3 syllabus, accounting for trade and cash or settlement discounts is required knowledge for this paper.

In practice, a seller should adopt one of the following approaches to deal with this situation depending upon whether or not it expects the customer to take advantage of the settlement discount:

Customer not expected to take the settlement discount

- Record the sale and receivable at the list price (less any trade discount), ignoring settlement discount

  Debit Receivables, and Credit Revenue

- When settlement discount is taken, record the cash receipt, reduce revenue by amount of discount allowed and settle the receivable

  Debit Cash, Debit Revenue, and Credit Receivables

- If settlement discount is not taken, record the cash receipt and settlement of the receivable

  Debit Cash, and Credit Receivables

Customer expected to take the settlement discount

- Record the sale and receivable at the list price (less any trade discount) and after settlement discount deducted

  Debit Receivables, and Credit Revenue

- When settlement discount is taken, record the cash receipt and settle the receivable

  Debit Cash, and Credit Receivables

- If settlement discount is not taken, record the cash receipt, settlement of the receivable and recognise the additional revenue received

  Debit Cash, Credit Receivables, and Credit Revenue

Seller perspective

Therefore, **in examination questions**, when dealing with transactions from the perspective of the seller, it will be made clear whether or not a credit customer is expected to take advantage of settlement discount terms for the purpose of calculating amounts invoiced and due from that customer, and to account for the subsequent cash receipt from that customer.

The following illustration shows the accounting requirements relating to settlement discounts from the perspective of the seller.

e.g

Illustration 1 – Settlement discount – seller perspective

An entity sold goods to a customer on credit at a list price of $200, and the customer was offered 3% settlement discount for settlement within ten days of the invoice date.

How should this be accounted for in the books of the seller if:

(a) the customer was not expected to take advantage of the early settlement discount terms offered?

(b) the customer was expected to take advantage of the early settlement discount terms offered?

Solution to Illustration 1

(a) The customer was not expected to take advantage of the early settlement discount.

The invoice would consist of the following amounts:

	$
List price	200
Less: 3% settlement discount – not applicable	Nil
Amount due from customer	200

If, as expected, the customer did not take advantage of the settlement discount available, the full amount of $200 should be received from the customer. Upon receipt of the amount due, this would be recorded as follows:

	$
Debit: Cash	200
Credit: Receivables	200

If, however, the customer did take advantage of the settlement discount terms, they would pay $194. The receivable of $200 must be cleared, even though only $194 has been received in full settlement. This would be recorded as follows:

	$
Debit: Cash (97% of $200.00)	194
Debit: Revenue	6
Credit: Receivables	200

(b) The customer was expected to take advantage of the early settlement discount.

The invoice would consist of the following amounts:

	$
List price	200
Less: 3% settlement discount	(6)
Amount due from customer	194

In this situation, settlement discount (along with any trade discount) is excluded from the accounting records of the seller. If, as expected, the customer paid within ten days to take advantage of the early settlement terms, the receipt of cash would be recorded as follows:

	$
Debit: Cash	194
Credit: Receivables	194

If, however, the customer did not take advantage of the early settlement terms, the full amount of $200 would be due. When received, the 'additional' cash receipt would be accounted for as if it was a cash sale as follows:

	$
Debit: Cash	200
Credit: Receivables	194
Credit: Revenue	6

Purchaser perspective

In examination questions, when dealing with transactions from the perspective of the purchaser, the purchaser will initially record the full cost of the goods and will then decide whether or not to take advantage of settlement discount terms offered by the seller. If the purchaser does not take advantage of the settlement discount offered, the gross amount is payable to the seller. If advantage is taken of the settlement discount terms offered, discount received should be recorded as a memorandum item in the cash payments book.

The following illustration considers the same information as used in Illustration 1 from the perspective of the purchaser.

Illustration 2 – Settlement discount – purchaser perspective

An entity sold goods to a customer on credit at a list price of $200, and the customer was offered 3% settlement discount for settlement within ten days of the invoice date.

How should this be accounted for in the books of the purchaser?

Solution to Illustration 2

The purchaser would initially record the purchase of goods as follows:

	$
Debit: Purchases	200
Credit: Payables	200

If the invoice was paid after the early settlement period, the full amount would be payable to the supplier, with the payment recorded as follows:

	$
Debit: Payables	200
Credit: Bank	200

Alternatively, if the invoice was paid within the 10-day early settlement period, $194 would be paid to the supplier in full settlement of the amount due, and discount received for $6 would be recorded as follows:

	$
Debit: Payables	200
Credit: Bank	194
Credit: Discount received	6

Test your understanding 3

George owes a supplier, Herbie, $2,000 and Herbie has offered George a cash discount of 3% if he makes payment within ten days. George took advantage of the early settlement discount offered and paid Herbie within ten days.

George sold goods to Iris for $3,400. George offers a cash discount to his customers of 2.5% if they pay within 14 days. Iris was expected to take advantage of the early settlement discount offered to her. However, Iris did not pay within 14 days and paid the full amount due after 30 days.

Required:

(a) **Produce the ledger accounts required for George to record his payment to Herbie and clear the amount payable.**

(b) **Produce the ledger accounts required for George to record the receipt from Iris and clear the amount receivable.**

Usually, any discount received from a supplier will be captured in the cash payments book (a book of prime entry) when a remittance advice is prepared and issued by the customer to the supplier. The remittance advice will identify the total amount due, the settlement discount deducted and the net amount paid to the supplier. It is at this point the customer will record that it has deducted settlement discount from the total amount due to the supplier. Your understanding of the cash payments book will be developed later in this chapter.

The income from discounts received is included in the statement of profit or loss immediately after gross profit and before expenses incurred.

Worked Example 5.B

Continuing with Worked Example 5.A suppose that XY also offered a settlement discount of 5 per cent for payment within ten days. From the buyer perspective, the full invoice cost of $200 is recorded in the accounting records. The ledger accounts of AB would appear as follows (as before):

Purchases

20X1		$			$
1 Jan	XY	200			

Payable XY

		$	20X1		$
			1 Jan	Purchases	200

If the account is not settled within 10 days, the full amount of $200 is payable. Subsequently, AB took advantage of the settlement discount offered and paid the amount due on 7 January.

Required:

Calculate the amount of settlement discount that AB is entitled to and show the ledger accounts to record settlement of the liability and the discount received if no separate purchase ledger control account is maintained.

Solution:

Five per cent is deductible, so only $190 is paid. The bank account will be credited with $190, and the account of XY will be debited as follows

Payable XY

20X1		$	20X1		$
7 Jan	Bank	190	1 Jan	Purchases	200

The account has been settled, and yet there is still a $10 credit balance in the payable ledger account, which gives the impression that there is still $10 owing to XY. This is not the case. The payable account for XY needs to reflect the elimination of any further liability due and also to record the discount received as follows:

Debit:	Payable XY	$10
Credit:	Discount received	$10

The ledger accounts after recording the cash discount received are as follows:

Payable XY

20X1		$	20X1		$
7 Jan	Bank	190	1 Jan	Purchases	200
	Discount received	10			

Discount received

		$	20X1		$
			1 Jan	XY	10

Presentation in the financial statements

Discount received is a form of income, and will be transferred to the statement of profit or loss at the end of the accounting period, to increase profit. Remember that discount allowed is adjusted against sales revenue to reduce profit and is not classified as an expense.

Using hypothetical figures discounts allowed and discounts received would appear in the statement of profit or loss as follows:

	$	$
Sales (after discount allowed of $400)		26,600
Opening inventory	1,500	
Purchases	5,000	
	6,500	
Less: Closing inventory	(1,700)	
		(4,800)
Gross profit		21,800
Add: Discount received		200
Less Expenses: Wages		(500)
Net profit		21,500

Note that CIMA has indicated that students will not be examined on accounting for sales tax and accounting for early settlement discount in the same question.

8 Organising the bookkeeping system

So far, the bookkeeping exercises have involved only a small number of transactions, and it was possible to keep all ledger accounts in one place, with no difficulty in locating a particular ledger account or transaction if required for any reason. Furthermore, producing a trial balance from a small number of ledger accounts is fairly quick, and any errors can easily be located by tracing through the entries again.

In larger organisations, a single ledger may not be sufficient to hold all the ledger accounts and it is common for the ledger accounts to be divided up into sections known as 'divisions of the ledger'.

A common division of the ledger is as follows:

- all receivable accounts are maintained in the **sales ledger** (also known as the receivables' ledger)
- all payable accounts are maintained in the **purchase ledger** (also known as the payables' ledger)
- all bank and cash accounts are maintained in a **cash book** with perhaps a separate **petty cash book**
- all other accounts are maintained in the **nominal ledger** (also known as the general ledger).

Note that the sales and purchase ledgers are individual accounts for each customer and supplier. It can be appreciated that if a business has many credit customers and suppliers, it would have a significant number of nominal ledger accounts. Therefore many businesses maintain a sales ledger control or total account and purchase ledger control or total account which form part of the double-entry bookkeeping system.

If control accounts are maintained within the nominal ledger, it is still necessary to maintain individual sales ledger and purchase ledger accounts for each customer or supplier for account management purposes. It is then possible to check the accuracy of the control account totals with the total of the individual sales and purchase ledger balances. If this is the case, the individual personal accounts within the sales and purchase ledgers are referred to a 'memorandum accounts' as they are not part of the double-entry system to record transactions in the nominal ledger. The composition of the control accounts, and how they relate to the personal ledger accounts of each customer or supplier is explained in more detail elsewhere in this publication.

Many organisations also maintain other books and records that, although not part of the nominal ledger, help to record and organise transactions in a systematic manner. These records are known collectively as **books of prime entry** ('prime' means 'first' – and the transactions are 'captured' here first, before being recorded in the nominal ledger accounts).

9 Books of prime entry

The ledger accounts within the nominal ledger are the main source of information used by an entity to prepare its financial statements. However, if an entity updated its ledger accounts each time a transaction occurred, the ledger accounts would quickly become cluttered and errors may be made, and consequently also difficult to identify. This would also be a very time consuming process.

Using day books all transactions are initially listed in an appropriate book of prime entry. Each book of prime entry is a list or summary of transactions, the monetary value of which is periodically totalled (daily/weekly etc. as required) as a basis for inclusion in the ledger accounts using the principles of double-entry bookkeeping.

Several books of prime entry exist, each recording a different type of transaction as follows:

Book of prime entry	**Transaction type**
Sales day book	Credit sales
Purchase day book	Credit purchases
Sales returns day book	Returns of goods sold on credit
Purchase returns day book	Returns of goods bought on credit
Cash book	All bank transactions
Petty cash book	All cash transactions 'notes and coins'
The journal	All transactions not recorded elsewhere

The books of prime entry do not form part of the double-entry bookkeeping system. They are simply a means of recording and summarising a number of similar transactions (e.g. all credit sales for the week ended 10 January 20X5), so that only the totals are posted into the appropriate nominal ledger accounts.

10 Sales and purchase day books

Sales day book

The sales day book summarises the daily sales made on credit terms (i.e. the goods are sold and payment will be received at a later date). This day book does not include cash sales which are recorded separately in the cash book.

A sales day book may look as follows:

Date	Invoice	Customer	Ledger Ref	Net $	Sales tax	Gross $
4.1.X6	1	Jake	RL3	4,500	900	5,400
4.1.X6	2	Bella	RL18	3,000	600	3,600
4.1.X6	3	Fizz	RL6	2,200	440	2,640
4.1.X6	4	Milo	RL1	10,000	2,000	12,000
4.1.X6	5	Max	RL12	500	100	600
Total for 4.1.X6				20,200	4,040	24,240

The total sales for the day of $20,200 will be recorded in the nominal ledger accounting ledgers using the principles of double-entry bookkeeping. Note that the day book will also record any sales tax charged by the entity on its credit sales.

The double-entry required for the total from the sales day book to the nominal ledger would be as follows:

Debit:	Receivables	$24,240
Credit:	Sales tax	$4,040
Credit:	Sales	$20,200

As well as the double-entry to the nominal ledger as above, each of the individual sales would also be recorded within the sales ledger, in each individual customer memorandum account.

Debit:	Jake	$5,400
Debit:	Bella	$3,600
Debit:	Fizz	$2,640
Debit:	Milo	$12,000
Debit:	Max	$600

Note that as the memorandum accounts are not part of the nominal ledger the principles of double-entry concept do not apply and, as such, there is no corresponding credit entry required.

Purchases day book

The purchase day book summarises the daily purchases made on credit terms (i.e. the goods are purchased and payment will be made at a later date). Cash purchases are recorded in the cash book. Note that not all of the suppliers may be registered for sales tax and so not all credit purchases will include sales tax.

A purchases day book may look as follows:

Date	Invoice	Customer	Ledger Ref	Net $	Sales tax	Gross $
4.1.X6	34	Harry	PL2	2,700	540	3,240
4.1.X6	11	Ron	PL37	145	0	145
4.1.X6	5609	Hermione	PL12	4,675	935	5,610
4.1.X6	2	Neville	PL9	750	150	900
4.1.X6	577	Draco	PL1	345	0	345
Total for 4.1.X6				8,615	1,625	10,240

The total purchases made on credit for the day will be entered into the accounting ledgers in double-entry format. Note that the day book will also record any sales tax charged by suppliers on the purchases made by the entity.

The double-entry to the nominal ledger for the total from the purchases day book would be as follows:

Debit:	Purchases	$8,615
Debit:	Sales tax	$1,625
Credit:	Payables	$10,240

Along with the double-entry to the nominal ledger as noted above, each of the individual credit purchases would also be recorded in memorandum individual supplier accounts within the purchase ledger as follows:

Credit:	Harry	$3,240
Credit:	Ron	$145
Credit:	Hermione	$5,610
Credit:	Neville	$900
Credit:	Draco	$345

As the memorandum accounts are not part of the nominal ledger, the principles of double-entry do not apply and, as such, there is no corresponding debit entry required.

Note: These ledgers may also be referred to as the 'receivables ledger' or 'payables ledger' respectively.

Maintenance of the sales and purchases ledgers, along with their reconciliation and agreement with the appropriate control account total, is dealt with in a subsequent chapter of this publication.

11 Sales and purchase returns day books

It is normal for customers to return unwanted goods to the supplier, perhaps because they have been damaged in transit, or the wrong goods were delivered. Equally a business entity may occasionally have reason to return unwanted or damaged goods to its suppliers.

Note that **sales returns may also be referred to as 'returns inwards'** which reflects the situation that goods have been returned in to the entity. Similarly, **purchase returns may be referred to as 'returns outwards'** to reflect the situation that goods have been returned by the entity.

Any returns made to credit suppliers (or returns received from credit customers) are recorded in separate day books as illustrated below.

Sales return day book

Date	Invoice	Customer	Ledger Ref	Net $	Sales tax	Gross $
14.1.X6	1	Jake	RL3	50	10	60
14.1.X6	2	Bella	RL18	450	90	540
14.1.X6	3	Fizz	RL6	390	78	468
14.1.X6	4	Milo	RL1	670	134	804
14.1.X6	5	Max	RL12	50	10	60
Total for 14.1.X6				1,610	322	1,932

The double-entry required for the total from the sales returns day book to the nominal ledger would be as follows:

Debit:	Sales returns	$1,610
Debit:	Sales tax	$322
Credit:	Receivables	$1,932

As well as the double-entry to the nominal ledger as above, each of the individual sales returns would also be recorded within the sales ledger, to each individual customer memorandum account. This time as the entries are for sales returns the accounts would be credited to reduce the amount showing as owing from each customer.

Credit:	Jake	$60
Credit:	Bella	$540
Credit	Fizz	$468
Credit:	Milo	$804
Credit:	Max	$60

Purchases returns day book

Date	Invoice	Supplier	Ledger Ref	Net $	Sales tax	Gross $
14.1.X6	112	Harry	PL2	600	120	720
14.1.X6	56	Ron	PL37	75	0	75
14.1.X6	7	Hermione	PL12	800	160	960
14.1.X6	890	Neville	PL9	50	10	60
14.1.X6	12	Draco	PL1	100	0	100
Total for 14.1.X6				1,625	290	1,915

The double-entry required for the total from the purchases returns day book to the nominal ledger would be as follows:

Debit:	Payables	$1,915
Credit:	Sales tax	$290
Credit:	Purchases returns	$1,625

As well as the double-entry to the nominal ledger as above, each of the individual purchases returns would also be recorded within the purchase ledger, to each individual supplier memorandum account. This time as the entries are for purchases returns the accounts would be debited to reduce the amount showing as owing to each supplier.

Debit:	Harry	$720
Debit:	Ron	$75
Debit:	Hermione	$960
Debit:	Neville	$60
Debit:	Draco	$100

Remember that returns inwards from customers and returns outwards to suppliers are each normally recorded in a separate book of prime entry. However, for entities which have very few sales returns and/or purchases returns, they may be recorded as 'negative amounts' in the sales day book and purchase day book respectively.

Worked Example 5.C

ABC, who is not registered to account for sales tax, had the following transactions during the first week of July 20X2:

1st	Bought goods on credit from JB cost $1,000
	Sold goods on credit to JSA for $800
2nd	Sold goods on credit to PB for $80
	Returned goods to JB because they were faulty $80
3rd	Bought goods on credit from AL cost $600
4th	JSA returned unwanted goods $200
5th	Returned goods to AL $120
6th	Sold goods on credit to CAL for $400
7th	CAL returned goods as unsuitable $120
	Sold goods on credit to BC for $240

Required:

Prepare the day books to record these transactions (You can ignore the memorandum accounts).

Solution

Purchases day book

Date	Doc. no	Personal details	Net	Sales Tax	Gross
			$	$	$
1 Jul	001	JB	1,000		1,000
3 Jul	002	AL	600		600
			1,600		1,600

Sales day book

Date	Doc. no	Personal details	Net	Sales Tax	Gross
			$	$	$
1 Jul	101	JSA	800		800
2 Jul	102	PB	80		80
6 Jul	103	CAL	400		400
7 Jul	104	BC	240		240
			1,520		1,520

Returns inwards day book

Date	Doc. no	Personal details	Net	Sales Tax	Gross
			$	$	$
4 Jul	901	JSA	200		200
7 Jul	902	CAL	120		120
			320		320

Returns outwards day book

Date	Doc. no	Personal details	Net	Sales Tax	Gross
			$	$	$
2 Jul	9001	JB	80		80
5 Jul	9002	AL	120		120
			200		200

Remember that we must still record the individual transactions in separate purchase and sales ledger accounts to enable identification of amounts owed to the entity from individual customers or owed by the entity to individual suppliers.

e.g

Illustration 3

Mr KNP runs a business providing equipment for bakeries. He always makes a note of sales and purchases on credit and associated returns, but he is not sure how they should be recorded in the accounting records. Ignore sales tax.

Mr KNP noted the following transactions during the first two weeks of August:

1st	Sold cake tins priced at $500 to BKW.
1st	Purchased equipment at a cost of $2,000 from wholesalers TPL.
2nd	Returned goods costing $150 to another supplier, ICO.
3rd	Sold equipment priced at $1,200 to JAF.
3rd	BKW returned goods to Mr KNP priced at $100.
4th	Sold a new oven priced $4,000 to VSW.
5th	Purchased baking trays at a cost of $600 from TTI.
8th	Purchased ovens at a cost of $10,000 from HSL.
8th	Mr KNP returned equipment costing $300 to TPL.
9th	Sold goods priced at $2,200 to POA.
11th	Sold oven-proof dishes to BKW priced at $600.

Required:

Write up the credit transactions entered into during the first two weeks of August 20X6 into the relevant day books on behalf of Mr KNP.

Solution:

Sales day book

Aug	Customer	$
1	BKW	500
3	JAF	1,200
4	VSW	4,000
9	POA	2,200
11	BKW	600
		8,500

Sales returns day book

Aug	Customer	$
3	BKW	100
		100

Purchases day book		
Aug	Supplier	$
1	TPL	2,000
5	TTI	600
8	HSL	10,000
		12,600

Purchases returns day book		
Aug	Supplier	$
2	ICO	150
8	TPL	300
		450

Extending the use of day books

The examples above assumed that only credit sales and credit purchases of goods for resale were entered in the day books. Many entities now extend the use of the purchase day book to include all expense invoices received (such as expenses for utilities) and the analysis of the purchase day book can be extended to accommodate this. Similarly, if an entity sells a range of products, the total of the sales day book can be analysed to record sales by product type or geographical regions.

As an example, consider a purchases day book that is used to record all the entity's purchases on credit as follows:

Date	Doc. no	Details	Purchases $	Stationery $	Heat and light $	Motor exps $	Sales tax $	Total $
1 Jan	001	ABC	1,000				175	1,175
2 Jan	002	XYZ		400			70	470
3 Jan	003	PQ	2,000				350	2,350
4 Jan	004	GLM				120	21	141
	005	ABC	4,000				700	4,700
5 Jan	006	XYZ		200			35	235
	007	GEL			600		105	705
6 Jan	008	RSM				240	42	282
7 Jan	009	GGA			400		70	470
		Totals	7,000	600	1,000	360	1,568	10,528

12 The cash book

The term 'cash book' dates back to when entities dealt only in cash transactions (i.e. notes and coins). Many business entities, unless they are consumer retail businesses, rarely deal in cash, so the term 'cash book' refers to any book that records monies received and paid.

At its simplest, the cash book is no more than an ordinary ledger account, used to record the movements in the bank account. Some entities use it to record cash movements as well as bank movements, by using two 'money' columns on each side to distinguish between transactions that have passed through the bank account and petty cash transactions respectively as follows:

Receipts					Payments				
Date	**Details**	**Ref.**	**Bank**	**Cash**	**Date**	**Details**	**Ref.**	**Bank**	**Cash**
			$	$				$	$
1 Jan	Balance b/d		400	50	3 Jan	ABC	00123	100	
4 Jan	XYZ	101	200		5 Jan	Wages			20
8 Jan	Cash sales			120	5 Jan	Office equipment	00124	300	
10 Jan	PQR	102	150		8 Jan	Advertising	00125	125	
	RST	102	170		12 Jan	Wages			30
14 Jan	Cash banked	103	50		14 Jan	Cash banked			50
					14 Jan	Balance c/d		445	70
			970	170				970	170
15 Jan	Balance b/d		445	70					

Discount columns in the cash book

The cash book can be used to record early settlement or prompt payment discounts that have been allowed to credit customers or received from credit suppliers. Early settlement discounts often involve a large number of small-value transactions, so it is possible that the nominal ledger (which contains all nominal ledger accounts), would soon fill up with the detail of a large number of small-value transactions. By adding an extra column to each side of the cash book, the early settlement discounts can be recorded at the point of either deducting discounts received from amounts due to credit suppliers or recognising discounts allowed deducted by credit customers on amounts due to the entity (which is when it becomes known). Remember that, when discounts allowed are accounted for by the seller, they are accounted for as an adjustment against revenue, rather than classified as an expense.

Worked Example 5.D

ZAD had a favourable balance of $216 on its business bank account as at the start of business on 1 May 20X8. The following is a list of bank transactions for the week ending 7 May 20X8:

2 May	Paid an insurance premium of $130 by cheque
3 May	Paid a supplier invoice for $99 from GDS after deducting 10% for early settlement
4 May	Received a cheque for $314 from FRD, a credit customer. FRD was settling an invoice early for $320 and was entitled to a $6 discount.
6 May	Paid employees' wages of $182 by cheque

Required:

Record these transactions in the cash book of ZAD.

Solution:

Date	Details	Bank	Disc all'd	Total	Date	Details	Bank	Disc rec'd	Total
		$	$	$			$	$	$
1 May	Balance b/d	216			2 May	Insurance	130		130
4 May	FRD	314	6	320	3 May	GDS	99	11	110
					6 May	Wages	182		182
					7 May	Balance c/d	119		
		530	6	320			530	11	422
8 May	Balance b/d	119							

The cash book shows the account balance at the start and end of the period and can also be used as the basis to make entries in the nominal ledger accounts of individual transactions e.g. using the payment made to GDS, the accounting entries would be:

		$
Debit:	GDS payable	110
Credit	Bank	99
Credit:	Discounts received	11

A preferable layout would be to record the entries in separate cash receipts and cash payments books and to analyse each entry ready for the double-entry process as follows:

Cash receipts book:

Date	Details	Bank	Sales Ledger	Disc all'd
		$	$	$
4 May	FRD	314	314	6

Cash payments book:

Date	Details	Bank	Insurance	Wages	Purchase Ledger	Discount rec'd
		$	$	$	$	$
2 May	Insurance	130	130			
3 May	GDS	99			99	11
6 May	Wages	182		182		
		411	130	182	99	11

As well as entering the amount of each payment and receipt in the bank columns, the amount would also be entered in one or other of the analysis columns. This means that when the cash book is totalled at regular intervals, it will be immediately apparent how much cash has been received from credit customers, how much paid to credit suppliers, how much paid in wages and so on. The totals can then be used to make nominal ledger and individual ledger account entries as appropriate.

The double entry required for the total from the cash receipts book in the nominal ledger would be as follows:

		$
Debit:	Bank	314
Debit:	Revenue (discounts allowed)	6
Credit:	Receivables (gross amount)	320

As well as the double entry to the nominal ledger, it is also necessary to reflect the amount received from FRD plus discount allowed in their individual customer account within our sales ledger.

Credit	FRD ($314 + $6)	$320

Note that as the memorandum accounts are not part of the nominal ledger the double-entry principle does not apply, and as such, there is no corresponding debit entry required.

The double-entry required for the total from the cash payments book to the nominal ledger would be as follows:

		$
Debit:	Insurance	130
Debit:	Wages	182
Debit:	Payables (gross amount)	110
Credit:	Discounts received	11
Credit:	Bank	411

As well as the double-entry to the nominal ledger as above, we would also need to reflect the liability reduced relating to credit supplier GDS to their individual supplier account within our purchases ledger.

Debit: GDS ($99 + $11) $110

Remember that as the memorandum accounts are not part of the nominal ledger the double-entry concept does not apply, and as such, there is no corresponding credit entry required within the purchase ledger.

13 The journal

In a bookkeeping system involving the use of books of prime entry, it is inevitable that there will be some transactions that do not correspond with the main books of prime entry used, that is, the day books and cash books. In order to complete the system, another book is needed in which to capture sundry items prior to recording them in the nominal ledger.

This book or record is called 'the journal' and is used to record a range of transactions, such as:

- the purchase or disposal of non-current assets
- depreciation charges
- the write-off of irrecoverable debts
- changes to the allowance for receivables
- accruals and prepayments
- the correction of errors
- opening entries when a new business entity is formed.

The journal is therefore a clear and straightforward method of setting out an accounting transaction by stating the double-entry required to record that transaction.

The journal is also used to correct errors in the accounting records. The correction of errors will be considered later in this publication.

The journal is used to record any transaction that does not get recorded in any of the other books of prime entry, i.e. transactions that are not sales or purchases on credit, and transactions not involving cash.

The journal has debit and credit columns. However, like the day books, it is not part of the double-entry system. It is merely a memorandum record of what is going to be recorded in the nominal ledger accounts for a particular transaction or adjustment. It is also common for journal entries to be authorised by a senior accountant. In the narrative to a journal entry it is good practice to add a brief comment or explanation about the transaction, and to cross reference it to other documentation.

It is common for a computer-based assessment question to ask for the journal entries for a transaction.

This may be used as an alternative to asking for the ledger account entries. You must, therefore, know how to present a journal and record the debits and credits of a transaction. A brief narrative should be given to explain the entry.

The basic layout is as follows:

Date	Account name	Dr	Cr	Explanation
		$	$	
31.12.X5	Non-current assets	3,000		Increase in non-current assets
	Payables		3,000	and payables due to purchase of NCA on credit terms

An alternative presentation is as follows:

Non-current asset $3,000 Debit to increase

Payables $3,000 Credit to increase

Increase in non-current assets due to purchase of NCA on credit terms.

Worked Example 5.E

A business entity entered into the following transactions:

1 May Purchased plant on credit from JSM for $1,000.

4 May Sold surplus office machinery for $800 to ABA on credit required. The machinery originally cost $1,000 and had been depreciated by $400.

Required:

State the journal entries required to record each of the transactions.

Solution:

The solution states the entries required to record the transactions. At this stage in your studies, you should focus upon understanding which accounts are affected by each transaction. Your understanding of recording transactions will be developed in the subsequent chapters when journal entries are used e.g. to record transactions relating to sales tax and irrecoverable debts.

Date	Account name	Dr	Cr	Explanation
		$	$	
1 May	Plant	1,000		Purchase of plant on credit, see invoice No. X123. Increase non-current assets and payables.
	JSM		1,000	
4 May	Office machinery at cost		1,000	Office machinery sold on credit, see invoice No. Y345. Transfer cost of office machinery asset and also accum dep'n to disposal account and match with amount due from ABA to determine profit on disposal.
	Office machinery accum dep'n	400		Profit on disposal is taken to the statement of profit or loss.
	ABA	800		
	Profit on disposal		200	

Test your understanding 4

What double-entry should be made to record the totals from the sales returns day book in the nominal ledger?

A	Dr	Receivables
	Cr	Returns inwards
B	Dr	Returns inwards
	Cr	Receivables
C	Dr	Returns inwards
	Cr	Payables
D	Dr	Returns outwards
	Cr	Payables

Authorisation of journal entries

As journal entries involving adjustments and transfer have no source documents to support them, it is vital that all such entries are authorised by a senior member of staff. This can be done by signing the journal entries, or by referencing them to other forms of authorisation, for example, letters, minutes and so on.

The following chapters will deal with more complex accounting entries and the journals required to record them in the ledgers.

14 Chapter summary

In this chapter you have studied:

- accounting for sales tax and discounts
- the books of prime entry
- how the books of prime entry form the basis for posting accounting entries into the nominal ledger.

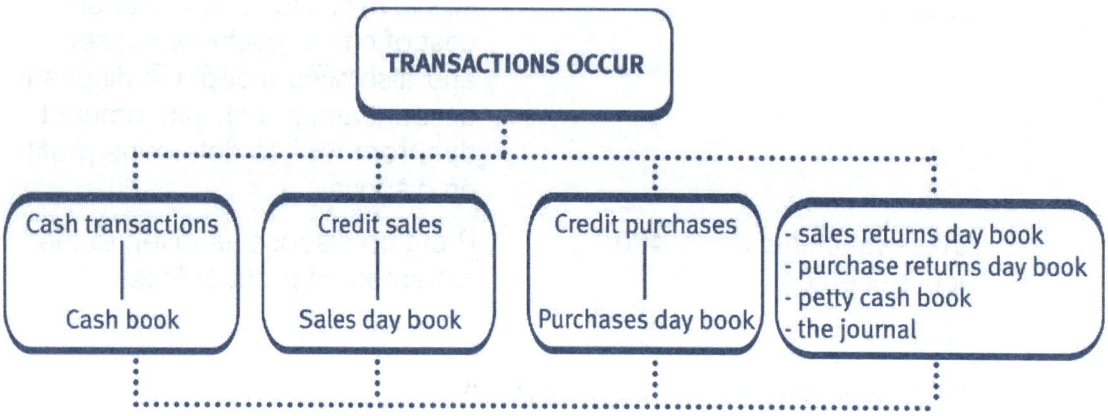

Test your understanding questions

Test your understanding 5

A book of prime entry is one in which:

A the rules of double-entry bookkeeping apply

B nominal ledger accounts are maintained

C transactions are entered prior to being recorded in the nominal ledger

D all personal accounts with customers and suppliers are maintained

Test your understanding 6

Which one of the following statements is correct?

A A ledger account is a book of prime entry

B All sales are recorded in the sales day book

C Settlement discount received is initially recorded in the cash book

D Purchase returns are recorded in the journal

Test your understanding 7

Which one of the following statements is correct?

A The sales account is credited with the total of sales made, including sales tax

B The sales account is credited with the total of sales made, excluding sales tax

C The sales account is debited with the total of sales made, including sales tax

D The sales account is debited with the total of sales made, excluding sales tax

Test your understanding 8

A business entity commenced trading with cash of $1,000. Inventory was purchased at a cost of $800 on credit (no sales tax). Half of the goods purchased were sold for $1,000 plus sales tax of 20%, the customer paying in cash immediately.

Required:

Insert words or values to complete the following statement:

The accounting equation after these transactions would consist of assets of ________, ________ liabilities of ________ equals capital of ________.

Available words and values:

plus/ less / $3,600 / $2,600 / $1,000 / $1,600

Test your understanding 9

A business entity purchased a machine on credit terms at a cost of $15,000 plus sales tax at 20%. The entity is registered with the tax authority to account for sales tax.

Required:

What are the accounting entries required to record this transaction?

Test your understanding 10

You have been provided with the following information relating to purchase costs. All costs are stated inclusive of the relevant rate of sales tax.

	Transaction	Gross $	Net $	Sales tax $
(a)	Purchase of equipment including sales tax at 25%	2,500.00		
(b)	Sale of goods including sales tax at 20%	1,200.00		
(c)	Heat and light costs including sales tax at 15%	266.80		
(d)	Vehicle repair costs including sales tax at 8%	273.78		
(e)	Purchase of raw materials including sales tax at 12%	2,764.72		

Required:

Calculate the net and sales tax amounts for each transaction noted above. In all cases, calculate your answers to the nearest cent.

Assets = liabilities + capital

Test your understanding 11

You have been provided with the following information relating to list selling prices. All prices are stated before accounting for any applicable trade discount and sales tax. In all cases, the rate of sales tax is 20%.

	Transaction 1	Transaction 2	Transaction 3
	$	$	$
List price (NET (excl Sales tax))	5,000	3,000	4,750
Rate of trade discount	20%	10%	10%
Amount of trade discount	~~1000~~	300	
Net price	4000		
Amount of sales tax	4800		
Invoice total	4800		

Required:

Based upon the information available, complete the information for each sale to determine the sales invoice total.

Test your understanding 12

You have been provided with the following information relating to purchase invoices. All invoice prices are stated after accounting for any applicable trade discount and sales tax. In all cases, the rate of sales tax is 20%.

	Transaction 1	Transaction 2	Transaction 3
	$	$	$
Supplier list price			
Rate of trade discount	10%	25%	20%
Amount of trade discount			1000
Net price			5000
Amount of sales tax			
Purchase invoice total	4,860	9,000	6,000

Required:

Based upon the information available, complete the information for each purchase invoice to determine the original list price of the supplier.

Test your understanding 13

The cash payments book

The following is an extract from the cash payments book of a business.

Date	Detail	Bank	Discount	Payables	Rent
		$	$	$	$
31.7.X6	MRA	1,400	100	1,400	
31.7.X6	Office	3,000			3,000
31.7.X6	MRB	210		210	
31.7.X6	MRC	1,600	80	1,600	
31.7.X6	Shop	400			400
		6,610	180	3,210	3,400

Required:

What accounting entries are required to post the totals from the cash book into the nominal ledger at 31 July 20X6, assuming control accounts are maintained?

Test your understanding 14

Which one of the following statements is correct?

A Only early settlement discount should always be deducted from an invoice amount before the invoice is accounted for by the seller

B Only trade discounts should always be deducted from an invoice amount before the invoice is accounted for by the seller

C Trade discount should be always deducted from an invoice amount after deducting early settlement discount before it is accounted for by the seller

D Both trade and early settlement discounts must always be deducted from an invoice amount before it is accounted for by the seller

Test your understanding 15

Dave purchased 20 items at a list price of $5 each. A trade discount of 10% was given and an early settlement discount of 2% was also offered for settlement within 10 days.

Required:

What amount did Dave pay for the goods if he took advantage of the early settlement discount? State your answer to the nearest cent.

$..................

Test your understanding 16

A business entity makes all of its purchases on credit.

At 1 January 20X1, there were payables brought forward from the previous year of $60,000. During 20X1, cash of $68,000 was paid to suppliers. Discounts received totalled $400 and the closing payables balance was $84,200.

Required:

What was the cost of purchases made during 20X1?

$....................

Test your understanding 17

A sole trader has not yet accounted for an early settlement discount received of $100.

When the correct accounting entries have been made, which one of the following statements is *correct*?

A Gross profit and net profit will increase by $100

B Gross profit and net profit will decrease by $100

C Gross profit will be unaffected but net profit will increase by $100

D Gross profit will be unaffected but net profit will decrease by $100

Test your understanding 18

A sole trader has not yet accounted for an early settlement discount allowed to a credit customer of $50.

When the correct accounting entries have been made, which one of the following statements is *correct*?

A Gross profit and net profit will increase by $50

B Gross profit and net profit will decrease by $50

C Gross profit will be unaffected but net profit will increase by $50

D Gross profit will be unaffected but net profit will decrease by $50

Test your understanding 19

NOP received an invoice from ABC for the supply of 40 units of a product at $5 each, less 25% trade discount, which were purchased on credit for resale. NOP paid this invoice, less an early settlement discount of 2%.

Which of the following accounting entries correctly records the initial purchase, and subsequent settlement of the amount due, in the accounting records of NOP?

			$			$
A	Dr	ABC	150	Cr	Purchases	150
	Dr	Cash	146	Cr	ABC	150
	Dr	Revenue	4			
B	Dr	Purchases	150	Cr	ABC	150
	Dr	ABC	150	Cr	Revenue	4
				Cr	Cash	146
C	Dr	Purchases	150	Cr	ABC	150
	Dr	ABC	150	Cr	Cash	147
				Cr	Discount received	3
D	Dr	ABC	200	Dr	Purchases	200
	Dr	Cash	147	Cr	ABC	200
	Dr	Discount received	53			

Test your understanding answers

Test your understanding 1

Oliver's books:

Debit	Cash	$900
Credit	Sales	$900

Net sale = $1,000 – (10% × $100)

Sam's books:

Debit	Purchases	$900
Credit	Cash	$900

Remember that the trade discount is deducted by the seller at the point of sale and excluded from the invoice.

Test your understanding 2

Purchases

20X1		$			
2 Dec	R Williams	280.00			
8 Dec	Samuel	525.00			
18 Dec	Amir	750.00			

Sales tax

20X1		$	20X1		
2 Dec	R Williams	56.00	10 Dec	Mary Smythe	80.00
8 Dec	Samuel	105.00	26 Dec	John Blair	160.00
18 Dec	Amir	150.00			

R Williams

		$	20X1		$
			2 Dec	Purchases	336.00

Samuel

		$	20X1		$
			8 Dec	Purchases	630.00

Amir

		$	20X1		$
			18 Dec	Purchases	900.00

Sales

	$	20X1		$
		10 Dec	Mary Smythe	400.00
		26 Dec	John Blair	800.00

Mary Smythe

20X1		$		$
10 Dec	Sales	480.00		

John Blair

20X1		$		$
26 Dec	Sales	960.00		

Test your understanding 3

(a)

Payables

	$		$
Cash (97% × $2,000)	1,940	Balance b/d	2,000
Discount received	60		
	2,000		2,000

Discount received

	$		$
		Payables	60

(b)

Receivables

	$		$
Balance b/d	3,315	Cash (97.5% × $3,400)	3,315
	3,315		3,315

Sales revenue

	$		$
		Cash (2.5% × $3,400)	85

Test your understanding 4

B

Test your understanding 5

C

A is incorrect as the rules of double entry do not apply to the books of prime entry. B is incorrect – ledger accounts are not maintained in books of prime entry. D is incorrect as personal accounts are ledger accounts that are maintained outside the main ledgers.

Test your understanding 6

C

A ledger account is not a book of prime entry. Cash sales are recorded in the cash book. Purchase returns are recorded in the purchase returns day book.

Test your understanding 7

B

Sales tax is excluded from sales and purchases accounts – therefore options A and C are incorrect. Sales represent revenue, and therefore the sales account is credited with the total of sales made, excluding sales tax.

Test your understanding 8

The accounting equation after these transactions would consist of assets of **$2,600**, **less** liabilities of **$1,000** equals capital of **$1,600**

	$		$
Assets (cash)	1,000	Capital	1,000
Transaction 1 (inventory purchased)	800	Profit (add to capital)	600
Transaction 2 (cash received)	1,200	Sales tax owing	200
Transaction 2 (cost of inventory sold)	(400)	Payables	800
Closing balance	2,600		2,600

Profit = Sales $1,000 (sales tax @20% also charged) – $400 (cost of half of goods purchased were sold) = $600

Assets $2,600 less liabilities $1,000 = capital $1,600

Test your understanding 9

Debit:	Property, plant and equipment	$15,000 (excluding sales tax)
Debit:	Sales tax account	$2,250 (sales tax amount)
Credit:	Payables	$17,250 (including sales tax)

Test your understanding 10

	Transaction	Gross $	Net $	Sales tax $
(a)	Purchase of equipment including sales tax at 25%	2,500.00	2,000.00	500.00
(b)	Sale of goods including sales tax at 20%	1,200.00	1,000.00	200.00
(c)	Heat and light costs including sales tax of 15%	266.80	232.00	34.80
(d)	Vehicle repair costs including sales tax of 8%	273.78	253.50	20.28
(e)	Purchase of raw materials including sales tax of 12%	2,764.72	2,468.50	296.22

Test your understanding 11

	Transaction 1 $	Transaction 2 $	Transaction 3 $
List price	5,000	3,000	4,750
Rate of trade discount	20%	10%	10%
Amount of trade discount	1,000	300	475
Net price	4,000	2,700	4,275
Amount of sales tax @20%	800	540	855
Invoice total	4,800	3,240	5,130

Test your understanding 12

	Transaction 1 (W1)	Transaction 2 (W2)	Transaction 3 (W3)
	$	$	$
Supplier list price	4,500	10,000	6,250
Rate of trade discount	10%	25%	20%
Amount of trade discount	450	2,500	1,250
Net price	4,050	7,500	5,000
Amount of sales tax	810	1,500	1,000
Purchase invoice total	4,860	9,000	6,000

(W1) Transaction 1 Sales tax = $4,860 / 120 × 20 = $810. Net price = $4,860 – $810 = $4,050. Trade discount = (4,050 / 90%) - $4,050 = $450. List price = $4,050 + $450 = $4,500.

(W2) Transaction 2 Sales tax = $9,000 / 120 × 20 = $1,500. Net price = $9,000 – $1,500 = $7,500. Trade discount = (7,500 / 75%) - $7,500 = $2,500. List price = $7,500 + $2,500.

(W3) Transaction 3 Sales tax = $6,000 / 120 × 20 = $1,000. Net price = $6,000 – $1,000 = $5,000. Trade discount = (5,000 / 80%) - $5,000 = $1,250. List price = $5,000 + $1,250 = $6,250.

Test your understanding 13

The cash transactions are recorded in total as follows:

Dr Payables ledger control account $3,210

Dr Rent expense $3,400

Cr Bank $6,610

The discount is recorded as follows:

Dr Payables ledger control account $180

Cr Discounts received $180

Entries must also be made to MRA, MRB and MRC's memorandum individual accounts in the payables ledger in order to reflect the payments made and discounts received.

Test your understanding 14

B

Trade discount is always deducted when preparing a sales invoice. Early settlement discount is deducted after trade discount at the point of sale, only if the customer is expected to take advantage of the early settlement discount terms. If the customer is not expected to take advantage of early settlement discount, it is not deducted at the point of sale when the sales invoice is prepared.

Test your understanding 15

$88.20

	$
Purchases (20 × $5)	100.00
Trade discount 10%	(10.00)
	90.00
Early settlement discount ($90 × 2%)	(1.80)
Amount paid	88.20

Test your understanding 16

$92,600

Payables

	$		$
Cash	68,000	Balance b/f	60,000
Discount received	400	Purchases (balance)	92,600
Balance c/f	84,200		
	152,600		152,600

Test your understanding 17

C

Discount received increases the net profit for the year.

Test your understanding 18

B

Discount allowed is accounted for as a reduction in revenue. Therefore, this will reduce both gross profit and net profit.

Test your understanding 19

C

Trade discount should always be deducted prior to accounting for an invoice, i.e. 40 units × $5 = $200 less 25% discount = $150 to debit purchases and credit ABC (payables).

When NOP settles the invoice and takes the discount it will make a payment of $150 less 2% = $147. This results in a Dr to the ABC account of $150 to clear the amount due and a Cr of $147 to the bank and a Cr of $3 to the discount received account.

Chapter

6

Accounting for accruals and prepayments

Chapter learning objectives

When you have completed this chapter, you should be able to:

- prepare accounting entries for accruals and prepayments.

1 Introduction

In this chapter you will learn to:

- how to calculate and account for accrued and prepaid expenses and
- how to calculate and account for accrued and prepaid income.

2 Accrued and prepaid expenses

To calculate the profit or loss for an accounting period, the accruals basis of accounting requires that we must include all income and expenditure relating to the accounting period, whether or not the cash has been received or paid or an invoice received. The profit or loss for an accounting period is therefore calculated as follows:

	$
Income earned	X
Expenditure incurred	(X)
Profit (loss)	X(X)

Accrued expense

An accrual arises when expenses of the business for the current accounting period have been incurred but not yet paid at the end of the financial year.

In this case, it is necessary to record the extra expense relevant to the year and create a corresponding statement of financial position liability (called an accrual) as follows:

		$
Debit	Expense account (SPL)	X
Credit	Accrual account (SOFP)	X

Often, the closing accrual is simply identified as a closing balance carried down at the end of the accounting period on the relevant expense account.

Accounting for an accrued expense therefore reduces profit.

e.g

Illustration 1

A business entity is preparing its financial statements for the year ended 31 December 20X1.

Required:

Prepare the heat and light account for the year ended 31 December 20X1 based upon the following information:

Bills received and paid during 20X1:

28 Feb	$460
31 May	$440
30 Aug	$390
30 Nov	$420
Bill received on 28 Feb 20X2	$450 (for the period 1 Dec. 20X1 to 28 Feb 20X2)

Solution:

Heat and light

20X1		$	20X1		$
28 Feb	Bank	460			
31 May	Bank	440			
30 Aug	Bank	390			
30 Nov	Bank	420			
31 Dec	Accrual	150	31 Dec	Statement of profit or loss	1,860
		1,860			1,860

The accrual of $150 represents one-third of the bill received on 28 February 20X2 (i.e. the amount applicable to the month of December 20X1). This amount will be credited to the accrual expenses account which will appear on the statement of financial position under current liabilities.

This ensures the correct amount is charged to the statement of profit or loss for the year 20X1.

At the beginning of the following year, 20X2, the accrual will be reversed, i.e. debit accrual account and credit heat and light account.

For the purposes of attempting questions in the exam, it is usually quicker to calculate and account for the accrued expense within the one ledger account working as follows:

Heat and light

20X1		$	20X1		$
28 Feb	Bank	460			
31 May	Bank	440			
30 Aug	Bank	390			
30 Nov	Bank	420			
31 Dec	Accrual c/d	150	31 Dec	Statement of profit or loss	1,860
		1,860			1,860
			20X2	Accrual b/d	150

Test your understanding 1

FGH has a business which incurred electricity charges for the year ended 31 December 20X1 of $24,000. FGH paid $18,000 during the year but will not pay the final quarter until January 20X2.

Required:

Prepare the nominal ledger account for the electricity expense account for the year ended 31 December 20X1.

Prepaid expense

A prepayment arises when expenses of the business, relating to the following year, have been paid in advance prior to the year end. In this case, it is necessary to remove the extra expense relevant to the following year and create a corresponding statement of financial position asset (called a prepayment):

Debit	Prepayment account (SOFP)	X
Credit	Expense account (SPL)	X

Accounting for a prepaid expense therefore increases profit.

e.g

Illustration 2

A business entity commenced trading on 1 March and pays rent quarterly in advance on 1 March, 1 June, 1 September and 1 December. The annual rental is $4,800.

	$
1 Mar	1,200
1 Jun	1,200
1 Sep	1,200
1 Dec	1,500

The annual rental was increased to $6,000 per annum with effect from 1 December 20X1. The accounting year end is 31 December.

Required:

Prepare the rent expense account for the accounting period ended 31 December 20X1.

Solution:

Rent expense

20X1		$	20X1		$
1 Mar	Bank	1,200			
1 Jun	Bank	1,200			
1 Sep	Bank	1,200	31 Dec	Prepayment	1,000
1 Dec	Bank	1,500	31 Dec	Statement of profit or loss	4,100
		5,100			5,100

The prepayment is for January and February 20X2, which is at the new rate of $500 per month. This amount will be debited to the prepayment expenses account which will appear on the statement of financial position under current assets. The charge to the statement of profit or loss can be confirmed as being 9 months at the old rate of $400 per month, and one month at the new rate of $500 per month, that is, $4,100.

At the beginning of the following year, 20X2, the prepayment will be reversed, i.e. credit prepayment account and debit rent payable account.

In the examination, as with an accrued expense, it will often be quicker to calculate and account for the prepaid expense within the one ledger account working as follows:

Rent expense

20X1		$	20X1		$
1 Mar	Bank	1,200			
1 Jun	Bank	1,200			
1 Sep	Bank	1,200	31 Dec	Prepayment	1,000
1 Dec	Bank	1,500	31 Dec	Statement of profit or loss	4,100
		5,100			5,100
20X2					
1 Jan	Prepayment b/d	1,000			

Test your understanding 2

The annual insurance charge for Asif is $24,000. Asif paid $30,000 on 1 January 20X1.

Required:

Show the entries in the insurance expense account for the year ended 31 December 20X1.

A proforma expense account would look like:

Expense

	$		$
Prepayment b/d (opening prepaid expense)	X	Accrual b/d (opening accrued expense)	X
Bank (amount paid in the year)	X	Statement of profit or loss	X
Accrual c/d (closing accrued expense)	X	Prepayment c/d (closing prepaid expense)	X
	X		X
Prepayment b/d (opening prepaid expense)	X	Accrual b/d (opening accrued expense)	X

3 Accrued and prepaid income

Accrued income

Accrued income arises when income has been earned in the accounting period, but not yet received. In this situation, it is necessary to record this income in the statement of profit or loss and create a corresponding asset in the statement of financial position as follows:

		$
Debit	Accrued income account (SOFP)	X
Credit	Income account (SPL)	X

Accounting for accrued income therefore increases profit.

Accrued income creates an additional current asset in the statement of financial position, along with additional income in the statement of profit or loss for the year.

e.g **Illustration 3**

A business entity earns bank interest income of $300 per month. During the year ended 31 December 20X6, bank interest of $3,000 has been received.

Required:

Calculate the bank interest income earned for the year ended 31 December 20X6 and the amount of accrued income to include in the statement of financial position at 31 December 20X6.

Solution:

The total amount credited to the statement of profit or loss for the year ended 31 December 20X6 should be $3,600 (i.e. 12 × $300).

The amount received during the year ended 31 December 20X6 was $3,000.

Therefore, accrued income to include within current assets in the statement of financial position at 31 December is $600 (i.e. $3,600 earned less $3,000 received).

Prepaid income

Prepaid income arises when income has been received during the current accounting period but which relates to the next accounting period. In this situation, it is necessary to remove this excess income from the statement of profit or loss for the current year and create a corresponding liability within current liabilities in the statement of financial position using the following accounting entries:

Debit	Income account (SP/L)	$X
Credit	Prepaid income (SOFP)	$X

Accounting for prepaid income therefore reduces profit.

Prepaid income creates an additional current liability in the statement of financial position, along with reduced income in the statement of profit or loss for the year.

e.g

Illustration 4

Commencing 1 July 20X5, a business entity rented out a property to a tenant at $5,000 per month. During the year ended 30 June 20X6, it received $64,000 cash from the tenant.

Required:

What was the rental income receivable for the year ended 30 June 20X6, and the liability for prepaid income received in the statement of financial position at 30 June 20X6?

Solution:

The total amount credited to the statement of profit or loss for the year ended 30 June 20X6 should be $60,000 (i.e. 12 × $5,000).

The cash received during the year ended 30 June 20X6 was $64,000.

Therefore, prepaid income to include within current liabilities in the statement of financial position at 30 June 20X6 was $4,000 (i.e. $64,000 received – $60,000 earned).

4 Application of accounting concepts

Accounting for accruals and prepayments represents application of the **accruals and matching concepts**. The idea is that the revenue earned during an accounting period is 'matched' in the statement of profit or loss with the expenses incurred in earning that revenue. So, the mere fact that something has been paid for during an accounting period does not necessarily mean that it has been consumed during that period in earning revenue, and therefore some adjustment is needed to the ledger accounts to fairly reflect what has been consumed.

Another important concept is the **realisation** concept, which states that we 'recognise' (i.e. account for) revenue only when it has been earned, not necessarily when cash is received from the customer. Additionally, consideration of the **prudence** concept requires that revenue and assets should not be recognised unless it can be measured (i.e. valued) reliably and it is probable that future economic benefits will be received. This is also the case for expenses and losses, but a degree of caution should be exercised in making any judgement, such that revenue and assets are not overstated whilst expenses and liabilities are not understated.

Some of the topics in this chapter are subjective and necessarily require assumptions and estimates to be made. For example, the calculation of an accrued expense for heat and light expense may be based upon taking a proportion of the value of an invoice received after the accounting period, say, using one-third of the value of an invoice covering a three-month period, even though this may not exactly reflect heat and power usage for that month. However, it is a reasonable basis for estimation of income or expense required for inclusion in the statement of profit or loss, and the associated entries required in the statement of financial position.

5 Chapter summary

In this chapter you studied the calculation an accounting entries required for:

- accruals and prepayments relating to expenses
- accruals and prepayments relating to income.

Both of these (especially accruals and prepayments relating to expenses,) are likely to appear in computer-based assessments involving either the preparation of ledger accounts or, more commonly, the preparation of financial statements.

The topics in this chapter are very important. The principles involved are also discussed and applied in more detail in subsequent chapters.

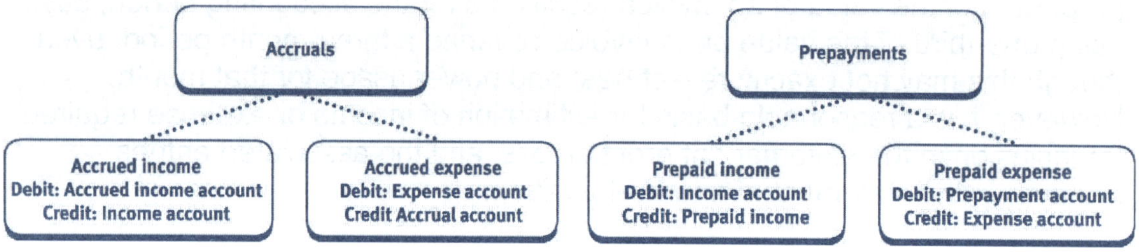

Test your understanding questions

Test your understanding 3

Rent paid on 1 October 20X2 for the year to 30 September 20X3 was $1,200 and rent paid on 1 October 20X3 for the year to 30 September 20X4 was $1,600.

Rent payable, as shown in the statement of profit or loss for the year ended 31 December 20X3, would be:

A $1,200

B $1,600

C $1,300

D $1,500

Test your understanding 4

Amounts paid for heat and light charges during the year amounted to $1,350. At 1 January 20X5, there was an unpaid invoice for $80, and an unpaid invoice at 31 December 20X5 of $70.

What was the charge to the statement of profit or loss for the year ended 31 December 20X5?

$..................

Test your understanding 5

An entity has an accounting year end of 30 September. On 1 January 20X6, the entity took out a loan of $100,000 with annual interest of 12 per cent. The interest is payable in equal instalments on the first day of April, July, October and January, in arrears.

How much should be charged to the statement of profit or loss for the year ended 30 September 20X6, and how much should be accrued on the statement of financial position?

Statement of profit or loss	Statement of financial position
$........................	$........................

Test your understanding 6

On 1 May 20X0, A paid a rent bill of $1,800 for the period to 30 April 20X1.

Required:

What is the charge to the statement of profit or loss and the entry in the statement of financial position for the year ended 30 November 20X0?

Statement of profit or loss	Statement of financial position	Accrual or Prepayment
$	$	

Test your understanding 7

TRO rents property to residential and commercial tenants. During the year ended 30 June 20X3, TRO received rent receipts from tenants totalling $256,000. Amounts for rent received in advance and in arrears at the beginning and end of the accounting year were as follows:

	30 June 20X2	30 June 20X3
	$	$
Rent received in advance	38,400	22,175
Rent received in arrears	25,600	24,200

Required:

What amount should be included for rental income in the statement of profit or loss of TRO for the year ended 30 June 20X3?

$..................

Test your understanding 8

UVW sublets part of its office accommodation. The rent is received quarterly in advance on 1 January, 1 April, 1 July and 1 October. The annual rent has been $30,000 for several years, but was increased to $36,000 from 1 October 20X5.

Required:

What amounts for rental income should appear in UVW's financial statements for the year ended 30 November 20X5?

Statement of profit or loss	Statement of financial position	Accrual or Prepayment
$......................	$......................	$......................

Test your understanding 9

The transactions on the electricity account for the year ended 30 April 20X6 were as follows:

Bills received and paid during the year:

30 June 20X5	$400
30 September 20X5	$350
31 December 20X5	$425
31 March 20X6	$450

Electricity accrued at 1 May 20X5 $250.

Which of the following are the appropriate entries for electricity in the financial statements for the year ended 30 April 20X6?

	Statement of profit or loss expense	Accrual at 30 April 20X6
A	$1,375	Nil
B	$1,525	$150
C	$1,675	$300
D	$1,825	$450

Test your understanding 10

BCD has an accounting year end of 31 December and pays $300 per quarter for electricity.

At 1 January 20X6 the statement from the electricity supplier showed that BCD had prepaid by $25. Bassett then received electricity bills for the next four quarters starting on 1 January 20X6 and ending on 31 December 20X6 for $350, $375, $275 and $300 respectively.

Which of the following are the correct entries for electricity in BCD's statement of profit or loss and statement of financial position for the year ended 31 December 20X6?

	Statement of profit or loss	Statement of financial position
A	$1,300	$75 accrual
B	$1,300	$75 prepayment
C	$1,200	$125 accrual
D	$1,200	$125 prepayment

Test your understanding answers

Test your understanding 1

Electricity

20X1		$	20X1		$
	Bank	18,000			
31 Dec	Accrual c/d	6,000	31 Dec	Statement of profit or loss	24,000
		24,000			24,000
			20X2	Accrual b/d	6,000

The charge to the statement of profit or loss must reflect the cost of electricity for the year, not the amount paid, i.e. $24,000. Therefore, we must make an accrual for $6,000 ($24,000 – $18,000). To make the accrual:

Debit: Electricity expense account

Credit: Accrual account

An accrual therefore increases the expense account, thus reduces profit. The accrual account will be shown on the statement of financial position as a current liability.

Test your understanding 2

Insurance expense

20X1		$	20X1		$
1 Jan	Bank	30,000	31 Dec	Prepayment c/d	6,000
			31 Dec	Statement of profit or loss	24,000
		30,000			30,000
20X2					
1 Jan	Prepayment b/d	6,000			

The charge to the statement of profit or loss must reflect the cost of insurance for the year, not the amount paid, i.e. $24,000. Therefore, we must recognise a prepayment for $6,000 ($30,000 – $24,000). To record the prepayment:

Debit: Prepayment account, and Credit: Insurance account

A prepayment therefore reduces the expense account, thus increases profit. The accrual account will be shown on the statement of financial position as a current liability.

Test your understanding 3

C

The year to 31 December 20X3 includes 3/4th of the rent for the year to 30 September 20X3 and 1/4th of the rent for the year to 30 September 20X4, that is:

(9/12 × $1,200) + (3/12 × $1,600) = $1,300.

Test your understanding 4

$1,340

The heat and light ledger account is as follows

Heat and light

	$		$
Paid during year	1,350	Outstanding invoice at 1.1.20X5	80
Outstanding invoice at 31.12.20X5	70	Statement of profit or loss	1,340
	1,420		1,420

Test your understanding 5

Statement of profit or loss $9,000

Statement of financial position $3,000.

The charge to the statement of profit or loss is $9,000 for 9 months' interest, at an annual rate of $12,000 (12 per cent of $100,000). The payment for the third quarter ending 30 September 20X6 is not paid until 1 October 20X6, so 3 months' interest is accrued, that is, $3,000.

Test your understanding 6

Statement of profit or loss $1,050 ($1,800 × 7/12)

Statement of financial position $750; Prepayment ($1,800 × 5/12)

We must remember the statement of profit or loss must reflect the amount due for the year 1 May to 30 November and the remainder of the $1,800 will have been paid in advance, i.e. prepaid.

Test your understanding 7

Rental Income

	$		$
1 July 20X2 Bal b/d	25,600	1 July 20X2 Bal b/d	38,400
		Cash received	256,000
Statement of profit or loss ß	270,825		
30 June 20X3 Bal c/d	22,175	30 June 20X3 Bal c/d	24,200
	318,600		318,600

Test your understanding 8

Statement of profit or loss = $31,000

((10/12 × $30,000) + (2/12 × $36,000))

Statement of financial position = $3,000.

The prepayment amount is part of the amount of $9,000 received on 1 October for the three months to 31 December 20X5: (3/9 × $9,000)

For UVW, this is prepaid deferred income i.e. income received in advance – a liability.

Test your understanding 9

B

Electricity

		$			$
30 Jun	Bank	400	1 May	Accrual b/d	250
30 Sep	Bank	350			
31 Dec	Bank	425			
31 Mar	Bank	450			
30 Apr	Accrual c/d	150	31 Dec	Statement of profit or loss	1,525
		1,775			1,775

Test your understanding 10

A

The statement of profit or loss must show the amount due for the year, i.e. $350 + $375 + $275 + $300 = $1,300. Bassett prepaid the year before which means he had a prepayment b/fwd and therefore an accrual of $75 will be required to balance the ledger account.

Electricity

		$			$
1 Jan	Prepayment b/d	25			
31 Mar	Bank	300			
30 Jun	Bank	300			
30 Sep	Bank	300			
31 Dec	Bank	300	31 Dec	Statement of profit or loss	1,300
31 Dec	Accrual c/d	75			
		1,300			1,300

Chapter

7

Accounting for payroll

Chapter learning objectives

When you have completed this chapter, you should be able to:

- prepare accounting entries for payroll

1 Introduction

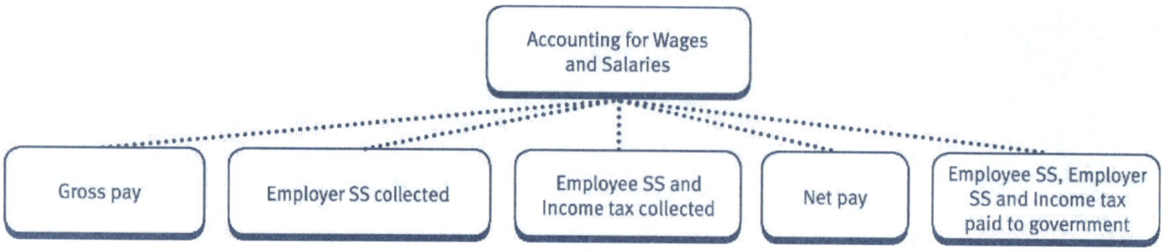

In this chapter you will learn:

- how to calculate and account for payroll costs.

In order to properly account and understand payroll costs, we need to understand the different factors involved in the calculation of gross pay of an employee (such as bonus or commission), and also the deductions from gross pay that may be required. In addition, this chapter also deals with the accounting entries required for payroll costs.

2 Accounting for payroll costs

Most business entities (other than sole traders and some partnerships) have employees working in the business. Those employees are paid wages and salaries and this chapter deals with the accounting entries required for payroll costs.

Wages and salaries paid to employees should be accounted for as an expense in the statement of profit or loss. Any tax and other amounts deducted from wages and salaries should be accounted for as liabilities until they have been paid over to the appropriate authority.

3 Accounting for wages and salaries

In this section we shall see how the wages cost is recorded in the ledger accounts of a business entity.

Gross pay and net pay

Worked Example 7.A

George is paid $5.50 per hour for a basic 36-hour week. Any overtime is paid at basic rate plus 50 per cent.

During a particular week, George worked for 42 hours.

The first step is to calculate the amount of George's gross earnings for that week:

		$
36 hours @ $5.50 per hour	=	198.00
6 hours @ $8.25 per hour	=	49.50
		247.50

George will have to pay income tax, and also in some countries, a social security (SS) contribution, which will be deducted from his gross earnings of $247.50. Let us assume that he will be liable to pay income tax at 25 per cent on all his weekly earnings in excess of $75 and, in addition, he will be liable to pay SS contributions of 9 per cent of his total earnings.

In addition to George's SS contributions, assume that his employer is also liable to pay a further 10.5 per cent SS contribution based upon George's gross earnings. The revised position is therefore:

	$	$
George's gross earnings		247.50
Less: Income tax 25% × ($247.50 – $75.00)	43.13	
Less: SS (9% × $247.50)	22.28	
		(65.41)
George's net earnings		182.09
Employer's SS contribution: 10.5% × $247.50		25.99

George's employer will deduct George's income tax and SS contributions and pay George his net earnings. The employer will then pay George's income tax and all of the SS contributions over to the government. Thus it can be seen that the total cost of employing George during for that week amounted to $273.49 (the total of George's gross earnings of $247.50 plus the employer's SS contributions of $25.99).

The accounting entries required to account for gross pay, deductions from payroll and employer SS contributions are as follows:

		$
Debit:	Gross wages expense	X
Credit:	Wages payable	X

Being accounting for the gross wages expense

		$
Debit:	Employer SS expense	X
Credit:	SS contribution	X

Being accounting for the employer SS obligation

		$
Debit:	Wages payable	X
Credit:	SS contribution and income tax payable	X

Being accounting for the employee SS and Income tax obligation deducted from gross pay

		$
Debit:	Wages payable	X
Credit:	Cash paid	X

Being accounting for the net pay to employees

		$
Debit:	SS contribution and income tax payable	X
Credit:	Cash paid	X

Being accounting for SS contribution and Income tax paid to the government/tax authority.

This wages cost will be recorded in the employer's ledger accounts as follows:

Gross wages expense

	$		$
Wages payable	247.50		

Employer SS expense

	$		$
Employer SS payable	25.99		

SS contributions and Income tax payable

	$		$
		Wages payable	65.41
		Employer SS	25.99

Wages payable

	$		$
Income tax & SS payable	65.41	Gross wages	247.50

Note that it is also possible to account for employer SS contributions as an addition to the gross wages expense account, rather than accounting for it as a separate expense. If this is done, the debit balance on the gross wages expense account will be closed off and transferred to the statement of profit or loss at the end of each accounting period. The total expense incurred by the employer will not change whichever method of accounting for employer SS contributions is adopted.

Note that the liability for wages payable is reduced by the amount of SS and income tax that George is obliged to pay. The remaining liability of $182.09 ($247.50 – $65.41) will be cleared when George is paid.

The total liability for SS contributions and income tax of $91.40 ($65.41 + $25.99) will be cleared when George's employer pays this amount to the government. Note that this total amount includes both George's liability and the employer liability.

Social security contributions are referred to as national insurance contributions in the UK.

Other deductions

The deductions of income tax and SS from George's gross wages by his employer are statutory or legally enforceable deductions. Meaning that George is required to pay these by law. However, George may also authorise his employer to make other deductions from his wages – these voluntary deductions are made from George's net earnings, as they do not affect his liability to income tax and SS.

For example, George's employer may have a sports and social club with a weekly membership fee of $1.25. George may also ask his employer to pay $20.00 a week directly into a savings plan (SP) scheme. The deductions will have the following effect:

	$	$
George's net earnings (as before)		182.09
Less:		
Sports and social club	1.25	
SP scheme	20.00	
		(21.25)
Net pay to be received by George		160.84

Wages payable

	$		$
Income tax payable	65.41	Gross wages	247.50
Sports club payable	1.25		
SP scheme payable	20.00		

Two further payable accounts would be required:

Sports club payable

	$		$
		Wages payable	1.25

SP scheme payable

	$		$
		Wages payable	20.00

The liability to pay the sports club and SP scheme will be eliminated when the employer pays them, which may be weekly or monthly.

Pension contributions

Many employees contribute to pension schemes by allocating a percentage of their gross pay to the pension fund, for example 5 or 6 per cent of their weekly or monthly earnings as appropriate. In some countries, this may be referred to as superannuation payments or retirement plans. This publication will use the term 'pension contributions' or 'pension plans' as appropriate. This amount is deducted from the employee's gross pay, and is payable to a pension fund managed by a separate entity.

Worked Example 7.B

Lesley earns $200 gross in week 21. Pension contributions are 5 per cent of weekly salary. The ledger entries to record this are as follows:

Debit: Wages payable = $10 (5% × $200)

Credit: Pension liability = $10

4 Chapter summary

In this chapter you have studied the bookkeeping and accounting treatment associated with wages and salaries.

This topic is likely to appear regularly in computer-based assessments involving either the preparation of ledger accounts or, more commonly, the preparation of financial statements.

Remember that this is an international exam and that the tax rates associated with employee wages and salaries will be given. However, make sure that you practise how to calculate and account for the appropriate tax using other rates.

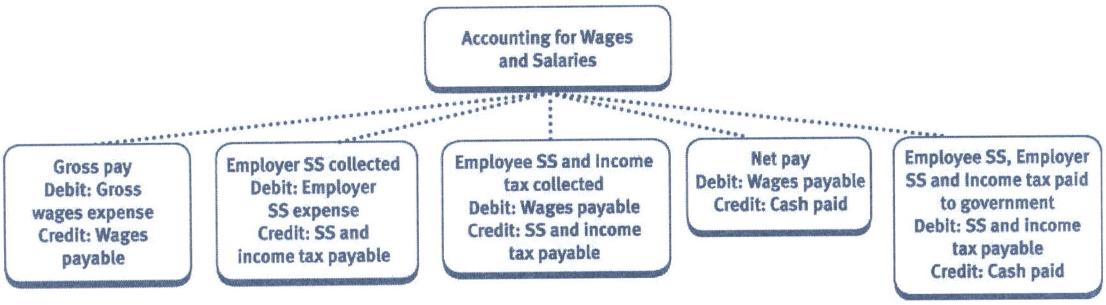

Test your understanding questions

Test your understanding 1

List the ledger entries required to record the following pay details, and the subsequent payment to the employee by cheque

Gross pay	$1,200
Social security contribution – employee's	9% of gross pay
Pension – Employee contribution	6% of gross pay
Income tax	$185
Social security contribution – employer's	10% of gross pay
Trade union subscription	$5

Test your understanding 2

At the end of the month, an entity needs to accrue for one week's wages. The gross wages amount to $500, tax amounts to $100, employer's social security contribution is $50, employees' social security contribution is $40, and employees' contributions to a pension scheme amount to $30. The ledger entries to record this accrual would be:

		$		$
A	Debit wages expense	500	Credit social security contribution payable	90
			Credit income tax payable	100
			Credit pension scheme payable	30
			Credit wages accrued	280

		$		$
B	Debit wages expense	550	Credit social security contribution payable	90
			Credit income tax payable	100
			Credit wages accrued	330
			Credit pension payable	30

C	Debit wages expense	280	Credit wages accrued	500
	Debit social security contribution expense	90		
	Debit income tax expense	100		
	Debit pension scheme expense	30		
D	Debit wages expense	330	Credit wages accrued	550
	Debit social security contribution expense	90		
	Debit income tax expense	100		
	Debit pension scheme expense	30		

Test your understanding 3

An employee is paid $3.50 per hour. Earnings of more than $75 a week are taxed at 20 per cent. Employees' social security contribution is 7 per cent, and employer's social security contribution is 10 per cent. During week 24, the employee works for 36 hours. The amounts to be charged to the statement of profit or loss and paid to the employee are:

	Statement of profit or loss	Paid to employee
A	$126.00	$94.38
B	$126.00	$106.98
C	$138.60	$94.38
D	$138.60	$106.98

Test your understanding 4

An employee has a gross monthly salary of $1,000. In September the tax deducted was $200, the employee's social security contribution was $60, and the employer's social security contribution was $100.

Required:

What was the charge to the statement of profit or loss for wages and salaries?

$..................

Test your understanding 5

B is a builder with ten employees. In April 20X1, he paid the following amounts:

	$
Net salaries paid after income tax and social security contributions/deductions	14,000
Income tax and employees' social security contributions for March	5,000
Employer's social security contributions for March 20X1	1,400

He owes the following amounts in respect of tax and social security contributions for April 20X1:

	$
Tax and employee's social security contributions	6,000
Employer's social security contributions	1,500

Required:

What was the total expense for employee costs included in the statement of profit or loss for April 20X1?

$..................

Test your understanding 6

An employee worked forty hours in week 25. The employee is paid at the standard rate of $10 per hour for the first 35 hours, and any additional hours are paid at standard rate plus 20%. The employee is liable to pay income tax on gross earnings at the rate of 30%. Both the employee and employer are obliged to pay social security contributions at the rate of 15% on gross earnings. In addition, the employee contributed $20 per week to a savings scheme which was deducted from his earnings by his employer.

Required:

(a) What was the net cash payment made to the employee for week 25?

(b) What was the total amount payable to the tax authority for income tax and social security contributions?

Test your understanding answers

Test your understanding 1

Gross wages	
Debit gross wages expense account	$1,200
Credit wages payable account	$1,200
SS employee's (9% × $1,200)	
Debit wages payable account	$108
Credit SS/tax payable account	$108
Pension (6% × $1,200)	
Debit wages payable account	$72
Credit pension payable account	$72
Income tax	
Debit wages payable account	$185
Credit SS/tax payable account	$185
SS employer's (10% × $1,200)	
Debit employers expenses account	$120
Credit SS/tax payable account	$120
Trade union expenses	
Debit wages payable account	$5
Credit trade union payable account	$5
Net pay ($1,200 – $108 – $72 – $5 – $185)	
Debit wages payable account	$830
Credit bank	$830

Test your understanding 2

B

A is incorrect as the employer's social security contributions has been deducted from the net wages accrued. C is incorrect as there has been no deduction from wages accrued for tax, social security contributions or pension contributions. Nor is there any record of liability for these items. D is similar, with the added error of employer's SS being included with wages accrued.

Test your understanding 3

D

Statement of profit or loss	$	Paid to employee	$
36 × $3.50	126.00	Gross pay	126.00
Employer's SS (10%)	12.60	7% SS	(8.82)
Gross wages cost	138.60	Tax	(10.20)
		Net pay	106.98

Test your understanding 4

$1,100

The charge for the salary in the statement of profit or loss is the gross salary plus the employer's social security contribution. This is $1,000 plus $100, a total of $1,100.

Test your understanding 5

$21,500

This is calculated using the April figures for net salary ($14,000), plus tax and SS for the employee ($6,000) and plus SS for the employer ($1,500).

The statement of profit or loss is always charged with the gross salary plus any additional costs to the employer, i.e. SS in this question.

Test your understanding 6

(a) **$205.50**

(b) **$246.00**

		$
Standard hours (35 × $10)		350.00
Overtime hours (5 × $10 × 1.2)		60.00
Gross earnings		410.00
Less: employee deductions		
Income tax ($410 × 30%)	123.00	
Employee social security contribution ($410 × 15%)	61.50	
Savings scheme deduction	20.00	
		(204.50)
Net cash paid to employee		205.50

The total payments for income tax and social security consist of the employee deductions as calculated above $184.50 ($123.00 + $61.50) plus the additional amount payable by the employer (a further $61.50). This gives a total of $246.00 payable for income tax and social security contribution.

Note that the amount deducted relating to the savings scheme is not income tax or social security contributions and will be paid separately to another external party, such as a bank, on behalf of the employee.

Chapter

8

Accounting for the issue of shares

Chapter learning objectives

When you have completed this chapter, you should be able to:

- prepare accounting entries for the issue of shares.

1 Introduction

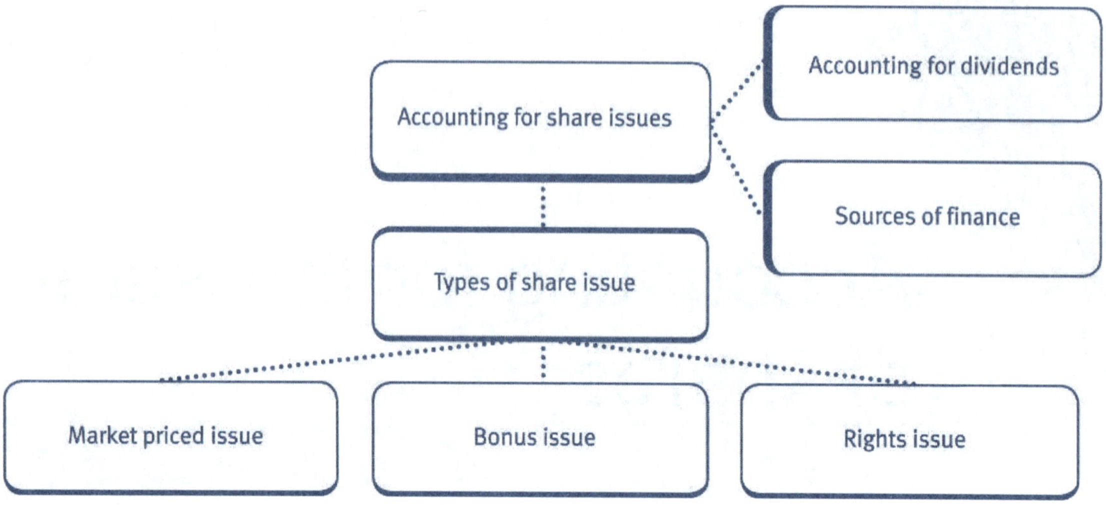

In this chapter, you will learn:

- sources of finance for a corporate entity
- accounting for the issue of shares
- accounting for dividends paid
- reserves and the statement of changes in equity.

Many business entities are constituted in the form of a limited liability company ('company' or 'corporate entity'). The nature of a corporate entity was considered briefly in Chapter 1 and you should refer back to refresh your memory if necessary. In this chapter we deal with some of the features of a corporate entity that have an impact on the content and presentation of its financial statements.

This chapter will focus upon the capital structure of a corporate entity (how it is financed) and, in particular, how to account for the issue of shares and the payment of dividends to its shareholders.

We also review an additional financial statement that a corporate entity is required to prepare as part of its annual financial statements – the statement of changes in equity.

The legal formalities relating to corporate entities are considered in BA4 Fundamentals of Ethics, Corporate Governance and Business Law.

Financial accounting issues relating to sources of finance and payment of dividends are relevant in subjects F1 Financial Reporting F2 Advanced Financial Reporting in the CIMA Professional qualification.

2 Sources of finance for a corporate entity

When considering the statement of financial position of a sole trader, we saw that the business entity was financed principally by the capital account of the sole trader. The statement of financial position of a corporate entity is similar to that of a sole trader, but it has a more formalised capital or equity structure as follows:

Sole trader – capital account	$	Corporate entity – equity structure	$
Capital b/fwd	X	Share premium	X
Add: Capital introduced (if any)	X	Revaluation surplus	X
Add: Profit (loss) for the year	X	Retained earnings	X
Less: Drawings for the year	(X)		
Capital c/fwd	X	Total equity	X

The capital structure of a sole trader and corporate entity can be compared. In effect, a sole trader has one capital account, although for the purpose of recording transactions, a separate drawings account may be used, which is then closed off annually to the capital account. A corporate entity always has a share capital account and a retained earnings account, and may also have share premium and/or revaluation surplus accounts.

The movements during the year in the equity accounts of a corporate entity are presented in a separate statement of changes in equity. The information presented above and included in the statement of financial position are the balances on those accounts at the accounting year end. The statement of changes in equity is discussed in more detail elsewhere in this chapter.

Both a sole trader and a corporate entity may raise finance in the form of loans (e.g. from a bank). In both cases, the loan will be classified as a liability in the statement of financial position.

Loan or debt finance

Debt

The main type of debt finance you are likely to come across is a loan note.

Loan notes

A loan note is the written acknowledgement of a debt by a corporate entity and normally contains details such as:

- the rate of interest and frequency of payment
- repayment of capital
- whether any security has been provided for the loan
- the lender's rights in the event of default by the borrower.

A loan note may be secured on some or all of the assets of the corporate entity. The provider of finance may be a single party, such as a bank, or a group who collectively have made the loan to the entity. This means that if the entity fails to repay the loan, or cannot keep up with the interest payments, the loan note holders can seize the assets on which their loan is secured and sell them to recover their money.

In accounting terms, a loan note is the same as a loan; it may be a current or non-current liability depending on the date of repayment of the principal. Interest payments are compulsory, irrespective of the level of profits, and are a normal expense, accounted for on an accruals basis (i.e. the full amount of interest arising during the accounting period must be charged in the statement of profit or loss, regardless of the date of payment of that interest).

3 Terminology

Equity

Equity is the net investment in the corporate made by the shareholders. It consists of all share capital and reserves accounts.

Share capital

The owners' investment is in the form of shares. The most common forms of share are ordinary shares and preference shares.

Ordinary ('equity') shares

These shares entitle the holders to the remaining distributable profits (i.e. retained earnings) at the discretion of the directors (and, upon liquidation of the entity, the remaining assets) after prior interests and claims have been settled e.g. payables and loans. Shareholders will receive this is the form of a dividend.

Preference shares

These shares usually entitle the holder to a fixed rate of dividend, subject to the conditions of issue and rank ahead of ordinary shares for payment of a dividend from available profits. Preference shareholders may also rank ahead of ordinary shareholders for repayment of capital in the event of liquidation of the entity.

Redeemable or irredeemable preference shares

Redeemable means the entity has agreed to buy back the shares from the shareholder at an agreed future date. In effect, it is really a type of loan and is classified and accounted for as debt i.e. as a current or non-current liability.

Irredeemable preference shares are classified and accounted for as equity shares. The reason for this is that, if they are not redeemable, they are very similar to ordinary shares.

Note that, for this syllabus, preference shares are normally regarded as being irredeemable. This means that they should be classified within equity, rather than as a liability, in the statement of financial position.

When preparing the financial statements, each of the above types of share capital should be presented as a separate source of finance in the statement of financial position.

When a corporate entity is formed, the legal formation documents state the authorised share capital of the entity. This is divided into a number of shares, each having a nominal value. The authorised share capital is the maximum number and type of shares that may be issued without obtaining prior permission from the entity's shareholders. The nominal value is also known as the face value or par value.

The **nominal or par value** is an arbitrary monetary value assigned to a share e.g. $1, 50c or 25c. This value remains fixed, whereas the market value of the share (the value at which the share is actively trading) fluctuates over time. The nominal value is often used when calculating dividend payments to shareholders.

Shares are first issued by an entity at an issue price. The issue price must be at least equal to the nominal value of the share, but often exceeds it. Any amount received by the entity in excess of the nominal value is accounted for in a separate **share premium account.**

Other terminology to be aware of:

- **Issued share capital** is that part of the authorised share capital share capital that has actually been allotted to shareholders following their application for shares. The number of issued shares is used in the calculation of dividends.
- **Called-up** share capital is that part of the issued capital paid by shareholders plus any further amounts that they have agreed to pay in the future.
- **Paid up** share capital is that part of the called-up capital which has been paid by shareholders by a specific date.

Note that for most entities not listed on a stock exchange, shares issued are normally paid up in full when they are first issued, rather than being paid in stages as described above.

4 Accounting for share issues

When a corporate entity issues shares, it may do so in several ways

- an issue at market price
- a rights issue
- a bonus issue.

Issue at market price

In the case of an issue at market price, the entity must always receive at least the nominal value per share. Any excess above nominal value received by the entity when the shares are first issued is classified as share premium.

The accounting entries to record the share issue would be:

		$
Debit	Bank account (issue price × no. shares)	X
Credit	Share capital account (nominal value × no. shares)	X
Credit	Share premium account (ß) (i.e. the difference between the issue price and the nominal value × no. of shares sold)	X

For example, consider the situation of an entity that issued 10,000 new ordinary shares, with a nominal value of 50c each, at an issue price of $2.50.

The accounting entries to record the share issue would be:

		$
Debit	Bank account ($2.50 × 10,000)	25,000
Credit	Share capital account ($0.50 × 10,000)	5,000
Credit	Share premium account (ß) ($2.00 × 10,000)	20,000

If you have been asked to account for the issue of shares, make sure that you allocate the total proceeds appropriately between share capital and share premium, particularly if the nominal value per share is not $1, as in this example. Alternatively, you could have been given equivalent information that, upon the issue of shares, the nominal value per share was $0.50 and share premium was $2 per share. You could then calculate that the cash received was $2.50 per share.

Rights issue

A rights issue is an offer by the entity to issue shares to current shareholders in proportion to their existing shareholding. A rights issue is normally made at less than market value to encourage shareholders to take up the share issue.

A rights issue is very similar to an issue at market price, and the accounting entries will be the same, with entries made in the share capital and share premium accounts as noted previously. However, the number of shares issued is in proportion to their existing shareholding, dependent upon the number of shares each shareholder currently owns.

For example, consider the situation of an entity that had issued share capital of 100,000 shares with a nominal value of 50c each. The issued share capital in the statement of financial position would be $50,000 (100,000 × 50c). If the entity now made a rights issue of 1 for 5 at a price of $1.25 per share, we would need to calculate the number of shares issued and then determine the cash received by the entity, allocated between share capital and share premium as follows:

Number of shares issued = 100,000/5 = 20,000 new shares of 50c nominal value issued

Cash received = 20,000 × $1.25 = $25,000

The accounting entries to record the rights issue would be:

		$
Debit	Bank account ($1.25 × 20,000)	25,000
Credit	Share capital account ($0.50 × 20,000)	10,000
Credit	Share premium account (ß) ($0.75 × 20,000)	15,000

Therefore, if an individual shareholder owned, say, 3,000 shares immediately prior to the rights issue, they would be eligible to acquire a further 600 shares (3,000/5) at a price of $1.25 per share.

As with an issue at market price, the entity must receive at least the nominal value per share upon issue, with any excess above nominal value is accounted for as share premium.

The advantages of a rights issue are as follows:

- it is usually cheaper for an entity to make a rights issue than an issue at market price as reduced regulatory and compliance costs are incurred.
- as the issue price is slightly lower than for an issue at market price, this acts as an incentive for shareholders to take up the rights issue and the entity is more likely to raise the full amount of capital it seeks.

The disadvantages of a rights issue are as follows:

- it is a more expensive way to raise capital than an issue of debt.
- it may not be fully subscribed (taken up) by the shareholders, leaving the entity with a shortfall in the amount of capital it was trying to raise.

The key difference in practical terms between an issue at market price and a rights issue will be the price at which the shares are issued by the entity. For a rights issue, it will be lower than for an issue at market price to encourage current shareholders to increase their shareholding in the entity.

Both the share capital and share premium accounts are included in the statement of financial position within the 'Equity' section.

Test your understanding 1

ALO issued 200,000 25c shares at a price of $1.75 each.

Required:

Prepare the ledger accounts to show this transaction.

Test your understanding 2

DOD had issued share capital of 10,000 ordinary shares of 50c nominal value each. It subsequently made a rights issue of '1 for 4' at 80c per share. The rights issue was fully taken up by the shareholders.

Required:

What accounting entries are required to account for the rights issue?

Bonus issue

A bonus issue is a 'free' issue of shares to current shareholders in proportion to their current shareholding i.e. the entity receives no cash or any other consideration in exchange for the share issue. In effect, it is a way for the entity to capitalise its reserves and increase the number of shares in issue.

A bonus issue would be accounted for as follows:

		$
Debit	Share premium/retained earnings (nominal value × no. shares)	X
Credit	Share capital account (nominal value × no. shares)	X

Note that the debit entry can be made into another account within equity. Ideally, a non-distributable reserve would be used, such as share premium or revaluation surplus. In the absence of any non-distributable reserves, it is acceptable to make the debit entry in the retained earnings account.

As with a rights issue, the number of new shares each shareholder would receive would be in proportion to their current shareholding. Suppose an entity had the following share capital and reserves balances immediately prior to making a bonus issue:

	$
Share capital @ $0.5 each	80,000
Share premium	15,000
Retained earnings	170,000
Total equity	265,000

If it made a bonus issue of '1 for 5' it would issue 32,000 new shares (($80,000 × 2)/5) with a nominal value of 50c per share, giving a monetary value of $16,000.

The accounting entries to record the bonus issue would be as follows:

		$
Debit	Share premium (use first as far as possible)	15,000
Debit	Retained earnings (use if insufficient share premium)	1,000
Credit	Share capital account (32,000 × 50c)	16,000

The resultant share capital and reserves balances would be:

	$
Share capital $0.50 each	96,000
Share premium	Nil
Retained earnings	169,000
Total equity	265,000

Note that the total of capital or equity remains unchanged at $265,000 after accounting for the bonus issue.

Suppose, for example, an individual held 3,500 shares each of 50c nominal value in that entity. The shareholder would receive 700 new shares (i.e. 3,500/5 = 700). As the entity received no cash or any other monetary benefit in exchange for the issue of shares, it follows that the total market value of the shareholding has not changed. However, the market value per share would fall to reflect the fact that there are now more shares in issue.

The advantages of a bonus issue are as follows:

- as the number of shares in issue has increased, the market value per share is now lower and makes them more marketable and more easily transferable.
- issued share capital is brought more into line with assets employed in the entity by reducing reserves and increasing share capital.

The disadvantage of making a bonus issue is as follows:

- the administration costs to the entity of making the bonus issue.

Test your understanding 3

ACO had the following capital structure at 31 December 20X3:

	$000
Issued share capital of $1 ordinary shares	1,000
Share premium account	800
Retained earnings	4,500
	6,300

On 14 January 20X4, it made a bonus issue of 1 share for 10.

Required:

What was the revised capital structure of ACO immediately following the bonus issue?

5 Accounting for dividends paid

Dividends

The amount paid to the entity's shareholders as a return for investing in the entity is known as a dividend.

Dividends are often paid in two instalments: one paid during the year is known as an **interim dividend**; the other, which is usually paid after the end of the financial year, is known as a **final dividend**.

- The total of the dividends paid in an accounting year is included in the statement of changes in equity (SOCIE) as a reduction in retained earnings.
- It is important that you understand that **dividends paid by a corporate entity are not an expense** included in the statement of profit or loss.

Note that dividends are accounted for in the financial statements on a **cash basis**. In effect, this usually means that, within the financial statements of a given year, it will account for the final dividend of the previous accounting year, together with the interim dividend of the current accounting year.

For example, consider an entity with an accounting year end of 31 December 20X5. When the final accounts for that year have been finalised in early 20X6, the directors will be in a position to decide upon an appropriate level of final dividend to pay (if any) to the shareholders, which will then be paid in 20X6.

Later in 20X6, the directors may decide to pay an interim dividend for 20X6 based upon, say, the management accounts for the six months to 30 June 20X6, which will then be paid before the end of the year. Therefore, the dividends accounted for in the financial statements (specifically the statement of changes in equity) for the year ended 31 December 20X6 is the final dividend for 20X5 plus the interim dividend for 20X6.

Note that this is a rather simplistic approach to accounting for dividends paid by a corporate entity, which is sufficient for the requirements of this subject. You will return to this topic in your subsequent study of financial accounting as you progress through your CIMA studies.

In practical terms, this means that, in most circumstances, the dividends paid in an accounting year will be the final dividend of the previous year and the interim dividend of the current year. A good rule of thumb to remember is that dividends are accounted for when they are paid.

e.g

Illustration 1

An entity has an accounting year end of 31 March. On 5 June 20X2 it paid a final dividend relating to the year ended 31 March 20X2 of $10,000. On 15 January 20X3, the entity paid an interim dividend of $6,000 relating to the year ended 31 March 20X3. It subsequently paid a final dividend of $8,000 relating to the year ended 31 March 20X3 on 18 June 20X3.

Required:

What amount should be included in the statement of changes in equity for dividends paid for the year ended 31 March 20X3?

Solution:

The dividends paid during the year ended 31 March 20X3 were as follows:

Final dividend re accounting year to 31 March 20X2 – paid 5 June 20X2	$10,000
Interim dividend re accounting year to 31 March 20X3 – paid 15 January 20X3	$6,000
Dividends paid in the accounting year to 31 March 20X3 –include in SOCIE	$16,000

Note that the payment made on 18 June 20X3 falls into the accounting year ended 31 March 20X4 and is therefore ignored in the current year.

e.g

Illustration 2

An entity has an accounting year end of 31 December. On 1 March 20X6, it paid a final dividend of $12,500 in relation to the year ended 31 December 20X5. On 15 November 20X6 it paid an interim dividend of $8,750 in relation to the accounting year ended 31 December 20X6 and subsequently paid a final dividend for 20X6 on 28 February 20X7 amounting to $11,350.

Required:

What was the amount of the dividends paid included in the statement of changes in equity for the year ended 31 December 20X6?

Solution:

Final dividend for 20X5	$12,500
Interim dividend for 20X6	$8,750
	$21,250

The $21,250 will appear in the trial balance for the year ended 31 December 20X6. The double entry will be debit 'dividends', credit 'bank'. Dividends paid do **NOT** appear in the statement of profit or loss as an expense but as a distribution of profit in the statement of changes in equity. This statement will be considered in more detail later in this chapter.

The final dividend for 20X6, paid in 20X7, will be accounted for in the statement of changes in equity in the financial statements for the year ended 31 December 20X7.

Further detail – dividends

Directors do not have to pay the dividends in two instalments – interim and final. Some entities may pay only one dividend payment after the end of the accounting year when annual financial statements have been prepared (if any dividend is paid at all). In this case, the dividend that will appear in the statement of changes in equity will be the dividend which was paid in the current year. For example, the financial statements for the year ended 31 December 20X4 will include the proposed dividend from the year ended 31 December 20X3 but paid in 20X4.

It should be noted that the directors do not have to propose any dividends – the payment of dividends is entirely at their discretion. If the shareholders are not happy with this situation, they would try to remove the directors and replace them with directors who were prepared to propose a dividend.

Dividends on ordinary shares

Ordinary shareholders are also known as equity shareholders. Their shares do not qualify for any special benefits, although they are entitled to vote at general meetings. An ordinary shareholder is not entitled to any particular dividend payment, although if the directors decide to declare a dividend it can be as small or as large as they see fit. The ordinary shareholders are regarded as the 'main' shareholders in a corporate entity. The profits that are retained in the entity belong to them, and would be repaid to them in the event that the corporate entity was liquidated after all prior claims have been settled.

Do take care, when computing dividends, to read the question carefully. If the question states that the ordinary dividend is to be 10¢ per share, you need to calculate how many shares are in issue. For example, if the share capital in the statement of financial position is described as 'Ordinary shares of 50¢' and they are stated at $500,000, then there are 1 million ordinary shares in issue ($500,000/0.50). The total dividend paid in this example would be 1 million × 10¢ = $100,000.

Dividends on preference shares

Preference shareholders are so known because they receive preferential treatment in the payment of dividends in comparison to ordinary shareholders, and in the repayment of capital in the event that the corporate entity ceases to exist. A preference share carries a fixed rate of dividend. The important point to remember is that if the ordinary shareholders are to receive a dividend, then the preference shareholders must first receive their dividend before any dividend is paid to ordinary shareholders.

There are many different types of preference shares and you will encounter these in more detail in your later studies. It is assumed that all preference shares are 'irredeemable', which means that the preference shares have no fixed repayment date. Consequently, to all intents and purposes, they have more similarity with ordinary shares than with debt finance.

In any questions which include preference shares, you should read the question carefully to ensure that your account for them correctly as either debt (if they are redeemable like a loan) or equity (if they are irredeemable like equity shares). It is likely that dividends on preference shares will have been paid and there will be no need to make any further adjustment.

Test your understanding 4

An entity has in issue $100,000 of ordinary shares at a par value of 10¢ each and 100,000 5 per cent irredeemable preference shares at a par value of 50¢ each. The entity paid a dividend of 5¢ per ordinary share.

Required:

What was the total amount paid out in dividends?

$...............

6 Reserves

- There are two types of reserves: capital reserves and revenue reserves.
- The difference between these is that capital reserves may not be distributed as dividends.
- Examples of capital reserves are share premium (see above) and revaluation surplus – created if a corporate entity revalues its non-current assets (usually land and buildings). Since the increase in value is based on a professional valuation and has not been realised by a sale, the increase in value (or profit) cannot be distributed to shareholders. For example, if a corporate entity had property in the statement of financial position at $200,000 and it was revalued to $275,000, the property would be increased to $275,000 in the statement of financial position and a revaluation surplus would be created for $75,000. Further detail on this topic is included in the chapters dealing with non-current assets.
- Revenue reserves are the accumulated and undistributed profits of a corporate entity. The most common is the balance remaining on retained earnings in the statement of changes in equity at the end of each year. However, the directors may decide to set aside a portion of the remaining profits into a separate reserve account, for other general or specific purposes. A specific reserve is used to identify the accumulation of profits for a specific future purpose. Despite the fact that several revenue reserve accounts may exist, they are all available to be used for the payment of dividends if the directors so decide.

It is important to realise that the existence of reserves does not indicate a fund of cash. The creation of a reserve is usually a bookkeeping transaction, debiting retained earnings reserve and crediting a general reserve.

7 Statement of changes in equity

We introduced the statement of changes in equity very briefly earlier in the chapter and now that we have discussed share capital, reserves and dividends in more detail, we can return to the statement of changes in equity. As the name implies, this statement shows the change in equity from the beginning of the year to the end of the year. Equity is the shareholders' capital in the corporate entity and comprises share capital and reserves. They may be increased by, for example:

- Share issues
- Total comprehensive income.

They may be decreased by, for example:

- Dividends paid in the accounting year.

There may be a transfer between reserves; this will not increase or decrease the total equity but will change the individual balances within equity.

A full example of a statement of changes in equity is as follows:

Statement of changes in equity of Hi Tech for the year ended 31 December 20X8

	Ordinary shares	**Share premium**	**Reval'n surplus**	**Ret earnings**	**Total**
	$000	$000	$000	$000	$000
Balance 1.1.X8	1,000	500	400	400	2,300
Profit for the year				600	600
Dividends				(200)	(200)
Shares issued	600	150			750
Revaluation of property			80		80
Balance 31.12.X8	1,600	650	480	800	3,530

Statement of financial position (extract) of Hi Tech as at 31 December 20X8

	$000
Equity	
Ordinary shares	1,600
Share premium	650
Revaluation surplus	480
Retained earnings	800
	3,530

These points are brought together in the following example. Note that this example is not in the form you would encounter in an examination but it is an excellent learning exercise.

Worked Example 8.A

An extract of the trial balance of ABC as at 30 September 20X2 is presented below:

	Debit	Credit
	$000	$000
Ordinary shares of $1 each		650
5% irredeemable preference shares of $1 each		100
Share premium		250
Revaluation surplus		250
Retained earnings at 1 October 20X1		432
10% loan note (repayable 20X9)		200
Preference dividend paid	5	

Notes:

1 The corporate entity made a profit after tax for the year ended 30 September 20X2 of $75,000, after accounting for an ordinary dividend paid of $31,000 as an administration expense.

2 The premises were revalued from a carrying value of $600,000 to $850,000 at 30 September 20X2.

3 On 30 September 20X2, the corporate entity made a rights issue of 1 ordinary share for 4 at an issue price of $1.50 per share. The rights issue was fully taken up by all shareholders.

Required:

Prepare the statement of changes in equity for the year ended 30 September 20X2.

Solution

Statement of changes in equity of ABC for the year ended 30 September 20X2

	Ord share capital $	Irred pref share capital $	Share premium $	Reval'n surplus $	Retained earnings $	Total $
Balance at 1 October 20X1	520	100	185	0	432	1,237
Ordinary shares – rights issue in the year	130		65			195
Comprehensive income for the year				250	106	356
Ordinary dividend paid					(31)	(31)
Preference dividend paid					(5)	(5)
Balance at 30 September 20X2	650	100	250	250	502	1,752

Notes:

- The revaluation of the premises occurs at the end of the year. The total of $250,000 in the revaluation surplus represents the change in carrying value of $600,000 to the revalued amount of $850,000. This revaluation is also presented as 'other comprehensive income' in the statement of total comprehensive income. Also, as the revaluation in the year equals the balance on revaluation surplus at 30 September 20X2, this means that there was a nil balance on revaluation surplus at the start of the year.
- The profit after tax for the year needs to be adjusted for the ordinary dividend paid that had been wrongly classified as an administration expense. Therefore, the correct profit after tax for the year is $106,000 ($75,000 + $31,000). The ordinary dividend paid is then accounted for as a deduction from retained earnings within the statement of changes in equity.
- Irredeemable preference shares are classified as equity.
- The 10% loan note is a liability and therefore not included in the statement of changes in equity

8 Chapter summary

In this chapter you have studied:

- the accounting treatment for certain transactions in the financial statements of corporate entities:
  - the issue of shares
  - the payment of dividends
  - loan notes
  - reserves.
- the bookkeeping entries to record the issue of shares
- the different types of finance such as ordinary share issues, loan notes, redeemable and non-redeemable preference shares

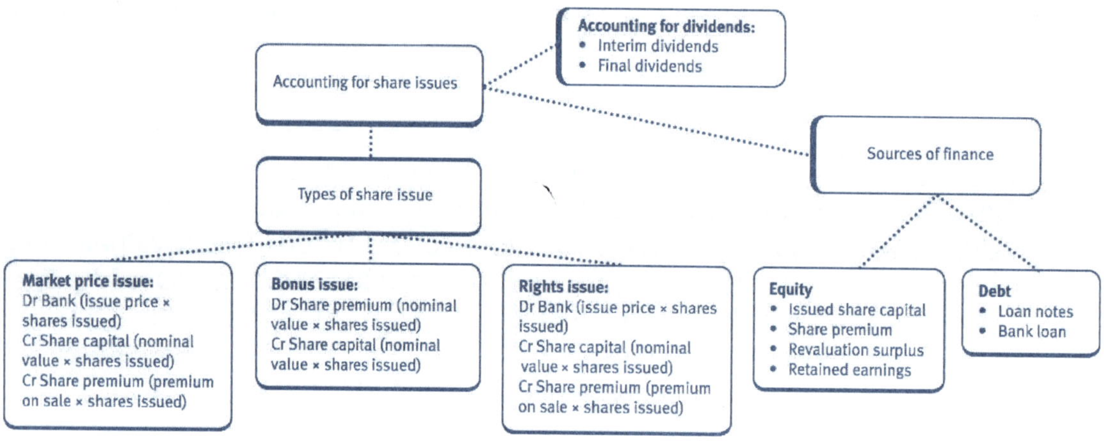

Test your understanding questions

Why add together?

Test your understanding 5

What are the correct ledger account entries required to record the issue of 380,000 $0.50 shares at a premium of 30¢, and paid for by cheque, in full?

Test your understanding 6

An entity issued share capital of two million ordinary shares of $1 each, at a premium of 50¢ each, raising capital of $3,000,000. The directors are considering proposing a total dividend payment of $120,000 for the year.

Required:

If the dividend was paid, what would be the dividend expressed as cents per share?

.... cents per share

Test your understanding 7

ADF issued 60,000 5 per cent irredeemable preference shares of $2 each and 350,000 ordinary shares with a nominal value of 50¢ each issued at a premium of 30¢ each.

During 20X6, an interim dividend of 6¢ per ordinary share plus the first half the preference dividend were paid.

A final dividend of 12¢ per ordinary shares was paid in February 20X7, along with the second half of the preference share dividend.

Required:

What were the dividends paid for inclusion in the statement of changes in equity for the year ended 31 December 20X6?

$...............

Test your understanding 8

Which two of the following would you expect to find in the statement of changes in equity in a corporate entity for the current year?

A Ordinary share dividend proposed during the previous year, and paid in the current year

B Ordinary share dividend proposed during the current year, and paid in the following year

C Directors' fees

D Auditors' fees

E Revaluation surplus

Test your understanding 9

What is the full impact of revaluation of a property upon the financial statements of an entity?

A Property in the statement of financial position increases and revaluation surplus is increased. Other comprehensive income is also disclosed.

B Property in the statement of financial position is increased revaluation surplus is increased. Other comprehensive income is not disclosed.

C Property in the statement of financial position is increased and the statement of profit or loss is increased. Other comprehensive income is also disclosed.

D Other comprehensive income is disclosed only

Test your understanding 10

*

The following is an extract from the equity section of the statement of financial position of KND as at 31 December 20X1:

	$
Share capital ($1 shares)	150,000
Share premium	50,000

During the year ended 31 December 20X2, KND issued 100,000 $1 shares at $3 each.

What was the balance on the share premium account as at 31 December 20X2?

A $200,000

B $250,000

C $350,000

D $300,000

Test your understanding 11

ADG has issued share capital of 800,000 ordinary shares of $1 each, which have been issued at a premium of 50¢ each, raising capital of $1,200,000. ADG is considering payment of a dividend of $120,000 for the current year.

Required:

If the dividend was paid, what would be the dividend per share?

.... cents per share.

Test your understanding 12

AEH has issued share capital of 50,000 5 per cent irredeemable preference shares of $2 each and 400,000 ordinary shares with a nominal value of 20¢ each.

The ordinary shares have been issued at a premium of 30¢ each. Interim dividends of 5¢ per ordinary share plus the first half of the preference dividend were paid during the current year.

A final dividend of 15¢ per ordinary shares was paid after the year end, along with the second half of the preference share dividend.

Required:

What was were the dividends paid in the year for inclusion in the statement of changes in equity?

$...............

Test your understanding 13

The following is an extract from the equity section of the statement of financial position of DNK as at 31 December 20X1:

	$
Share capital ($1 shares)	250,000
Share premium	100,000

During the year ended 31 December 20X2, DNK issued 120,000 $1 shares at $3.50 each.

Required:

What is the balance on the share premium account as at 31 December 20X2?

$..............

not added together.

Test your understanding answers

Test your understanding 1

Cash

	$		$
Share capital/premium (200,000 × $1.75)	350,000		

Share capital

	$		$
		Cash (200,000 × 25c)	50,000

Share premium

	$		$
		Cash (350,000 – 50,000)	300,000

Test your understanding 2

The number of shares issued = 10,000/4 = 2,500

DOD received cash of: 2,500 × $0.80 = $2,000

The accounting entries to record the share issue were:

		$
Debit	Bank account ($0.8 × 2,500)	2,000
Credit	Share capital account ($0.5 × 2,500)	1,250
Credit	Share premium account (ß) ($0.3 × 2,500).	750

Test your understanding 3

Revised capital structure of ACO is as follows:

	$000
Issued share capital of $1 ordinary shares (1,000 + 100)	1,100
Share premium account (800 – 100)	700
Retained earnings	4,500
	6,300

The number of bonus shares issued was 100,000 (i.e. 1,000,000/10). The accounting entries to record the bonus issue would be

	$000
Debit: Share premium	100
Credit: Share capital	100

Note that, ACO would choose to debit a non-distributable reserve (e.g. share premium or revaluation reserve) if available, rather than retained earnings if possible. The reason for this is that, by using a non-distributable reserve, retained earnings are not reduced which can otherwise be used for payment of a dividend.

The bonus issue would be disclosed in the statement of changes in equity (covered in subsequent section within chapter) in the accounting year in which it occurred i.e. the year ended 31 December 20X4.

Test your understanding 4

The share capital consists of:

	$
Irredeemable preference shares, 100,000 at 50¢	50,000
Ordinary shares, 1,000,000 at 10¢	100,000

The preference dividend amounts to 5 per cent of $50,000, that is $2,500, and the ordinary dividend amounts to 5¢ × 1 million shares = $50,000, giving a **total dividend of $52,500.**

Remember that irredeemable preference shareholders must first receive their dividend before a dividend can be paid to the ordinary shareholders.

Test your understanding 5

	Debit	**Credit**
Bank (380,000 × $0.80)	304,000	
Share capital (380,000 × $0.50)		190,000
Share premium (380,000 × $0.30)		114,000

Test your understanding 6

6¢ per share

Dividends are declared and paid based upon the nominal value per share in issue.

If the entity has 2,000,000 shares with a nominal value of $1 each in issue, then the dividend per share will be:

The total dividend of $120,000/2,000,000 = 6¢ per share.

Test your understanding 7

$24,000

Ordinary dividend = 350,000 shares × $0.06 interim) = $21,000
Irredeemable preference dividend = 60,000 shares × $2 = $120,000 × 5% × 1/2 = $3,000

The total dividend paid was $24,000.

Note: Ordinary dividends are payable **per share** and preference dividends are payable **on nominal value.**

Test your understanding 8

A & E

Dividends proposed are included in the statement of changes in equity only when they are paid. Directors' and auditors' fees are normal business expenses and appear in the statement of profit or loss and other comprehensive income. Revaluation surplus is one of the components of equity which is included in the statement of changes in equity.

Test your understanding 9

A

Property in the statement of financial position and revaluation surplus are increased. Other comprehensive income is also disclosed as the revaluation in the year does not affect the profit after tax for the year.

Test your understanding 10

B

The excess of the issue price about nominal value will be recorded in the share premium, i.e. 100,000 × ($3 – $1) = $200,000. This amount will increase the opening balance of $50,000 to $250,000.

Test your understanding 11

15¢ per share.

Dividends are declared only on issued shares, and are based on the nominal value.

If the entity has $800,000 share capital with a nominal value of $1 each = 800,000 shares

The total dividend of $120,000/800,000 = 15¢ per share.

Test your understanding 12

$22,500.

Ordinary dividend = $20,000 (400,000 shares × 0.05 interim).
Irredeemable preference dividend = $2,500 (50,000 shares × $2 = $100,000 × 5% × ½).

Note: Ordinary dividends are payable **per share** and preference dividends are payable **on nominal value.**

Test your understanding 13

$400,000

The excess of the issue price about nominal value will be recorded in the share premium, i.e. 120,000 × ($3.50 – $1) = $300,000. This amount will increase the opening balance of $100,000 to $400,000.

Chapter

9

Accounting for irrecoverable debts and allowances for receivables

Chapter learning objectives

When you have completed this chapter, you should be able to:

- prepare accounting entries for irrecoverable debts and allowances for receivables.

1 Introduction

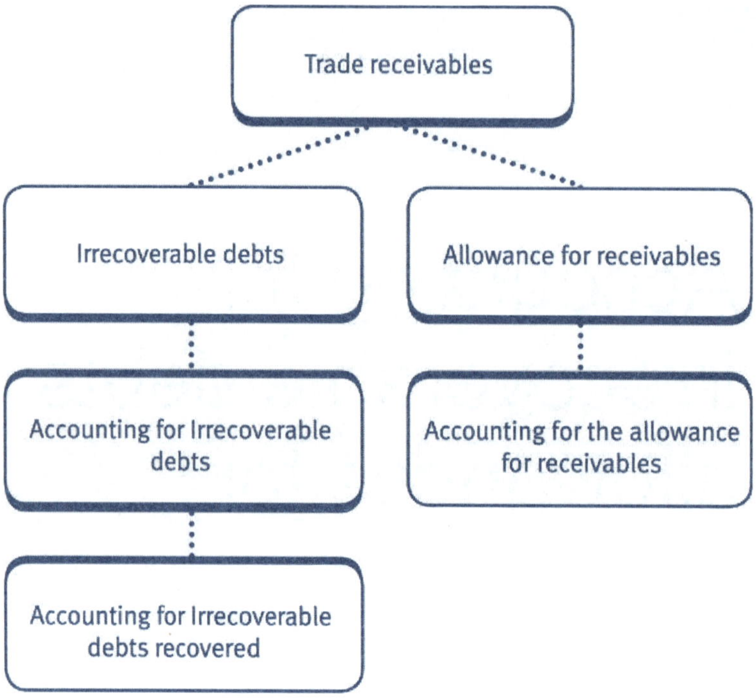

In this chapter, you will learn:

- the definition of an irrecoverable debt
- how to account for an irrecoverable debt
- the definition of an allowance for receivables
- how to account for an allowance for receivables.

When a business entity sells goods on credit, it assumes that the customer will subsequently pay in full for those goods. However, sometimes a customer does not pay in full, or even at all, and thus it is incorrect to retain the balance as an asset or to treat the sale as having generated profit.

There may also be occasions when a business entity considers that some of its credit customers may fail to pay the amounts due in full and are therefore considered to be doubtful, although not yet regarded as irrecoverable.

Both of these situations need to be considered when preparing the financial statements.

2 Accounting for irrecoverable debts

When it becomes known that a customer is unlikely to pay, (perhaps because it becomes known that the customer is in financial difficulties) the receivable balance must be removed (since it is no longer an asset of the business entity) and transferred to the statement of profit or loss as an expense of the period in which the irrecoverable debt arises. This may also be referred to as a bad debt.

The double entry is:

		$
Debit	Irrecoverable debts expense account	X
Credit	Receivables/Sales ledger control account	X

Worked Example 9.A

X sold goods to Y on credit on 1 January 20X1 valued at $350. On 30 November 20X1, X was advised that Y was unable to pay the debt.

Required:

Account for the irrecoverable debt in the accounting records of X.

Solution:

Prior to X receiving this information the SLCA account was as follows:

Sales ledger control account

		$			$
1 Jan	Sales	350			

However, now it is necessary to remove the asset and instead treat the outstanding balance as an expense. The entries are shown below:

Sales ledger control account

		$			$
1 Jan	Sales	350	30 Nov	Irrecoverable debts exp	350

Irrecoverable debts expense

		$			$
30 Nov	Sales ledger control account	350			

There may be circumstances where only part of the debt needs to be written off as an expense. For example, if Y had paid $200 on 30 June 20X1 and only the balance needed to be written off, then the accounts would appear as follows:

Sales ledger control account

		$			$
30 Nov	Sales ledger control account	350	30 June	Bank	200
			30 Nov	Irrecoverable debts expense	150
		350			350

Irrecoverable debts expense

		$			$
30 Nov	Sales ledger control account	150			

3 Irrecoverable debts recovered

It is possible that debts that have previously been written off may later be paid to the entity. If this happens, then the entries made to write off the debt as an expense must be reversed before recording the receipt of the payment from the customer.

The double entry will be:

Debit:	Receivables/Sales ledger control account	$X
Credit:	Irrecoverable debts expense account	$X

This entry reinstates the debt to enable the business entity to allocate the cash received from the customer.

The payment can then be allocated to the receivables/sales ledger control account as follows:

Debit:	Bank account	$X
Credit:	Receivables/Sales ledger control account	$X

We have now made a debit and credit entry to the receivables/sales ledger control account of equal amounts. Therefore, we could take a shortcut double entry as follows

Debit:	Bank account	$X
Credit:	Irrecoverable debts expense account	$X

Worked Example 9.B

P sold goods to Q on credit valued at $500. Q did not pay and his debt was written off in 20X0. The original ledger account entries were as follows:

Sales ledger control account

20X0	$	20X0	$
Balance b/d	500	Irrecoverable debts exp	500

Irrecoverable debts expense

20X0	$	20X0	$
Sales ledger control account	500	Statement of profit or loss	500

On 31 December 20X1, Q paid the debt in full. The entries required to record this in the ledger accounts are shown below:

Sales ledger control account

20X0	$	20X0	$
Balance b/d	500	Irrecoverable debts exp	500
20X1		20X1	
Irrecoverable debts	500	Bank	500

Irrecoverable debts expense

	$	20X1	$
		Sales ledger control account	500

The credit balance on the irrecoverable debts expense account will be credited to the statement of profit or loss at the end of 20X1.

Sometimes a part payment of a debt previously written off is made. If Q had paid $200 as full and final settlement, then the entries made would have been:

Sales ledger control account

20X0	$	20X0	$
Balance b/d	500	Irrecoverable debts exp	500
20X1		20X1	
Irrecoverable debts	500	Bank	200
		Irrecoverable debts exp	300
	500		500

Irrecoverable debts expense

20X1	$	20X1	$
Sales ledger control account	300	Sales ledger control account (irrecoverable debt brought back)	500
	____		____

The reason for reinstating the full amount of the original debt and then writing off the resulting $300 is so that if P were to trade with Q again in the future it would be clear that an irrecoverable debt arose from their previous trading activities. If only the part of the debt settled was reinstated, then it may appear that no irrecoverable debt actually occurred.

4 Allowance for receivables

While some debts are definitely irrecoverable – it is known for certain that the customer will not be able to pay – others may be only doubtful. In this case it would not be appropriate to eliminate the receivable balance because the credit customer may pay after all. But we have to recognise that the value of the asset 'trade receivables' is probably less than it appears to be. The technique used is to create an **allowance for receivables.**

The double entry will be:

Debit:	Irrecoverable debts expense account	$X
Credit:	Allowance for receivables account	$X

Prudence concept

Both writing off irrecoverable debts and accounting for allowances for receivables are in accordance with the concept of **prudence**, which you will learn more about this elsewhere in this publication. Adopting a prudent approach is simply ensuring that profits and assets are not overstated, by estimating likely losses and decreases in assets as soon as they become apparent.

This estimate can be prepared using a number of different techniques, such as:

- using experience and knowledge of customers and the economic climate
- listing all receivables ledger account balances and analysing them individually for their ability to pay
- preparing a schedule of receivables account balances according to the length of time that their debt has been outstanding, and using different percentages depending on the age of the debt. This is known as an 'aged receivables schedule'.

For the BA3 exam it is likely that you will be given a % to apply to the total receivables balance which when calculated will represent the allowance required, the detailed review and calculation of allowances are outside the BA3 syllabus.

Worked Example 9.C

Age of debt	**Amount** ($)
Less than 1 month	8,000
1–2 months	3,000
2–3 months	700
More than 3 months	140
	11,840

The required allowance is equivalent to 5% of the outstanding receivables balance = $592 ($11,840 × 5%).

Irrecoverable debts expense

20X1	$	20X1	$
Allowance for receivables	592		

Allowance for receivables

20X1	$	20X1	$
		Irrecoverable debts exp	592

When the allowance for receivables is first created, the ledger account entries are as shown above.

The balance on the irrecoverable debts account is transferred to the statement of profit or loss at the end of the period. Thus the balance on this account will be reduced to nil at the end of the accounting period.

The balance on the allowances account is used to decrease the value of total receivables included in the statement of financial position at the end of the accounting period. The net balance on the statement of financial position will be total receivables less the allowance for receivables. This balance on allowance for receivables will remain in the ledger accounts.

Note that no entries are made in the individual receivables accounts for the allowance.

Once the allowance has been created it must be reviewed periodically (e.g. monthly, quarterly or annually) and increased or decreased depending on the circumstances of the business entity.

For example, if the above allowance were to be decreased by $73 ($592 - $519) in 20X2, then the accounting entries would appear as follows:

Irrecoverable debts expense

		20X2	$
		Allowable for receivables	73

Allowable for receivables

20X2	$	20X2	$
Irrecoverable debts exp	73	Balance b/d	592
Balance c/d	519		
	592		592
		20X3	
		Balance b/d	519

Note that it is possible to avoid the use of the irrecoverable debts account if the entry is only made once a year, since the statement of profit or loss can be debited directly, but most modern accounting systems provide monthly profit statements for internal management use, and in these circumstances it is common to use the ledger accounts shown.

It is important to remember that only the **movement** on the allowance account is transferred to the irrecoverable debts expense account.

Always remember to write off all irrecoverable debts before the allowance for receivables is calculated and accounted for.

The accounting entries required to **increase an allowance** are as follows:

Debit:	Irrecoverable debts expense account	$X
Credit:	Allowance for receivables account	$X

The accounting entries required to **decrease an allowance** are as follows:

Debit:	Allowances for receivables account	$X
Credit:	Irrecoverable debts expense account	$X

Test your understanding 1

The allowance for receivables for each year end was as follows:

31 December 20X0	$1,500
31 December 20X1	$1,100
31 December 20X2	$1,650
31 December 20X3	$2,000

Required:

Write up the allowance for receivables account for each of the years 20X0 to 20X3 inclusive.

Test your understanding 2

On 31 August 20X4, the total receivables of Henry Higgins was $10,000 and the balance on the allowance for receivables account at that date was $200. Of the total receivables it was considered that $500 was irrecoverable and should be written off. A closing allowance for receivables equivalent to 3% of remaining receivables is required.

At 31 August 20X5, the total of receivables balances had fallen to $8,000, of which $100 was considered to be irrecoverable and should be written off.

Required:

- Show the irrecoverable debts account at 31 August 20X4 and 20X5.
- Show the allowance for receivables account at 31 August 20X4 and 20X5.
- 3 Show the relevant figures in the statements of financial position for the 2 years 20X4 and 20X5.

Further detail

Payments received after creating allowance for receivables

Because there is no adjustment made in the account of the receivable when an allowance is made there is no need to make any particular entries if that receivable eventually pays. The adjustment to the allowance of the previous accounting period will take place when the current year total receivables are assessed for the likelihood of being paid, and that debt will be ignored in the calculation of the allowance for the current year. It is accepted that, in making allowances, there is some doubt as to the absolute accuracy of the estimates made. An over-allowance or an under-allowance can occur, but provided that these do not make a significant (material) difference to the view portrayed by the financial statements, no action is taken.

5 Application of accounting concepts

An important convention that affects accounting is the **prudence** concept, which states that revenue and assets should not be recognised unless they can be reliably measured and it is probable that future economic benefits will be received. In addition, revenue and assets should not be overstated.

Accounting for irrecoverable debts and allowances for receivables represents application of the **prudence concept.** Trade receivables, is an asset in the statement of financial position and should not be overstated. Therefore, if any debts are regarded as irrecoverable, they should be removed from the trade receivables balance and written off as an expense. Similarly, an allowance for receivables should be recognised when there is reason to believe that there may not be full recovery of amounts due from customers.

Some of the topics in this chapter are subjective and require assumptions and estimates to be made. For example, at precisely what point in time should a receivable be regarded as irrecoverable? Similarly, at what point should an allowance be made against a receivable, and for what amount? If a prudent estimate or judgement is made, it is likely to be a reasonable basis for inclusion in the financial statements. For this reason, Chapter 1 discusses various sources of guidance, concepts and principles used by accountants when preparing accounting information.

6 Chapter summary

In this chapter you studied the bookkeeping and accounting treatment of the following transactions:

- irrecoverable debts
- allowances for receivables.

Both of these are likely to appear in computer-based assessments requiring either the preparation of ledger accounts or, more commonly, the preparation of financial statements.

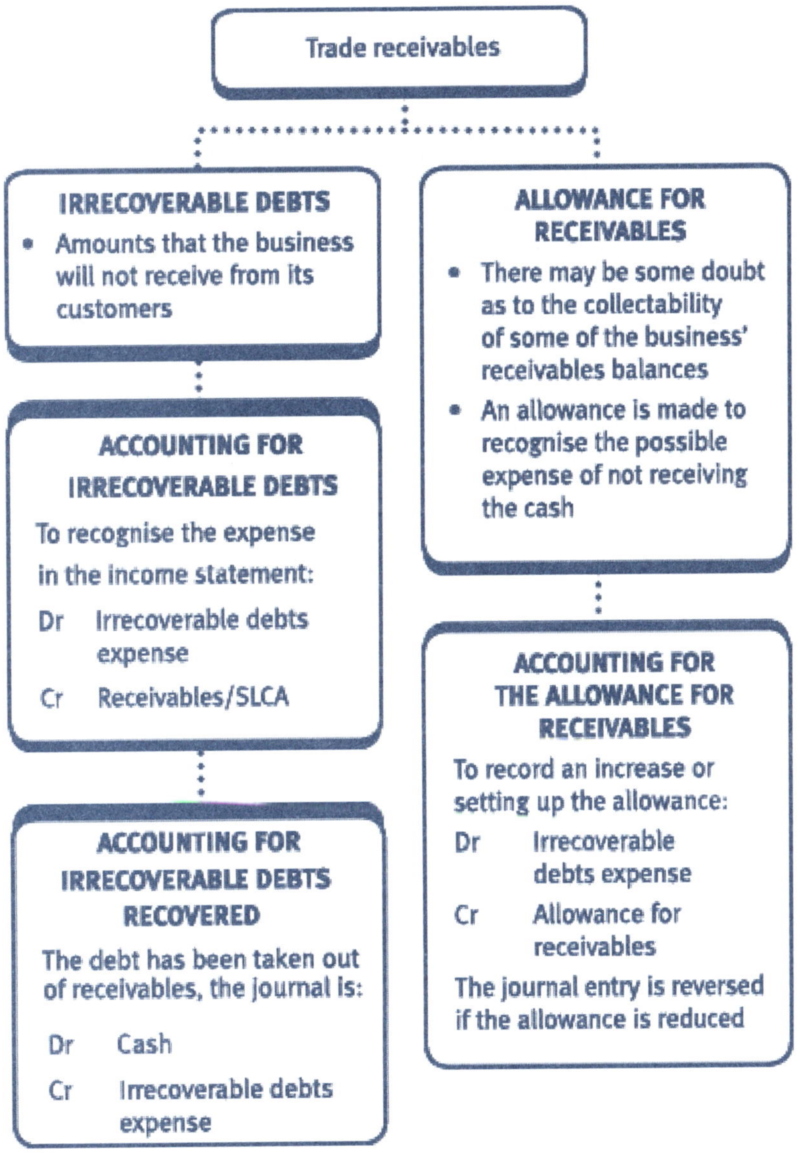

Test your understanding questions

Test your understanding 3

A decrease in the allowance for receivables would result in:

A an increase in liabilities

B a decrease in working capital

C a decrease in net profit

D an increase in net profit

Test your understanding 4

An entity wishes to have an allowance of $4,000, which would make the allowance of 33 1/3% higher than the current allowance.

What figure would appear in the statement of profit or loss for irrecoverable debts?

$........................... Debit or Credit (delete which does not apply)

Test your understanding 5

At 30 April 20X6 Gary had a sales ledger control account balance of $50,000 and an allowance for receivables of $800. Following a review of individual receivables accounts, Gary wishes to write off an irrecoverable debt of $1,000 and adjust his allowance to $2,450.

What will be the charge to the statement of profit or loss for the year ended 30 April 20X6?

A $1,000

B $2,650

C $3,450

D $3,250

Test your understanding 6

At 31 March Savi has a sales ledger control account balance of $82,500. Following a review of receivables' account balances, Savi has decided to write off irrecoverable debts amounting to $4,750.

Savi would like to make an allowance for $1,800. The current balance on the allowance for receivables account is $2,000. Savi also received $300 from a debt that had been written off in a previous accounting year.

What is the charge to the statement of profit or loss in respect of irrecoverable debts and allowances and the net receivables shown on the statement of financial position?

	Statement of profit or loss	Statement of financial position
A	$4,250	$75,950
B	$4,450	$77,750
C	$4,450	$75,950
D	$4,250	$77,750

Test your understanding 7

At the start of the year Joe had an allowance of $700 against receivables. During the year $450 of this amount went bad and $150 was received; the balance remained unpaid at the year end. At the year-end it was decided to provide for a new debt of $240.

What was the total charge to the statement of profit or loss for irrecoverable debts and allowances for the year?

A $450

B $90

C $300

D $690

Test your understanding 8

Doris currently has a sales ledger control account balance of $47,800 and an allowance for receivables of $1,250. She received $150 in respect of half of a debt that she had provided against. She now believes the other half of the debt to be irrecoverable and wishes to write it off. She also wishes reduce her allowance to $950.

What was the total charge to the statement of profit or loss for irrecoverable debts and allowances for the year?

A $150 debit

B $150 credit

C $300 debit

D $300 credit

Test your understanding 9

At the year-end Hardeep has a sales ledger control account balance of $100,000 and an allowance for receivables of $5,000. He has not yet accounted for a receipt of $500 in respect of a debt which he had previously provided against or a receipt of $1,000 in respect of a debt which had been written off in the previous year. Hardeep wishes his allowance for receivables to be $6,965.

What balances will be shown in receivables and irrecoverable debts in the statement of profit or loss at the year end?

	Sales ledger control account	Irrecoverable debts expense
A	$98,500	$1,965
B	$99,500	$1,965
C	$98,500	$965
D	$99,500	$965

Test your understanding answers

Test your understanding 1

Allowance for receivables account

20X0		$	20X0		$
31 Dec	Balance c/d	1,500	31 Dec	Increase in allowance	1,500
20X1			20X1		
31 Dec	Decrease in allowance	400	1 Jan	Balance b/d	1,500
	Balance c/d	1,100			
		1,500			1,500
20X2			20X2		
			1 Jan	Balance b/d	1,100
31 Dec	Balance c/d	1,650	31 Dec	Increase in allowance	550
		1,650			1,650
20X3			20X3		
			1 Jan	Balance b/d	1,650
31 Dec	Balance c/d	2,000	31 Dec	Increase in allowance	350
		2,000			2,000
			20X4		
			1 Jan	Balance b/d	2,000

Test your understanding 2

Irrecoverable debts

20X4		$	20X4		$
31 Aug	Receivables/SLCA	500	31 Aug	Statement of profit or loss	585
31 Aug	Allowance for receivables	85			
		585			585
20X5			20X5		
31 Aug	Receivables/SLCA	100	31 Aug	Allowance for receivables	48
				Statement of profit or loss	52
		100			100

Allowance for receivables

20X4		$	20X4		$
			1 Sept	Balance b/d	200
31 Aug	Balance c/d	285	31 Aug	Irrecoverable debts	85
		285			285
20X5			20X5		
31 Aug	Irrecoverable debt	48	1 Sept	Balance b/d	285
31 Aug	Balance c/d	237			
		285			285
			20X6		
			1 Sept	Balance b/d	237

Statement of Financial Position extracts		
20X4	$	
Trade receivables (10,000 – 500)	9,500	
Less: allowance	(285)	
Net receivables		9,215
20X5	$	
Trade receivables (8,000 – 100)	7,900	
Less: allowance	(237)	
Net receivables		7,663

Test your understanding 3

D

The change in allowance for receivables is taken to the statement of profit or loss – an increase is debited and therefore decreases net profit, while a decrease is credited and therefore increases net profit. The resultant balance on the allowance for receivables account is deducted from total receivables (current assets), which in turn affects working capital. A decrease in the allowance would increase net profit, and would also increase current assets. The latter is not one of the options, therefore D is the answer.

Test your understanding 4

The answer is **Debit $1,000**

Allowance now = $4,000

This allowance is 33 1/3 higher than before, i.e. represents 133.33333%.

The allowance was therefore previously $4,000/133.3333 × 100 = $3,000

This represents an increase of $1,000 and a charge to the statement of profit or loss.

Test your understanding 5

B

Allowance now = $2,450

Allowance was = $800

The statement of profit or loss charge will be the irrecoverable debt of $1,000 + movement of the allowance of $1,650 ($2,450 – $800) = $2,650

Test your understanding 6

A

Sales ledger control account = $82,500 – $4,750 = $77,750.

Allowance required is $1,800. Allowance was previously $2,000. The allowance must be reduced by $200 resulting in a credit to the statement of profit or loss for the year.

Total charge to the statement of profit or loss = $4,750 (irrecoverable debt) – $200 (allowance reduction) – $300 (irrecoverable debt recovered) = $4,250.

SLCA balance in statement of financial position = $77,750 (new receivables balance) – $1,800 (allowance) = $75,950.

Test your understanding 7

B

Allowance b/d $700 – $450 irrecoverable – $150 recovered = allowance c/d $100 + $240 = $340.

This has resulted in a decrease in the allowance from $700 to $340 = $360. The decrease will be credited to the statement of profit or loss. The charge to the statement of profit or loss will be $450 (irrecoverable debt) – $360 (decrease in allowance) = $90.

Test your understanding 8

B

Sales ledger control account = $47,800 – $150 irrecoverable – $150 paid = $47,500.

Allowance = $950. This has resulted in a decrease in the allowance from $1,250 to $950 = $300. The decrease will be credited to the statement of profit or loss. The charge to the statement of profit or loss will be $150 (irrecoverable debts) – $300 (decrease in allowance) = $150 credit.

Test your understanding 9

D

Sales ledger control account = $100,000 – $500 = $99,500. The allowance now required is $6,965, and was previously $5,000. Statement of profit or loss = increase in allowance $1,965 ($6,965 –$5,000) – $1,000 (irrecoverable debt recovered) = $965

Chapter

10

Accounting for inventory

Chapter learning objectives

When you have completed this chapter, you should be able to:

- prepare accounting entries for inventory in accordance with IAS 2 *Inventories.*

1 Introduction

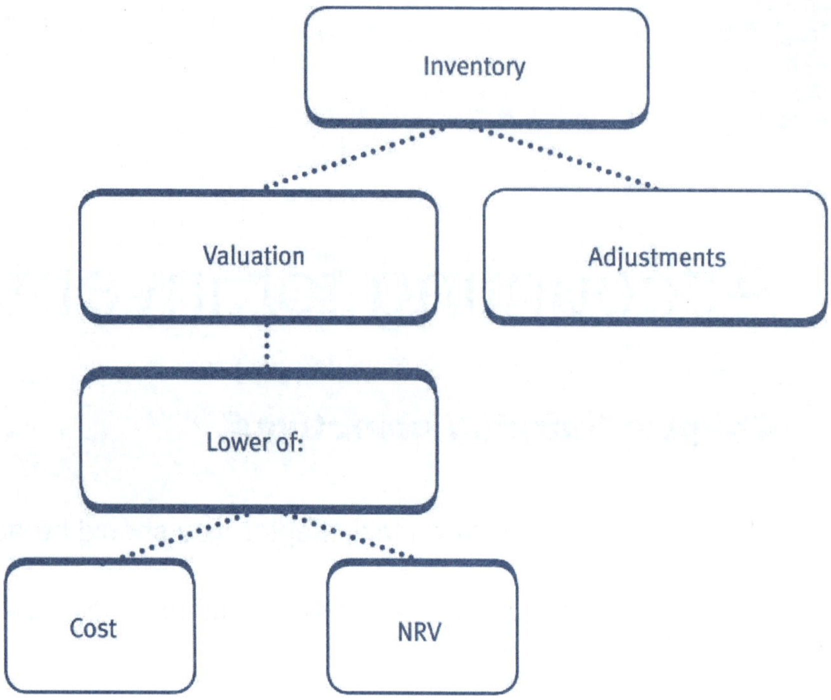

In this chapter, you will learn:

- the importance of the inventory valuation
- the accounting entries required for inventory in the financial statements
- how inventory is valued.

Inventory consists of:

- goods purchased for resale
- consumable stores (such as oil)
- raw materials and components (used in the production process)
- partly finished goods (usually called work in progress – WIP)
- finished goods (which have been manufactured by the business entity) or items purchased for resale.

2 Inventory in the financial statements

We saw in earlier chapters how opening and closing inventory was used to calculate the cost of sales in the statement of profit or loss and therefore directly affect the level of profit or loss made in an accounting period.

Measurement of inventory is also important as it is one of the assets in the statement of financial position at each reporting date.

The ability to alter the profit of an entity by changing its inventory measurement explains the need to regulate the methods that can be used when valuing inventory.

When calculating gross profit we match the revenue generated from the sales of goods in the year with the costs of purchasing or manufacturing those goods. You should understand that the costs of the unused inventory should not be included in this figure. These costs are carried forward to the next accounting period where they will be matched against revenue generated on goods that are sold in that period.

The goods carried forward to the next accounting period are classified as assets on the statement of financial position.

Matching concept

The carrying forward of unused inventory is an application of the matching concept. This is an extension of the accruals concept. Inventory costs are matched against the revenues they help to generate.

3 Year-end adjustments

At the end of the financial year two basic adjustments are required to recognise opening and closing inventory correctly in the financial statements:

b/f

1 Inventory brought forward from the previous year is assumed to have been used to generate assets for sale. It must be removed from inventory assets and recognised as an expense in the current accounting period as follows:

   Debit: Opening inventory in costs of sales – increase Expense

   Credit: Inventory assets – reduce asset

c/f

2 The unused inventory at the end of the accounting period is removed from purchase costs and carried forward as an asset into the next accounting period as follows:

   Debit: Inventory assets – increase asset

   Credit: Closing inventory in cost of sales ← reduce expense

When these accounting entries have been recorded, cost of sales is correctly stated by including the opening inventory and excluding the closing inventory. **The inventory ledger account shows the closing inventory for the asset remaining at the end of the accounting period.**

Ledger accounts

If a business entity has been trading for more than one year, there will be a balance on the inventory account at the start of the accounting period, which will be a debit balance (representing an asset). Let us assume opening inventory of $500. The inventory account at the start of the accounting period would appear as follows:

Inventory

20X1		$			$
1 Jan	Balance b/f	500			

At the end of the year, when the statement of profit or loss is prepared, the starting point is to prepare the trading account in which gross profit for the accounting period is calculated. The opening inventory valuation is transferred into the trading account by crediting the inventory account and debiting the trading account. The inventory account then appears as follows:

Inventory

20X1		$			$
1 Jan	Balance b/f	500	31 Dec	Trading account	500

The inventory account now has no balance, so it can be 'closed off'.

As the preparation of the trading account continues, it will be necessary to determine the value of the inventory at the end of the accounting period. The inventory valuation is used by the bookkeeper, who then debits the inventory account with the new valuation, and credits the trading account. Let us assume an example of closing inventory of $430.

The inventory account now appears as follows:

Inventory

20X1		$			$
1 Jan	Balance b/f	500	31 Dec	Trading account	500
31 Dec	Trading account	430			

The trading account would now look as follows:

Trading Account

20X1		$	20X1		$
1 Jan	Opening inventory	500	31 Dec	Sales	X
31 Dec	Purchases	X		Closing inventory	430

The trading account thus brings together the revenue and costs of the trading function for a specified period of time, and by comparing them calculates the **gross profit**, being the balance remaining on the account.

This balance is then transferred to the statement of profit or loss account.

Here is an example of a trading account using hypothetical values for sales, returns and purchases in addition to the above mentioned opening and closing inventory.

Trading account for the year ended 31 December 20X1

	$	$
Sales		9,400
Less: Sales returns		(300)
		9,100
Opening inventory	500	
Purchases	6,400	
	6,900	
Less: Closing inventory	(430)	
		(6,470)
Gross profit		2,630

4 Valuation of inventory

IAS 2 *Inventories* requires inventory to be **valued at the lower of cost and net realisable value** (NRV) for each separate item or product.

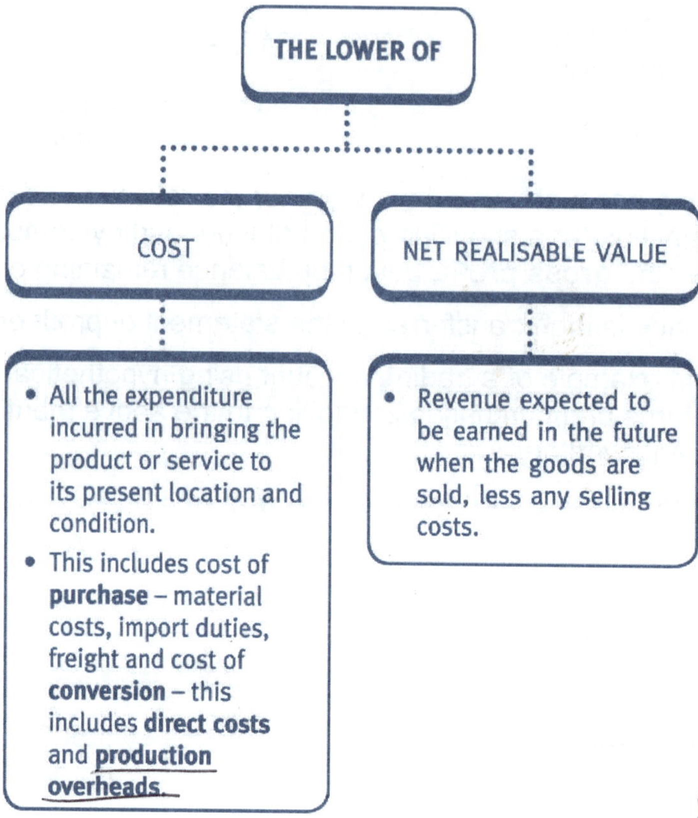

Cost includes **'all costs of purchase, costs of conversion and other costs incurred in bringing the inventories to their current location and condition'** (IAS 2 para 10).

According to IAS 2 costs which must be **excluded** from the cost of inventory are:

- overheads (with the exception of production overheads)
- selling costs
- storage costs
- abnormal waste of materials, labour or other costs
- administrative overheads.

5 Consideration of cost and NRV

Product X is purchased at a cost of $5 per unit and is normally sold to customers for $9 per unit. Due to a change in market conditions, product X can now only be sold for $6 per unit, subject to incurring packaging and delivery costs of $1.50 per unit.

Required:

How is inventory valued in this situation?

Solution:

Determine the lower of cost and net realisable value for product X as follows:

	$
Cost	5.00
Net realisable value ($6 – $1.50)	4.50

In other words, when the items are eventually sold for $6 per unit, there will be a loss of $0.5 per unit as follows:

	$	$
Selling price		6.00
Less: purchase cost	5.00	
Less: packaging and delivery costs	1.50	
		(6.50)
		(0.50)

By valuing product X at its net realisable value of $4.50 per unit we have recognised the foreseeable loss of $0.50 per unit immediately, rather than waiting until the goods have been sold in the next accounting period.

The fall in value should be recognised as soon as it is known about. Suppose that we bought 100 units of the above item, and sold 60 in the first month, with the remainder carried forward to the next month. The calculation of the loss in the first month would be as follows:

	$	$
Sales (60 × $6.00)		360
Less: Cost of sales		
Purchases (100 × $5.00)	500	
Packaging costs (60 × $1.50)	90	
	590	
Less: Closing inventory (40 × $4.50)	(180)	(410)
Loss		(50)

The whole of the loss is accounted for in the first month, not just the loss on the units sold. In the second month, assuming all of the remaining items were sold, the result would be as follows:

	$	$
Sales (40 × $6.00)		240
Less: Cost of sales		
Opening inventory (as above)	180	
Packaging costs (40 × $1.50)	60	
		(240)
Profit/(Loss)		–

This treatment is an example of applying the convention of **'prudence'**, which is considered further at the end of this chapter.

Test your understanding 1

SCO sells three products – Basic, Super and Luxury. The following information was available at the year-end:

	Basic $ per unit	Super $ per unit	Luxury $ per unit
Original cost	6	9	18
Estimated selling price	9	12	15
Selling and distribution costs	1	4	5
	Units	**Units**	**Units**
Units in inventory	200	250	150

Required:

What was the value of inventory at the year end?

$...........

6 Methods of calculating the cost of inventory

So far, we have considered a definition of cost that includes all costs incurred in bringing the inventory to its present location and condition.

Business entities also need a working assumption to apply this this definition to determine the cost of inventory at a specific date in time.

For example, although we may know the unit cost of a product each time it is purchased, if there are many purchases and sales during an accounting period, it may be problematic to determine precisely the cost of the items sold and the cost of any remaining inventory.

How do we know precisely which items have been sold and what is the cost of the remaining inventory?

A business entity may keep precise and detailed records of inventory identification, receipt and issue, including the order of receipt and issue, but this would be unusual. Instead, business entities apply an assumption regarding the purchase and issue of inventory to enable them to determine the order of usage or issue as a basis for determining the cost of inventory on a reasonable basis as follows:

Method	**Key points**	
Method Unit cost	This is the actual cost of purchasing identifiable units of inventory	Only used when items of inventory are individually distinguishable and of high value
FIFO, – first in, first out	For costing purposes, the first items of inventory received are assumed to be the first ones sold	The cost of closing inventory is the cost of the most recent purchases of inventory.
AVCO – average cost	The cost of an item of inventory is calculated by taking the average of all inventory held	The average cost can be calculated on a periodic basis or a continuous basis
LIFO – last in, first out	For costing purposes, the last items of inventory received are assumed to be the first ones sold	The cost of closing inventory is the cost of the oldest remaining items purchased

IAS 2 does not permit the use of LIFO (last in, first out) but you need to be aware of it and the impact its application has upon the financial statements. During a time of rising costs, the valuation of closing inventory using the LIFO method will be lower than if valued using the FIFO method as older (and lower cost) items are presumed to remain in inventory at the end of the accounting period. Consequently, application of LIFO will potentially increase cost of sales for the current accounting period and, in effect, carry forward a closing inventory valuation based upon low, out-of-date purchase prices. The LIFO method of inventory valuation is therefore regarded as inappropriate and not permitted by IAS 2.

*

Periodic weighted average cost

With this inventory valuation method, an average cost per unit is calculated based upon the cost of opening inventory plus the cost of all purchases made during the accounting period. This method of inventory valuation is calculated at the end of an accounting period when the total quantity and cost of purchases for the period is known.

an average cost per unit = cost of opening inventory + the cost of all purchases

* calculate at end of period.

Continuous weighted average cost

With this inventory valuation method, an updated average cost per unit is calculated following each purchase of goods. The costs of any subsequent sales are then accounted for at that weighted average cost per unit. This procedure is repeated whenever a further purchase of goods is made during the accounting period.

Note: When using either of the two methods of weighted average cost to determine inventory valuation, it is possible that small rounding differences may arise. They do not affect the validity of the approach used and can normally be ignored.

Further detail

The value of inventory is obtained at a particular point in time – there are two ways to achieve this: either physically measure the quantity of inventory held at that time and then value it, or record the movement of inventory on a regular basis and verify such records randomly over a period of time. These inventory records are then used as the basis of the measurement.

Physical inventory count

The physical measurement of the quantity of inventory held at a particular time is known as a physical inventory count or stock-taking. It is not always possible to count inventory at the time required and in these circumstances cut-off procedures are applied to ensure that inventory movements between the date of the count and the year-end are allocated to the correct accounting period.

Example

On 3 June, a physical inventory count was carried out that revealed XYZ held 405 units of inventory. According to the entity's records it received a delivery of 250 units on 2 June and had sold 110 units between 1–3 June.

Required:

Calculate the number of units in inventory on 31 May.

Solution:

The inventory that existed on 31 May was therefore:

	Units
Quantity as per physical inventory count on 3 June	405
Add: Units sold/used before physical inventory count	110
Less: Units received before the physical inventory count	(250)
Inventory on 31 May	265

The cost measurement of these items is then obtained by multiplying the quantity by the cost per unit.

This technique is most common in small entities. Larger entities keep records of the movement of inventory using bin cards or stores ledger cards, but even so they should physically check their inventories from time to time and compare it with the inventory recorded on the bin or stores ledger card, and make any necessary investigations and/or adjustments to ensure that it is reliable.

A bin card is a document, traditionally made of cardboard, on which the movement of inventory is manually recorded. It is called a bin card because in storekeeping terminology a 'bin' is the location of an item in the stores. This record is usually kept with the items in the stores so that any movement of the inventory is recorded as it occurs.

The stores ledger card is similar except that in addition to recording quantities, cost values are also recorded so that the value of inventory can be identified at any time.

Each item of inventory has its own inventory reference code and bin card/stores ledger card.

e.g

Illustration 1

Consider the following information regarding the movements of inventory during March:

1 March	Opening inventory = Nil
2 March	Purchased 10 units @ $3 each
7 March	Purchased 20 units @ $4 each
10 March	Sold 15 units @ $8 each
13 March	Bought 20 units @ $5 each
17 March	Sold 5 units @ $8 each

Using these figures we can calculate that the inventory remaining after these transactions was 30 units. The difficulty is in measuring the cost of those units. Is the remaining inventory made up of items bought recently, or is it made up of items bought earlier? Or is a mixture of the two? How do we know?

Required:

(a) Prepare a summary of the receipt and issue of inventory, applying the FIFO principle, together with a trading account for March.

(b) Prepare a summary of receipt and issue of inventory, applying the LIFO principle, together with a trading account for March.

Note that part (b) is to aid your understanding of the LIFO valuation method. It is unlikely that you will be required to perform calculations in the exam relating to LIFO.

Solution – FIFO inventory valuation

FIFO Method

One method of summarising receipts and issue of inventory, including their cost and sales value, is to prepare a stores ledger card. Note that the card is 'ruled off' each time there is an 'issue' of inventory.

Note also that the cost per unit of each issued is based upon the oldest items of inventory available as at that date. For example, of the 15 units issued on 10 March, 10 were costed at $3 per unit as they were purchased on 1 March, with the remaining 5 units costed at $4 each, which is the next oldest purchase, made on 2 March.

	Receipts			Issues			Balance		
Date	**Units**	**$/unit**	**$**	**Units**	**$/unit**	**$**	**Units**	**$/unit**	**$**
1 Mar							Nil		Nil
2 Mar	10	3	30				10	3	30
7 Mar	20	4	80				20	4	80
10 Mar				10	3	30			
				5	4	20	15	4	60
13 Mar	20	5	100				20	5	100
17 Mar				5	4	20	10	4	40
							20	5	100
Totals	50		210	20		70	30		140

This cost formula gives a closing inventory cost of $140 and the cost of sales (obtained by totalling the cost of each issue) amounted to $70. Using this cost formula, the trading account would be as follows:

	$	$
Sales (20 units @ $8)		160
Opening inventory	Nil	
Purchases	210	
	210	
Less: closing inventory	(140)	
Cost of sales		(70)
Gross profit		90

Solution – LIFO inventory valuation

LIFO method

Again, a stores ledger card can be produced to record the number of units received and issued, together with their associated purchase cost and sales value. The LIFO method of inventory valuation assumes that the items bought most recently are those used or issued first. Again, this assumption is made only for costing purposes; it does not have any connection with the physical usage of the inventory.

Note that the number of units in inventory at the end of the month is the same as when using the FIFO method. What is different is the valuation of those 30 units. They are costed based upon the most recent receipt at that date. For example, the issue of 15 units on 10 March are costed at $4 per unit based upon the most recent purchase made on 7 March.

	Receipts			Issues			Balance		
Date	**Units**	**$/unit**	**$**	**Units**	**$/unit**	**$**	**Units**	**$/unit**	**$**
1 Mar							Nil		Nil
2 Mar	10	3	30				10	3	30
7 Mar	20	4	80				20	4	80
10 Mar				15	4	60	10	3	30
							5	4	20
13 Mar	20	5	100				20	5	100
17 Mar				5	5	25	10	3	30
							5	4	20
							15	5	75
Totals	50		210	20		85	30		125

This method of determining the cost of inventory gives a closing inventory cost of $125 and the cost of sales (obtained by totalling the cost of each issue) amounted to $85. Using this cost formula, the trading account would be as follows:

	$	$
Sales (20 units @ $8)		160
Opening inventory	Nil	
Purchases	210	
	210	
Less: closing inventory	(125)	
Cost of sales		(85)
Gross profit		75

You can see that this results in a **higher cost of sales** total than with the FIFO cost formula, and hence a lower gross profit, in times of inflation or rising prices. It also results in a lower closing inventory figure, as the inventory is valued at earlier prices. **The LIFO cost formula is not acceptable when preparing financial statements for external reporting although it may be useful for management accounts.** It can be argued that the profit calculated using the LIFO method of valuing inventory is more realistic than the FIFO cost formula, as it values cost of sales at a value nearer to the current cost of replacing the inventory sold with new inventory. The major drawback, however, is that LIFO consequently understates the value of closing inventory as it uses older, 'out of date' costs to value closing inventory.

e.g

Illustration 2

INV has closing inventory of 5 units at a cost of $3.50 per unit at 31 December 20X5. During the first week of January 20X6, INV entered into the following transactions:

Purchases

- 2 January – 5 units at $4.00 per unit
- 4 January – 5 units at $5.00 per unit
- 6 January – 5 units at $5.50 per unit.

INV sold 7 units for $10.00 per unit on 5 January.

Required:

(a) Calculate the value of the closing inventory at the end of the first week of trading using the following inventory valuation methods:

1 FIFO

2 periodic weighted average cost

3 continuous weighted average cost.

(b) Prepare the trading account of INV to determine gross profit for the first week of trading using each method of inventory valuation.

Solution:

(a) **Inventory valuation**

FIFO basis

With this method of inventory valuation it is assumed that the oldest items of inventory are sold first, thereby leaving the business entity with the most recently purchased items. This provides the most recent valuation for the remaining items of inventory as it uses a recent purchase price to value the majority of goods.

When INV sells the 7 units on 5 January we assume it sells the oldest items first. Therefore INV will sell all 5 units of opening inventory, plus purchased 2 units purchased on 2 January. This leaves INV with the following items:

	$
2 January – 3 units × $4.00 =	12.00
4 January 5 – units × $5.00 =	25.00
6 January 5 – units × $5.50 =	27.50
Closing inventory cost	64.50

Periodic AVCO basis

With this inventory valuation method, we work out an average cost per unit based upon the cost of opening inventory plus the cost of all purchases made during the accounting period as follows:

Average cost per unit: ((5 × $3.50) + (5 × $4.00) + (5 × $5.00) + (5 × $5.50))/20 units = $4.50 per unit

Closing inventory cost = 13 units × $4.50 = $58.50

Cost of sales = 7 units × $4.50 = $31.50

Continuous AVCO basis

With this inventory valuation method we work out an updated average cost per unit each time a purchase of inventory is made. Any subsequent sales are accounted for at that average cost per unit until the next purchase is made and a new average cost per unit is calculated.

The best way to deal with this is to prepare a schedule dealing with transactions in date order as follows:

Date	Transaction	Units		Cost	Total cost
				$	$
1 Jan X6	Op inventory	5		3.50	17.50
2 Jan X6	Purchase	5		4.00	20.00
		10	(37.50/10) =	3.75	37.50
4 Jan X6	Purchase	5		5.00	25.00
		15	(62.50/15) =	4.17	62.50
5 Jan X6	**Sale at cost**	**(7)**		4.17	**(29.19)**
		8			33.31
6 Jan X6	Purchase	5		5.50	27.50
7 Jan X6	Cl inventory	13	(60.81/13) =	4.68	60.81

(b) **Trading accounts**

FIFO basis	$	$
Sales (7 units × $10.00)		70.00
Cost of sales:		
Opening inventory (5 units × $3.50)	17.50	
Purchases (5 units × $4.00) + (5 units × $5.00) + (5 units × $5.50)	72.50	
	90.00	
Less: closing inventory (see part (a)	(64.50)	
		(25.50)
Gross profit		44.50

Periodic AVCO basis	$	$
Sales (7 units × $10.00)		70.00
Cost of sales:		
Opening inventory (5 units × $3.50)	17.50	
Purchases (5 units × $4.00) + (5 units × $5.00) + (5 units × $5.50)	72.50	
	90.00	
Less: closing inventory (see part (a)	(58.50)	
		(31.50)
Gross profit		38.50

Continuous AVCO basis	$	$
Sales (7 units × $10.00)		70.00
Cost of sales:		
Opening inventory (5 units × $3.50)	17.50	
Purchases (5 units × $4.00) + (5 units × $5.00) + (5 units × $5.50)	72.50	
	90.00	
Less: closing inventory (see part (a)	(60.81)	
		(29.19)
Gross profit		40.81

Test your understanding 2

On 1 July 20X6 an entity, PIN, had 10 items of inventory at a unit cost of $8.50. PIN then made the following purchases and sales during a six-month accounting period to 31 December 20X6:

Purchases:	**Quantity**	**Unit cost**	**Total cost**
Date		$	$
14 Oct X6	15	9.00	135.00
22 Nov X6	25	9.20	230.00
13 Dec X6	20	9.50	190.00
	60		555.00

Sales: Date	Quantity	Unit price $	Total sale $
23 Aug X6	7	12.00	84.00
20 Oct X6	10	12.25	122.50
30 Nov X6	15	12.50	187.50
24 Dec X6	18	13.00	234.00
	50		628.00

Required:

Based upon the available information, calculate the closing inventory valuation at 31 December 20X6 using:

(a) periodic weighted average cost

(b) continuous weighted average cost.

Issues and receipts

Take care when doing exercises that require you to calculate purchases, cost of sales and/or closing inventory. Ensure that you clearly identify purchases/receipts of inventory at purchase cost and that the cost of any despatches/sales are costed based upon the appropriate valuation basis, whether it is FIFO, or AVCO using either the periodic weighted average cost or continuous average cost basis.

If you also need to calculate sales revenue, perhaps to also calculate gross profit, this should be done as a separate exercise.

Test your understanding 3

MLO had inventory on 1 January 20X1 consisting of 400 articles bought at $4 each. Its purchases during the month of January consisted of 800 articles at $4.20 each purchased on 8 January, and 2,000 articles at $3.80 each on 18 January. MLO sold 2,400 articles at $5.00 each on 28 January. Forty of those sold were returned in perfect condition on 31 January. MLO values inventory at cost, using the 'first in, first out' method.

Required:

(a) Ascertain, by means of an inventory account:

- the number of articles held in inventory on 31 January 20X1
- the unit cost and total cost of the inventory.

(b) Prepare the trading account for the month ended 31 January 20X1.

7 Application of accounting concepts

When accounting for inventory, application of the relevant accounting requirements represents application of the prudence and matching concepts.

Application of prudence requires that inventory is valued at the lower of cost and net realisable value for each separate product or item. This means that some products or items are valued at cost when they are expected to be used or sold profitably, whilst other items will be valued at net realisable value if they are not expected to be sold or used in a way which recovers their cost, perhaps because they are obsolete or damaged.

In the statement of profit or loss, the cost of purchases is adjusted to include opening inventory and exclude closing inventory to determine the cost of goods sold during an accounting period. This represents application of the matching concept as the cost of goods sold is matched against the sales revenue generated during an accounting period, to determine the gross profit made.

8 Chapter summary

In this chapter you were introduced to the importance of accounting for inventory in the financial statements and how it should be valued. In particular your studies included:

- year-end adjustments
- inventory in the financial statements
- inventory valuation
- inventory records.

The accounting requirements of IAS 2 are relevant in subject F1 Financial Reporting in the CIMA Professional Qualification.

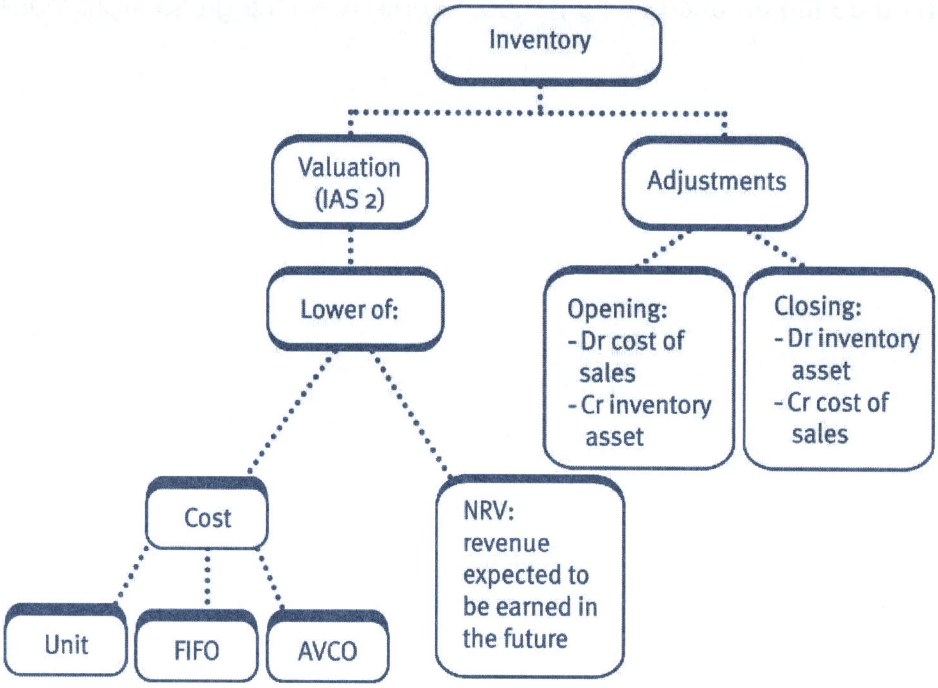

Test your understanding questions

Test your understanding 4

Opening inventory for a business entity was 10 units at $2 each. Purchases made during the accounting period were 30 units at $3 each. Two issues of inventory were made during the accounting period, for 12 units and 8 units respectively.

Required:

What was the value of closing inventory if the business entity applies the FIFO basis of inventory valuation?

$...........

Test your understanding 5

In times of rising prices, the FIFO cost formula for inventories cost, when compared with the average cost method, will usually produce:

A a higher profit and a lower closing inventory value

B a higher profit and a higher closing inventory value

C a lower profit and a lower closing inventory value

D a lower profit and a higher closing inventory value

Test your understanding 6

A business entity uses the periodic weighted average cost method to value inventory. On 1 October 20X8, there were 60 units in inventory valued at $12 each. On 8 October, 40 units were purchased for $15 each, and a further 50 units were purchased for $18 each on 14 October. On 21 October, 75 units were sold for $1,200.

Required:

What is the value of closing inventory at 31 October 20X8?

$...........

Test your understanding 7

The inventory record card for component X includes the following details:

1 Feb	50 units in inventory at a cost of $40 per unit
7 Feb	100 units purchased at a cost of $45 per unit
14 Feb	80 units sold
21 Feb	50 units purchased at a cost of $50 per unit
28 Feb	60 units sold

Required:

Using the FIFO basis of inventory valuation, what was cost of inventory at 28 February?

$............

What was the cost of goods sold for February?

$............

Test your understanding 8

When measuring inventory at cost, which of the following shows the correct method of arriving at cost?

	Include inward carriage costs	Include production overheads
A	Yes	No
B	No	Yes
C	Yes	Yes
D	No	No

Test your understanding 9

At 31 December 20X1, a business entity has an item of inventory which cost $100 to manufacture. Due to damage, the entity will need spend $50 to repair the item before it can be sold for $120.

What is the value of inventory to be included in the statement of financial position at 31 December 20X1?

A $100

B $150

C $120

D $70

Test your understanding 10

XYZ uses the periodic weighted average cost method to determine the value of its inventory. At 30 September 20X3, it had inventory of 100 units at a total cost of $1,005.

During October 20X3, it made the following inventory purchases and sales:

Date	Transaction	Units	Unit cost or selling price $
3 October	Purchase	25	12.00
10 October	Sale	40	20.00
17 October	Purchase	25	15.00

Required:

What was the value of inventory at 31 October 20X3?

$...........

What was the gross profit for the month of October 20X3?

$...........

Test your understanding 11

FGH uses the continuous weighted average cost method to determine the value of its inventory. At 1 April 20X6 it had 100 units of inventory which had cost $10 per unit. During April 20X6, the following purchases and sales of inventory took place:

During April 20X6, it made the following inventory purchases and sales:

Date	Transaction	Units	Unit cost or selling price $
5 April	Purchase	25	12.00
13 April	Sale	40	18.00
22 April	Purchase	25	11.72

Required:

What was the value of inventory at 30 April 20X6?

$...........

What was the cost of goods sold for April 20X6?

$...........

Test your understanding answers

Test your understanding 1

	Cost	NRV	Lower of cost and NRV	Units	Cost
	$	$	$		$
Basic	6	8	6	200	1,200
Super	9	8	8	250	2,000
Luxury	18	10	10	150	1,500
					4,700

Test your understanding 2

(a) **Periodic weighted average cost per unit**

Total cost = cost of opening inventory + cost of purchases during the accounting period.

Total cost = (10 × $8.50) + $555.00 purchases = $640.00

Periodic weighted average cost = $640/70 units = $9.14

Closing inventory = 70 units – 50 units sold = 20 units × $9.14 = $182.80

(b) **Continuous weighted average cost per unit**

Date	**Transaction**	**Units**		**Cost** $	**Total cost** $
1 Jul X6	Op inventory	10		8.50	85.00
23 Aug X6	Sales	(7)		8.50	(59.50)
		3			25.50
14 Oct X6	Purchase	15		9.00	135.00
		18	(160.50/18) =	8.92	160.50
20 Oct X6	Sale at cost	(10)		8.92	(89.20)
		8			71.30
22 Nov X6	Purchase	25		9.20	230.00
		33	(301.30/33) =	9.13	301.30
30 Nov X6	Sales at cost	(15)		9.13	(136.95)
		18			164.35
13 Dec X6	Purchase	20		9.50	190.00
		38	(354.35/38 =	9.32	354.35
24 Dec X6	Sales at cost	(18)		9.32	(167.76)
31 Dec X6	**Cl inventory**	**20**		**9.32**	**186.40**
			Rounding – ignore	0.19	

Test your understanding 3

(a) The best way to deal with this is to prepare a schedule dealing with transactions in date order as follows:

	Receipts			Issues			Balance		
Date	**Receipts Units**	**$/unit**	**Cost $**	**Units**	**$/unit**	**Cost $**	**Units**	**$/unit**	**Valuation**
1 Jan	Op inventory						400	4.00	1,600
8 Jan	800	4.20	3,360				1,200	4.20	3,360
18 Jan	2,000	3.80	7,600				2,000	3.80	7,600
28 Jan				400	4.00	1,600			
				800	4.20	3,360			
				1,200	3.80	4,560	800	3.80	3,040
31 Jan	40	3.80	152				840	3.80	3,192

Inventory at 31 January = 840 items with unit cost of $3.80, giving a total valuation of $3,192.

(b) **Trading account for the year ended 31 January 20X1**

	$	$
Sales		12,000
Less: Sales returns		(200)
		11,800
Opening inventory	1,600	
Purchases	10,960	
	12,560	
Less: Closing inventory	(3,192)	
		(9,368)
Gross profit		2,432

Test your understanding 4

FIFO means the oldest inventory will be issued first leaving the most recent purchases. The first issues (12 units) would use up the opening inventory of 10 units and 2 units of the purchases at $3 each, leaving 28 units at $3 each. The next issues would be of $3 units, leaving closing inventory of 20 units at $3 each, valued at $60.

Test your understanding 5

B

The closing inventory figure reduces the cost of goods sold figure, which in turn increases the gross profit.

Therefore, a higher closing inventory figure means a lower cost of goods sold figure, and hence a higher gross profit. In times of rising prices, the FIFO cost formula will produce higher closing inventory values, and therefore a higher gross profit figure.

Test your understanding 6

Purchases	Cumulative quantity	Cumulative cost – $
1 October (60 × $12)	60	720
8 October (40 × $15)	100	1,320
14 October (50 × $18)	150	2,220
Issues		
21 October (75 × $14.80*)	(75)	(1,110)
Closing inventory	75	1,110

Periodic average cost = $2,220 / (60+40+50) = $2,220 / 150 = $14.80*

Test your understanding 7

FIFO means the oldest inventory will be issued first leaving the most recent purchases in stock. There were 60 units in inventory at 28 February (50 + 100 – 80 + 50 – 60). These are deemed to comprise the 50 units purchased on 21 February at cost $50 per unit = $2,500, and 10 units from the units purchased on 7 February at $45 per unit = $450, which is $2,950 in total.

Closing inventory = (10 × $45) + (50 × $50) = $2,950

Cost of goods sold = (50 × $40) + (30 × $45) + (60 × $45) = $6,050

Test your understanding 8

C

The cost of inventory should include all costs in getting inventory to its location and condition. Therefore it will include both carriage inwards and production overheads.

Test your understanding 9

D

The closing inventory should always be valued at the lower of cost and NRV.

The cost is $100 and the NRV = expected selling price of $120 less costs to sell of $50 = $70.

Test your understanding 10

Periodic weighted average cost = Total cost / total units

Total cost = $1,005 + (25 × $12) + (25 × $15) = $1,680

Total units = 100 + 25 + 25 = 150

Therefore: $1,680/150 units = $11.20 per unit.

Closing inventory = 100 + 25 + 25 – 40 = 110 units × $11.20 = $1,232.00

Sales revenue = (40 × $20) = $800

Cost of sales = $1,680 – $1,232 = $448

Gross profit = $800 – 448 = $352

Test your understanding 11

For this method of inventory valuation, remember that a new average cost must be calculated immediately following each purchase. Any sales made are then accounted for at the newly calculated weighted average cost.

Date	Transaction	Units		Cost	Total cost
				$	$
1 Apr	Op inventory	100		10.00	1,000.00
5 Apr	Purchase	25		12.00	300.00
		125	(1,300/125) =	10.40	1,300.00
13 Apr	Sale	(40)		10.40	(416.00)
		85		10.40	884.00
22 Apr	Purchase	25		11.72	293.00
30 Apr	Balance c/fwd	110	(1,177/110) =	10.70	1,177.00

Cost of goods sold = (40 × $10.40) = $416.00

Chapter

11

Non-current assets: Acquisition and depreciation

Chapter learning objectives

When you have completed this chapter, you should be able to:

- define tangible and intangible non-current assets
- classify expenditure as capital or revenue
- prepare accounting entries to record the acquisition and depreciation of tangible non-current assets
- calculate depreciation using different methods
- prepare accounting entries to record the acquisition and amortisation of intangible non-current assets
- prepare extracts from financial statements dealing with non-current assets.

1 Introduction

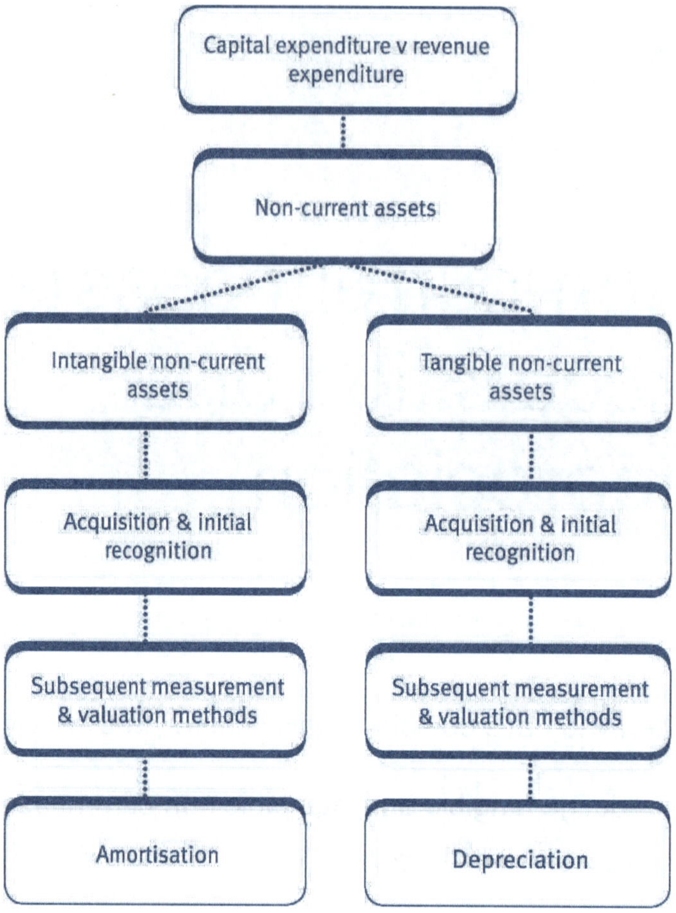

In this chapter you will learn:

- the distinction between tangible and intangible non-current assets
- the distinction between capital expenditure and revenue expenditure
- how to account for the purchase of a tangible non-current asset
- how to calculate and account for depreciation
- how to account for intangible non-current assets
- valuation of intangible non-current assets.

2 Non-current assets – tangible and intangible

Non-current assets are distinguished from current assets because they:

- are a resource acquired by an entity with the intention of using it to earn revenue for more than one accounting period
- are not normally acquired for resale
- could be tangible or intangible
- are used to generate income directly or indirectly for a business entity
- are not normally liquid assets (i.e. not easily and quickly converted into cash without a significant loss in value).

Examples of tangible non-current assets include land, buildings, motor vehicles, machinery and equipment.

Examples of intangible non-current assets include goodwill, development costs, licences and patents.

3 Capital and revenue expenditure

A business entity's expenditure may be classified as one of two types:

- capital expenditure – expenditure likely to increase the future earning capability of the entity or
- revenue expenditure – expenditure associated with maintaining the entity's present earning capability

CAPITAL EXPENDITURE

- Expenditure on the acquisition of non-current assets required for use in the business, not for resale.
- Expenditure on existing non-current assets aimed at increasing their earning capacity.

Capital expenditure is long-term in nature as the business intends to receive the benefits of the expenditure over a long period of time.

REVENUE EXPENDITURE

- Expenditure on current assets.
- Expenditure relating to running the business (such as administration costs).
- Expenditure on maintaining the earning capacity of non-current assets e.g. repairs and renewals.

Revenue expenditure relates to the current accounting period and is used to generate revenue in the business.

Illustration 1

Consider the situation where a computer is repaired by replacing a faulty CD drive and a faulty hard drive. The replacement CD drive is identical to that which it replaced. The faulty hard drive had a storage capacity of 500 megabytes; its replacement is a 5 gigabyte (i.e. 5,000 megabyte) unit. At the same time a scanner facility is added.

How should these 'repair' costs be classified?

The replacement of the faulty CD drive with an identical unit is clearly a repair, and as such will be treated as an expense.

The fitting of the scanner facility is clearly not a repair because the computer did not have a scanner facility previously. This is an addition to the asset, the cost of which should be capitalised.

It is the cost of the hard disk drive that presents the classification problem. To the extent that it replaced the original hard drive it is a repair, but the new drive has ten times the capacity of the original. As it also enhances the storage capacity of the computer it is capital expenditure. Thus this cost must be divided; part of it is treated as an expense and the remainder as capital expenditure.

The distinction between capital and revenue expenditure is important because of the implications for the financial statements. Revenue expenditure will be reflected in full in the measurement of profit in the period in which it is incurred. In contrast, capital expenditure will be reflected in an increase in asset values in the statement of financial position. This will diminish over the life of the asset as it is depreciated (see later), with a corresponding reduction in the profit reported.

Test your understanding 1

Classify each of the following items of expenditure as either capital expenditure or revenue expenditure.

	Item of expenditure	Classification
A	Repainting of a building	
B	Installation of a new central heating system	
C	Repainting of a delivery van	
D	Providing drainage for a new piece of water-extraction equipment	
E	Legal fees incurred on the purchase of land	
F	Carriage costs for a replacement component part for a piece of machinery	

4 Acquisition of a non-current asset

According to IAS 16 *Property, Plant and Equipment*, the cost of a non-current asset is any amount incurred to acquire the asset and bring it into working condition.

Includes

Capital expenditure such as:

- purchase price
- delivery costs
- legal fees
- subsequent expenditure that enhances the productive capacity of an asset
- trialling, testing and installation costs

Excludes

Revenue expenditure such as:

- repairs and maintenance
- repainting
- administration
- subsequent expenditure that maintains the productive capacity of an asset
- general overheads
- wastage
- employee training costs

The correct double entry to record the purchase is:

Debit	Non-current asset account	$X
Credit	Cash/bank/payable account	$X

A separate cost account should be kept for each class or category of non-current asset, e.g. motor vehicles, fixtures and fittings etc.

Subsequent expenditure

Subsequent expenditure on the non-current asset can only be recorded as part of the cost (i.e. capitalised), if it enhances the benefits of the asset, i.e. increases the revenues capable of being generated by the asset.

An example of subsequent expenditure which meets this criterion, and so can be capitalised, is an extension to a shop building which provides extra selling space.

An example of subsequent expenditure which does not meet this criterion is repair work. Any repair costs must be debited to the statement of profit or loss, i.e. expensed.

5 Depreciation

- The cost of the non-current asset will contribute to the ability of an entity to earn revenue for a number of accounting periods. It would be unfair if the total cost was treated as an expense in the statement of profit or loss in the year of acquisition.
- Instead, if a non-current asset has a finite life, the cost is spread over all of the accounting periods in which the asset is expected to be making a contribution to earnings (this is known as the asset's **useful life**).
- The process by which this is achieved is called **depreciation.**
- **IAS 16 *Property, Plant and Equipment***, defines depreciation as **'the measure of the cost or revalued amount of the economic benefits of the tangible non-current asset that has been consumed during the period'** (IAS 16 para 6).
- In simple terms, depreciation spreads the cost or revalued amount of the asset over the accounting periods in which it is expected to be used.
- Depreciation matches the cost of using a non-current asset to the revenues generated by that asset over its useful life.
- According to IAS 16 depreciation must also be matched to the pattern of use of the asset and should be periodically reviewed to ensure that it is still appropriate.
- This is achieved by recording a depreciation charge each year, the effect of which is two-fold ('the dual effect'), i.e. reduce the statement of financial position value of the non-current asset by accumulated depreciation to reflect its use or wearing out. Record the annual depreciation charge as an expense in the statement of profit or loss to match to the revenue generated by the non-current asset in that accounting period.
- Note that land is not subject to depreciation as this is regarded as having an infinite useful life.

Further detail on depreciation

We will consider the calculation of depreciation in detail in the next section. For now, we will focus upon the main principles of accounting for depreciation.

- When we acquire a non-current asset, we debit an account called 'non-current assets' or 'plant and machinery' or another suitable description and credit cash (or payables).
- If we prepared a set of financial statements immediately after purchasing a non-current asset we would display the balance on the asset account – the cost of the asset – on the statement of financial position. It would not appear as an expense in the statement of profit or loss at all, because we have not yet begun to 'consume' it in earning revenue.

- During the accounting periods that the asset is in use – its useful life – we must allocate its original cost on some reasonable basis. An appropriate proportion of the cost must be recorded as an expense – called depreciation charge – in the statement of profit or loss of each accounting period concerned.
- We achieve this by, in effect, changing the carrying amount of the asset in the statement of financial position. Each year we calculate or estimate that some proportion of the original cost has now been 'consumed' or used up in operating the business. This proportion is transferred to the statement of profit or loss, where it is accounted for as an expense, and the amount remaining on the statement of financial position is correspondingly reduced. (This remaining balance is referred to as the **carrying amount or carrying value of the asset**.)
- Eventually we reach a point where the whole of the original cost has been consumed and the carrying amount or carrying value for the asset on the statement of financial position has declined to zero (or perhaps to some small residual value that may be realised on disposal).

It is extremely important to understand this basic notion of depreciation as a means of allocating the cost of a non-current asset over a number of accounting periods. It has nothing whatever to do with 'valuing' the asset, in the sense of estimating what its fair value might be at the end of each accounting period. (Fair value is the estimated amount for which an asset could be sold.) Indeed, it is not likely, in general, that the carrying amount or value of a non-current asset is anything like an approximation to its fair value. Nor does depreciation have anything to do with providing a fund for replacing the non-current asset when it is consumed.

The process of transferring amounts from statement of financial position to statement of profit or loss each year does not in any sense generate funds for the entity. It may indeed be desirable to plan ahead for asset replacement by setting aside cash for the purpose, but this is an exercise quite separate from the process of charging depreciation.

6 Calculating depreciation

There are a number of methods that accountants use to calculate or estimate the annual depreciation charge on a non-current asset. The two most common methods used are:

- straight-line and
- reducing balance.

IAS 16 says that **'the depreciation method applied to an asset should reflect the pattern in which the assets future economic benefits are expected to be consumed'** (IAS 16 para 60).

In this section we will use the same basic information relating to an individual non-current asset:

Cost – 1 January 20X4	$10,000
Estimated useful life	5 years
Estimated residual value at the end of its useful life (residual value)	$3,280

The straight-line method

- This method charges the same amount each accounting period to the statement of profit or loss over the expected useful life of the asset.
- If the depreciation charge was illustrated on a graph it would be a straight line parallel to the horizontal axis (hence the name of the method).
- Buildings are commonly depreciated using this method because entities will commonly get the same usage from a building every year.
- The amount to be charged to each accounting period is calculated as follows:

$$\text{Depreciation per annum} = \frac{\text{Original cost} - \text{estimated residual value}}{\text{Estimated useful life}}$$

OR

% × (Cost – estimated residual value)

Residual value: the estimated disposal value of the asset at the end of its useful life.

Useful life: the estimated number of years during which the entity will use the asset.

Carrying amount (CA) = original cost of the non-current asset less accumulated depreciation on the asset to date.

$$\frac{\$10{,}000 - \$3{,}280}{5} = \$1{,}344$$

This would be presented in the annual financial statements as follows:

			SOFP	
	Cost	**Acc Dep'n**	**Carrying amount**	**SP/L Dep'n charge**
Year end	$	$	$	$
31 Dec 20X4	10,000	1,344	8,656	1,344
31 Dec 20X5	10,000	2,688	7,312	1,344
31 Dec 20X6	10,000	4,032	5,968	1,344
31 Dec 20X7	10,000	5,376	4,624	1,344
31 Dec 20X8	10,000	6,720	3,280	1,344

Note the following points:

- the historical cost of the asset remains unchanged
- the accumulated depreciation provision increases by $1,344 each year i.e. by the annual depreciation charge
- the net carrying amount of the asset decreases by $1,344 annually
- the same annual charge of $1,344 is made in the statement of profit or loss.

In relation to straight-line depreciation, you may be asked to determine an appropriate rate to use, based upon given information, and also to calculate amounts for inclusion in the financial statements

Ledger accounts

The example above shows the depreciation account in respect of the individual asset used in the example: however, each asset would not normally have a separate ledger account. Whilst it is necessary to calculate the depreciation of each asset separately, it is usual for the ledger accounts to summarise the depreciation charge and the accumulated depreciation in respect of different categories of assets such as buildings, motor vehicles, and plant and equipment.

The reducing-balance method

- Some assets give a greater service – and therefore depreciate more – in their early years than they do in later years. For this reason, it is considered reasonable to charge a higher amount of depreciation in the earlier years. This method of depreciation is known as the reducing-balance method.
- Annual depreciation charge = X % × carrying amount (CA). Note that there is no need to deduct the residual value when calculating reducing balance depreciation.
- The reducing balance method results in a constantly reducing depreciation charge throughout the life of the asset. This is used to reflect the expectation that the asset will be used less and less, or will be less productive, as it ages.
- This is a common method of depreciation for vehicles, where it is expected that they will provide less service to the entity as they age because of the increased need to service/repair them as their mileage increases.

The decision as to which rate of reducing balance depreciation should be applied to the asset should be designed to write off the cost of the asset over its expected useful life to the entity. Normally this would take into account any expected residual value of the asset, and so there would be no need to deduct the expected residual value in the calculation of depreciation. Note however that the rate, when determined, is initially applied to the cost of the asset.

It is unlikely that you would be required to determine the rate of reducing balance depreciation to apply to assets, although you would be expected to be able to calculate amounts to include in the financial statements based upon information provided.

Calculation of the annual depreciation charge can be illustrated by use of the data from the previous example and using a reducing balance rate of 20%.

	$	
Original cost	10,000	
Year 1 depreciation	2,000	(20% of $10,000)
	8,000	
Year 2 depreciation	1,600	(20% of $8,000)
	6,400	
Year 3 depreciation	1,280	(20% of $6,400)
	5,120	
Year 4 depreciation	1,024	(20% of $5,120)
	4,096	
Year 5 depreciation	819	(20% of $4,096)
	3,277	

This would be presented in the annual financial statements as follows:

	Cost	**Acc Dep'n**	**SOFP Carrying amount**	**SP/L Dep'n charge**
Year end	$	$	$	$
31 Dec 20X4	10,000	2,000	8,000	2,000
31 Dec 20X5	10,000	3,600	6,400	1,600
31 Dec 20X6	10,000	4,880	5,120	1,280
31 Dec 20X7	10,000	5,904	4,096	1,024
31 Dec 20X8	10,000	6,723	3,277	819

Note the following points:

- The historical cost of the asset remains unchanged.
- The accumulated depreciation provision increases each year by the amount of the annual depreciation charge.
- The net carrying amount of the asset decreases annually.
- A reduced annual depreciation charge is made in the statement of profit and loss each year.

Further detail

If all initial estimates and assumptions relating to a non-current asset are reliable, then at the end of the asset's useful life the remaining carrying amount should equal its estimated residual value of $3,280 subject to any difference caused by rounding the percentage to be used for the amounts of annual depreciation.

The double-entry bookkeeping will be the same in principle as that illustrated earlier for the straight-line method. Clearly, though, the amount charged as an expense and the corresponding reduction in the value of the asset will be different depending on the method of depreciation used, until the end of the asset's useful life.

We can summarise the two methods as follows:

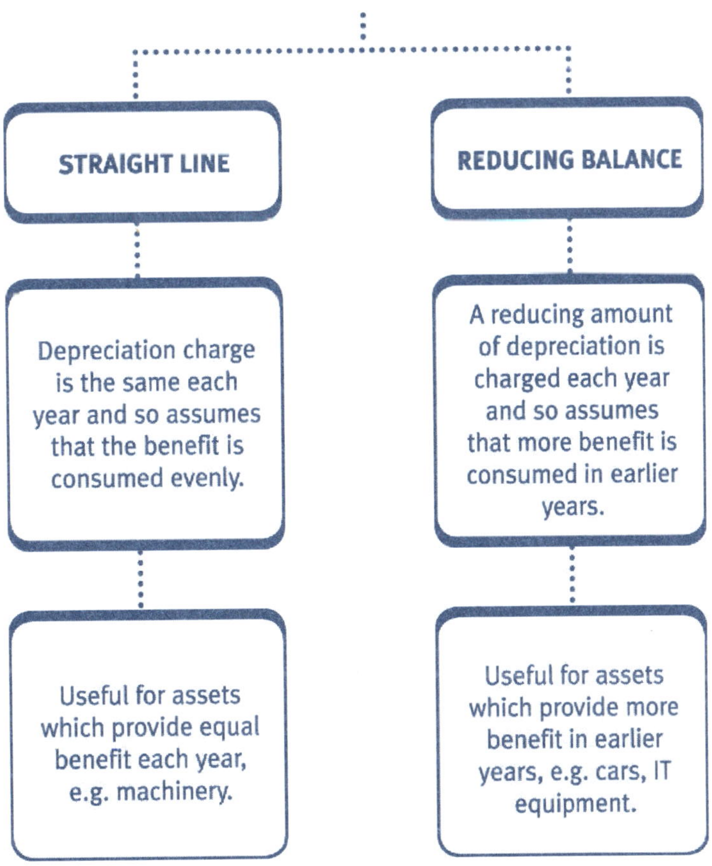

Test your understanding 2

KLM owns and operates a successful pizza business since 20X1.

KLM bought the following assets as the pizza business grew:

- a new oven for the kitchen at a cost of $2,000 (purchased 1 December 20X4)
- a van for deliveries at a cost of $18,000 (purchased 1 June 20X4).

KLM depreciated the oven at 10% straight line and the van at 25% reducing balance. A full year's depreciation is charged in the year of purchase and none in the year of disposal.

Required:

What was the total depreciation charge for the year ended 31 October 20X6?

A $2,531

B $2,700

C $4,231

D $2,731

Calculate your answer to the nearest $1.

7 Accounting for depreciation

Whichever method of depreciation is used, the accounting entries required are the same.

The ledger entries to record the depreciation charges for the year are as follows:

Debit	Depreciation expense account	$X
Credit	Accumulated depreciation account	$X

- The depreciation expense account is a statement of profit or loss account and therefore is not cumulative.
- The accumulated depreciation account is a statement of financial position account and as the name suggests is cumulative, i.e. reflects all depreciation charged to date.
- On the statement of financial position it is shown as a deduction against the cost of non-current assets:

	$
Cost	X
Accumulated depreciation	(X)
Carrying amount (CA)	X

Continuing with the earlier example of an asset which cost $10,000 with an estimated residual value of $3,280 and an estimated useful life of five years, the balance on the accumulated depreciation account will increase each year as follows:

Accumulated depreciation

		$
31 Dec X4	Statement of profit or loss	1,344
31 Dec X5	Statement of profit or loss	1,344
31 Dec X5	Accumulated depreciation balance	2,688
31 Dec X6	Statement of profit or loss	1,344
31 Dec X6	Accumulated depreciation balance	4,032

The asset would be included as a non-current asset in the statement of financial position as follows:

	Cost	less	Accum. dep'n	=	Carrying amount
	$		$		$
31 Dec 20X4	10,000		(1,344)		8,656
31 Dec 20X5	10,000		(2,688)		7,312
31 Dec 20X6	10,000		(4,032)		5,968

The depreciation expense account will be transferred to the statement of profit or loss and should only reflect the depreciation for the **current year**.

The accumulated depreciation account will be shown on the statement of financial position and offset against the cost of non-current assets. The accumulated depreciation account should always reflect the **cumulative** depreciation on the asset.

Test your understanding 3

A business entity has an accounting year end of 30 April. A machine was purchased on 1 May 20X0 for $1,000 cash and was depreciated using the reducing balance basis of 20 per cent per annum.

Required:

Prepare the ledger accounts or accounts to reflect the first three years of ownership. Note that statement of profit or loss and statement of financial position extracts are not required.

The machine-hour method/units of production method

Some non-current assets depreciate according to their usage. If the asset has a measurable 'life' in terms of the number of hours it is likely to be used, or the number of units of output it is likely to produce, then the depreciation charge can be calculated based upon usage information.

For example, a computer printer cost $1,000 and may have an expected total output of 50,000 sheets, with no residual or scrap value. If it printed 12,000 sheets in a given year, it could be said to have used up (12,000/50,000 × $1,000) $240 of its cost in that year. This reflects using up the cost of the printer over its productive life to the entity.

Depreciation in the year of acquisition and disposal

If a non-current asset is purchased or disposed of during an accounting period, there are two ways in which the depreciation charge may be calculated. It can be assumed that either:

- a full year of depreciation is charged in the year of purchase, and none in the year of disposal, irrespective of when in the year the asset was acquired or disposed, or
- a monthly or pro-rata depreciation charge is charged in the year of purchase and disposal, based upon the number of months the asset was owned during each accounting period under review.

You should always read questions carefully to identify which assumption should be applied

Test your understanding 4

A business entity has an accounting year end of 31 December. On 1 April 20X3, it purchased an asset for $14,000. The asset is expected to have a useful life to the entity of five years, with an expected residual value of $2,000. Depreciation is charged on a straight-line basis with a proportionate charge in the year of purchase and disposal. The machine was sold on 30 September 20X6.

Required:

What was the annual depreciation charge included in the financial statements for each accounting year that the entity owned the asset?

8 Accounting for intangible non-current assets

IAS 38 *Intangible Assets* defines an intangible asset as **'an identifiable non-monetary asset without physical substance'** (IAS 38 para 8).

An asset is identifiable if it is separable, or arises through contractual or other legal rights.

- Intangibles can either be purchased or internally generated, e.g. brand names.
- As a general rule, purchased intangibles are capitalised whereas internally generated intangibles are not recognised in the financial statements.
- When the cost and expected useful life of an intangible asset can be reliably estimated, it must be amortised to select the using up or wearing out of that asset.

In effect, amortisation is really the same as depreciation but a term used in relation to intangible assets. The asset cost is reduced by the accumulated amortisation provision in the statement of financial position and there is an annual amortisation charge in the statement of profit or loss.

Examples of intangible assets include:

- goodwill
- development costs
- brands
- copyrights
- licences and trademarks.

What is goodwill?

Goodwill is the difference between the fair value of a business entity as a whole and the aggregate of the fair values of its separable and identifiable assets and liabilities. This implies that it is not possible to identify goodwill separately from the entity, and this is largely because it is an intangible asset.

Purchased goodwill is calculated as follows when the whole of a business entity has been acquired:

	$
Fair value of consideration paid (purchase price)	X
Less: Fair value of net assets (i.e. assets less liabilities)	(X)
Purchased goodwill – an intangible asset	X

The definition and calculation above identifies that goodwill is the value placed upon a business entity in excess of the sum of its individual net assets.

Therefore, goodwill represents the value of the entity continuing as a going concern, as compared with the sum of its individual net assets. In practical terms, a monetary value can be placed upon the fair value of the net assets acquired and the purchase price, leaving goodwill as a residual value.

However, it could be said to be more than that. All established business entities have some goodwill. Goodwill comprises a number of nebulous elements such as having established business contacts, good staff relations, the right to occupy and use land and buildings and so on. All of these have a value, which may change over time – the difficulty lies in placing a value on them.

Purchased and non-purchased goodwill

When a business entity first commences trading, it is either created by its owners or purchased from an existing entity. In the latter case there will have been a certain amount of negotiation over the purchase price. The vendors will obviously seek to obtain the highest price possible, whereas the purchaser will seek to minimise the price. It is likely, however, that the final price will be greater than the purchaser's valuation of the separable net assets taken over. This is accepted because the price includes the rights to the existing entity's customer base, such as its name, staff experience and expertise, and so on. This difference is the goodwill and, more precisely, is said to be **purchased goodwill.**

However, whether the entity is created as a new start-up business or is the result of the acquisition of another entity, new goodwill is earned or created by the new owners over a period of time. This is known as **non-purchased goodwill.**

Accounting treatment

- The accounting treatment of purchased goodwill is for the purchaser to place a fair value on the net assets (i.e. assets–liabilities) of the business entity acquired and to consider the difference between the sum of these values and the total purchase price to be goodwill.
- This amount is debited to the goodwill ledger account and is classified as an intangible non-current asset on the statement of financial position. The purchaser will hope that the value of the goodwill will at least be maintained and that, if he were to sell the business, they would be paid for its goodwill.

However, it is important to note, when applying the concept of prudence, that assets should not be overstated. It could be that the factors which caused goodwill to exist in the past, for example location and customer base or some particular competitive advantage, no longer applies and that the value of goodwill is now less than the price paid for it.

- It is therefore necessary to estimate, on an annual basis, the value of goodwill.
- If the current estimated value is less than the amount in the statement of financial position, then goodwill is said to be 'impaired'.
- Impairment occurs when the value of a non-current asset is less than its carrying amount in the statement of financial position.
- In this situation, goodwill is reduced to its new lower value and the difference (the 'impairment') is charged to the statement of profit or loss as an expense.

It may be noted that impairment can also apply to tangible and intangible non-current assets. This will occur when the carrying amount of an asset is overstated in a statement of financial position. Impairment of non-current assets is considered in more detail in the following chapter.

Non-purchased goodwill

Non-purchased (or 'internal') goodwill is **not recognised** in the statement of financial position. The reason for this is that it is not possible to obtain a reliable measurement of its value. In the case of purchased goodwill, the fact that someone has paid for goodwill does mean that it had a value and that it was measured by the price paid at the date of purchase. In the case of internal goodwill, there has been no such external transaction and there is no reliable basis on which internal goodwill can be valued.

e.g

Illustration 2

WXY recently acquired the assets and liabilities of ACE for $1,500,000. The assets and liabilities acquired were valued by WXY as follows:

	$
Land and buildings	750,000
Plant and equipment	240,000
Inventories	65,000
Receivables	38,000
Payables	(41,000)
	1,052,000

Required:

Calculate the value of goodwill upon purchase of ACE.

Solution:

The difference between the sum of the individual net assets $1,052,000 and the purchase price $1,500,000 is goodwill. In this illustration the value of goodwill is $448,000.

If in the future WXY values the goodwill at only $400,000, then the impairment of $48,000 will be charged to the statement of profit or loss and the goodwill asset in the statement of financial position will be reduced to $400,000.

9 Valuation of intangible assets

Intangible assets affect the value of a business entity and challenge our use of the historical cost convention. They are all items that cause accountants difficulty in their valuation, mainly because of the subjective nature of the value of such items. The general principle on which all intangibles are valued is whether or not they have the potential to earn profits in the future. In other words, do they provide an economic benefit to the entity, and that can be quantified with a reasonable degree of accuracy?

We will now consider one particular intangible asset in order to appreciate the difficulties involved and the approach to be taken in its valuation.

The valuation of research and development costs

Some business entities spend money on research and development (R&D), and this presents difficulties for accountants.

Research

IAS 38 *Intangible Assets* defines research as **"original and planned investigation undertaken with the prospect of gaining new scientific or technical knowledge and understanding"** (IAS 38 para 8). All research expenditure **must be written off** to the statement of profit or loss as it is incurred.

- It is not possible to apply the matching concept as it is not yet probable that such expenditure will lead to (and can be matched against) future economic benefits (i.e. revenues and profits) for the entity.
- Therefore, in accordance with the prudence concept, such expenditure must be written off as it is incurred.
- Note that any capital expenditure on tangible non-current assets to undertake research activity should be capitalised and depreciated as normal.

Development expenditure

IAS 38 *Intangible Assets* defines development as **"the application of research knowledge...to a plan or design for the production of new or substantially improved materials, devices, products....before the start of commercial production or use"** (IAS 38 para 8).

Development expenditure is a particular class of research expenditure that meets certain criteria and which therefore enables a separate accounting treatment to be applied to it.

- In accordance with IAS 38 development expenditure **must be capitalised** as an intangible asset on the statement of financial position provided that all of the following criteria are met:
  - **S**eparate project
  - **E**xpenditure identifiable and reliably measured
  - **C**ommercially viable
  - **T**echnically feasible
  - **O**verall profitable
  - **R**esources available to complete.
- Any development expenditure capitalised must then be amortised over its useful life to the entity.
- If the above criteria are not met, development expenditure is treated as research activity and must be written off to the statement of profit or loss as it is incurred.
- If research expenditure has been written off as an expense, it cannot be reinstated as an asset.

Amortisation

Like any other non-current asset, an intangible asset should be written off over its expected useful life to the entity.

If the expected useful life of an intangible asset is finite, capitalised development costs must be amortised once commercial exploitation begins. Amortisation is simply the term given to writing off an intangible non-current asset over its estimated useful life – in effect, it is equivalent to depreciation of a tangible non-current asset.

The amortisation method used should reflect the pattern in which the asset's economic benefits are consumed by the enterprise. If that pattern cannot be determined reliably, the straight-line method should be used.

An intangible asset with an indefinite useful life should not be amortised. An asset has an indefinite useful life if there is no foreseeable limit to the period over which the asset is expected to generate net cash inflows for the entity. Instead, the intangible asset is subject to an annual impairment review to ensure that its carrying amount in the financial statements does not exceed its recoverable amount (i.e. the expected future benefits from that asset).

Accounting for amortisation of intangible assets

Intangible assets are normally amortised on a straight-line basis, unless there is a good reason to do otherwise.

This illustration makes use of much of the same information used earlier in the chapter that dealt with the calculation of, and accounting for, depreciation on a tangible non-current asset. You should notice that the only change from the earlier illustration is the change of some terminology, to reflect that fact that a tangible asset is subject to depreciation, whereas an intangible asset is subject to amortisation. In addition, it is usual for an intangible asset to be retained and used for all of its estimated useful life, and therefore regard its estimated residual value as nil.

Cost – 1 January 20X4	$10,000
Estimated useful life	5 years
Estimated residual value at the end of its useful life (residual value)	Nil

Key points to note include:

- This method charges the same amount each accounting period to the statement of profit or loss over the expected useful life of the asset.
- If the amortisation charge was illustrated on a graph it would be a straight line parallel to the horizontal axis (hence the name of the method).
- Licences are commonly depreciated using this method because entities will commonly get the same usage from a licence every year.
- The amount to be charged to each accounting period is calculated as follows:

$$\text{Amortisation per annum} = \frac{\text{Original cost} - \text{estimated residual value}}{\text{Estimated useful life}}$$

OR

% × (Cost – estimated residual value)

Using the information above, the annual depreciation charge would be

$$\frac{\$10{,}000 - \$\text{nil}}{5} = \$2{,}000$$

This would be presented in the annual financial statements as follows:

	Cost	Acc Amort'n	SOFP Carrying amount	SP&L Amort'n charge
Year end	$	$	$	$
31 Dec 20X4	10,000	2,000	8,000	2,000
31 Dec 20X5	10,000	4,000	6,000	2,000
31 Dec 20X6	10,000	6,000	4,000	2,000
31 Dec 20X7	10,000	8,000	2,000	2,000
31 Dec 20X8	10,000	10,000	Nil	2,000

Note the following points:

- The historical cost of the asset remains unchanged.
- The accumulated amortisation provision increases by $2,000 each year i.e. by the annual amortisation charge.
- The net carrying amount of the asset decreases by $2,000 annually.
- The same annual charge of $2,000 is made in the statement of profit or loss.

In relation to straight-line depreciation, you may be asked to determine an appropriate rate to use, based upon given information, and also to calculate amounts for inclusion in the financial statements.

10 Application of accounting concepts

Accounting for the purchase of non-current assets, represents application of the **matching** concept. As non-current assets are used in the business over a number of accounting periods, their usage is reflected by an annual depreciation charge in the statement of profit or loss.

11 Chapter summary

In this chapter, we considered some of the accounting issues associated with non-current assets.

Note that the accounting requirements of IAS 16 relating to property, plant and equipment are relevant to subject F1 Financial Reporting in the CIMA Professional qualification. The accounting requirements of IAS 38 relating to intangible assets are relevant to subject F2 Advanced Financial Reporting in the CIMA Professional Syllabus.

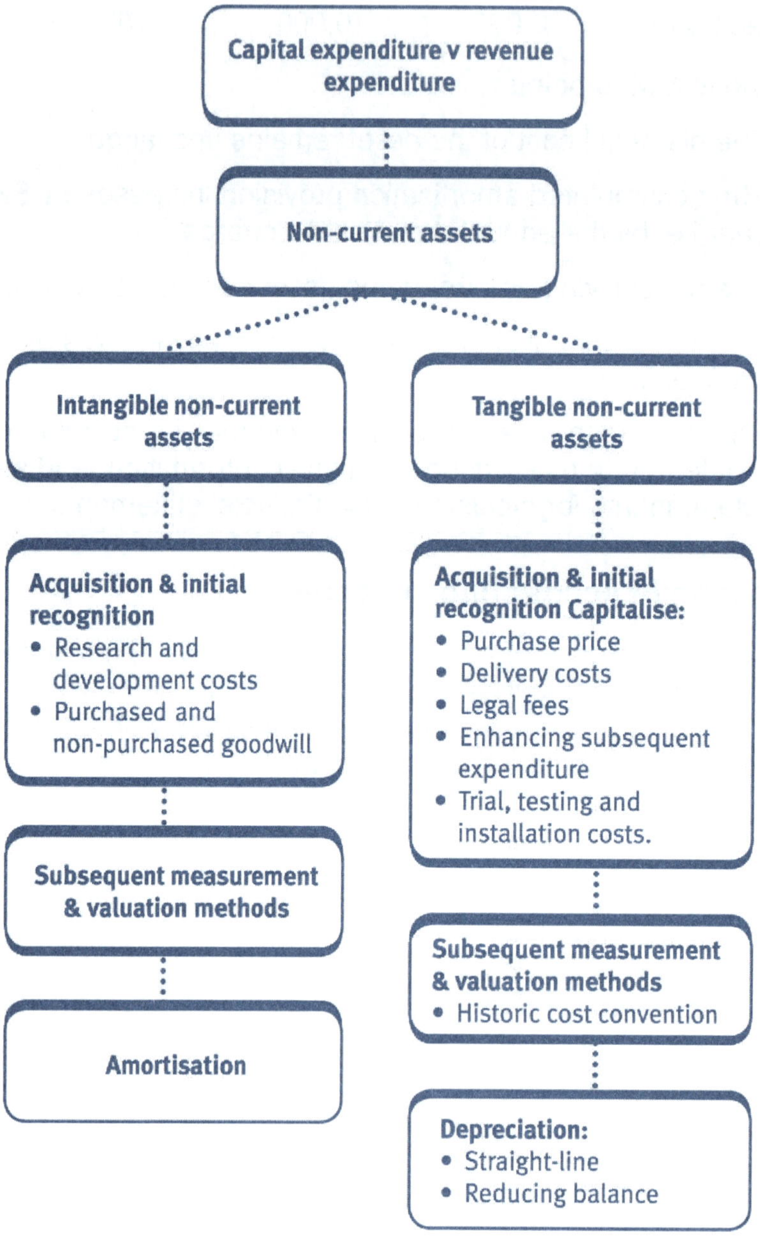

Test your understanding questions

Test your understanding 5

The most appropriate definition of depreciation is:

A a means of determining the decrease in fair value of an asset over time

B a means of allocating the cost of an asset over a number of accounting periods

C a means of setting funds aside for the replacement of the asset

D a means of estimating the fair value of the asset

Test your understanding 6

The phrase 'carrying amount' or 'carrying value' when applied to non-current assets means that

A the assets are shown in the statement of financial position at their original cost

B the assets are valued at their likely selling price

C the assets have been depreciated using the reducing-balance method

D the assets are shown in the statement of financial position at their cost less accumulated depreciation

Test your understanding 7

UVW bought a new printing machine. The cost of the machine was $80,000. The installation costs were $5,000 and the employees received training on how to use this particular machine, at a cost of $2,000. Before using the machine to print customers' orders, a test was undertaken and the paper and ink used in the test cost $1,000.

Required:

What should be the cost of the machine in UVW's statement of financial position?

$................

Test your understanding 8

KMO purchased a new pulping machine at a purchase price of $150,000. The installation costs were $10,000 and the employees received specific training on how to use this particular machine at a cost of $5,000. Before the pulping machine was used in normal operations, it was subject to a compulsory safety test at a cost of $3,000. The machine was expected to have an eight-year estimated useful life, with an estimated residual value of $8,000.

Required:

What is the cost of the pulping machine capitalised in the statement of financial position?

$................

What is the annual depreciation charge associated with the pulping machine?

$................

Test your understanding 9

A business entity acquired a licence at a cost of $25,000 on 1 July 20X3 which gave it the exclusive right to use a particular production process for ten years from the date of purchase. The licence is amortised over its expected useful life, with a proportionate charge in the year of acquisition.

Required:

What is the amortisation charge relating to the licence for the year ended 31 March 20X4?

$................

Test your understanding 10

A non-current asset was purchased at a cost of $4,800 on 1 January 20X4. It is subject to an annual depreciation charge of 20% on a reducing balance basis.

Required:

What is the carrying amount of the asset at 31 December 20X7?

$ .... (answer to the nearest $1)

Test your understanding 11

Classify each of the following items of expenditure as either capital expenditure or revenue expenditure.

	Item of expenditure	Classification
A	Delivery costs of a machine purchased	
B	The replacement of broken windows in a factory	
C	The purchase of a car for resale by a car sales business	
D	Annual servicing costs of an office printer	

Test your understanding 12

Which of the following statements regarding goodwill is NOT correct?

A Goodwill is classed as an intangible non-current asset

B Goodwill is the excess of the value of a business as a whole over the fair value of its separable net assets

C Purchased goodwill may be shown on the statement of financial position and may be reduced by impairment

D Non-purchased goodwill is a liability

Test your understanding 13

Which of the following statements explains what is meant by capital expenditure?

A Expenditure on non-current assets, including repairs and maintenance

B Expenditure on any type of asset

C Expenditure relating to amounts withdrawn from the business entity

D Expenditure relating to the acquisition or improvement of non-current assets

Test your understanding 14

A business entity buys an item of machinery for long-term use. Which of the following is NOT capital expenditure?

A The purchase price of $1,000

B Delivery fees of $125

C $350 spent on training employees to use the machine

D $500 incurred testing the machine

Test your understanding answers

Test your understanding 1

	Item of expenditure	Classification
A	Repainting of a building	Revenue expenditure
B	Installation of a new central heating system	Capital expenditure
C	Repainting of a delivery van	Revenue expenditure
D	Providing drainage for a new piece of water-extraction equipment	Capital expenditure
E	Legal fees incurred on the purchase of land	Capital expenditure
F	Carriage costs for a replacement component part for a piece of machinery	Revenue expenditure

Test your understanding 2

D

	20X6 $
Oven	
$2,000 × 10%	200
Van	
20X4: $18,000 × 25% = $4,500	
20X5: ($18,000 – $4,500) × 25% = $3,375	
20X6: ($18,000 – $4,500 – $3,375) × 25% = $2,531	2,531
Total	2,731

Test your understanding 3

Machine at cost

20X0	.	$		.	$
1 May	Cash	1,000			

Accumulated depreciation for machinery

20X1		$			$
30 May	Balance c/f	200	30 Apr	Statement of profit or loss	200
20X2			20X2		
			1 May	Balance b/f	200
30 Apr	Balance c/f	360	30 Apr	Statement of profit or loss	160
		360			360
			20X3		
20X3			1 May	Balance b/f	360
30 Apr	Balance c/f	488	30 Apr	Statement of profit or loss	128
		488			488
			20X4		
			1 May	Balance b/f	488

Workings:

20X1 – $1,000 × 20% = $200

20X2 – ($1,000 – $200) × 20% = $160

20X3 – ($1,000 – $200 – $160) × 20% = $128

Test your understanding 4

The annual depreciation charge should be: ($14,000 – $2,000)/5 years = $2,400.

Year ended	Calculation	Depn charge
31 Dec X3	$2,400 × 9/12	$1,800
31 Dec X4	Full year	$2,400
31 Dec X5	Full year	$2,400
31 Dec X6	$2,400 × 9/12	$1,800

Note: Accounting for disposal of non-current assets will be considered in the following chapter.

Test your understanding 5

B

Depreciation never provides a fund for the replacement of the asset, nor does it aim to show assets at their fair values.

Test your understanding 6

D

Non-current assets should, except in certain circumstances, be depreciated over their expected useful life. Answer A would almost never be appropriate. Assets are rarely valued at their expected selling price –if this is more than their cost, this would be imprudent, and if less than cost would contravene the 'going concern' convention, which is discussed in a later chapter. The method of depreciation is irrelevant.

Test your understanding 7

	$
Cost of machine	80,000
Installation	5,000
Testing	1,000
	86,000

All costs necessarily incurred to bring the non-current asset into use must be capitalised.

Test your understanding 8

Cost of pulping machine $163,000

Annual depreciation charge $19,375

Capitalised cost = $150,000 + $10,000 + $3,000 = $163,000

Annual depreciation charge = ($163,000 – $8,000)/8 years = $19,375

Note that staff training costs are excluded from the capitalised cost. The cost of the compulsory safety test is capitalised as, without incurring this cost, the asset cannot be brought into operational use.

Test your understanding 9

$1,875

Annual amortisation charge was ($25,000/10 years) = $2,500 × 9/12 = $1,875

However, during the year ended 31 March 20X4, the asset had been owned for only 9 months. Therefore, the annual amortisation charge should be prorated by 9/12 to arrive at the amortisation charge for the year ended 31 March 20X4.

Test your understanding 10

$1,966 (to the nearest $1)

By 31 December 20X7, the asset has been used in the business for four years. Therefore, the carrying amount of the asset at that date was:

$4,800 × 80% = $3,840 × 80% = 3,072 × 80% = 2,457.6 × 80% = $1,966.08

Test your understanding 11

	Item of expenditure	**Classification**
A	Delivery costs of a machine purchased	Capital expenditure
B	The replacement of broken windows in a factory	Revenue expenditure
C	The purchase of a car for resale by a car sales business	Revenue expenditure
D	Annual servicing costs of an office printer	Revenue expenditure

Note that the purchase of a car by a car sales business is a purchase for resale, rather than the acquisition of a non-current asset to be used in the business over a number of years. This answer would be different, for example, if the vehicle purchased was a transporter vehicle used to deliver cars to customers.

Test your understanding 12

D

A, B and C are all correct, in most situations.

Test your understanding 13

D

Test your understanding 14

C

Chapter

12

Non-current assets: Revaluation, impairment and disposal

Chapter learning objectives

When you have completed this chapter, you should be able to:

- account for the revaluation of a non-current asset
- account for the impairment of a non-current asset
- prepare accounting entries to record the disposal of tangible non-current assets, including part exchange transactions
- calculate the profit or loss on the disposal of a non-current asset
- prepare a non-current asset register.

1 Introduction

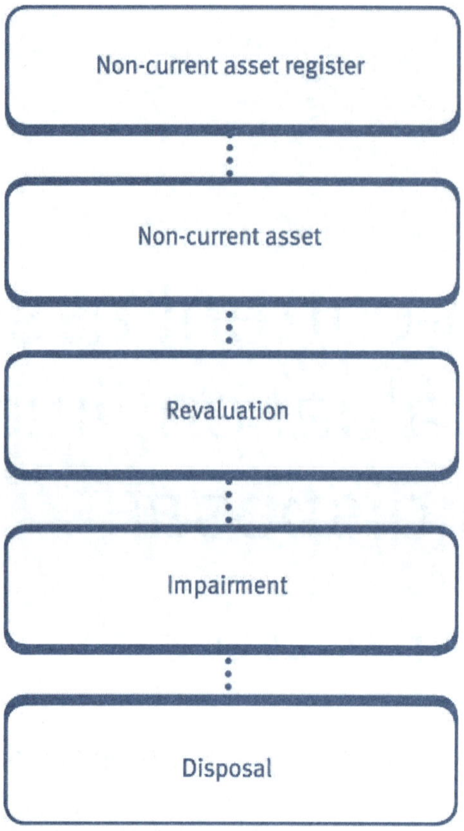

In this chapter you will learn how to:

- account for the revaluation of a non-current asset
- account for the impairment of a non-current asset
- account for disposal of a non-current asset
- prepare the non-current asset register.

2 The revaluation of tangible non-current assets

IAS 16 *Property, Plant and Equipment* permits entities to account for tangible non-current assets at either cost or fair value.

The fair value of an asset is usually its market value – i.e. the price at which it could be sold for at a given point in time.

If an asset is revalued, any accumulated depreciation at the date of the revaluation should be written off to the revaluation surplus account. IAS 16 says that **'If an asset's carrying amount is increased as a result of a revaluation, the increase shall be recognised in other comprehensive income and accumulated in equity under the heading of revaluation surplus'** (IAS 16 para 39). This will be considered in more detail in later chapters.

In accordance with IAS 16 depreciation will then be calculated based on the **revalued amount** using the remaining useful life of the asset as at the revaluation date.

IAS 16 says that **'if an item of property, plant and equipment is revalued, the entire class of property, plant and equipment to which that asset belongs shall be revalued'** (IAS 16 para 37). For example, if buildings are revalued, all other buildings must be accounted for using the revaluation basis so that a consistent accounting treatment is adopted. Note that, if an entity has a significant number of assets accounted for using the revaluation model, it is not necessary to revalue all assets on the same date. For example, there could be a 'rolling programme' of revaluation to ensure that all relevant assets are revalued at regular intervals.

The frequency of revaluation will depend upon market conditions and will normally be carried out by an independent, professionally qualified person.

Note also that other classes of non-current asset, such as fixtures and fittings, can continue to be accounted for using the cost model.

Steps to account for a revaluation:

1 Restate the asset cost to the revalued amount and transfer the increase to revaluation surplus account.

2 Remove any accumulated depreciation provision at the revaluation date and transfer to the revaluation surplus account.

3 Recalculate the current year depreciation charge on the revalued amount.

e.g

Illustration 1

On 31 December 20X2, a building which originally cost $100,000, and which had a carrying amount of $70,000, was revalued to $120,000. At that date, the remaining useful life of the building was considered to be 12 years and the building was depreciated using the straight-line basis.

Required:

Prepare the ledger account entries required to account for the revaluation of the building and calculate the depreciation charge based upon the revalued amount.

Solution:

First we must revalue the asset from cost to the revalued amount. This is an increase of $20,000 ($100,000 increases to $120,000). The accounting entry would be to debit the asset account and credit the revaluation surplus account. Note that the asset account can no longer be referred to as a cost account as the asset is now recorded at valuation.

Debit	Non-current asset account	$20,000
Credit	Revaluation surplus account	$20,000

The next step is to remove the accumulated depreciation from the books at the revaluation date. As the original cost of the asset was $100,000 and the carrying amount in the accounts is currently $70,000, accumulated depreciation must be $30,000. To remove this we must debit the accumulated depreciation account and credit the revaluation surplus account.

Debit	Accumulated depreciation account	$30,000
Credit	Revaluation surplus account	$30,000

The revaluation surplus now has two credit entries, $20,000 and $30,000. This $50,000 represents the increase in value of the building from its carrying amount in the accounts before the revaluation of $70,000, to the revalued amount of $120,000. This accumulated surplus is part of the capital or equity of the entity and included in the capital or equity section of the statement of financial position. You will learn more about the capital structure of a corporate entity as you continue your studies for this subject. The bookkeeping entries related to this example are as follows:

Building at cost or valuation

20X2		$	**20X2**		$
1 Jan	Balance b/f	100,000	31 Dec	Balance c/f	120,000
31 Dec	Revaluation surplus	20,000			
		120,000			120,000
20X3					
1 Jan	Balance b/f	120,000			

Accumulated depreciation – building

20X2		$	**20X2**		$
31 Dec	Revaluation surplus	30,000	1 Jan	Balance b/f	30,000
		30,000			30,000

Revaluation surplus

20X2		$	**20X2**		$
31 Dec	Balance c/f	50,000	31 Dec	Building cost or val'n	20,000
				Accum dep'n	30,000
		50,000			50,000
			20X3		
			1 Jan	Balance b/f	50,000

The future depreciation charge will be based on the revalued amount of $120,000, i.e. $120,000/12 years remaining life = £10,000 p.a.

Test your understanding 1

JKL purchased a building on 1 January 20X3 at a cost of $470,000. The building was depreciated on a straight-line basis at 2% per annum. On 1 January 20X8, the building was revalued to $485,000.

What accounting entries are required to account for this revaluation?

		$		$
A	Debit Non-current asset	15,000	Credit Revaluation surplus	71,400
	Debit Accumulated depreciation	56,400		
B	Debit Non-current asset	15,000	Credit Revaluation surplus	62,000
	Debit Accumulated depreciation	47,000		
C	Debit Revaluation surplus	71,400	Credit Non-current asset	15,000
			Accumulated depreciation	56,400
D	Debit Revaluation surplus	62,000	Credit Non-current asset	15,000
			Accumulated depreciation	47,000

Test your understanding 2

HIJ revalued its premises on 1 January 20X7 to $1,600,000. The premises had been purchased on 1 January 20X1 at a cost of $900,000 and depreciation was charged at 2% per annum on a straight-line basis.

Required:

What was the balance on the revaluation surplus account after accounting for the revaluation?

A $750,000

B $790,000

C $808,000

D $826,000

Test your understanding 3

At 30 June 20X4, LMN had cost of $15.6 million for property plant and equipment and $4.8 million for accumulated depreciation on buildings. At that date, the land and buildings were revalued to $16.5 million.

Required:

What is the revaluation surplus arising upon accounting for this revaluation?

$ ....

3 Impairment of tangible non-current assets

An asset may be impaired if its recoverable amount is less than its carrying amount in the financial statements.

Indications that an asset may be impaired include:

- obvious damage
- obsolescence
- lack of use, so that the asset is not creating value for the entity.

The recoverable amount of an asset represents the best use of that asset and is the higher of:

- net selling price (fair value less costs to sell) or
- value in use (generated by continuing to use the asset in the business – normally given in the question).

If an asset has been identified as impaired, its carrying amount must be reduced to its recoverable amount and the fall in value is transferred to the statement of profit or loss as an expense (think of it as an extra depreciation charge in that year).

For an asset which is not depreciated, the journal entry would be as follows:

Debit	Statement of profit or loss expense account	$X
Credit	Non-current asset account	$X

For an asset which is depreciated, it is acceptable to account for the impairment charge as if it was an additional depreciation charge as follows:

Debit	Statement of profit or loss expense account	$X
Credit	Accumulated depreciation and impairment account	$X

In this situation, the new carrying amount of the asset would be = Cost – accumulated depreciation and impairment charges.

e.g

Illustration 2

At 31 December 20X5, HKM had a non-current asset which had cost $15,000 and on which accumulated depreciation was $10,000. Information collated for an impairment review at that date identified that its fair value was $4,900 and costs to sell were $600. The value in use of the non-current asset was $4,800.

Required:

What was the extent of impairment recognised in HKM's financial statements at 31 December 20X5?

Solution:

$200 impairment

An asset should be stated at the lower of carrying amount or its recoverable amount, where recoverable amount is the higher of either value in use or fair value less costs to sell. Carrying amount = $5,000 ($15,000 – $10,000).

Recoverable amount is the higher of either fair value less costs to sell of $4,300 ($4,900 – $600) or value in use of $4,800. Therefore the recoverable amount is $4,800.

Finally, compare the carrying amount of $5,000 with recoverable amount of $4,800. As carrying amount exceeds recoverable amount, there is impairment of $200 and this should be accounted for as follows:

Debit Impairment charge (P/L) $200

Credit Accumulated depreciation and impairment charges (SOFP) $200.

Test your understanding 4

At 30 June 20X3, CEG had a non-current asset which had cost $25,000 and on which accumulated depreciation was $15,000. Information collated for an impairment review at that date identified that its fair value was $10,200 and costs to sell were $800. The value in use of the non-current asset was $9,200.

Required:

What was the extent of impairment recognised in CEG's financial statements at 30 June 20X3?

4 Accounting for the disposal of a non-current asset

- At the end of the asset's life it will be either abandoned or sold. This is known as a 'disposal' in accounting terminology. IAS 16 says that **'the carrying amount of an item of property, plant and equipment shall be derecognised on disposal or when no future economic benefits are expected from its use or disposal'** (IAS 16 para 67).
- IAS 16 says that **'the gain or loss arising from the derecognition of an item of property, plant and equipment shall be determined as the difference between the net disposal proceeds, if any, and the carrying amount of the item'** (IAS 16 para 71).
- The difference is referred to as the **profit or loss arising on the disposal of the asset**. It effectively represents the extent to which the depreciation charged during the life of the asset was incorrect.
- The profit or loss on disposal will be treated as a statement of profit or loss item.

If the **proceeds** received on disposal **are less than the carrying amount,** the difference is a **loss** on disposal, which is treated as an expense in the statement of profit or loss.

If the proceeds received on disposal are **greater than the carrying amount,** the difference is a **profit** on disposal, which is treated as income in the statement of profit or loss.

A quick method of calculating the profit or loss on disposal of a non-current asset is to compare the carrying amount of the asset with the disposal proceeds as follows:

			$
Disposal proceeds			X
Less:	Carrying amount of non-current asset at disposal date:		
	Cost of non-current asset	X	
Less:	Accumulated depreciation up to disposal date	(X)	
			(X)
Profit (or loss) on disposal of non-current asset			X or (X)

In some questions, you may be provided with the carrying amount of the non-current asset at disposal date, or be provided with separate information relating to the asset cost along with the accumulated depreciation on that asset to date. Alternatively, you may need to calculate the accumulated depreciation up to the date of disposal prior to calculating the profit or loss on disposal.

This approach, if sufficient information is available, avoids the need to prepare ledger accounts as part of your workings or calculations. However, you may be required to calculate specific figures as part of a question requirement, so it is important that you also understand the accounting entries required to deal with the disposal of a non-current asset.

There is a three step approach when accounting for the disposal of a non-current asset:

Step 1 – remove the cost of the asset from the books and transfer to the disposal account.

Debit	Disposal account	$X
Credit	Non-current asset account	$X

Step 2 – remove the accumulated depreciation from the books and transfer to the disposal account.

Debit	Accumulated depreciation account	$X
Credit	Disposal account	$X

Step 3 – record the cash proceeds

Debit	Cash account	$X
Credit	Disposal account	$X

The balance on the disposal account represents the profit or loss on disposal and should be transferred to the statement of profit or loss:

Disposal of NCA account

	$		$
Non-current asset (cost or valuation)	X	Accumulated depreciation	X
		Bank/cash	X
Profit ß (to SPL)	X	Loss ß (to SPL)	X
	X		X

Note: The non-current asset account is normally accounted for at cost; however it could be accounted for at a revalued amount. Whether a non-current asset has been accounted for at cost or at its revalued amount, accounting for its disposal is an identical procedure to determine the profit or loss arising on that disposal.

e.g **Illustration 3**

R purchased a machine at a cost of $25,000 on 1 April 20X2. The machine was sold for $6,500 on 31 March 20X6. At that date, accumulated depreciation on the machine amounted to $17,000.

Required:

What was the profit or loss on disposal of the machine?

Solution:

		$
Sale proceeds		6,500
Less: Carrying amount of machine at disposal date:		
Cost of machine	25,000	
Less: accumulated depreciation	(17,000)	
		(8,000)
Loss on disposal		(1,500)

e.g

Illustration 4

X purchased a van on 1 January 20X4 for $10,000. At the date of purchase, it was estimated that the van would have an estimated resale value of $400 after 6 years' use. The van was depreciated on a straight-line basis, applying a pro-rata charge in the year of acquisition and disposal.

The van was sold on 30 June 20X6 for $5,500.

Required:

Calculate the profit or loss on disposal of the van.

Solution:

The amount of depreciation charged each year was:

$$\frac{\text{Original cost} - \text{estimated residual value}}{\text{Estimated useful life}} = \frac{\$10{,}000 - \$400}{6} = \$1{,}600$$

X owned the asset for 2 years and 6 months, thus the total depreciation charged since acquisition is $1,600 × 2.5 = $4,000. This means that the carrying amount or value at the date of the disposal was $10,000 –$4,000 = $6,000.

Since the sale proceeds only amounted to $5,500 there is a 'loss on disposal' of $500.

The bookkeeping entries related to this example are as follows:

Van at cost

20X4		$	20X2		$
1 Jan	Bank	10,000	31 Dec	Balance c/f	10,000
		10,000			10,000
20X5			20X5		
1 Jan	Balance b/f	10,000	31 Dec	Balance b/f	10,000
		10,000			10,000
20X6			20X6		
1 Jan	Balance b/f	10,000	30 Jun	Disposal	10,000

Accumulated depreciation – van

		$			$
			20X4		
			31 Dec	Depreciation	1,600
			20X5		
			31 Dec	Depreciation	1,600
20X6			20X6		
30 Jun	Disposal	4,000	30 Jun	Depreciation	800
		4,000			4,000

Non-current asset disposal – van

20X6		$	20X6		$
30 Jun	Van at cost	10,000	30 Jun	Accumulated depreciation – van	4,000
				Bank	5,500
				Loss (to statement of profit or loss)	500
		10,000			10,000

Test your understanding 5

A non-current asset that was purchased on 23 March 20X1 for $3,500. Its residual value was expected to be $200, and its expected useful life was 4 years. The asset was sold on 18 January 20X4 for $1,300. A full year's depreciation should be charged in the year of purchase, and none in the year of disposal. The entity's year end is 31 December.

Required:

Write up the relevant accounts to account for this non-current asset.

A comprehensive example

A business entity purchased the following machines:

- Machine A on 3 February 20X1, at a cost of $1,000
- Machine B on 18 March 20X2, at a cost of $1,200
- Machine C on 27 June 20X3, at a cost of $2,000.

Each of the machines had an expected residual value of $nil and they are all depreciated using the straight-line basis over 10 years, with a full year's depreciation in the year of purchase and none in the year of disposal. Machine A was sold for $720 on 30 June 20X4. The entity's accounting year-end is 31 December.

Annual depreciation was calculated as follows:

- Machine A $100
- Machine B $120
- Machine C $200.

Required:

Write up the ledger accounts to account for the three machines.

Solution:

Because there are three machines bought at different times, it is a good idea to tabulate the depreciation as follows:

Year	Machine A	Machine B	Machine C	Total
	$	$	$	$
20X1	100	Nil	Nil	100
20X2	100	120	Nil	220
20X3	100	120	200	420
20X4	Nil	120	200	320

The total column gives the depreciation to be charged each year. Remember to dispose of Machine A in 20X4. The ledger accounts are as follows:

Machines at cost

20X1		$	20X1		$
3 Feb	Cash	1,000	31 Dec	Balance c/f	1,000
20X2			20X2		
1 Jan	Balance b/f	1,000			
18 Mar		1,200	31 Dec	Balance c/f	2,200
		2,200			2,200

20X3			20X3		
1 Jan	Balance b/f	2,200			
27 Jun	Cash	2,000	31 Dec	Balance c/f	4,200
		4,000			4,200
20X4			20X4		
1 Jan	Balance b/f	4,200	30 Jun	Disposals a/c	1,000
			31 Dec	Balance c/f	3,200
		4,200			4,200
20X4					
1 Jan	Balance b/f	3,200			

Accumulated depreciation – machines

20X1		$	20X1		$
3 Feb	Balance c/f	100	31 Dec	Statement of profit or loss	100
20X2			20X2		
			1 Jan	Balance b/f	100
31 Dec	Balance c/f	320	31 Dec	Statement of profit or loss	220
		320			320
20X3			20X3		
			1 Jan	Balance b/f	320
31 Dec	Balance c/f	740	31 Dec	Statement of profit or loss	420
		740			740
20X4			20X4		
30 Jan	Disposals a/c	300	1 Jan	Balance b/f	740
31 Dec	Balance c/f	760	31 Dec	Statement of profit or loss	320
		1,060			1,080
			20X5		
			1 Jan	Balance b/f	760

Non-current asset – disposals

20X4		$	20X4		$
30 Jun	Machines at cost	1,000	30 Jun	Accumulated dep'n-machine	300
31 Dec	Statement of profit or loss	20	30 Jun	Cash	720
		1,020			1,020

The profit on disposal is credited to the statement of profit or loss.

5 Disposal using a part-exchange agreement (PEA)

A part exchange agreement arises when an old asset is provided in part payment for a new one, the balance of the new asset is then paid in cash or a payable created for the liability outstanding.

The procedure to record this transaction is very similar to the three-step process used for a cash disposal. The first two steps are identical; however, steps 3 and 4 are as follows:

Step 3 – record the **part-exchange value or proceeds**

Debit	Non-current asset cost account	$X
Credit	Disposal account	$X

Step 4 – record the **cash payment or payable** (as appropriate)

Debit	Non-current asset cost account	$X
Credit	Cash/Payables	$X

If the balance on the part exchange agreement was not paid in cash and the entity was given credit then the credit entry to the journal in step 4 would be to the payables account instead of the cash account.

The balance on the disposal account still represents the profit or loss on disposal and should be transferred to the statement of profit or loss.

Test your understanding 6

TYR operates a car repair business. When it started business on 1 January 20X2, it bought a compressor machine for $5,000. All machinery is depreciated using the straight-line method at a rate of 20% pa, with a full year charged in the year of purchase and none in the year of disposal.

As the business expanded, TYR decided to replace the current compressor with a new, more efficient, machine. A new machine was purchased on 18 December 20X5, with the current compressor traded-in as part of the agreement as follows:

Part exchange allowance for old machine $2,500 Balance to be paid in cash for new machine $6,000

Required:

Prepare the ledger account entries for the year ended 31 December 20X5 to reflect this transaction.

6 The non-current asset register

Purpose of the non-current asset register

The register is a list of non-current assets owned by the business entity. It is not part of the double-entry accounting system but is part of the internal control system of the entity. The register enables key information relating to an individual asset to be easily identified, such as its location, type/description and cost.

Most entities own a number of non-current assets and in large entities their control is vital to its efficient running and management.

Management will need to be aware of:

1 the location of each asset

2 the extent to which it is used

3 the repairs that have been carried out on the asset and the cost of those repairs

4 the expiry dates of any licences permitting the entity to use the asset.

Content of the non-current asset register

The register normally contains the following information relating to each individual non-current asset:

- the asset register/serial/code number – this should be a sequential number from the register and marked/identified on the asset
- the date of purchase
- the supplier name and contact details
- asset description e.g. AK200 milling machine
- the asset location and department e.g. Leeds foundry, Dept. 2
- the initial cost of the asset
- the estimated residual value of the asset
- the estimated useful life and/or depreciation method of the asset e.g. 20% straight-line
- the annual depreciation charge
- the accumulated depreciation to date (updated each year)
- the carrying amount of the asset (updated each year)
- disposal date
- disposal proceeds
- details of any grants received to assist with the purchase of the asset.

Normally an individual employee would be responsible for maintaining and updating the register, which should be agreed or reconciled periodically with the information in the nominal or general ledger. If there are any discrepancies between the information contained in the register and of that contained in the nominal ledger, it should be investigated and rectified.

Format of the non-current asset register

The register may be maintained as either a manual record or in computerised form. Whichever form of register is adopted, the information recorded and maintained should be the same.

An extract of the non-current asset register for Barker or the year ended 31 December 20X5 could be as follows:

Reg No	*Description*	*Location*	*Supplier Date*	*EUL yrs*	*Dep'n method*	*Cost* $	*Est Res Value* $	*Acc Dep'n b/f* $	*Dep'n charge X5* $	*Carrying amount 31/12/X5* $	*Disp value*	*Disp value* $
3456	AK200 miller	Leeds	Aze Co 01/01/X2	5	25% SL	10,000	2,000	4,000	2,000	4,000		
3457	A30 shaper	Crewe	Que Co 01/07/X3	4	20% SL	9,000	1,000	3,000	2,000	4,000		
3458	P42 driller	Hull	Rye Co 01/04/X4	10	10% SL	70,000	6,000	4,800	6,400	58,800		

The equivalent extract from Barker's non-current asset register for the year ended 31 December 20X6 could be as follows:

Reg No	*Description*	*Location*	*Supplier Date*	*EUL yrs*	*Dep'n method*	*Cost*	*Est Res Value*	*Acc Dep'n b/f*	*Dep'n charge X5*	*Carrying amount 31/12/X5*	*Disp value*	*Disp value*
						$	$	$	$	$		$
3456	AK200 miller	Leeds	Aze Co 01/01/X2	5	25% SL	10,000	2,000	6,000	Nil		01/01/X6	4,500
3457	A30 shaper	Crewe	Que Co 01/07/X3	4	20% SL	9,000	1,000	5,000	2,000	2,000		
3458	P42 driller	Hull	Rye Co 01/04/X4	10	10% SL	70,000	6,000	11,200	6,400	52,400		

Note the following points based upon the two extracts:

- the accumulated depreciation brought forward and the current year depreciation charge for each asset is identified in the register
- the accumulated depreciation brought forward is updated each year – e.g. year ended 31 December 20X6 asset 3457 accumulated depreciation brought forward = $5,000 (i.e. $3,000 + $2,000 re 20X5)
- a new carrying amount is calculated for each non-current asset still owned at the end of each year
- no depreciation was charged on asset 3456 in 20X6 as it was disposed of on 1 January 20X6
- the annual depreciation charge for the year will be included in the statement of profit or loss of $10,400 in 20X5 and $8,400 in 20X6
- in 20X6, there is a profit on disposal of asset 3456 of $500 ($4,500 – ($10,000 – $6,000)) which will be included in the statement of profit or loss for that year.

The non-current asset register

The efficiency of the entity can be greatly improved if the register is stored on a computer. Specialist computer packages exist for the recording of an entity's non-current assets, but much the same effect can be obtained by using a spreadsheet or database program, particularly in smaller entities or where the information is recorded within each department.

In the context of a non-current asset register, each asset would be given a code number. There should be a separate record on the computer file for each non-current asset, and within each record there would be a field for each data item to be recorded. The asset code would normally be used as the key field so that the record of any particular asset could be located easily.

The use of a computerised non-current asset register would allow the calculation of depreciation to be automated and various reports could be produced showing, for example:

- the depreciation charge for the accounting period analysed by asset and by department as required
- a list of assets requiring servicing
- a list of assets at a particular location
- the extent of any repair expenditure on each asset
- a list of assets continuing in use beyond their estimated useful life.

The use of a computerised system greatly improves the speed and accuracy of reporting and allows management to design different reports specific to their needs. These needs will vary for different managers and the use of a computerised system means that the basic data needs to be entered only once, and the computer can then arrange it in different ways in order to produce the report required.

Test your understanding 7

A non-current asset register is:

A an alternative name for the non-current asset ledger account

B a list of the physical non-current assets rather than their financial cost

C a schedule of planned maintenance of non-current assets for use by the plant engineer

D a schedule of the cost and other information about each individual non-current asset

Test your understanding 8

A non-current asset register had a total carrying amount of $67,460 for all non-current assets. A non-current asset which cost $15,000 was sold for $4,000, making a loss on disposal of $1,250. No entries have been made in the non-current asset register for this disposal.

Required:

What will be the balance on the non-current asset register when it has been updated to reflect this transaction?

A $42,710

B $51,210

C $53,710

D $62,210

7 Application of accounting concepts

Accounting for the impairment of a non-current asset represents application of the **prudence** concept to ensure that assets are not overstated in the financial statements.

Although revaluation of non-current assets is permitted, it is subject to accounting requirements which ensure that such revaluations are credible and do not exceed their recoverable amount. For non-current assets such as a building, the revalued amount is depreciated over its remaining expected useful life, which represents continued application of the **matching** concept.

8 Chapter summary

In this chapter, we considered accounting issues associated with tangible non-current assets. These issues can be summarised as:

- accounting entries to record the disposal of tangible non-current assets with cash and/or part exchange proceeds
- accounting entries to record the revaluation of tangible non-current assets
- accounting entries to record the impairment of tangible non-current assets
- the control of tangible non-current assets.

The accounting requirements of IAS 16, along with accounting for impairments, are relevant in subject F1 Financial Reporting in the CIMA Professional Qualification.

Test your understanding questions

Test your understanding 9

A business entity bought a machine at a cost of $5,000 on 1 January 20X1, which had an expected useful life of 4 years and an expected residual value of $1,000. The asset was depreciated using the straight-line basis, with a proportionate charge in the year of acquisition and disposal. On 31 December 20X3, the machine was sold for $1,600.

Required:

What was the amount to be entered in the 20X3 statement of profit or loss for profit or loss on disposal?

$......................... .

Test your understanding 10

An entity's non-current asset register had a carrying amount or value of $135,600. The non-current asset account in the nominal ledger had a carrying amount or value of $125,600. Upon investigation, it was identified that the difference was due to an asset disposal not yet removed from the non-current asset register.

Which of the following would account for the difference between the register and nominal ledger account?

A An asset with disposal proceeds of $15,000 and a profit on disposal of $5,000

B An asset with disposal proceeds of $15,000 and a carrying amount or value of $5,000

C An asset with disposal proceeds of $15,000 and a loss on disposal of $5,000

D An asset with disposal proceeds of $5,000 and a carrying amount or value of $5,000

Test your understanding 11

A machine cost $9,000. It had an expected useful life of 6 years, and an expected residual value of $1,000. It was depreciated at 30 per cent per annum using the reducing-balance basis. A full year's depreciation was charged in the year of purchase, with none in the year of disposal. During year 4, it was sold for $3,000.

Required:

What was the profit or loss on disposal?

$......................... .

Test your understanding 12

A non-current asset was disposed of for $2,200. It had been purchased exactly 3 years previously for $5,000, and had an expected residual value of $500. The non-current asset had been depreciated using the reducing-balance basis, at 20 per cent per annum.

Required:

What was the profit or loss on disposal?

$........................

Test your understanding 13

A van was purchased by a newsagent business in May 20X0 as follows

	$
Cost	10,000
Annual vehicle licence tax	150
Total	10,150

The entity has an annual accounting year end of 31 December. The van has been depreciated at 25 per cent per annum using the reducing-balance method, charging a full year's depreciation in the year of purchase and none in the year of sale. The van was traded in for a replacement vehicle in August 20X3 at an agreed value of $5,000.

Required:

What was the profit or loss on disposal of the van during the year ended December 20X3 (give your answer to the nearest $1)?

$........................

Test your understanding 14

The carrying amount of RST's non-current assets was $200,000 at 1 August 20X0. During the year ended 31 July 20X1, RST sold non-current assets for $25,000 on which it made a loss of $5,000. The depreciation charge for the year ended 31 July 20X1 was $20,000.

Required:

What was the carrying amount or value of non-current assets at 31 July 20X1?

$........................

Test your understanding 15

An entity purchased a car at a cost of $12,000 on 1 April 20X0 which has been depreciated at 20 per cent each year, straight line, assuming a nil residual value. The depreciation policy of the entity is to charge a full year's depreciation in the year of purchase and no depreciation in the year of sale. The car was traded in for a replacement vehicle on 1 August 20X3 for an agreed value of $5,000.

Required:

What was the profit or loss on the disposal of the vehicle for the year ended 31 December 20X3?

$........................

Test your understanding 16

At 1 January 20X6 MDP had motor vehicles which cost $15,000. On 31 August 20X6 MDP sold a motor vehicle which had originally cost $8,000. MDP purchased a new motor vehicle which cost $10,000 on 30 November 20X6.

MDP's policy is to depreciate motor vehicles at the rate of 25 per cent per annum using the straight-line basis, with a proportionate charge in the year of purchase and disposal.

What was the depreciation charge for the year ended 31 December 20X6?

A $3,750

B $3,291

C $4,250

D $3,500

Test your understanding 17

A business entity has an accounting year end of 30 June. A non-current asset was purchased on 1 July 20X3 for $2,400 and depreciated at 20 per cent per annum using the reducing balance method. A full year's charge is made in the year of purchase and none in the year of disposal. On 1 July 20X6 it was sold for $1,200.

Required:

What was the profit or loss on disposal?

A A loss on disposal of $240.00

B A loss on disposal of $28.80

C A profit on disposal of $28.80

D A profit on disposal of $240.00

Test your understanding 18

OLY's machinery cost account had a balance of $5,000 at 1 January 20X6. During the year OLY entered into the following transactions:

28 February – disposed of machine which cost $300 31 March – acquired a machine which cost $1,000

OLY depreciates machines at the rate of 10 per cent per annum using the straight-line method, based upon the number of months' ownership.

Required:

What was the depreciation charge in respect of the machinery for the year ended 31 December 20X6?

A $500

B $550

C $570

D $467

Test your understanding answers

Test your understanding 1

B

The asset has been held for 5 years between from the date of purchase to the revaluation date. Accumulated depreciation is therefore $47,000 ($470,000 / 50 × 5 years). The carrying amount of the asset at the date of revaluation was $423,000 ($470,000 – $47,000). The cost of the asset needs to be increased by $15,000 to $485,000 so that it is now stated at revaluation amount, the accumulated depreciation account balance is eliminated and there is a resulting revaluation surplus included within equity of $62,000 by the following accounting entries:

	$		$
Debit Non-current asset	15,000	Credit Revaluation surplus	62,000
Debit Accumulated depreciation	47,000		

Test your understanding 2

C

The bookkeeping entries related to this example are as follows:

Building at cost/valuation

20X7		$	20X7		$
1 Jan	Balance b/f	900,000	1 Jan	Balance c/f	1,600,000
1 Jan	Revaluation surplus	700,000			
		1,600,000			1,600,000
20X7					
1 Jan	Balance b/f	1,600,000			

Accumulated depreciation – building

20X7		$	20X7		$
1 Jan	Revaluation surplus	108,000	1 Jan	Balance b/f	108,000
		108,000			108,000

Revaluation surplus

20X7		$	20X7		$
31 Dec	Balance c/f	808,000	1 Jan	Building at cost/val'n	700,000
				Accum depn	108,000
		808,000			808,000
			20X8		
			1 Jan	Balance b/f	808,000

The accumulated depreciation at the revaluation date = 6 years, i.e. $900,000 × 2% × 6 = $108,000. This represents the depreciation from the purchase date 20X1 up to and including 20X6. The future depreciation charge for 20X7 will be based on the revalued amount of $1,600,000.

Test your understanding 3

$5.7 million

The carrying amount of the land and buildings at the date of the revaluation was $10.8 million ($15.6m – $4.8m). The revaluation surplus arising is the difference between the revalued amount and the current carrying amount i.e. $5.7 million ($16.5m –$10.8m).

Test your understanding 4

$600 impairment

An asset should be stated at the lower of carrying amount or recoverable amount, where recoverable amount is the higher of either value in use or fair value less costs to sell. Carrying amount = $10,000 ($25,000 – $15,000).

Recoverable amount is the higher of either fair value less costs to sell of $9,400 ($10,200 – $800) or value in use of $9,200 – in this case $9,400.

Finally, compare the carrying amount of $10,000 with the recoverable amount of $9,400. As recoverable amount is less than carrying amount, the asset is impaired by $600 and should be written down to its recoverable amount of $9,400 as follows:

Debit Impairment charge (P/L) $600

Credit Accumulated depreciation and impairment charges (SOFP) $600

Test your understanding 5

Non-current assets at cost

20X1		$	20X4		$
23 Mar	Balance b/f	3,500	18 Jan	Disposal	3,500

Accumulated depreciation

		$	20X1		$
			31 Dec	Statement of profit or loss	825
			20X2		
			31 Dec	Statement of profit or loss	825
20X4			20X3		
18 Jan	Disposals a/c	2,475	31 Dec	Statement of profit or loss	825
		2,475			2,475

Non-current asset disposals

20X4		$	20X4		$
18 Jan	NCA at cost	3,500	18 Jan	Accumulated depreciation	2,475
31 Dec	Profit on disposal	275		Proceeds	1,300
		3,775			3,775

Workings:

$$\frac{\text{Original cost – estimated residual value}}{\text{Estimated useful life}} = \frac{\$3,500 - \$200}{4} = \$825 \text{ pa}$$

The depreciation policy is to charge full depreciation in the year of acquisition (20X1) and nothing in the year of disposal (20X4), hence three years' depreciation has been charged.

Note: The cost account amount of $3,500 and the accumulated depreciation account would be carried forward each year as a balance on the account, until the year of disposal 20X4. This has not been done in this question, simply to make the ledger account look neater for presentation purposes. However, it is important to remember this would be done in practice.

Test your understanding 6

Non-current assets at cost

		$			$
20X2			20X2		
1 Jan	Cash	5,000	31 Dec	Balance c/f	5,000
20X5			20X5		
1 Jan	Balance b/f	5,000	18 Dec	Disposals	5,000
18 Dec	PEA	2,500			
	Cash	6,000	31 Dec	Balance c/f	8,500
		13,500			13,500
20X6					
1 Jan	Balance b/f	8,500			

Accumulated depreciation

		$			$
			20X2		
			13 Dec	Statement of profit or loss	1,000
			20X3		
			31 Dec	Statement of profit or loss	1,000
20X4			20X4		
31 Dec	Balance c/f	3,000	31 Dec	Statement of profit or loss	1,000
		3,000			3,000
20X5			20X5		
18 Dec	Disposals a/c	3,000	1 Jan	Balance b/f	3,000
31 Dec	Balance c/f	1,700	31 Dec	Statement of profit or loss	1,700
		4,700			4,700
			20X6		
			1 Jan	Balance b/f	1,700

Non-current assets disposals

20X5		$	20X5		$
18 Jan	Cash	5,000	18 Dec	Accumulated depreciation	3,000
31 Dec	Profit on disposal	500	18 Dec	PEA	2,500
		5,500			5,500

Workings:

Old compressor depreciation = $5,000 × 20% = $1,000 p.a. The depreciation policy is to charge full depreciation in the year of acquisition (20X2) and nothing in the year of disposal (20X5), hence three years' depreciation has been charged.

New compressor depreciation = $8,500 × 20% = $1,700 p.a. The depreciation policy is to charge full depreciation in the year of acquisition (20X5).

Test your understanding 7

D

Test your understanding 8

D

The non-current asset register balance of $67,460 must be reduced by the carrying amount of the asset disposed, i.e. $5,250 = $62,210. The register represents the carrying amount of all non-current assets owned by the entity.

If the asset was sold for $4,000 which resulted in a loss of $1,250, the asset had a carrying amount of $5,250 at the date of disposal.

Test your understanding 9

The answer is: **$400**

The profit or loss on disposal is the difference between the carrying amount at the time of disposal and the disposal proceeds. An excess of disposal proceeds over carrying amount indicates a profit on disposal, while an excess of carrying amount over disposal proceeds indicates a loss on disposal.

The annual depreciation on the machine is calculated as:

$$\frac{\text{Cost} - \text{residual value}}{\text{Useful life}} = \frac{5{,}000 - 1{,}000}{4 \text{ years}} = 1{,}000 \text{ per year}$$

Depreciation by 31 December 20X3 would be 3 × $1,000 = $3,000, therefore the carrying amount of the machine at the date of disposal would be $2,000. Disposal proceeds were $1,600; therefore there was a loss on disposal of $400.

Test your understanding 10

A

The difference between the two records is $10,000. Therefore the disposed asset must have had a carrying amount or value of this amount. B and D are clearly wrong, and C would produce a carrying amount or value of $20,000.

Test your understanding 11

	$	
$9,000 × 0.7 × 0.7 × 0.7 =	3,087	(carrying amount or value)
Proceeds of sale	(3,000)	
Loss on disposal	87	

Test your understanding 12

	$	
$5,000 × 0.8 × 0.8 × 0.8 =	2,560	(carrying amount or value)
Receipt	(2,200)	
Loss on disposal	360	

Note that, when the reducing balance method of calculating depreciation is used, the relevant percentage is applied to the initial cost of the non-current asset.

Test your understanding 13

	$
Cost	10,000
20X0 Depreciation	(2,500)
	7,500
20X1 Depreciation	(1,875)
	5,625
20X2 Depreciation	(1,406)
	4,219
20X3 Part-exchange	(5,000)
Profit	781

Test your understanding 14

	$	$
Carrying amount at 1 August 20X0		200,000
Less: Depreciation		(20,000)
Non-current assets disposed of – proceeds	25,000	
Loss on disposal	5,000	
Therefore carrying amount of non-current assets disposed of		(30,000)
Carrying amount at 31 July 20X1		150,000

Test your understanding 15

	$
Cost	12,000
20X0 Depreciation	(2,400)
	9,600
20X1 Depreciation	(2,400)
	7,200
20X2 Depreciation	(2,400)
	4,800
20X3 Part-exchange	(5,000)
Profit	200

Test your understanding 16

B

Cost $15,000 1 January 20X6 to 31 August 20X6 = 8 months

Cost $15,000 – $8,000 = $7,000 1 September to 31 December 20X6 = 4 months

Addition $10,000 1 December 20X6 to 31 December 20X6 = 1 month

Depreciation charge =

$15,000 × 25% × 8/12 = $2,500

$7,000 × 25% × 4/12 = $583

$10,000 × 25% × 1/12 = $208

Total depreciation charge for the year = $3,291

Test your understanding 17

B

	$
Cost	2,400.00
Year end 30 June 20X4 – depreciation 20%	(480.00)
	1,920.00
Year end 30 June 20X5 – depreciation 20%	(384.00)
	1,536.00
Year end 30 June 20X6 – depreciation 20%	(307.20)
Carrying amount at disposal date – 1 July 20X6	1,228.80
Disposal proceeds	(1,200.00)
Loss on disposal	28.80

Test your understanding 18

B

Cost $5,000 1 January 20X6 to 28 February 20X6 = 2 months

Cost $5,000 – $300 = $4,700 1 March to 31 December 20X6 = 10 months

Addition $1,000 1 April 20X6 to 31 December 20X6 = 9 months

Depreciation charge =

$5,000 × 10% × 2/12 = $83

$4,700 × 10% × 10/12 = $392

$1,000 × 10% × 9/12 = $75

Total depreciation charge for the year = $550

Chapter

13

Accounting reconciliations

Chapter learning objectives

When you have completed this chapter, you should be able to:

- prepare bank reconciliation statements
- prepare petty cash statements under an imprest system
- prepare sales and purchase ledger control account reconciliations.

1 Introduction

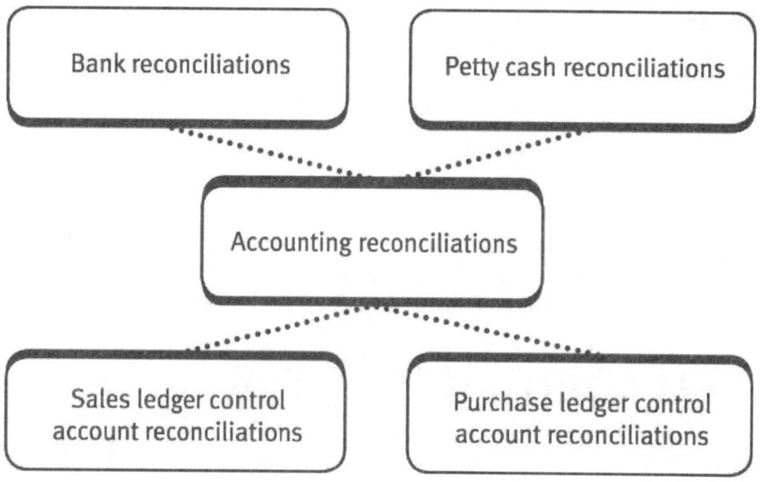

In this chapter you will learn:

- to prepare bank reconciliation statements
- to prepare petty cash statements under an imprest system
- to prepare sales and purchase ledger control account reconciliations.

No bookkeeping system can be guaranteed to be entirely free of errors. Human beings are fallible, and even automated and computerised systems are less than perfect. For example, a computer cannot possibly know that a supplier has sent you an invoice that you haven't received, perhaps because it was lost in the post, or that it contains incorrect information.

In this chapter we consider a number of ways in which the bookkeeping system can be checked for reliability, and ways in which errors and omissions can be rectified.

2 The need for financial controls

Financial controls are needed to:

- **Provide a check on the accuracy** of entries made in the ledgers. It is very easy to make a mistake posting entries, i.e. errors of omission, duplication, principle etc. (refer to previous chapters). The control accounts check the accuracy of the postings made in both the personal accounts (sales and purchase ledger) and the nominal ledger. As a point of reference, a personal account is the account of an individual receivable or payable. The sales and purchase ledgers comprise all individual receivables' and payables' personal accounts respectively, each of which can be totalled to identify the total amount due to the entity from credit customers, or the total amount owed to credit suppliers.

  The bank reconciliation checks the accuracy of the bank's records and the cashbook maintained by the entity and may highlight receipts and payments that have been missed, e.g. bank charges and direct debits.

- **Reduce the risk of fraud or error in the accounting records** – by having people performing different duties we reduce the risk of fraud or error, e.g. one person does not record all entries relating to a single transaction from start to finish. The purchases ledger would be maintained by one person and then the nominal ledger by another. This prevents someone creating a fictitious expense and payables account to enable them to make a payment in order to obtain cash from the business dishonestly.

Other means by which errors or omissions may be prevented (or identified if they occur) include the performance of an audit and understanding the different types of fraud or error that may occur. The role of internal and external audit, along with the nature of error and fraud, are considered in detail in Subject BA4 Fundamentals of Ethics, Corporate Governance and Business Law.

Reconciliations

A reconciliation is a comparison of records to identify differences and to effect agreement. There are several types of reconciliation that can be carried out.

- Reconciling the accounts of the entity with records received from other entities. Common reconciliations of this type are:
  - bank reconciliations, where the bank account maintained by the entity is reconciled with the statement issued by the bank
  - use of the petty cash imprest system to account for petty cash transactions and balances
  - supplier reconciliations, where the ledger account maintained by the entity is reconciled with a statement of the ledger account in the supplier's books.
- Reconciling groups of ledger account balances with a control account. Control accounts are considered in more detail later in this chapter.

Each of these reconciliations is considered in more detail and demonstrated in this chapter.

3 Bank reconciliation statements

This is an essential 'must know' topic.

Before we progress on to dealing with how transactions are recorded in the cash book, it may be helpful to consider the banking system and the different types of transaction that may pass through a bank account.

The banking system

Today's banking system is highly automated, with large numbers of transactions conducted electronically. Although many entities use automated or direct payments, many entities still use cheques to make payments, and paying-in slips to make deposits into their bank accounts.

Some common methods of transacting business through a bank account are as follows:

- **By cheque** – The **drawer** makes out a cheque to the person being paid (the **payee**). The cheque is entered in the drawer's ledger accounts at once, and sent to the payee. The payee pays it into their own bank account some days later, using a paying-in slip to record its details and that of other cheques paid in at the same time. The bank clearing system passes it to the drawer's bank for approval and payment, with the result that it is taken out of the drawer's bank account. This is known as **presenting a** cheque for payment. Until the cheque is accepted by the drawer's bank, it is considered to be **uncleared** and the bank has the right to return it as **dishonoured** if there is something amiss with it, or there are insufficient funds in the drawer's account. The time delay between making out a cheque and it being cleared depends on various factors, such as postal delays, administrative delays, holiday periods and so on. Each cheque has a reference or serial number by which it can be identified.
- **By the bank automated clearing system (BACS)** – This avoids use of the postal system and the writing of numerous cheques by creating a transfer between the bank accounts of different entities. It is a faster means of payment and it is also more cost-effective when there are regular payments to the same people. The account holder produces a list of the payments to be made at any particular time. There are also specialised types of automated payments suitable for the immediate transfer of funds both within a country and on an international basis.
- **By direct debit or standing order** – These work in a similar manner to each other, and are suitable for regular payments to a particular person. The bank makes the transfer automatically.
- **By bank-initiated transactions** – This will include transactions such as charging fees for maintaining or operating a bank account (bank charges), interest paid on overdrawn balances, interest received, charges for dealing with dishonoured cheques and so on.

An entity may both make and receive payments by any of these methods.

The purpose of a bank reconciliation

The purpose of a bank reconciliation statement is to check the accuracy of an entity's bank account record by comparing it with the record of the account held by the bank.

When dealing with the preparation of cash and bank account records we saw that there is often a timing delay between the transaction occurring (and therefore being recorded in the cash book) and being processed by the bank. This is often the case with cheques issued to pay credit suppliers – it may take a day or two in the post to arrive at the supplier's premises, and then another few days for the cheque to be presented and cleared by the banking system. It is this timing difference that is usually the cause of any difference between the two balances.

However, there are some transactions of which the entity will not be aware until they receive their bank statement. These include bank charges, commissions and dishonoured cheques (where the drawer's bank has refused to honour the cheque drawn upon it), and may also include direct debit and standing order transactions if the account holder has not been separately notified of them.

In order to ensure that both the bank and the entity accounting records are correct, a comparison is made of the two sets of records and a reconciliation statement produced.

Note debits and credits are reversed on the bank statement because it is recorded from the bank's point of view. If you have money in a bank account, the bank owes that money to you. In effect, from the bank's perspective, you are a creditor and they must repay that money to you when you request payment. Many banks now apply user-friendly terms such as 'receipts' and 'payments' or 'money in' and 'money out' which are easier for most people to understand.

Differences between the bank statement and the cash book

When attempting to reconcile the bank statement with the cash book, there are three differences between the cash book and bank statement:

- unrecorded items
- timing differences
- errors

Further details

Unrecorded items

These are items included in the bank statement but not in the cash book. This could be due to the fact the entity has forgotten to include them or they were not aware of them until the bank statement was received. These include:

- bank charges and interest paid
- direct debits
- standing orders
- receipts direct into the bank account
- interest received
- dishonoured cheques.

These items must now be recorded in the cash book to bring it up to date.

Timing differences

These items have been recorded in the cash book, but due to the bank clearing process have not yet been recorded on the bank statement:

- outstanding/unpresented cheques – cheques sent to suppliers but not yet cleared by the bank
- outstanding/uncleared deposits – cheques received by the entity by not yet cleared by the bank.

The bank statement needs to be adjusted for these items as follows:

	$
Balance as per bank statement	X
Less: unpresented cheques	(X)
Plus: uncleared deposits	X
Balance as per revised cash book	X

Errors

Errors can be found in either the cash book or the bank statement but must be adjusted appropriately.

Authorising bank payments

All payments out of the bank account should be authorised by a senior member of staff. Two signatories may be required for amounts above a specified value, e.g. $50, although any limit set will depend upon individual business needs and circumstances.

All items to be paid should be evidenced by source documents, such as receipts or invoices that have been approved for payment.

The steps taken to perform a bank reconciliation are as follows:

Step 1 – Tick off all items in **both** the cash book and the bank statement.

Step 2 – Update the cash book for unticked items in the bank statement to bring the cash book up to date.

Step 3 – Prepare the bank reconciliation with the remaining unticked items in the cash book.

Note on the presentation of bank statements – there is no standard method of presenting bank statements. Some bank statements will use 'debit'/'credit' headings which are presented from the perspective of the bank. Other bank statements may use different wording, such as 'money in'/'money out', to present the same information.

Worked Example 13.A

The following is an extract from the cash book of ABX for the month of June:

	$		$
Balance b/f	9,167	Purchase ledger	1,392
Sales ledger	4,023	Rent payable	2,613
Cash sales	2,194	Interest payable	981
Sales ledger	7,249	Cheques cashed	3,290
		Balance c/f	14,357
	22,633		22,633

ABX's bank statement for the same period was as follows:

	Money out	Money in	Balance
	$	$	$
Opening balance			7,645
Deposit 000212		2,491	10,136
Cheque 000148	969		9,167
Insurance D/D	2,413		6,754
Deposit 000213		4,023	10,777
Cheque 000149	1,392		9,385
Cheque 000150	2,613		6,772
Cheque 000152	3,290		3,482
Deposit 000214		2,194	5,676
Bank charges	563		5,113

Required:

Reconcile the balances in the cash book and the bank statement at the end of the month.

Solution:

Step 1 – compare the entries shown in the cash book with those on the bank statement and match them. This is shown below where letters have been used to match the items together

	$		$
Balance b/f	9,167	Purchase ledger (c)	1,392
Sales ledger (a)	4,023	Rent payable (d)	2,613
Cash sales (b)	2,194	Interest payable	981
Sales ledger	7,249	Cheques cashed (e)	3,290
		Balance c/f	14,357
	22,633		22,633

ABX's bank statement for the same period was as follows:

	Money out	Money in	Balance
	$	$	$
Opening balance			7,645
Deposit 000212		2,491	10,136
Cheque 000148	969		9,167
Insurance D/D	2,413		6,754
Deposit 000213		4,023 (a)	10,777
Cheque 000149	1,392 (c)		9,385
Cheque 000150	2,613 (d)		6,772
Cheque 000152	3,290 (e)		3,482
Deposit 000214		2,194 (b)	5,676
Bank charges	563		5,113

When the matching is complete there will usually be items on the bank statement that are not included in the cash book, and items entered in the cash book that are not included on the bank statement.

Some of these may relate to the previous period – in this example the opening balances were not the same. There is a deposit (reference 000212) and a cheque (number 000148) that are not in the cash book for June. A simple calculation shows that these items represent the difference between the opening balances in the cash book and bank statement at 1 June. These are, therefore, timing differences that do not affect the bank reconciliation at 30 June.

Step 2 – There are some items on the bank statement that have not yet been entered in the cash book. These are the direct debit for insurance and the bank charges. The cash book balance needs to be updated and amended for these items:

	$	$
Balance as shown in cash book		14,357
Less:		
Insurance	2,413	
Bank charges	563	
		(2,976)
Amended cash book balance		11,381

Step 3 – The remaining differences between the amended cash book balance and the bank statement balance are caused by timing differences on those items not matched above:

	$
Balance as per bank statement	5,113
Add: Uncleared deposit	7,249
	12,362
Less: Unpresented cheque	(981)
Balance as per cash book	11,381

You should note that this statement commenced with the balance as per the bank statement and reconciled it to the balance shown in the cash book.

Remember that the **revised** cash book figure is always the bank figure used in the statement of financial position.

Illustration 1

You have been presented with the following information relating to an entity:

	$
Balance as per cash book	1,245
Unpresented cheques	890
Bank charges not entered in cash book	100
Receipts not yet credited by bank	465
Dishonoured cheque not entered in cash book	170
Balance as per bank statement	1,400

Required:

Prepare a statement that shows any necessary corrections to the cash book balance and a statement that reconciles the bank statement balance with the corrected cash book balance.

Solution:

	$
Original cash book balances	1,245
Less: Amounts not yet entered in the cash book	
Bank charges	(100)
Dishonoured cheque	(170)
Corrected cash book balance	975
Balance per bank statement	1,400
Add: Outstanding deposits	465
Less: Unpresented cheques	(890)
Balance as per corrected cash book	975

Test your understanding 1

Cash book (bank columns only)

		$			$
1 Jan	Balance	600	18 Jan	D Anderson	145
13 Jan	Umberto	224	28 Jan	R Patrick	72
13 Jan	L Bond	186	30 Jan	Parveen	109

		Debit $	Credit $	Balance ($)
1 Jan	Balance			635
3 Jan	H Turner	35		600
13 Jan	Umberto		224	824
23 Jan	D Anderson	145		679
31 Jan	Standing order	30		649

Required:

Using the information provided:

(a) prepare a corrected cash book

(b) prepare a bank reconciliation statement.

4 Petty cash reconciliation under imprest system

Previous chapters of this publication dealt with the books of prime entry, including the petty cash book. Like the cash book, it should be subject to regular reconciliation with the underlying receipts, vouchers and remaining cash balance.

Normally, petty cash is controlled by an imprest system, whereby there is a predetermined cash float which is periodically reimbursed from the main bank account. It is then possible to reconcile the imprest amount with the balance of cash held plus receipts and vouchers supporting petty cash payments. Just as the cash payments book may include a column for sales tax paid on purchases made, the petty cash book may also have a similar column as part of the analysis of payments made.

Petty Cash

Controls over petty cash

As petty cash consists of notes and coins, it is important that it is safeguarded from loss or theft. This usually involves only authorised person(s) having access to the petty cash float and only authorised person(s) being able to authorise such payments.

The following controls and security over petty cash would normally be applied in most business entities:

- The petty cash float must be kept in a secure petty cash box.
- The petty cash box must be secured in a safe when not required.
- The person(s) responsible for petty cash must be reliable and understand their responsibilities.
- All petty cash expenditure must be supported by invoices or receipts.
- Petty cash vouchers must be signed by the claimant and the person authorising the payment or reimbursement of expense.
- Regular spot checks must be carried out to ensure that the petty cash float and supporting records are accurate.

Petty cash book

In this book the business entity will record (usually) small cash transactions. The cash receipts will be recorded together with the payments which will be analysed in the same way as a cash book.

An imprest system will be adopted for the petty cash book. An amount is withdrawn from the bank account which is referred to as a ‘petty cash float’. This ‘float’ will be used to pay for the various sundry expenses. The petty cash book cashier will record any payments.

> Any expenditure must be evidenced by an expense receipt and the petty cashier will attach a petty cash voucher to each expense.
>
> At any point in time the cash together with the expense vouchers should agree to the total float. At the end of the period the petty cash float is 'topped up' by withdrawing an amount from the bank totalling the petty cash payment made during the period.

Worked Example 13.B

Beechfield makes use of a petty cash book as part of their bookkeeping system. The following is a summary of the petty cash transactions for the month of November 20X9.

		$
1 Nov	Opening petty cash book float received from cashier	350
2 Nov	Cleaning materials	5
3 Nov	Postage stamps	10
6 Nov	Envelopes	12
8 Nov	Taxi fare	32
10 Nov	Petrol for delivery van	17
14 Nov	Typing paper	25
15 Nov	Cleaning materials	4
16 Nov	Bus fare	2
20 Nov	Visitors' lunches	56
21 Nov	Mops and brushes for cleaning	41
23 Nov	Postage stamps	35
27 Nov	Envelopes	12
29 Nov	Visitors' lunches	30
30 Nov	Photocopying paper	40

Required:

Prepare a petty cash book for the month using analysis columns for stationery, cleaning, entertainment, travel and postage. Show clearly the receipt of the amount necessary to restore the float and the balance brought forward for the start of the following month.

Solution

Debit ($)	Date	Details	Total ($)	Stat'y ($)	Cleaning ($)	Ent'ment ($)	Travel ($)	Post ($)
350	1 Nov	Cashier						
	2 Nov	Materials	5		5			
	3 Nov	Stamps	10					10
	6 Nov	Envelopes	12	12				
	8 Nov	Taxi	32				32	
	10 Nov	Petrol	17				17	
	14 Nov	Paper	25	25				
	15 Nov	Materials	4		4			
	16 Nov	Bus fare	2				2	
	20 Nov	Lunches	56			56		
	21 Nov	Mops, etc.	41		41			
	23 Nov	Stamps	35					35
	27 Nov	Envelopes	12	12				
	29 Nov	Lunches	30			30		
	30 Nov	Paper	40	40				
321	30 Nov	Cashier						
	30 Nov	Balance c/d	350					
671			671	89	50	86	51	45

The totals of the various expense columns are then debited to those accounts in the nominal ledger.

The accounting entries will be to **debit the analysed expense accounts and credit bank**.

The amount reimbursed is equal to the amount paid from the petty cash, i.e. $321. This will be taken from the bank account into petty cash.

Test your understanding 2

Explain briefly the operation of the imprest system of controlling petty cash

Test your understanding 3

The petty cash imprest is restored to $100 at the end of each week. The following amounts were paid out of petty cash during the week:

Stationery	$14.10
Travel costs	$25.50
Office refreshments	$12.90
Sundry payables	$28.80

Required:

What is the amount required to restore the imprest to $100?

$.......81.30.....

Test your understanding 4

The petty cash imprest is restored to $80 at the end of each week. The following amounts were paid out of petty cash during the week:

Office stationery	$11.04
Local train fares to attend meetings	$13.70
Office cleaning materials	$25.50
Office refreshments	$24.00

Required:

What is the amount required to restore the imprest to $80?

$......................

Reconciliation of suppliers' statements

Many suppliers send monthly statements to their customers, showing the position of that customers account in their own records, and this provides an ideal opportunity to check the accuracy of the entity's records with those of another. A reconciliation of payable balances to supplier statements is no different in principle from performing a bank reconciliation as shown below.

Example

Included in the payables ledger of JCO, is the following account that disclosed the amount owing to one of its suppliers, NAL, at 31 May 20X4 as $472.13.

Payables ledger – NAL

20X4		$	20X4		$
18 May	Purchase returns	36.67	1 May	Balance b/f	862.07
27 May	Purchase returns	18.15	16 May	Purchases	439.85
27 May	Adjustment (overcharge)	5.80	25 May	Purchases	464.45
31 May	Discount received	24.94	25 May	Adjustment (undercharge)	13.48
31 May	Bank	1,222.16			
31 May	Balance c/f	472.13			
		1,779.85			1,779.85

NAL has sent a statement to JCO which identifies the transactions that have occurred between the two entities and the balance due from JCO at 31 May 20X4 as follows

JCO in account with NAL – Statement of account

20X4		**Debit $**	**Credit $**	**Balance $**
1 May	BCE			1,538.70 Dr
3 May	DISC		13.40	1,525.30 Dr
	CHQ		634.11	891.19 Dr
5 May	ALLCE		29.12	862.07 Dr
7 May	GDS	256.72		1,118.79 Dr
10 May	GDS	108.33		1,227.12 Dr
11 MAY	GDS	74.80		1,301.92 Dr
14 May	ADJ	13.48		1,315.40 Dr
18 May	GDS	162.55		1,477.95 Dr
23 May	GDS	301.90		1,779.85 Dr
25 May	ALLCE		36.67	1,743.18 Dr
28 May	GDS	134.07		1,877.25 Dr
29 May	GDS	251.12		2,128.37 Dr
30 May	GDS	204.80		2,333.17 Dr
31 May	GDS	91.36		2,424.53 Dr
31 May	BCE			2,424.53 Dr

Abbreviations: BCE – balance; CHQ – cheque; GDS – goods; ALLCE – allowance; DISC – discount; ADJ – adjustment.

Note the balance outstanding on the statement prepared by NAL is a debit balance. This reflects the situation that NAL is owed $2,424.53 by JCO as at 31 May 20X4

Required:

Prepare a statement reconciling the closing balance on the supplier's account in JCO's payables ledger with the closing balance shown on the statement of account submitted by the supplier (NAL).

Solution:

As we saw with bank reconciliation statements the technique is to match the items first and then construct a reconciliation statement

Payables ledger – NAL

20X4		$	20X4		$
18 May	Purchase Returns (a)	36.67	1 May	Balance b/f	862.07
27 May	Purchase Returns (r)	18.15	16 May	Purchases (b)	439.85
27 May	Adjustment (overcharge) (t)	5.80	25 May	Purchases (c)	464.45
31 May	Discount Received (s)	24.94	25 May	Adjustment (undercharge)	13.48
31 May	Bank (s)	1,222.16			
31 May	Balance c/f	472.13			
		1,779.85			1,779.85

JCO in account with NAL – Statement of Account

20X4		Debit $	Credit $	Balance $
1 May	BCE			1,538.70 Dr
3 May	DISC		13.40 (q)	1,525.30 Dr
	CHQ		634.11 (p)	891.19 Dr
5 May	ALLCE		29.12 (p)	862.07 Dr
7 May	GDS	256.72 (b)		118.79 Dr
10 May	GDS	108.33 (b)		1,227.12 Dr
11 MAY	GDS	74.80 (b)		1,301.92 Dr
14 May	ADJ	13.48 (d)		1,315.40 Dr
18 May	GDS	162.55 (c)		1,477.95 Dr
23 May	GDS	301.90 (c)		1,779.85 Dr
25 May	ALLCE		36.67 (a)	1,743.18 Dr
28 May	GDS	134.07 (q)		1,877.25 Dr
29 May	GDS	251.12 (q)		2,128.37 Dr
30 May	GDS	204.80 (q)		2,333.17 Dr
31 May	GDS	91.36 (q)		2,424.53 Dr
31 May	BCE			2,424.53 Dr

The items marked 'p' reconcile the opening balances.

Reconciliation statement

	$	$
Account balances per JCO payables ledger		472.13
Add:		
Goods despatched by supplier not entered in ledger (q)	681.35	
Returns not yet recognised by supplier (r)	18.15	
Payments/discounts not yet recognised by supplier (s)	1,247.10	
Adjustment not yet recognised by supplier (t)	5.80	
		1,952.40
Balance as per supplier statement from NAL		2,424.53

Test your understanding 5

A supplier sends you a statement showing a balance outstanding of $14,350. Your own records show a balance outstanding of $14,500.

The reason for this difference could be that:

A the supplier sent an invoice for $150 that you have not yet received

B the supplier has allowed you discount of $150 that you have not yet entered in your records

C you have paid the supplier $150 that he has not yet accounted for

D You have returned goods which cost $150 that the supplier has not yet accounted for

5 Control accounts

Control accounts are an essential 'must know' topic.

- Control accounts are nominal ledger accounts that summarise a large number of transactions. As such, they are part of the double entry system.
- They are used to prove the accuracy of the ledger accounting system.
- They are mainly used with regard to receivables – **sales ledger control account** and payables – **purchases ledger control account.**

It is essential that routinely there are reconciliations to ensure that the sales ledger control account and the purchase ledger control account match back not only to the relevant statements, but also to the memorandum accounts. This is known as a control account reconciliation.

We will now look at each of the control accounts in turn.

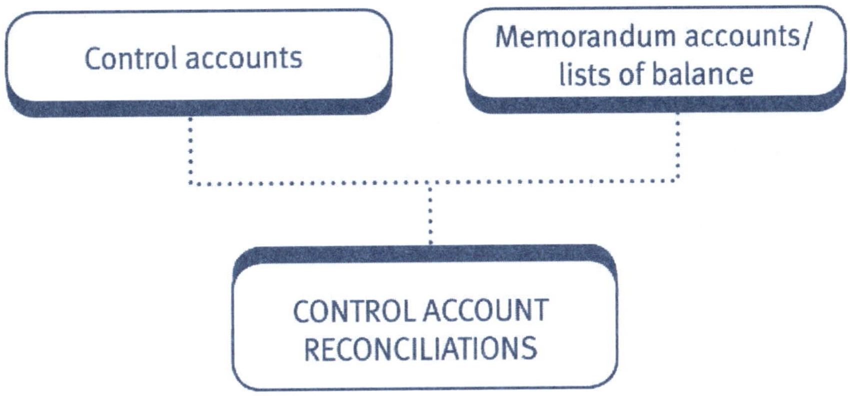

The sales ledger control account (receivables) may include any of the following entries:

Sales ledger control account

20X1		$	20X1		$
1 Jan	Balance b/f	X	31 Jan	Sales returns daybook	X
31 Jan	Sales daybook	X	31 Jan	Cash book receipts	X
31 Jan	Dishonoured cheque	X	31 Jan	Irrecoverable debts	X
			31 Jan	Contra entry	X
			31 Jan	Balance c/f	X
		X			X
1 Feb	Balance b/f	X			

Note that, for completeness, this proforma control account includes reference to irrecoverable debts. An irrecoverable debt is an amount outstanding from a credit customer that the entity does not expect to recover. It is explained and illustrated in more detail in the chapter dealing with irrecoverable debts and allowances for receivables.

Note also that the control account refers to contra entries. A contra entry is an agreed amount set-off between the sales ledger control account and the purchases ledger control account. It may occur when one entity and another both buy and sell to each other on credit, and they offset an agreed amount due between them, rather than both entities sending payment to each other. This will reduce the balance outstanding on both the sales ledger control account and the purchases ledger control account (see below). The amount of any contra agreed with another entity should also be recorded in the personal accounts maintained in the sales ledger and purchases ledger respectively.

The purchases ledger control account (payables) may include any of the following entries:

Purchase ledger control account

20X1		$	20X1		$
1 Jan	Cash book paid	X	1 Jan	Balance b/f	X
31 Jan	Discount received	X	31 Jan	Purchase daybook	X
31 Jan	Contra entry	X			
31 Jan	Purchase returns daybook	X			
31 Jan	Balance c/f	X			
		X			X
		X	1 Feb	Balance b/f	X

Worked Example 13.C

An entity had four receivables, with the following balances at 1 January 20X1:

	$
Khan	437
P Binns	1,046
J Harris	93
C Bloggs	294
Total	1,870

The sales daybook for January was as follows:

Sales daybook

Date	**Customer**	**Total $**
20X1		
10 Jan	J Harris	235
17 Jan	P Binns	470
23 Jan	Khan	705
		1,410

The sales returns daybook for January was as follows:

Sales returns daybook

Date	**Customer**	**Total $**
20X1		
12 Jan	J Harris	94
23 Jan	P Binns	141
		235

The cash book (debit side) for the same month included the following entries:

Received from receivables

Date	Details	Total $
20X1		
14 Jan	C Bloggs	130
18 Jan	P Binns	600
		730

Required:

Write up the personal accounts in the sales ledger and the control account, and reconcile the control account to the total of the sales ledger balances.

Solution:

Sales ledger accounts (personal accounts) – memorandum accounts

Khan

20X1		$	20X1		$
1 Jan	Balance b/f	437			
23 Jan	Invoice	705	31 Jan	Balance c/f	1,142
		1,142			1,142
1 Feb	Balance b/f	1,142			

P Binns

20X1		$	20X1		$
1 Jan	Balance b/f	1,046	16 Jan	Cash	600
17 Jan	Invoice	470	23 Jan	Sales returns	141
			31 Jan	Balance c/f	775
		1,516			1,516
1 Feb	Balance b/f	775			

J Harris

20X1		$	20X1		$
1 Jan	Balance b/f	93	12 Jan	Sales return	94
10 Jan	Invoice	235	31 Jan	Balance c/f	234
		328			328
1 Feb	Balance b/f	234			

C Bloggs

20X1		$	20X1		$
1 Jan	Balance b/f	294	14 Jan	Cash	130
			31 Jan	Balance c/f	164
		294			294
1 Feb	Balance b/f	164			

A list of receivables' balances extracted at 31 January 20X1 was as follows:

	$
Khan	1,142
P Binns	775
J Harris	234
C Bloggs	164
Total	2,315

The sales ledger control account can be compiled from the total of the entries made to the individual receivables accounts, using the totals in the various books of prime entry, as follows:

Sales ledger control account

20X1		$	20X1		$
1 Jan	Balance b/f	1,870	31 Jan	Sales returns daybook	235
31 Jan	Sales daybook	1,410	31 Jan	Cash book Received	730
			31 Jan	Balance c/f	2,315
		3,280			3,280
1 Feb	Balance b/f	2,315			

The individual postings to the sales ledger should exactly equal the total postings made to the nominal ledger. It follows that if we add up the balances on all the personal accounts in the sales ledger we should reach a total that exactly equals the balance on the receivables control account in the nominal ledger. The same applies in the case of the purchase ledger. By performing this exercise at regular intervals we are, in effect, checking that postings to the ledgers are accurate. The exercise is sometimes regarded as performing a 'trial balance' on the ledgers.

The status of the control account

The status of a control account is not an easy concept to grasp. Particular care should be taken to ensure that you understand this issue as it is the basis of many computer-based assessment questions.

So far, we have considered that the double-entry is completed by entering each transaction in the receivables personal accounts in the sales ledger, and entering the totals of sales, returns, sales tax and cash received in the nominal ledger. Now that we have introduced a control account, it might appear that we are duplicating the entries in the sales ledger. Obviously, this cannot happen, as the ledger accounts will be out of balance. We cannot have **both** the receivables accounts and the control account as part of the double-entry system. Therefore, either one or the other of these must be treated as being outside the double-entry system. The records that are outside the double-entry system are known as **memorandum accounts.**

In computerised systems, it is common for the sales ledger to be a separate component of the bookkeeping system, and for the control account to exist in the nominal ledger. Note that it is acceptable to regard the control account as a memorandum account, with the sales ledger balances part of the double-entry system.

e.g

Illustration 2

Briefly explain the meaning of each of the entries in the following receivables account:

P Richmond

		$			$
1 Jan	Balance b/f	465	13 Jan	Cheque	465
6 Jan	Sales	240			
8 Jan	Sales	360	17 Jan	Returns	40
			31 Jan	Balance c/f	560
		1,065			1,065
1 Feb	Balance b/f	560			

Solution:

- 1 January: balance. P Richmond owes this amount at 1 January.
- 6/8 January: sales. P Richmond has been sold goods and services to those values on credit.
- 13 January: cheque. P Richmond has paid $465 by cheque to clear an amount of $465. It is likely that this was in payment of the opening balance on 1 January.
- 17 January: P Richmond has returned goods and been allocated a credit of $40 to be offset against the amount owing.
- 31 January: balance $560. P Richmond owes this amount at 31 January

Worked Example 13.D

You obtain the following information for the year ended 30 November 20X8 from the books of original entry of an entity:

Cash book

	$
Cash and cheques from customers	294,406
Discounts received	3,415
Cash and cheques paid to suppliers	233,078
Customer's cheque dishonoured	251

The following totals have been extracted from the daybooks for the year:

According to the audited financial statements for the previous year, receivables and payables as at 30 November 20X7 were $44,040 and $63,289, respectively.

	$
Purchases daybook	247,084
Sales daybook	306,580
Sales returns daybook	6,508
Purchases returns daybook	4,720

Required:

Prepare the relevant control accounts for the year ended 30 November 20X8, entering the closing balances for receivables and payables.

Solution:

Sales ledger control account

	$		$
Balance b/f	44,040	Cash and cheques	294,406
Sales	306,580	Sales returns	6,508
Cheque dishonoured	251	Balance c/f	49,957
	350,871		350,871

Purchase ledger control account

	$		$
Discounts received	3,415	Balance b/f	63,289
Cash and cheques	233,078	Purchases	247,084
Purchases returns	4,720		
Balance c/f	69,160		
	310,373		310,373

The entries in the control accounts reflect respectively the effect of the transactions on the value of receivables (sales ledger control account) and payables (purchase ledger control account).

In the sales ledger control account the debit entries are those transactions that cause the asset of receivables to increase, whereas decreases are recorded on the credit side of the control account.

In the purchase ledger control account the debit entries are those transactions that cause the liability of payables to decrease, whereas increases are recorded on the credit side of the control account.

It may also help to review the following summary to refresh your memory:

Debit	**Credit**
Increases in assets	Decreases in assets
Decreases in liabilities	Increases in liabilities

Note that the transactions are entered individually in the personal accounts of the customers and the totals in the control account.

You should also note that every entry in the personal accounts should also be included in the control account and vice versa – if the control account balance agrees with the total of the individual account balances it is highly likely that the double-entry has been posted correctly. Note, however, that if a transaction is posted to the wrong personal account this will not be found by the reconciliation of the control account balance.

Illustration 3

You have been presented with the following information relating to an entity:

	$
Opening receivables	23,750
Closing receivables	22,400
Cash sales	14,000
Receipts from receivables	219,500
Irrecoverable debts written off	2,250
Dishonoured cheques	2,500

Required:

Ascertain the value of credit sales from the available information:

Sales ledger control account

	$		$
Opening receivables	23,750	Receipts	219,500
Sales	**?**		
Dishonoured cheques	2,500	Irrecoverable debts w/off	2,250
		Closing receivables	22,400
	244,150		244,150

The sales figure is the only unknown value in the sales ledger control account. It can be calculated as a balancing figure, that is $244,150 – $23,750 – $2,500 = $217,900.

Note: cash sales are not relevant to the sales ledger control account.

Contra entries

When one entity is both a supplier and a customer of another entity it is common for an agreement to be made to set off the sums receivable and payable, and for a single payment to be sent between the parties to settle the net balance. The entry to record the setting off of the balances is known as a contra entry.

Worked Example 13.E

The following accounts are taken from the accounting records of ZR:

Sales ledger

AP

	$		$
Balance b/f	1,815		

Purchase ledger

AP

	$		$
		Balance b/f	792

Required:

Account for a contra entry between the sales and purchase ledger accounts of AP in the books of ZR so that the smaller account balance is cleared.

Solution:

The balance of $792 in the purchases ledger is set off against the sales ledger balance using a contra entry:

Sales ledger

AP

	$		$
Balance b/f	1,815	Purchases ledger (contra)	792

Purchases ledger

AP

	$		$
Purchase ledger (contra)	792	Balance b/f	792

AP would send a cheque to ZR for $1,023 to clear its sales ledger balance.

The same entries must be made in the control accounts: that is, debit the purchase ledger control account with $792, and credit the sales ledger control account with $792. Note that it is always the smaller of the two balances that is transferred, but the entries of 'debit purchase ledger' and 'credit sales ledger' always occur.

The contra would also be entered in the journal (as it is book of prime entry), but remember that the journal is not part of the double-entry system.

Credit balances in the sales ledger; debit balances in the purchase ledger

Normally, sales ledger accounts have debit balances, and purchase ledger accounts have credit balances. But it can happen that the reverse occurs. For example, a receivable may have paid his invoice, and then returns some goods that are faulty. The accounting entries for the returned items would be to debit returns inwards and credit the receivable – which means that he acquires a credit balance. The same might occur with a supplier, whereby you have paid his invoice and later returned goods. Strictly speaking, receivables with credit balances are payables (and similarly, payables with debit balances would be regarded as receivables) but it is not normal to move them from one ledger to the other.

Thus it is possible to have credit balances in the sales ledger and debit balances in the purchase ledger. Very often, these balances are eliminated when the customer orders more goods, or we order goods from the supplier. But sometimes it happens that there will be no further transactions, and a refund will be required. With receivables, the entries are to debit the receivable and credit bank, and with payables the entries are to credit the payable and debit bank.

Test your understanding 6

You have extracted the following information from the accounting records of a business entity:

	$
Opening balances	Debit 14,500, credit 125
Sales on credit	27,500
Sales returns	850
Cash sales	420
Cheques received from receivables	20,280
Dishonoured cheques	750
Contras to the purchases ledger	340
Refunds to credit customers	125

Required:

Compile a sales ledger control account from the available information to determine the closing balance on the control account.

The control account and allowance for receivables

An allowance for receivables is made when it is considered that not all of the credit customers may honour their debts in full. This differs from an irrecoverable debt where there is evidence that the amount due will not be collected. Calculation of, and accounting for, the allowance for receivables is dealt with in a separate chapter dealing with accounting for irrecoverable debts and allowances for receivables.

In the context of preparing a sales ledger control account reconciliation, the important point to remember is that **no entries are made in the receivables ledger accounts** for allowances for receivables, and therefore no entry is made in the sales ledger control account either.

The allowance for receivables and irrecoverable debts are considered in more detail in a later chapter of this publication.

Advantages of control accounts

- They check the accuracy of the ledger accounts that they control.
- They enable 'segregation of duties' by allocating the job of maintaining the sales/purchase ledger to one person, and the job of maintaining the control account to another person, thereby reducing the risk of undetected fraud.
- They enable the trial balance to be prepared more speedily, as the receivables and payables total can be extracted from the control accounts rather than waiting for the individual accounts to be balanced and totalled.
- They enable speedier identification of reasons why the trial balance may not balance – if the control account disagrees with its ledger balances, it prompts investigation into the entries in that area.

Reconciling control accounts and ledger accounts

The control account must be checked against the total of balances in the relevant ledger, on a regular basis, and any difference between the two must be investigated and rectified. Assuming that the control account has been prepared using totals from the books of prime entry, it is usual to 'work backwards' through the tasks that have been carried out, before checking individual entries. The sequence for a sales ledger control account could be as follows:

(i) Rework the balance on the control account; check that irrecoverable debts have been entered, contras have been properly recorded, and that the account does not contain the allowance for receivables.

(ii) Check that all totals have been correctly transferred from the books of prime entry to the control account.

(iii) Recalculate the list of receivable balances (look especially for credit balances listed as debits, check contras and irrecoverable debts written off).

(iv) Recalculate the columns in the books of prime entry (look at the sequence of invoice numbers to see if any are missing; look also in the cash book for refunds made to receivables). If the balances are still incorrect, it will be necessary to start looking at entries in detail:

- cross-check the net, sales tax and totals for each invoice/credit note in the daybooks
- cross-check the total for each receipt in the cash book
- cross-check the calculation of the balances on the individual receivable accounts
- cross-check the entry of each invoice, credit note, receipt and so on in the receivable accounts.

In computerised systems there is much less chance of arithmetical error, but omissions and mispostings can still occur.

When the errors have been identified, corrections must be made to the sales ledger accounts, the control account or both as appropriate.

Worked Example 13.F

Cathy maintains a sales ledger control account. At 31 March 20X1, the balance on the control account was calculated as being $128,545, whilst the total of individual balances extracted from the sales ledger was $128,476. An examination of the books and records revealed the following:

(i) The total of $29,450 for sales in the sales daybook had been posted as $29,540.

(ii) The credit balance of $128 on a receivable account had been listed as a debit balance.

(iii) An irrecoverable debt of $240 had been correctly written off in the receivable account, but no entry had been made in the control account.

(iv) A credit balance of $95 in the purchase ledger had been set off against the same person's balance in the sales ledger, but no entries had been made in the control account.

(v) The total on the debit side of a receivable account had been overcast by $100.

Required:

Reconcile the sales ledger control account balance with the list of sales ledger balances.

Solution:

Each adjustment is likely to affect either the control account or the individual balances; it is also possible that an error affects both.

Adjustments to receivables balance	$
Total per original list	128,476
(ii) credit balance listed as debit (2 × $128)	(256)
(v) debit side overcast	(100)
Revised total	128,120

Adjustments to the control account (probably easiest to show this as a ledger account):

	$		$
Balance b/f	128,545	Error in sales daybook (i)	90
		Irrecoverable debts w/off (ii)	240
		Contra (iv)	95
		Revised balance c/f	128,120
	128,545		128,545

6 Chapter summary

In this chapter we prepared a number of accounting reconciliations designed to ensure the reliability of the accounting records, in particular:

- the preparation of bank reconciliations
- the preparation of petty cash imprest statements
- the preparation of sales and purchase ledger control account reconciliations.

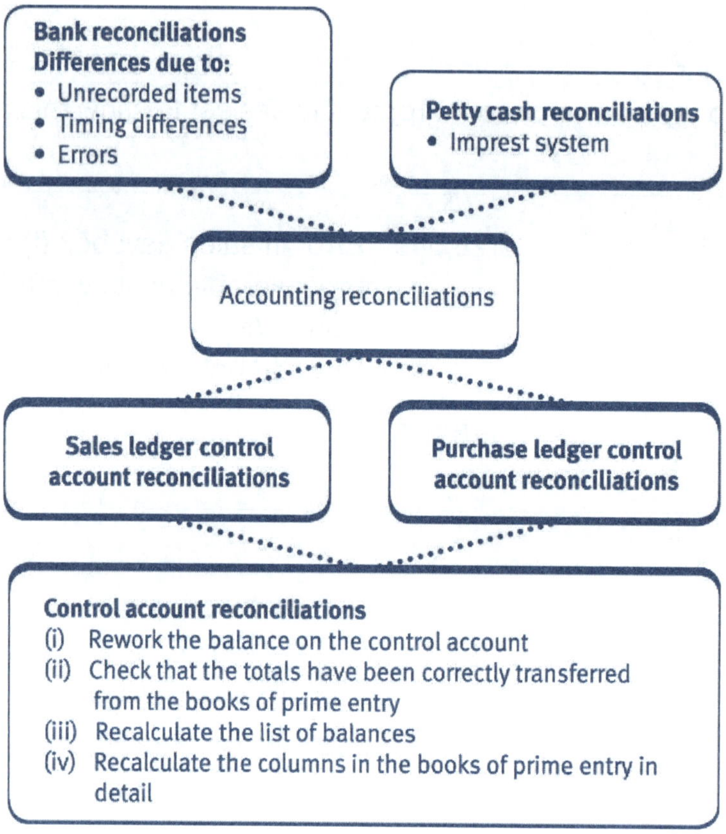

Test your understanding questions

Test your understanding 7

The cash book shows a bank balance of $5,675 overdrawn at 31 August 20X5. It is subsequently discovered that a standing order for $125 has been entered twice, and that a dishonoured cheque for $450 has been debited in the cash book instead of credited.

What is the correct bank balance?

$...............

Test your understanding 8

Your cash book at 31 December 20X3 shows a bank balance of $565 overdrawn. On comparing this with your bank statement at the same date, you discover that

- a cheque for $57 drawn by you on 29 December 20X3 has not yet been presented for payment
- a cheque for $92 from a customer which was paid into the bank on 24 December 20X3 has been dishonoured on 31 December 20X3.

The correct bank balance to be shown in the statement of financial position at 31 December 20X3 is:

$...............

Test your understanding 9

Your firm's cash book at 30 April 20X8 shows a balance at the bank of $2,490. Comparison with the bank statement at the same date reveals the following differences:

	$
Unpresented cheques	840
Bank charges not in cash book	50
Receipts not yet credited by the bank	470
Dishonoured cheque not in cash book	140

The correct bank balance at 30 April 20X8 is:

$...............

Test your understanding 10

The following information relates to a bank reconciliation.

(i) The bank balance in the cash book before taking the items below into account was $8,970 overdrawn.

(ii) Bank charges of $550 on the bank statement have not been entered in the cash book.

(iii) The bank has credited the account in error with $425, which belongs to another customer.

(iv) Cheque payments totalling $3,275 have been entered in the cash book but have not been presented for payment.

(v) Cheques totalling $5,380 have been correctly entered on the debit side of the cash book but have not been paid in at the bank.

What was the balance as shown by the bank statement before taking the items above into account?

$...............

Test your understanding 11

When reconciling the payables' ledger control account with the list of payables ledger balances of M, the following errors were found:

- the purchase daybook had been overstated by $500
- the personal ledger of a supplier had been understated by $400.

What adjustment must be made to correct these errors?

	Control account	List of payables ledger balances
A	Cr $500	Decrease by $400
B	Dr $500	Increase by $400
C	Dr $400	Increase by $500
D	Cr $400	Decrease by $500

Test your understanding 12

Which one of the following statements is true in relation to bank reconciliations?

A Uncleared deposits are deducted from the balance on the bank statement

B Dishonoured cheques are adjusted for by debiting the cash book

C Unrecorded direct credits are adjusted by debiting the cash book

D Bank errors are adjusted for in the cash book

Test your understanding 13

Z's bank statement shows a balance of $825 overdrawn. The bank statement includes bank charges of $50, which have not been entered in the cash book. There are unpresented cheques totalling $475 and deposits not yet credited of $600. The bank statement incorrectly shows a direct debit payment of $160, which belongs to another customer.

The figure for the bank balance in the statement of financial position should be:

$.......... overdrawn.

Test your understanding 14

Which of the following should NOT be credited to the sales ledger control account?

A Sales returns

B Refunds of over-payments to customers

C Contras

D Irrecoverable debts

Test your understanding 15

When the individual accounts in Rylan's receivables ledger are added up, they total $301,450.

What will be the balance on the receivables ledger after correcting the following errors?

- The total on the sales day book was under-cast by $5,000.
- A contra with the purchase ledger control account for $300 which was recorded in the sales ledger control account but not in the receivables ledger.

A $301,150

B $306,150

C $306,450

D $306,750

Test your understanding 16

JAG's bank statement shows an overdrawn balance of $410. This does not agree to the cash book. The following reconciling differences are noted:

- There are unpresented cheques of $300.
- The bank debited $1,000 from JAG's account instead of from Jim's account.
- JAG has made no accounting entries for bank charges of $70.

What is the balance on the cash book when it has been updated?

A $1,710 Cr

B $290 Dr

C $290 Cr

D $1,110 Dr

Test your understanding 17

You have been provided with the following information:

	$
Receivables at 1 January 20X3	10,000
Receivables at 31 December 20X3	9,000
Total receipts during 20X3 (including cash sales of $5,000)	85,000

What was the value of sales made on credit during 20X3?

$...............

Test your understanding answers

Test your understanding 1

Cash book

		$			$
1 Jan	Balance b/f	600	18 Jan	D Anderson	145
13 Jan	Umberto	224	28 Jan	R Patrick	72
31 Jan	L Bond	186	30 Jan	Parveen	109
			31 Jan	Standing order	30
			31 Jan	Balance c/f	654
		1,010			1,010
1 Feb	Balance b/f	654			

Bank reconciliation statement at 31 January

	$
Balance as per bank statement	649
Add: Uncleared deposits	186
Less: Unpresented cheques (109 + 72)	(181)
Balance as per cash book	654

Test your understanding 2

The imprest system of controlling petty cash is based on a set 'float' of cash that the petty cashier commences with. This amount is used to pay for small items during the coming week or month, for which a petty cash voucher should be prepared. At the end of the period (or when the cash runs out), the vouchers can be totalled and the amount spent is reimbursed to the petty cashier so as to commence the next period with the same 'float'.

Test your understanding 3

	$
Stationery	14.10
Travel	25.50
Refreshments	12.90
Sundry payables	28.80
	81.30

Test your understanding 4

	$
Office stationery ($9.20 × 1.20)	11.04
Local train fares to attend meetings	13.70
Office cleaning materials	25.50
Office refreshments	24.00
Total petty cash payments made and imprest to be reimbursed	74.24
Balance of cash retained by petty cash cashier at end of the week	5.76
	80.00

Test your understanding 5

B

The supplier's records show a smaller amount owing than your own records. This could not be due to an invoice not received as this would further increase the amount owing according to your records. If you have paid the supplier, this would further reduce the balance in his records. If you have returned goods, this would also reduce the balance in his records. Discount allowed by the supplier will be discount received in your records, which will reduce the balance in your records to agree with the supplier statement.

Test your understanding 6

Sales ledger control account

	$		$
Opening balances	14,500	Opening balances	125
Sales on credit	27,500	Sales returns	850
Dishonoured cheques	750	Cheques received	20,280
Refunds	125	Contras to purchase ledger	340
		Closing balances	21,280
	42,875		42,875

Test your understanding 7

The correct bank balance can be found as follows:

	$	
Cash book balance	5,675	overdrawn (credit)
Correct standing order error	125	debit
Reverse error of dishonoured cheque	450	credit
Enter dishonoured cheque correctly	450	credit
Correct balance	6,450	overdrawn

Test your understanding 8

The cash book balance needs adjusting for the dishonoured cheque, and the bank balance needs adjusting for the unpresented cheque. The correct balance for the statement of financial position is therefore:

$565 overdrawn + dishonoured cheque $92 = $657 overdrawn

Test your understanding 9

	$
Original cash book figure	2,490
Adjustment re: charges	(50)
Adjustment re: dishonoured cheque	(140)
	2,300

Test your understanding 10

Cash book	$	**Bank statement**	$
Balance	(8,970)	Balance (β)	(11,200)
Bank charges	(550)	Credit in error	(425)
		Unpresented cheques	(3,275)
		Outstanding deposits	5,380
	(9,520)		(9,520)

Test your understanding 11

B

Test your understanding 12

C

Uncleared deposits are cheques received by the entity not yet cleared by the bank. Once cleared they will increase the bank statement amount as part of the bank reconciliation.

Dishonoured cheques are cheques not cleared by the bank as the customer has insufficient funds to meet the payment. These amounts will reduce the cash book balance when the cash book is updated prior to the bank reconciliation.

Bank errors are adjusted on bank statement amount as part of the bank reconciliation.

Test your understanding 13

	$
Bank statement – overdrawn	(825)
Unpresented cheques	(475)
Deposits outstanding	600
Direct debit error	160
Bank balance – overdrawn	(540)

Test your understanding 14

B

Test your understanding 15

A

	$
Balance as receivables' ledger	301,450
Contra entry allowed adjustment	(300)
Correct bank/cash book balance	301,150

The casting error in the sales day book will affect only the control account and not the individual accounts in the receivables' ledger.

Test your understanding 16

B

	$
Balance as per bank statement (overdrawn)	(410)
Unpresented cheques	(300)
Bank error	1,000
Correct bank/cash book balance in hand (debit balance)	290

Test your understanding 17

Sales can be found by constructing a mini sales control account:

Sales ledger control account

	$		$
Receivables at 1.1.X3	10,000	Receipts, less cash sales	80,000
Sales	?	Receivables at 31.12.X3	9,000
	89,000		89,000

Sales = $79,000 (balancing item)

Chapter

14

Incomplete records

Chapter learning objectives

When you have completed this chapter, you should be able to:

- prepare financial statements from incomplete records.

1 Introduction

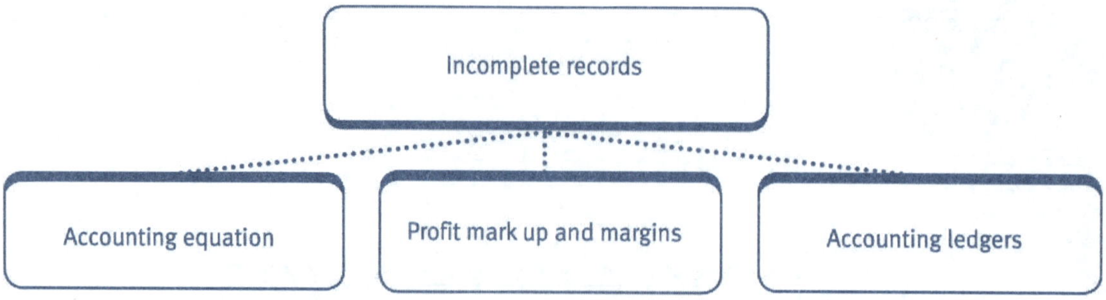

In this chapter, you will learn:

- to calculate missing figures using the accounting equation
- to calculate missing figures using profit margins and mark-ups
- to calculate missing figures using accounting ledgers.

So far, we have considered the preparation of financial statements from a complete set of ledger accounts, with the results summarised in the trial balance. But not every business entity uses the full system of daybooks, ledger accounts and so on. In particular, in small business entities, there may not be management time or the financial expertise available. Even in larger business entities it occasionally happens that accounting records are lost, damaged or destroyed. For all these reasons it may sometimes be necessary to prepare financial statements from the limited information available.

The content of this chapter should be considered important for the examination, as it provides a good test of your knowledge of bookkeeping, which is essential to pass the computer-based assessment. The ability to prepare financial statements from incomplete records may be regarded as more difficult than from complete records, which you have studied in the previous chapters.

2 Accounting equation method

If a business entity does not maintain its accounting records in double-entry form, with the production of a trial balance, the preparation of the statement of profit or loss and statement of financial position may require some figures to be ascertained from other records and information. For example, a common situation arises when the sole proprietor of a business entity has not kept records of his drawings from the entity, but there are other figures available that would enable the drawings figure to be determined.

The accounting equation is usefully employed in this situation:

Assets = Liabilities + Capital

From this the value of capital can be calculated at any time. A change in the value of capital can be caused by only three things:

1 an introduction/withdrawal of capital
2 net profit or loss for the period
3 drawings.

THE ONLY 3 THINGS THAT CHANGE CAPITAL.

Thus, if the opening and closing values of capital are known then, provided that the value of profit and of capital introductions/withdrawals are known, the value of drawings can be calculated or determined as a missing figure.

In a business entity that does not keep full ledger accounts, there may be several figures that need to be determined with the aid of other figures that can be verified. There are several techniques to identify these missing figures.

Test your understanding 1

A sole trader had a capital account balance of $10,000 at 1 April 20X4 and a capital account balance of $4,500 at 31 March 20X5. During the year ended 31 March 20X5, period the owner introduced capital of $4,000 and withdrew $8,000 for her own use.

Required:

What was the profit or loss for the year ended 31 March 20X5?

$...1500...

3 Gross profit mark-up and margin

Gross profit **mark-up means the profit is based on the cost of sales**, e.g. mark-up of 25% means 25% has been added to the cost of sales to find the selling price. In a 25% mark-up situation the following cost structure would apply:

	$	%
Sales	750	125
Cost of sales	600	100
Gross profit	150	25

This means that if we are given the cost of $600 in the question and the mark-up of 25% we can calculate the selling price of $750 by adding 25% to the cost of $600. We can also calculate the cost if we are given the selling price by dividing the selling price by 125 and multiplying it by 100.

In a mark-up situation the **cost will always represent 100%** and the selling price will always represent 100 plus the mark-up%.

Gross profit **margin means the profit is based on the selling price**, e.g. margin of 25% means 25% of the selling price is profit. In a 25% margin situation the following cost structure would apply:

	$	%
Sales	800	100
Cost of sales	600	75
Gross profit	200	25

This means that if we are given the selling price of $800 in the question and the margin of 25% we can calculate the cost of $600 by taking 25% from the selling price of $800. We can also calculate the selling price if we are given the cost by dividing the cost by 75 and multiplying it by 100.

In a margin situation the selling **price will always represent 100%** and the cost will always represent 100 less the margin%.

Test your understanding 2

A business entity achieved a 25% margin on sales made of $150,000 for the year ended 30 June 20X2. The inventory valuation was $10,000 at 1 July 20X1 and $20,000 at 30 June 20X2.

Required:

What was the cost of purchases for the year ended 30 June 20X2?

$..........

Prepare the trading account for the year ended 30 June 20X2 based upon the available information.

Test your understanding 3

A business entity applied a 30% mark-up on goods sold during the year ended 30 September 20X6. For that year, it had sales revenue of $169,000. The inventory valuation was $15,000 at 1 October 20X5 and $12,000 at 30 September 20X6.

Required:

What was the cost of purchases for the year ended 30 September 20X6?

$..........

Prepare the trading account for the year ended 30 September 20X6 based upon the available information.

4 Calculate missing figures using the accounting ledgers

The balancing figure approach, using ledger accounts, uses incomplete records and information to derive additional information as follows:

Ledger account	Missing figure
Receivables	Credit sales, Money received from receivables
Payables	Credit purchases, Money paid to payables
Cash at hand	Drawings, Money stolen
Cash at bank	Cash sales, Cash stolen

In effect, by recreating a ledger account as a summary of transactions, any one missing figure can be determined as a balancing figure if all other items are known. Therefore, you should ensure that you are familiar with the layout and content of the various control accounts considered in earlier chapters.

Sales figures

It is common for entities that do not keep full bookkeeping records to find that some figures regarding sales are unavailable. It might be that opening receivables lists have been mislaid, or cash sales have not been recorded, or amounts written off as irrecoverable may have been overlooked.

Preparing the equivalent of a sales ledger control account will enable the missing figure to be determined. Of course, it will not be a 'proper' sales ledger control account, because there is unlikely to be a sales ledger, but the technique is the same.

The idea is to insert into the ledger accounts all known information, and then to derive the missing information as a balancing figure.

To take sales as an example:

- the opening figure for receivables is probably known – it is the figure that appeared in last year's statement of financial position
- the figure for closing receivables is probably known – they are the customers who owe the business money at the year end
- bank statements should indicate the amount received from customers in the form of cheques and other types of receipts (though we may have to look back through all the statements for the accounting period in order to derive this information)
- there may be records of cash sales (e.g. till rolls) that will indicate the amounts received from cash customers
- by entering all these known amounts into the sales total account, it is possible to derive a sales figure for the period as a balancing figure.

Note that, although we normally exclude cash sales from the sales ledger control account, it is permissible to include them in the 'sales total account' in order to derive total sales, whether for cash or on credit.

This can be simplified using the following ledger account:

Sales ledger control account

20X1		$			$
1 Jan	Balance b/d	X	In year	Bank – cash from customers	X
In year	**Sales (balancing figure)**	**X**	In year	Irrecoverable debt written off	X
			In year	Contra with PLCA	X
			31 Dec	Balance c/d	X
		X			X

Note that this control account includes all possible items that may be relevant. It may be that, in a given question, not all items are relevant and therefore preparation of the control account is less detailed than it otherwise would be.

Test your understanding 4

Jaswinder knows that his receivables at 1 January 20X1 were $27,000, and during the year he received $142,000 in cheques from customers. He wrote off an irrecoverable debt of $5,000 during the year, and his closing receivables at 31 December 20X1 amount to $24,500. In addition. Jaswinder agreed with some customers, who were also suppliers, that he would contra $500 of the amounts they owed him them with their payables balances.

Required:

Calculate the value of Jaswinder's sales for the year ended 31 December 20X1.

Purchases figures

These are calculated in the same way as sales figures.

This can be simplified using the following ledger account

Purchase ledger control account

20X1		$	20X1		$
In year	Bank – cash paid to suppliers	X	1 Jan	Balance c/d	X
In year	Contra with SLCA	X	In year	**Purchases (balancing figure)**	**X**
In year	Discounts received	X			
31 Dec	Balance c/d	X			
		X			X

Note that this control account includes all possible items that may be relevant. It may be that, in a given question, not all items are relevant and therefore preparation of the control account is less detailed than it otherwise would be.

Test your understanding 5

At 1 January 20X1, Jaswinder had payables of $12,050, and his payables at 31 December 20X1 were $14,450, During 20X1, he made bank payments of $98,500 and received discount of $385 for early settlement of some of the amounts due. In addition. Jaswinder agreed with some suppliers, who were also customers, that he would contra $500 of the amounts he owed them with their receivables balances.

Required:

Calculate the cost of Jaswinder's purchases for the year ended 31 December 20X1.

Expenses figures

As with sales and purchases, a ledger account is prepared and includes the known figures, with the missing figure deduced as the figure required to make the account balance.

Expense account

20X1		$	20X1		$
1 Jan	Balance b/d	X	1 Jan	Balance b/d	X
In year	Bank	X	In year	**Statement of profit or loss (balancing figure)**	X
In year	Balance c/d	X	In year	Balance c/d	X
		X			X

Test your understanding 6

During 20X1, Jaswinder paid several amounts for electricity which totalled $550. On 1 January 20X1, he knew that $120 was owed for electricity consumed in the previous year, and on 31 December 20X1 he knew that $140 had been consumed in the current year, but not yet billed.

Required:

Calculate Jaswinder's charge for electricity in the statement of profit or loss for the year ended 31 December 20X1.

Cash and bank summaries

It is common for incomplete records questions to commence with a summary of the cash and bank transactions. Such a summary is called a **receipts and payments account**. Very often, there is a missing figure in these – commonly the figure for owner's drawings. Preparing such a summary (which is in effect just a copy of the cash book) enables the missing figure to be determined.

This can be simplified using the following ledger accounts:

Cash at bank

20X1		$	20X1		$
1 Jan	Balance b/d	X	In year	Cash paid to suppliers PLCA	X
In year	Cash received from customers SLCA	X	In year	Expenses	X
In year	Bankings from cash at hand	X	**In year**	**Drawings (balancing figure)**	**X**
In year	Sundry income	X	31 Dec	Balance c/d	X
		X			X

Cash at hand

20X1		$	20X1		$
1 Jan	Balance b/d	X	In year	Cash purchases	X
			In year	Cash expenses	X
In year	Cash sales	X	In year	Cash banked	X
			In year	**Cash drawings (balancing figure)**	**X**
In year	Sundry other receipts	X	31 Dec	Balance c/d	X
		X			X

5 Chapter summary

In this chapter we reviewed and applied the main techniques required to prepare financial statements from incomplete records, including the use of mark-up and margin information.

In addition, this chapter developed your knowledge and understanding of topics introduced in previous chapters, in particular:

- the preparation of control accounts
- the distinction between capital and revenue transactions
- adjustments for accruals and prepayments
- the accounting equation.

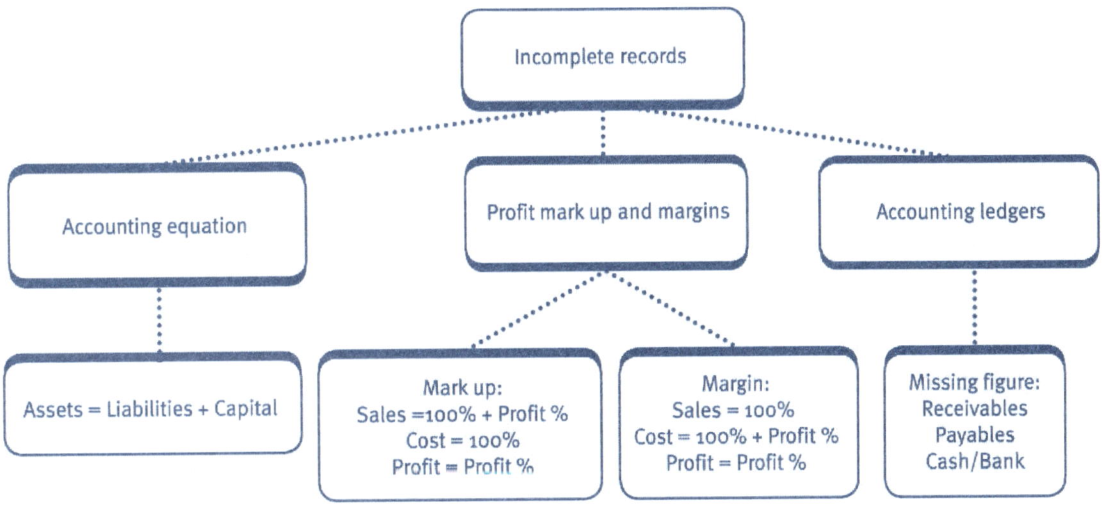

Test your understanding questions

Test your understanding 7

Carol owns a shop and provided you with the following information relating to the year ended 31 December 20X6:

Inventory valuation at 1 January 20X6 was $3,500 and $1,350 at 31 December 20X6. Carol made purchases during the year at a cost of $10,000. Carol estimated that she made a gross profit margin on sales of 40%.

Required:

What was the value of sales for the year ended 31 December 20X6?

$...........

Test your understanding 8

Kara provided you with information relating to her business entity for the year ended 30 April 20X4. At that date, she had payables of $137,800. During the year ended 30 April 20X4, she paid $542,300 to her suppliers of and received discount of $13,200. Kara returned faulty goods to her suppliers had cost $27,500. At 1 May 20X3, payables were $142,600.

Required:

What was the cost of purchases made by Kara during the year ended 30 April 20X4?

$...........

Test your understanding 9

A business entity has a receivables balance at 1 January 20X1 of $40,000. During the year cash of $38,000 was received from customers, irrecoverable debts written off amounted to $1,200. At 31 December the receivables were $43,000.

Required:

What was the value of sales made during the year ended 31 December 20X1?

$...........

Test your understanding 10

At 1 January 20X1 the opening inventory of a business entity was $10,000. The business entity made purchases of $80,000 during the year and had closing inventory at 31 December 20X1 of $6,000. It applied a mark-up of 30% on goods sold.

Required:

What was its sales revenue for the year ended 31 December 20X1?

$...........

Test your understanding 11

At 1 May 20X7 BCD had an opening accrual of $353 for motor expenses. During the year to 30 April 20X8 BCD paid invoices for motor expenses of $4,728. BCD also needs to account for accrued expenses of $257 at 30 April 20X8.

Required:

What amount should BCD include in its statement of profit or loss for motor expenses for the year ended 30 April 20X8?

$...........

Test your understanding 12

NAJ is preparing its trial balance at 31 March 20X3. At 1 April 20X2 NAJ had an accrual of $327 for heat and light charges. During the year to 31 March 20X3 NAJ paid invoices for heat and light charges of $8,750. At 31 March 20X3, NAJ had an accrued expense of $389.

Required:

What expense should NAJ include in its statement of profit or loss for the year ended 31 March 20X3 for heat and light?

$...........

Test your understanding 13

OXE had a trade receivables balance of $64,700 at 1 May 20X6 and $69,500 at 30 June 20X7. During the year, there were cash sales of $96,400 and cash received from receivables of $553,300. During the year, discounts received totalled $17,260. Irrecoverable debts of $12,325 were written off.

Required:

What value of credit sales did OXE make during the year ended 30 June 20X7?

$...........

Test your understanding 14

ELO has estimated that, at 31 August 20X4, it had the following assets and liabilities:

	$
Non-current assets	34,750
Trade payables	8,633
Inventory	4,245
Bank overdraft	1,039
Trade receivables	11,948

At 31 August 20X4 it was noted that ELO also had an accrual for rent of £750 which had yet not been accounted for.

Required:

What was ELO's capital balance as at 31 August 20X4?

$...........

Test your understanding 15

An entity had a cash book opening balance of $485 credit. The following transactions then took place:

- cash sales $1,450
- receipts from customers of $2,400
- payments to payables of $1,800
- dishonoured cheques from customers amounting to $250.

Required:

What was the closing balance in the cash book after the above transactions had been accounted for?

$...........

Test your understanding 16

The following totals appear in the day books of a business entity, which is registered to account for sales tax, for March 20X8:

	Goods exc. sales tax	Sales tax
	$	$
Sales day book	40,000	7,000
Purchases day book	20,000	3,500
Sales returns day book	2,000	350
Purchases returns day book	4,000	700

Both opening inventory at 1 March and closing inventory at 31 March were each valued at $3,000.

Required:

What was the gross profit for March 20X8?

$............

Test your understanding answers

Test your understanding 1

$1,500 loss

Closing capital = opening capital + profit – loss + capital introduced – drawings

4,500 = 10,000 +/– profit/loss + 4,000 – 8,000

4,500 = 6,000 +/– profit/loss

Therefore, the missing figure must be a loss of $1,500 to make the equation balance.

Test your understanding 2

	$	$	%
Sales		150,000	100
Cost of sales			
Opening inventory	10,000		
Purchases **(balancing figure)**	122,500		
Closing inventory	(20,000)		
		112,500	75
Gross profit		37,500	25

This question is based on margin which means the profit is based upon a percentage of the sales value. In cost structure terms this means the sales are 100% and profit 25% respectively, and cost of sales must represent 75%. When we have calculated the total amount for cost of sales as 75% of $150,000 we can work out the purchases as the missing or balancing amount.

Test your understanding 3

	$	$	%
Sales		169,000	130
Cost of sales			
Opening inventory	15,000		
Purchases **(balancing figure)**	127,000		
Closing inventory	(12,000)		
		130,000	100
Gross profit		39,000	30

This question is based on mark-up which means that the gross profit is calculated based upon a percentage of cost of sales. In cost structure terms this means the cost of sales is 100%, sales represent 130% of cost of sales and gross profit is 30% of cost of sales. When we have calculated the total for cost of sales as $130,000 (100/130 × $169,000) we can work out the purchases as the missing or balancing amount.

Test your understanding 4

This can be done by drawing up a sales ledger control account, and inserting the known figures. The unknown figure for sales can then be determined as the figure required to balance the account

Sales ledger control account

20X1		$	20X1		$
1 Jan	Balance b/d	27,000	In year	Bank	142,000
In year	**Sales (balancing figure)**	**145,000**	In year	Irrecoverable debt written off	5,000
			In year	Contra with PLCA	500
			31 Dec	Balance c/d	24,500
		172,000			172,000

Test your understanding 5

This can be done by drawing up a sales ledger control account, and inserting the known figures. The unknown figure for sales can then be determined as the figure required to balance the account

Purchase ledger control account

20X1		$	20X1		$
In year	Bank payments	98,500	1 Jan	Bank	12,050
In year	Discounts received	385			
In year	Contra with SLCA	500	In year	**Purchases (balancing figure)**	**101,785**
31 Dec	Balance c/d	14,450			
		113,835			113,835

Test your understanding 6

The missing statement of profit or loss figure is $570.

Electricity

20X1		$	20X1		$
In year	Bank payments	550	1 Jan	Balance b/d	120
31 Dec	Balance c/d	140	31 Dec	**Statement of profit or loss (balancing figure)**	**570**
		690			690

Test your understanding 7

$20,250

	$	$	$
Sales **(balancing figure)**		20,250	100
Cost of sales			
Opening inventory	3,500		
Purchases	10,000		
Closing inventory	(1,350)		
		12,150	60
Gross profit		8,100	40

This question is based on margin which means the profit is based on sales. In cost structure terms this means the sales are 100% and profit 40%, hence cost of sales must represent 60%. When we have calculated the total amount for cost of sales as 60% of $12,150 we can work out the sales as 12,150/60 × 100 = $20,250.

Test your understanding 8

$578,200

This can be done by drawing up a purchase ledger control account, and inserting the known figures. The unknown figure for purchases can then be determined as the figure required to balance the account.

Purchase ledger control account

	$		$
Bank	542,300	Balance b/d	142,600
Discounts received	13,200	**Purchases (balancing figure)**	**578,200**
Purchase returns	27,500		
Balance c/d	137,800		
	720,800		720,800

Test your understanding 9

$42,200

This can be done by drawing up a sales ledger control account, and inserting the known figures. The unknown figure for sales can then be determined as the figure required to balance the account.

Sales ledger control account

20X1		$	20X1		$
1 Jan	Balance b/d	40,000	In year	Bank	38,000
In year	**Sales (balancing figure)**	**42,200**			
			In year	Irrecoverable debts written off	1,200
			31 Dec	Balance c/d	43,000
		82,200			82,200

Test your understanding 10

$109,200

	$	$	$
Sales **(balancing figure)**		109,200	130
Cost of sales			
Opening inventory	10,000		
Purchases	80,000		
Closing inventory	(6,000)		
		84,000	100
Gross profit		25,200	30

This question is based on mark-up which means the profit is based on cost of sales. In cost structure terms this means the cost of sales are 100% and profit 30%, hence sales must represent 130%. When we have calculated the total amount for cost of sales as 100% of $84,000 we can work out the sales as the balancing amount.

Test your understanding 11

$4,632

Cash paid in year $4,728 – Accrual b/f $353 + Accrual c/f $257 = $4,632 charge for the year

Test your understanding 12

$8,812

Expense for the year: amounts paid in the year $8,750 – opening accrual $327 + closing accrual $389 = $8,812 expense for the year.

Test your understanding 13

$570,425

Note – discounts received are credited to other income and debited to payables, they do not affect the receivables account.

	$	$
Balance b/f	64,700	
Cash received re credit sales		553,300
Credit sales – bal fig	570,425	
Irrecoverable debts		12,325
Balance c/f		69,500
	635,125	635,125

Test your understanding 14

$40,521

	$
Non-current assets	34,750
Inventory	4,245
Trade receivables	11,948
Trade payables	(8,633)
Bank overdraft	(1,039)
Accrual to account for	(750)
Capital balance at 31 August 20X4	40,521

Test your understanding 15

The calculation is as follows:

	$
Opening overdraft	(485)
Add: Receipts ($1,450 + $2,400)	3,850
	3,365
Less: Payments	(1,800)
	1,565
Less: Dishonoured cheques	(250)
	1,315

Test your understanding 16

Reconstruction of the trading account:

	$	$
Sales		40,000
Less: Sales returns		(2,000)
		38,000
Less: Opening inventory	3,000	
Purchases	20,000	
Purchases returns	(4,000)	
Closing inventory	(3,000)	
		(16,000)
Gross profit		22,000

Chapter

15

Accounting errors and suspense accounts

Chapter learning objectives

When you have completed this chapter, you should be able to:

- explain the nature of accounting errors
- prepare accounting entries for the correction of errors.

1 Introduction

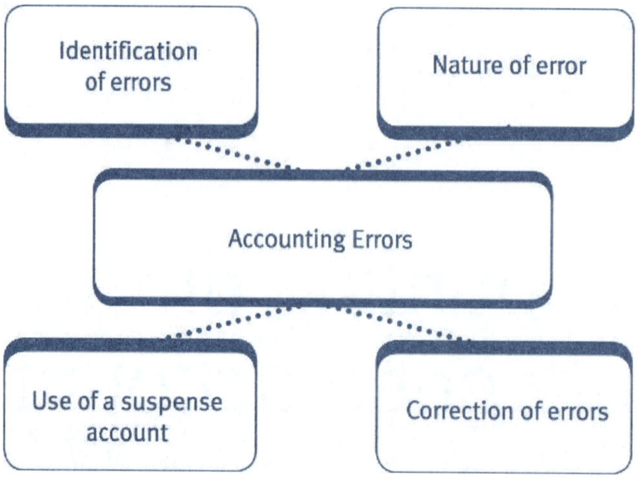

In this chapter you will learn how to:

- identify and understand the nature of accounting errors
- use a suspense account
- make accounting entries required to correct errors.

No bookkeeping or accounting system can be guaranteed to be entirely free from error, whether it is manual, computerised, or a combination of both. Therefore, it is important that you understand the nature of accounting errors, how they may occur and how they may be corrected, including the use of a suspense account where appropriate.

2 The nature of accounting errors

In previous chapters of this publication, a trial balance was extracted from the ledger accounts and a statement of profit or loss and statement of financial position was prepared. However, it is possible that the accounting records may contain errors or omissions, even if the trial balance is in agreement. This may occur in any type of accounting system, whether it is manual, computerised or a combination of both

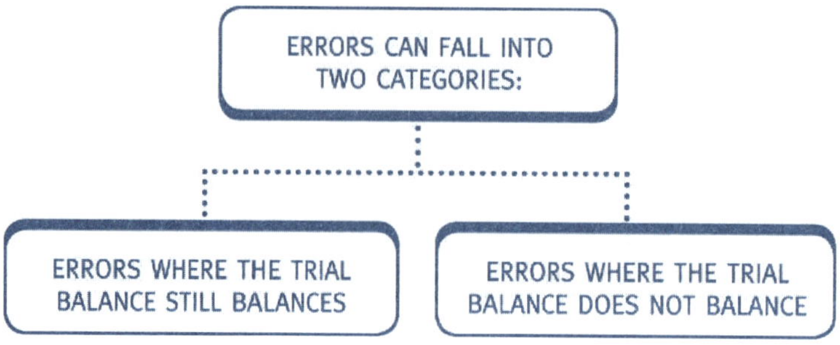

Errors and omissions where the trial balance still agrees

There are a number of errors that may have been made that do not prevent the trial balance from agreeing. These are:

- Errors of **omission**, where a transaction has been completely omitted from the ledger accounts.
- Errors of **commission**, where one side of the transaction has been entered in the wrong account (but of a similar type to the correct account, for example, entered in the wrong asset account, or in the wrong expense account). An error of commission would not affect the calculation of profit, or the position shown by the statement of financial position.
- Errors of **principle**, where the correct and incorrect accounts are of different types, for example, entered in the purchases account instead of a non-current asset account. This type of error would affect the calculation of profit, and the position shown by the statement of financial position.
- Errors of **original entry**, where the wrong amount has been used for both the debit and credit entries.
- **Reversal** of entries, where the debit has been made to the account that should have been credited and vice versa.
- **Duplication** of entries, where the transaction has been posted twice.
- **Compensating errors,** where two or more transactions have been entered incorrectly, but cancelling each other out, for example, electricity debited $100 in excess, and sales revenue has also been credited with $100 in excess.

In all of these cases, an account has been debited and an account has been credited with the same amount, so the trial balance will still be in agreement, even though it contains incorrect entries.

Consequently, any errors identified will need to be corrected, usually by recording the required accounting entries in the journal and then making the required entries in the ledger accounts.

When trying to decide the accounting entries required to rectify an error, it may be helpful to adopt the following approach:

- What should the double entry have been?
- What was the double entry actually made?
- What correction is required?

Note that one part of each of the correcting entries will almost certainly be to the suspense account.

Test your understanding 1

A business entity entered into a number of transactions which had not been properly recorded as follows:

1 A cash sale of $100 was not recorded.

2 Rates expense of $500, paid in cash has been debited to the rent account in error.

3 A non-current asset purchase of $1,000 on credit has been debited to the repairs expense account rather than an asset account.

4 A rent bill of $1,200 paid in cash has been debited to the rent account as $1,400 and a casting error on the sales account has resulted in sales being overstated by $200.

5 A cash sale of $76 has been recorded as $67.

6 A cash sale of $200 has been debited to sales and credited to cash.

Required:

State the journal entries required to correct each error or omission.

Errors and omissions where the trial balance does not agree

Some errors and omissions will result in the trial balance not being in agreement. Examples of these errors or omissions include:

- **Posting only one part of the double-entry** required to record a transaction, for example, posting only the debit (or credit) entry into the ledger accounts.
- **Posting a different value of debits and credits** to record a transaction, for example, making a transposition error and posting $1,234 as the debit entry and $1,243 as the credit entry into the ledger accounts.
- **Arithmetic errors** in calculating the balance on individual ledger accounts.
- An **opening balance has not been brought down** correctly.
- **Extraction error** – the balance on the trial balance does not agree the ledger account balance – either because it has not been recorded correctly in the trial balance, or because a debit balance has been recorded as a credit balance or vice versa.

In these situations, it is good practice to open a suspense account and record the amount of the difference from the trial balance in the suspense account.

The use of a suspense account allows financial statements to be prepared subject to the correction of the errors. The prudent approach is to treat a debit balance as an expense (rather than an asset) and a credit balance as a liability (rather than income). When, following investigation, the reason(s) for the suspense account difference have been identified correcting entries can be recorded in the journal and included in the ledger accounts.

3 Accounting entries for the correction of errors

Irrespective of the nature of an accounting system, if there are errors or omissions in the accounting records, they need to be corrected. The following procedure should be used when the trial balance is not in agreement, to correct such errors or omissions:

- calculate the difference between the total of debits and total of credits in the trial balance
- if the total of debits exceeds the total of credits, post the difference to the credit side of the suspense account
- if the total of credits exceeds to total of debits, post the difference to the debit side of the suspense account
- identify the error(s) which account for the suspense account difference
- record correcting entries in the journal
- update the ledger accounts and clear the suspense account.

Remember, when trying to decide the accounting entries required to rectify an error, it may be helpful to adopt the following approach noted earlier in the chapter:

- What should the double entry have been?
- What was the double entry actually made?
- What correction is required?

Note that one part of each of the correcting entries will almost certainly be to the suspense account.

Worked Example 15.A

On 31 December 20X1 a trial balance was extracted from the ledgers of Marcon and the total of the debit side was found to be $77 less than the total of the credit side. A suspense account was opened to record the difference. Later, the following errors were discovered:

1. A cheque for $150 paid to Bond had been correctly entered in the cash book but not in Bond's account or the control account.
2. The purchases account had been undercast by $20.
3. A cheque received for $93 from Smith had been correctly entered in the cash book but had not been entered in Smith's account.

Required:

(a) Record the journal entries required to clear the difference on the suspense account, including explanatory narrative.

(b) Prepare the suspense account to confirm that the suspense account difference has been rectified.

Solution:

The journal entries and resulting entries in the suspense account are as follows:

Journal

	Dr	Cr
	$	$
Bond	150	
Suspense		150
(Being correction of an error whereby only one entry was posted)		
Purchases	20	
Suspense		20
(Being correction of an error of addition in the purchases account)		
Suspense	93	
Smith		93
(Being correction of an error whereby only one entry was posted)		

Suspense

	$		$
From trial balance	77	Bond	150
Smith	93	Purchases	20
	170		170

Test your understanding 2

The following trial balance was extracted from the books of Jane Smith as at 31 March 20X1:

	Dr	Cr
	$	$
Premises	50,000	
Motor vans	7,400	
Sundry receivables	1,680	
Sundry payables		2,360
Purchases	160,260	
Sales		200,490
Wages	12,000	
Drawings	1,600	
Capital		30,000
	232,940	232,850

As the trial balance totals did not agree, the difference was posted to a suspense account. The following errors were discovered:

1 The purchase of a motor van had been entered in the motor van account as $3,860 instead of $3,680.

2 The total of the purchases book $32,543 had been posted to the purchases account as $32,453.

3 The owner had withdrawn $140 for private use during March that had been debited to the wages account.

Required:

Based upon the available information, prepare the following:

(a) journal entries to correct the errors, and

(b) the suspense account written up and balanced.

4 Prevention and detection of errors and omissions

So far, we have considered the different types of error which may occur when recording accounting transactions and whether or not they affect the trial balance. We have also considered how those errors or omissions, having been identified, can then be corrected in the accounting records.

It is also reasonable to consider how errors and omissions in accounting records can be prevented or detected. There are a number of procedures and controls that an entity may introduce to help prevent and detect errors and omissions in accounting records. These procedures and controls, including audit, form part of the syllabus for BA4 Fundamentals of Ethics, Corporate and Legal Governance and are considered in detail in that Subject.

5 Chapter summary

This chapter has outlined the nature of accounting errors and the preparation of accounting entries for the correction of errors

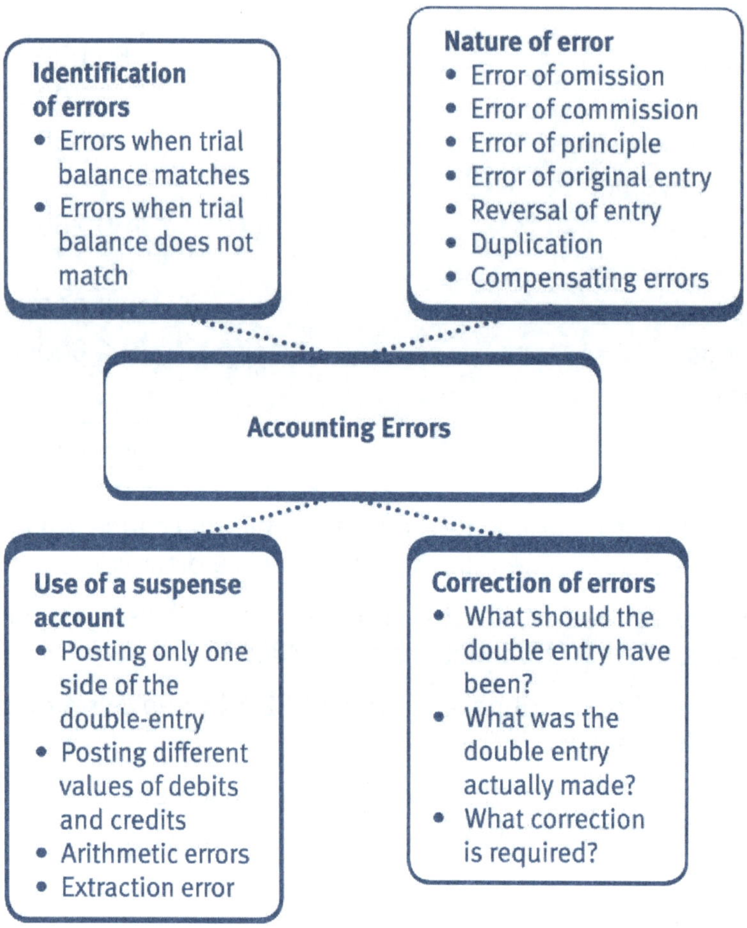

Test your understanding questions

Test your understanding 3

Following preparation of a trial balance, it was found not to agree, and a suspense account was opened with a credit balance of $130.

Which two of the following statements would each explain this difference?

A Omission of a sale of $130 from the sales account

B Recording a purchase of $130 twice in the purchases account

C Failure to record payment by a credit supplier of $130

D Recording an electricity bill paid of $65 by debiting the bank account and crediting the electricity account

E Omission of the insurance expense ledger account balance of $130 from the trial balance

Test your understanding 4

After calculating your profit for 20X3, you discover that:

- a non-current asset which had cost $50,000 had been included in the purchases account
- stationery purchased for $10,000 had been included as closing inventory of raw materials, instead of as inventory of stationery.

Drag and drop words and values from the available list to complete the following statement:

These two errors had the effect of ________ gross profit by $________ and ________ net profit by $________.

Available words:

overstating/understating/$40,000/$50,000/$60,000

Test your understanding 5

The debit side of OPQ's trial balance totals $1,200 more than the credit side.

Which of the following errors would fully account for the difference?

A The petty cash balance of $1,200 has been omitted from the TB

B A receipt of $1,200 for interest receivable has been omitted from the records

C $600 paid for plant maintenance has been correctly entered into the cash book and credited to the plant cost account

D Bank interest received of $600 has been debited to the bank interest expense account

Test your understanding 6

Bond's trial balance failed to agree and a suspense account was opened for the difference. The following errors were found in Bond's accounting records:

1 In recording the sale of a non-current asset, cash received of $33,000 was credited to the disposals account as $30,000.

2 An opening liability of $340 had been omitted.

3 Cash of $8,900 paid for plant repairs was correctly accounted for in the cash book but was credited to the plant cost account.

4 A cheque for $12,000 paid for the purchase of a machine was debited to the machinery account as $21,000.

Which of the errors will require an entry to the suspense account to correct them?

A (1), (3) and (4) only

B All

C (1) and (4) only

D (2) and (3) only

Test your understanding 7

For each of the errors notes below, match it with the type of error from the available list.

	Error	Type of error
A	A transaction has not been recorded	
B	One side of a transaction has been recorded in the wrong account, and that account is of a different class from the correct account	
C	One side of a transaction has been recorded in the wrong account, and that account is of the same class as the correct account	
D	A transaction has been recorded using the wrong amount	

Type of error:

Error of original entry/Error of commission/Error of omission/Error of principle

Test your understanding 8

When a transaction is credited to the correct ledger account, but debited incorrectly to the repairs and renewals account instead of to the plant and machinery account, what type of error is this?

A An error of omission

B An error of commission

C An error of principle

D An error of original entry

Test your understanding 9

If a purchase return of $48 has been wrongly posted to the debit side of the sales returns account, but has been correctly entered in the supplier's account, what would the total of the trial balance show?

A The credit side to be $48 more than the debit side

B The debit side to be $48 more than the credit side

C The credit side to be $96 more than the debit side

D The debit side to be $96 more than the credit side

Test your understanding 10

The debit side of a trial balance totals $50 more than the credit side.

What could cause this difference in the trial balance?

A A purchase of goods for $50 being omitted from the payables account

B A sale of goods for $50 being omitted from the receivables account

C An invoice of $25 for electricity being credited to the electricity account

D A receipt for $50 from a receivable being omitted from the cash book

Test your understanding 11

An invoice from a supplier of office stationery has been debited to the rent account.

What type of error is this?

A An error of commission

B An error of original entry

C A compensating error

D An error of principle

Test your understanding 12

Which one of the following is an error of principle?

A A gas bill credited to the gas account and debited to the bank account

B The purchase of a non-current asset credited to the asset at cost account and debited to the payables account

C The purchase of a non-current asset debited to the purchases account and credited to the payables account

D The payment of wages debited and credited to the correct accounts, but using the wrong amount

Test your understanding 13

What would be the result of recording the purchase of computer stationery by debiting the computer equipment at cost account?

A An overstatement of profit and an overstatement of non-current assets

B An understatement of profit and an overstatement of non-current assets

C An overstatement of profit and an understatement of non-current assets

D An understatement of profit and an understatement of non-current assets

Test your understanding 14

Which one of the following statements best explains the purpose of the trial balance?

A The purpose of the trial balance is to check the arithmetical accuracy of the entries made to the ledger accounts

B The purpose of the trial balance is to help prepare the statement of profit or loss

C The purpose of the trial balance is to help prepare the statement of financial position

D The purpose of the trial balance is to prove that the accounting ledgers contain no errors

Test your understanding answers

Test your understanding 1

	What should the double entry have been?	What was the double entry?	Correcting journal
1	Dr cash $100 Cr sales $100		Dr cash $100 Cr sales $100 to record both sides of the sale correctly
2	Dr rates $500 Cr cash $500	Dr rent $500 Cr cash $500	Dr rates $500 to record the rates expense correctly Cr rent $500 to reverse the incorrect debit to the rent account
3	Dr NCA asset $1,000 Cr payables $1,000	Dr repairs $1,000 Cr payables $1,000	Dr NCA asset $1,000 to record the asset correctly Cr repairs $1,000 to reverse the incorrect debit to the repairs account
4	Dr rent $1,200 Cr cash $1,200	Dr rent $1,400 Cr cash $1,200	Cr rent $200 to reverse the extra £200 debited to the rent account Dr sales $200 to correct the casting error
5	Dr cash $76 Cr sales $76	Dr cash $67 Cr sales $67	Dr cash $9 Cr sales $9 to record the extra $9 sales not previously recorded
6	Dr cash $200 Cr sales $200	Dr sales $200 Cr cash $200	Dr cash $400 Cr sales $400 to firstly reverse the error of $200 and then record the sale of $200 correctly in both accounts

Test your understanding 2

Journal entries

		Dr ($)	Cr ($)
Item 1	Suspense account	180	
	Motor vans		180
Item 2	Purchases	90	
	Suspense account		90
Item 3	Drawings	140	
	Wages		140

Suspense account

	$		$
Motor van	180	Balance from TB	90
		Purchases	90
	180		180

Test your understanding 3

A and B

Only A & B would account for the suspense account difference.

Test your understanding 4

These two errors had the effect of **understating** gross profit by **$40,000** and **understating** net profit by **$50,000.**

Including a non-current asset in the purchases account has overstated purchases, and hence has overstated cost of goods sold; this has the effect of understating gross profit. Including stationery inventory with closing inventory of raw materials has the effect of increasing closing inventory of raw materials, which then understates the cost of goods sold, and hence overstates gross profit. So, gross profit has been understated by $50,000 and overstated by $10,000 – a net understatement of $40,000.

Inventory of stationery should reduce the total of stationery expenses in the statement of profit or loss. Omitting to consider the closing inventory of stationery of $10,000 will overstate expenses and therefore understate net profit.

The effect on net profit will consist of the understatement of gross profit (this also affects net profit) due to the non-current asset error and also the overstatement of the stationery expense resulting in a total understatement of net profit by $50,000.

Test your understanding 5

D

A and C would result in the credit side of the TB being $1,200 higher than the debit side.

B would have no effect on the TB since neither the debit nor the credit side of the transaction has been accounted for.

Test your understanding 6

B

An entry to the suspense account is required wherever an account is missing from the trial balance or the initial incorrect entry did not include an equal debit and credit.

Test your understanding 7

	Error	**Type of error**
A	A transaction has not been recorded	Error of omission
B	One side of a transaction has been recorded in the wrong account, and that account is of a different class from the correct account	Error of principle
C	One side of a transaction has been recorded in the wrong account, and that account is of the same class as the correct account	Error of commission
D	A transaction has been recorded using the wrong amount	Error of original entry

Test your understanding 8

C

This is a straightforward test of your knowledge of the types of errors that can exist. If the wrong account is used, and this results in an incorrect statement of profit, then an error of principle has been made. Debiting the repairs and renewals account results in an extra charge for expenses in the statement of profit or loss, when the item should be included as a non-current asset on the statement of financial position

Test your understanding 9

D

A purchase return should be credited to the purchase returns account. If it has been debited to an account (whether the correct account or not), and also debited to the supplier's account (which is correct), then two debit entries will have been made with no corresponding credit. $96 (2 × $48) will have been debited, and nothing credited. Thus, the debit side will exceed the credit side by $96.

Test your understanding 10

A

B and D are incorrect as they would result in a lower debit side. C is incorrect because it would result in a higher credit side.

Test your understanding 11

A

An error of commission occurs where an entry is made in the wrong account, but that account is the same category as the correct account. Office stationery is an expense, so too is rent. Profit will be correct but the individual totals will be incorrect.

Test your understanding 12

C

An error of principle is where one side of an entry has been recorded in the wrong account, and where that account is classified differently to the correct account. In this case, debiting a non-current asset to the purchases account would result in the profit calculation being incorrect, and the value of assets shown on the statement of financial position being incorrect.

Test your understanding 13

A

Stationery is an expense and should be used to reduce profits; therefore profits would be overstated. Computer equipment is shown in the statement of financial position, and therefore the figure for non-current assets would be overstated.

Test your understanding 14

A

The purpose of a trial balance is to check the arithmetical accuracy of the entries made to the ledger accounts, that is, that the total of debit entries equals the total of credit entries. It is not proof that the ledger accounts are free from error. The statement of profit or loss and statement of financial position are prepared from the ledger account balances.

Chapter

16

The financial statements of single entities

Chapter learning objectives

When you have completed this chapter, you should be able to:

- prepare financial statements from trial balance for a single entity
- account for income tax in corporate entity financial statements.

1 Introduction

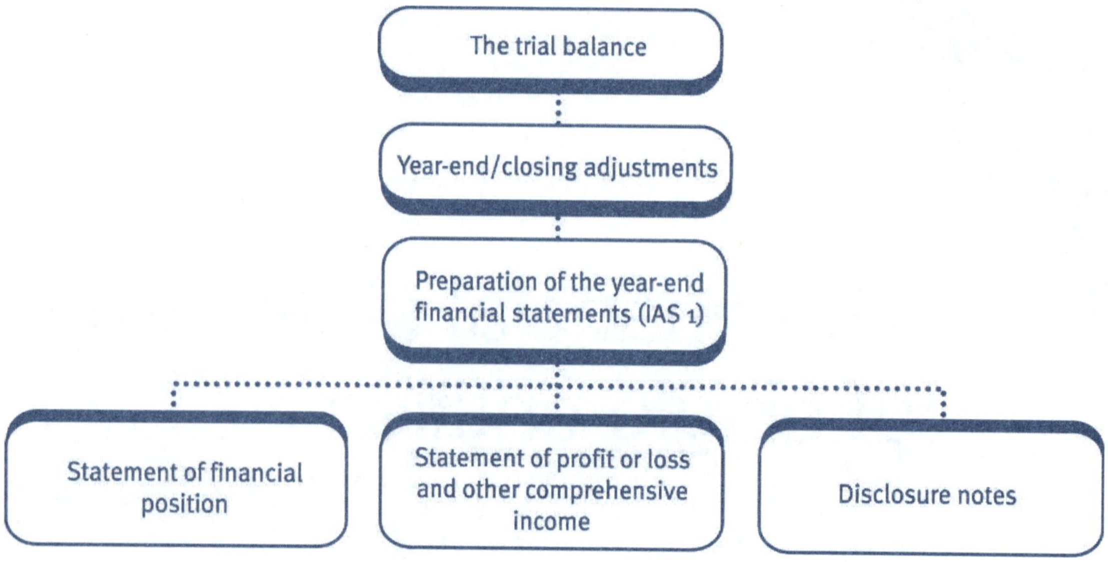

In this chapter, you will learn:

- the accounting requirements of IAS 1 *Presentation of Financial Statements*
- the accounting treatment of corporate income tax in corporate entity financial statements.

This chapter builds upon the content of earlier chapters which covered the preparation of financial statements from a trial balance. In this chapter we discuss some of the more formalised requirements of corporate entity financial statements. IAS 1 *Presentation of Financial Statements* deals with the format, classification and disclosure of information in corporate entity financial statements. This chapter also deals with the accounting treatment of corporate income tax in financial statements.

2 IAS 1 Presentation of Financial Statements

The required formats for published corporate entity financial statements are provided by IAS 1. This requires the following financial statements to be presented:

- a statement of profit or loss and other comprehensive income
- a statement of financial position
- a statement of changes in equity
- a statement of cash flows (covered later in this publication).

The only statements additional to those of a sole trader are the statement of changes in equity and the statement of cash flows. The statement of changes in equity shows the changes in the components (or elements) of equity during the twelve-month accounting period under review, where equity is equivalent of the 'capital' of a sole trader.

3 Statement of profit or loss and other comprehensive income

We introduced the statement of profit or loss and other comprehensive income very briefly earlier in the publication. We now return to this subject to discuss it in more detail. In previous chapters we have referred to the statement of profit or loss when discussing the revenue and expenses in sole proprietors. In limited companies this is referred to as the statement of comprehensive income. The statement of comprehensive income has two sections – the 'statement of profit or loss' section and the 'other comprehensive income' section. The statement of profit or loss section is similar to that of sole proprietors, except for differences in terminology and taxation noted earlier in the chapter. The 'statement of profit or loss' section includes all items from 'Sales' to 'Profit for the period'.

The section for 'other comprehensive income' can contain several items and you will learn about these later in your studies at more advanced levels. With regard to the assessment for this paper, there is **only one item you need to know**, and that is the revaluation of property. If a corporate entity revalued a property, then the **amount of the gain or surplus would be included as an item of 'other comprehensive income'**.

This gain or surplus is added to the profit for the period to give 'total comprehensive income for the period'. An illustration of this is given below:

Statement of comprehensive income of ABC for the Year Ended 30 June 20X8

	$000
Revenue	1,000
Cost of sales	(640)
Gross profit	360
Operating expenses (e.g. rent, power, telephone, etc.)	(100)
Operating profit	260
Investment income	5
Finance cost	(20)
Profit before tax	245
Income tax	(80)
Profit for the period	165
Other comprehensive income:	
Surplus on property revaluation in the year	25
Total comprehensive income for the period	190

Although the first section has been referred to above as the 'statement of profit or loss' section, this title does not appear in the statement. A corporate entity may choose to present its statement of profit or loss and other comprehensive income as two separate statements. In this case the two statements are called the 'statement of profit or loss' and the 'statement of profit or loss and other comprehensive income'. The title 'statement of profit or loss' does appear, and the statement of comprehensive income begins with the profit for the period.

The two statements would be presented as follows:

Statement one:

Statement of profit or loss and other comprehensive income of ABC for the Year Ended 30 June 20X8

Statement of profit or loss

	$000
Revenue	1,000
Cost of sales	(640)
Gross profit	360
Operating expenses (e.g. rent, power, telephone, etc.)	(100)
Operating profit	260
Investment income	5
Finance cost	(20)
Profit before tax	245
Income tax	(80)
Profit for the period	165

Statement two:

Statement of comprehensive income

Profit for the period	165
Other comprehensive income:	
Surplus on property revaluation in the year	25
Total comprehensive income for the period	190

As can be seen above, there is little difference in practice between the two presentations. In this subject, it will normally be assumed that a single statement is prepared and this will be referred to as the 'statement of comprehensive income'. There will only rarely be an 'other comprehensive income' section, as this only applies when there has been a revaluation of property during the year.

The total comprehensive income for the year will be shown in the statement of changes in equity, analysed between profit for the period and the net surplus on property revaluation in the year. For purposes of the assessment, you should be aware of the following:

- a statement of profit or loss, then only a statement of profit or loss showing profit after tax for the year is required
- a statement of profit or loss and other comprehensive income, showing total comprehensive income for the year, then either:
  - a statement with two sections is required, as in the first illustration above, or
  - two statements are required, as in the second illustration above.
- other comprehensive income', then just this section of a comprehensive income statement is required.

In general, the exam will make clear from the amount of information given and the nature of the question the exact format required to answer the question.

4 Statement of financial position

This summarises the asset, liability and equity balances (i.e. the financial position of the company) at the end of the accounting period.

Statement of financial position

Assets	$000	$000
Non-current asset		
Land	X	
Buildings	X	
Office equipment	X	
		X
Current assets		
Inventory	X	
Receivables	X	
Bank balance	X	
Cash in hand	X	
		X
		X
Capital + liabilities		
Capital		X
Non-current liabilities		
Bank loan		X
Current liabilities		
Payables		X
		X

5 Statement of changes in equity

We introduced the statement of changes in equity very briefly earlier in the publication and now that we have discussed financial statements of single entities in more detail, we can return to the statement of changes in equity.

The statement of changes in equity represents movements in the owners' interests in the company. As equity helps the shareholders' value their wealth it is important to ensure that they understand any movements in these balances. For this reason a statement of changes in equity is required.

A full example of a statement of changes in equity is as follows:

Statement of changes in equity

	Ordinary shares	Share premium	Reval'n surplus	Ret earnings	Total
	$000	$000	$000	$000	$000
Balance 1.1.X8	X	X	X	X	X
Profit for the year				X	X
Dividends				(X)	(X)
Shares issued	X	X			X
Revaluation of property			X		X
Balance 31.12.X8	X	X	X	X	X

6 Tax in corporate entity accounts

We can see from the above example of the statement of profit or loss and other comprehensive income that an additional item appears in the financial statements of companies – that of taxation. In the case of a sole trader this is a personal expense, and so does not appear in the financial statements. In contrast, in the case of a corporate entity, it is liable to pay tax on its profits and tax is therefore accounted for in the financial statements just like any other expense or liability. At the end of each year an estimate is made by the entity of the amount of its taxation liability and an accrual is made in its accounts as follows:

		$
Debit	Taxation expense account	X
Credit	Taxation liability account	X

When the liability is finally agreed with the tax authority there may be a difference between the accrual and the amount actually paid to settle the liability. Any difference between the accrual and the amount paid is adjusted in the following year financial statements.

For example, if in the current year the tax liability was estimated at $100,000 but only $95,000 was required to subsequently settle the liability, there would be an over-provision for tax. Therefore, the over-provision is released back into the statement of profit or loss to reduce the tax charge in the following year.

To summarise:

The statement of financial position liability = the current year's tax estimate (what we expect to pay based upon the profit for the year)

The statement of profit or loss and other comprehensive **income tax expense = the current year's tax estimate + under-provision from the previous year or – over-provision from the previous year.**

In this publication, tax on corporate entity profits is referred to by the generic term 'income tax' though in different countries it may have another name, for example corporation tax in the UK. Also take care to ensure that you do not confuse income tax paid by corporate entities with the income tax paid by employees on their wages and salaries – they are quite separate issues.

Test your understanding 1

RVL estimated its income tax charge for the year ended 30 June 20X3 at $230,000. In early 20X4, RVL's tax advisor settled the liability with the tax authority at $222,000. The difference arose because the financial statements were finalised some time before the tax computation was finalised and submitted to the tax authority. Therefore RVL had to make a prudent estimate of the potential tax liability to include in its financial statements for the year ended 30 June 20X3.

For the year ended 30 June 20X4, RVL estimated its income tax liability at $265,000, but is unsure as to how this should be reflected in the financial statements.

Required:

Which of the following represents the correct presentation of information in the financial statements for the year ended 30 June 20X4?

	SOFP	SPLOCI
	Income tax liability	**Income tax expense**
A	$257,000	$265,000
B	$273,000	$265,000
C	$265,000	$257,000
D	$265,000	$273,000

Worked example 16.A

Note: The following question is not in the form or style that you would expect to face in the real examination. However, it is a good learning exercise and should help you to understand how a basic set of financial statements are prepared from the information available.

The following trial balance has been extracted from the ledgers of JKL at 31 March 20X3:

	$	$
Sales (all on credit)		647,400
Inventories (1 April 20X2)	15,400	
Trade receivables and payables	82,851	41,936
Purchases (all on credit)	321,874	
Carriage in	13,256	
Carriage out	32,460	
Electricity	6,994	
Local business tax	8,940	
Wages and salaries	138,292	
Postages and stationery	6,984	
Rent	14,600	
Sales tax control		16,382
Employees' income tax control		4,736
Motor vehicles		
At cost	49,400	
Cumulative depreciation		21,240
Bank deposit account	90,000	
Bank current account	77,240	
Ordinary shares of $1 each		50,000
Retained earnings		76,597
	858,291	858,291

The following notes are also relevant:

(i) Inventory at 31 March 20X3 was valued at a cost of $19,473.

(ii) Prepaid rent amounted to $2,800.

(iii) Accruals are estimated as follows:

Electricity – $946

Wages and salaries – $2,464

(iv) Depreciation on motor vehicles is to be calculated at 25 per cent per annum using the reducing-balance method.

(v) Accrued interest on the bank deposit account amounts to $7,200.

(vi) An accrual for income tax of $30,000 is to be made on the profits for the year.

Required:

(a) Prepare JKL's statement of profit or loss for the year ended 31 March 20X3.

(b) Prepare JKL's statement of financial position at 31 March 20X3.

Solution:

(a) **Statement of profit or loss of JKL for the year ended 31 March 20X3**

	$000	$000
Sales		647,400
Opening inventory	15,400	
Purchases	321,874	
Carriage inwards	13,256	
Closing inventory	(19,473)	
		(331,057)
Gross profit		316,343
Carriage outwards	32,460	
Electricity (6,994 + 946)	7,940	
Local business tax	8,940	
Wages and salaries (138,292 + 2,464)	140,756	
Postage and stationery	6,984	
Rent (14,600 – 2,800)	11,800	
Depreciation of vehicles (49,400 – 21,240) × 25%	7,040	
		(215,920)
Operating profit		100,423
Interest receivable		7,200
Profit before tax		107,623
Income tax		(30,000)
Profit for the period		77,623

(b) **Statement of financial position of JKL as at 31 March 20X3**

Assets	**Cost** $000	**Acc. depreciation** $000	**Carrying amount** $000
Non-current assets			
Motor vehicles	49,400	(28,280)	21,120
Current assets			
Inventories	19,473		
Receivables	82,851		
Interest receivable	7,200		
Prepayment	2,800		
Bank deposit account	90,000		
Bank current account	77,240		
			279,564
			300,684
Equity and liabilities			
Ordinary shares of $1 each			50,000
Retained earnings			154,220
			204,220
Current liabilities			
Payables	41,936		
Accrual for expenses (946 + 2,464)	3,410		
Income tax	30,000		
Sales tax	16,382		
Employees' income tax	4,736		
			96,464
			300,684

Workings:

Retained earnings: $76,597 + $77,623 = $154,220

7 Chapter summary

In this chapter you have studied:

- the preparation of financial statements from trial balance for a single entity, including:
  - the accounting requirements of IAS 1 *Presentation of Financial Statements*
  - the accounting treatment of income tax in corporate entity financial statements.

Note that the accounting requirements of IAS 1, including the format of the financial statements, are relevant in subject F1 Financial Reporting in the CIMA Professional Qualification.

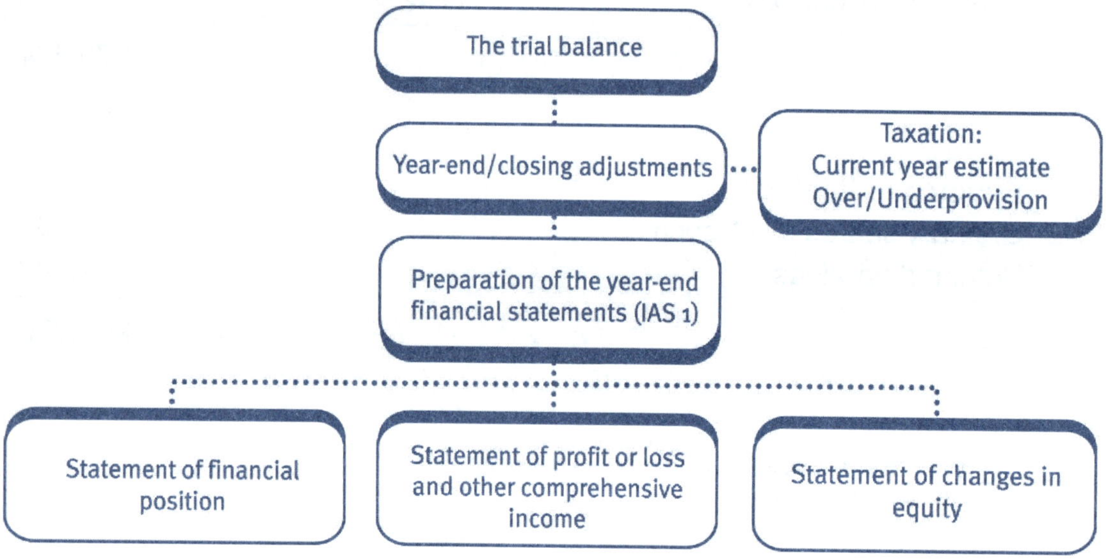

Test your understanding questions

Test your understanding 2

Which one of the following would you expect to find in the statement of changes in equity in a corporate entity for the current year?

A Ordinary dividend proposed during the current year, but paid in the following year

B Ordinary dividend proposed during the previous year, but paid in the current year

C Directors' fees

D Auditors' fees

Test your understanding 3

Match the financial statement in which each of the following items will be disclosed:

	Item	Financial statement
A	Dividend paid by a corporate entity to its shareholders in the year	
B	Corporate income tax liability	
C	Loss on disposal of a non-current asset	
D	Surplus arising on revaluation of land and buildings in the year	
E	Corporate income tax charge	
F	The issue of ordinary shares in the year	

Choice of financial statement available:

Statement of financial position/Statement of profit or loss/Statement of other comprehensive income/Statement of changes in equity

Test your understanding 4

Which two of the following items are not included in a corporate entity statement of profit or loss?

A Salaries paid to directors

B Dividend paid to shareholders

C Income tax expense

D Revaluation surplus for the year

E Audit fee

Test your understanding 5

In July 20X2 POK paid its prior year tax bill of $103,000. The estimate of the income tax liability included in the financial statements for the year ended 31 December 20X1 was $100,000.

POK estimated that it would have an income tax liability for the year ended 31 December 20X2 of $150,000.

Required:

What was the income tax expense and liability included in POK's financial statements for the year ended 31 December 20X2?

$.............. income tax expense

$.............. income tax liability

Test your understanding 6

At 31 March 20X5, ROM had a liability outstanding for income tax of $15,500. During the year ended 31 March 20X6, the outstanding income tax liability was agreed and paid at $14,750, and the liability for the year ended 31 March 20X6 was estimated as $16,300.

Required:

What was the income tax expense and liability included in ROM's financial statements for the year ended 31 March 20X6?

$.............. income tax expense

$.............. income tax liability

Test your understanding 7

UVW estimated its income tax charge for the year ended 30 September 20X3 at $185,000. In February 20X4, UVW agreed and settled the liability with the tax authority at $189,000. For the year ended 30 September 20X4, UVW estimated its income tax liability at $180,000, but is unsure as to how this should be reflected in the financial statements.

Required:

Which of the following represents the correct presentation of information in the financial statements for the year ended 30 September 20X4?

	SOFP	SPLOCI
	Income tax liability	**Income tax expense**
A	$189,000	$185,000
B	$185,000	$180,000
C	$176,000	$176,000
D	$180,000	$184,000

Test your understanding 8

The following question is not in the form or style that you would expect to face in the real examination. It requires you to identify or calculate specific amounts for inclusion in the financial statements, or to state accounting entries required. Each of the individual requirements could form the basis of a question in the objective test examination and it is therefore a good learning exercise that should help you to understand the issues involved when preparing financial statements for an entity.

The accountant of FID has started to prepare the financial statements for the year ended 31 December 20X6. The items included in the trial balance as at 31 December 20X6 were as follows:

	$000
Land	100
Buildings	120
Plant and machinery	170
Accumulated depreciation of plant and machinery	120
$1 Share capital	100
Retained earnings	200
Receivables	200
Payables	110
Inventory	190
Operating profit	83
5% Loan notes	180
Allowance for receivables	3
Cash at bank and in hand	12
Suspense (may be a debit or a credit balance)	???

Notes (i) – (vi) are relevant to the preparation of the financial statements:

(i) The sales ledger control account figure, which is used in the trial balance, does not agree with the total of the sales ledger balances. A contra of $5,000 has been entered correctly in the individual ledger accounts but has been entered on the wrong side of both control accounts.

The balance of $4,000 on sales returns account has inadvertently been omitted from the trial balance, though correctly entered in the ledger records.

(ii) A standing order of receipt from a regular customer for $2,000, and bank charges of $1,000, have been completely omitted from the accounting records.

(iii) A receivable for $1,000 is to be written off. The allowance for receivables balance is to be increased to $5,000.

(iv) It was discovered that the closing inventory valuation included some items valued at $2,000 which were damaged and worthless.

(v) The loan notes were issued on 1 September 20X6 and no payment of interest had been made by 31 December 20X6.

(vi) A dividend of 10c per share was proposed before the year end, but not paid until 31 January 20X7.

Required:

(a) Prepare a trial balance as at 31 December 20X6 and identify the balance on the suspense account.

(b) Prepare the journal entries to correct the suspense account balance.

(c) Calculate the charge to the statement of profit or loss for irrecoverable debts and allowance for receivables.

(d) Calculate the accrual required for interest on the 5% loan notes.

(e) State the journal adjustment required to account for the standing order receipt and the bank charges omitted from the accounting records.

Test your understanding 9

The following is an extract from the trial balance of a business entity for the year ended 31 December 20X4.

	Debit	Credit
	$	$
Opening inventory	28,000	
Sales		310,000
Purchases	225,000	
Returns	22,000	26,000
Carriage inwards	7,000	
Carriage outwards	8,000	

You are also advised that the value of inventory at 31 December 20X4 was $23,000.

Required:

Using some or all of the figures above, what was the gross profit for the year ended 31 December 20X4?

$..............

Test your understanding answers

Test your understanding 1

C

The statement of financial position liability at 30 June 20X4 should always be the liability estimated based upon the profit for that year i.e. $265,000.

The statement of profit or loss expense represents the current year estimated charge less the over-provision for the previous year, i.e. $265,000 – ($230,000 – $222,000) = $257,000.

Test your understanding 2

B

Dividends proposed are included in the statement of changes in equity when they are paid. The dividend should be approved at the annual general meeting and subsequently paid. Directors' and auditors' fees are normal business expenses and appear in the statement of profit or loss and other comprehensive income.

Test your understanding 3

	Item	**Financial statement**
A	Dividend paid by a corporate entity to its shareholders in the year	Statement of changes in equity
B	Corporate income tax liability	Statement of financial position
C	Loss on disposal of a non-current asset	Statement of profit or loss
D	Surplus arising on revaluation of land and buildings in the year	Statement of other comprehensive income
E	Corporate income tax charge	Statement of profit or loss
F	The issue of ordinary shares in the year	Statement of changes in equity

The corporate income tax charge is included in the statement of profit or loss in arriving at profit after tax for the year. The corporate income tax liability is included within current liabilities in the statement of financial position.

The dividend paid by a corporate entity to its shareholders is included in the statement of changes in equity. The loss on disposal of a non-current asset is included in the statement of profit or loss in arriving at profit after tax for the year.

The issue of ordinary shares in the year will be disclosed in the statement of changes in equity. Note that the balance on the ordinary share capital account at the end of the accounting period will be disclosed in the statement of financial position – this will not be the same amount as the nominal value of shares issued in the year (or even the total proceeds raised if the shares were issued at a premium) if there were already ordinary shares in issue.

The surplus arising upon revaluation of land and buildings in the year is included in the statement of other comprehensive income. Note that the balance on the revaluation surplus account at the end of the accounting period will be disclosed in the statement of financial position – this will not be the same amount as the revaluation surplus arising in the year if land and buildings have been revalued in an earlier accounting period.

Test your understanding 4

B and D

Revaluation surplus is an item of other comprehensive income, accounted for after profit after tax for the year. Dividends paid are accounted for in the statement of changes in equity.

Test your understanding 5

$153,000 income tax expense and $150,000 income tax liability

The statement of profit or loss tax expense represents this year's estimate plus any under-provision (or less any over-provision) for the previous year. In the case of POK, it has paid **more** for the previous year than previously estimated, hence made an under-provision in the previous year which must be **added** to the current year estimate.

Tax expense for 31 December 20X2 = $150,000 + $3,000 under-provision = $153,000

Test your understanding 6

$15,550 income tax expense and $16,300 income tax liability

The statement of financial position liability at 31 March 20X6 should always be the liability estimated based upon the profit for that year i.e. $16,300.

The statement of profit or loss expense represents the current year estimated liability less the over-provision for the previous year, i.e. $16,300 – ($15,500 – $14,750) = $15,550.

Test your understanding 7

D

The statement of financial position liability at 30 September 20X4 should always be the liability estimated based upon the profit for that year i.e. $180,000.

The statement of profit or loss charge represents the current year estimated charge plus the under-provision for the previous year, i.e. $180,000 + ($189,000 – $185,000) = $184,000.

Test your understanding 8

(a) **Trial balance as at 31 December 20X6**

	Debit	Credit
	$000	$000
Land	100	
Buildings	120	
Plant and machinery	170	
Accumulated depreciation on non-current assets		120
Issued share capital @ $1 each		100
Retained earnings at 31 December 20X5		200
Receivables	200	
Payables		110
Inventory	190	
Draft operating profit for the year		83
5% Loan notes		180
Allowance for receivables		3
Cash at bank and in hand	12	
Suspense account – balancing figure	**4**	
	796	796

(b) The balance on the suspense account was $4,000 debit. Within note 1 of the question you were advised that the sales returns ledger account balance had been omitted from the trial balance, which will be corrected by the following:

Debit: Sales Returns $4,000, and Credit: Suspense $4,000.

The consequence will be that, if credit customers have returned goods, we can no longer include the value of those items as sales revenue, therefore sales (and consequently profit for the year) will be reduced by $4,000.

(c) The charge to the statement of profit or loss for irrecoverable debts is $1,000 plus the increase in allowance for receivables of $2,000 ($5,000 – $3,000) = $3,000 total charge.

(b) The accrual for loan note interest is $3,000 (4/12 × 5% × $180,000).

(e)

	$	$
Bank ($2,000 – $1,000) i.e. net increase of $1,000 in bank balance	1,000	
Bank charges expense	1,000	
Receivables ledger control account		2,000

Test your understanding 9

Draw up the following:

	$	$	$
Sales			310,000
Less: Returns			(22,000)
			288,000
Less: Cost of sales			
Opening inventory		28,000	
Purchases	225,000		
Carriage inwards	7,000		
	232,000		
Less: Returns	(26,000)		
Net purchases		206,000	
		234,000	
Less: Closing inventory		(23,000)	
			211,000
Gross profit			77,000

Common errors include:

- reversing returns
- not adding carriage inwards to the cost of purchases (or deducting it)
- adding carriage outwards to the cost of purchases.

Chapter

17

The manufacturing account

Chapter learning objectives

When you have completed this chapter, you should be able to:

- prepare basic manufacturing accounts.

1 Introduction

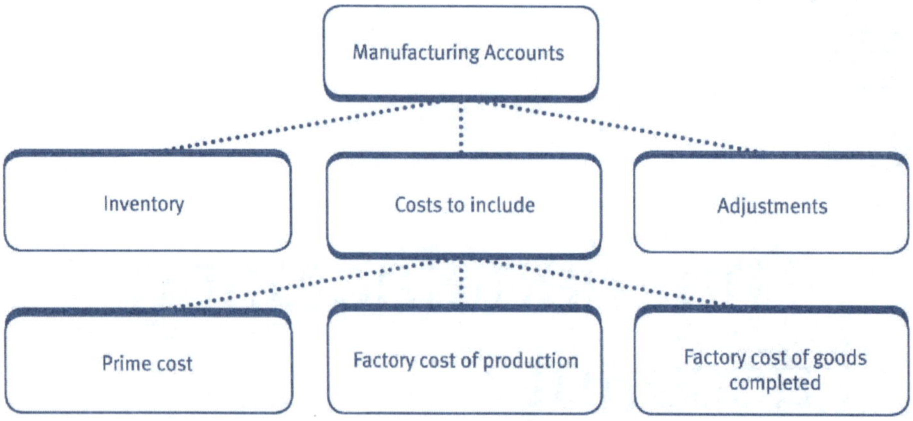

In this chapter, you will learn:

- why manufacturing accounts are needed
- the costs to include in a manufacturing account
- the form and content of a manufacturing account.

In the chapters studied so far, you have considered business entities that purchase goods for onward sale to customers – in other words, with retail and wholesale traders. We now turn our attention to manufacturing business entities.

In most respects the financial statements of a manufacturing entity show no major or fundamental differences from what you have already studied. Its statement of financial position will be very similar, although it is worth noting that the asset of inventory in a manufacturing entity is likely to comprise raw materials, work-in-progress and finished goods.

In addition, the scale of business activities of a manufacturing entity is often larger than for other trading entities. They may own factories that contain lots of plant and equipment, whereas a trading entity may operate from smaller rented premises and not have the same need for plant and equipment other than office equipment and delivery vans. Ultimately, both types of business entity own and use non-current assets, and have current assets of inventory, receivables and cash and bank balances. Note that retail business will have non-current assets (premises, fixtures and fittings etc.), and current assets of inventory and cash and bank balances, but will be unlikely to have receivables as their sales are usually on a cash basis.

The statement of profit or loss will be almost identical. The one exception is that instead of the cost of finished goods purchased in the year, the trading account will show the cost of finished goods manufactured in the year.

It is this final item that leads to the one major difference in the financial statements of a manufacturing entity in comparison with a trading entity. Establishing the cost of finished goods manufactured in the year is not such a simple process as finding the total of finished goods purchased by a retailer.

Indeed, it requires a new account – **the manufacturing account** –to arrive at this cost.

The manufacturing account, in an identical way to the trading account, is a sub-section of the statement of profit or loss. The name 'manufacturing account' does not appear within the statement of profit or loss but it is nevertheless a very important element of the statement of profit or loss.

2 Why is a manufacturing account needed?

Manufacturers may sell their finished products directly to the public, or may sell them to another trading entity such as a wholesaler or retailer. The statement of profit or loss is used to bring together the income and expenditure of trading and operating the entity, and this still applies to a manufacturing entity. However, the calculation of the cost of goods sold by a retail or wholesale entity is relatively straightforward, that is, opening inventory, plus purchases, less closing inventory. Calculating the cost of goods manufactured is often more detailed than this, as the manufacturing entity will incur not only the cost of materials but also labour costs and other expenses incurred during the manufacturing process. The manufacturing account is used to bring together the costs of manufacturing during the accounting period.

Inventory in manufacturing entities

The manufacturing process will involve three stages:

Stage 1 The acquisition of raw materials.

Stage 2 The modification or processing of those materials, with the addition of labour costs and other expenses.

Stage 3 The production of finished goods.

However, some raw materials purchased during an accounting period will still be unmodified at the end of the accounting period, whilst some will only be partly modified. In addition, there will be some finished goods produced during the accounting period that remain unsold. The business entity may also buy-in ready-made items for sale. Therefore, at the beginning and end of an accounting period, there could be four types of inventory included in the statement of financial position as follows:

- bought-in goods – those bought-in as finished goods for sale to customers
- finished goods – those manufactured by the entity for sale to customers
- work in progress – i.e. partly completed goods, and
- raw materials – purchased from suppliers and not yet used in the manufacturing process.

It is important to remember that the trading account must still be used to show the sales revenue earned and the cost of goods sold, not the cost of goods manufactured. The trading account will therefore bring together opening inventory of finished goods, plus the cost of completed goods manufactured during the accounting period, less closing inventory of finished goods. The manufacturing account will contain all of the manufacturing costs, with adjustments for opening and closing inventory of raw materials and work in progress.

It is also important to appreciate that the manufacturing account is used solely to bring together expenses – it does not include any sales revenues.

3 Costs to include in the manufacturing account

We have already mentioned that the cost of raw materials is contained within the manufacturing account. The calculation of raw materials consumed in the manufacturing process is exactly the same as the calculations you have previously used in the trading account of retail and wholesale entities, that is:

- opening Inventory of raw materials
- plus purchases of raw materials (including carriage inwards and less returns)
- less closing Inventory of raw materials.

However, other manufacturing costs must now also be considered.

The following terms are considered key to understanding the manufacturing account.

Other direct costs

A direct cost is one that can be identified with units of production; very often it is a cost that varies according to the level of production. You will learn more about this cost behaviour in your studies of subject BA2 Fundamentals of Management Accounting. Obviously, raw materials costs are direct costs in that they directly vary with the level of production.

Examples of other direct costs are:

- **Direct labour (also known as production labour).** The wages and associated costs of those producing the goods
- **Direct expenses.** These are other costs that can be identified with units of production. These are more difficult to establish, as most expenses are more general in nature, but examples of direct expenses might be equipment hire for a special production run, power costs for a particular machine, and royalties payable on the production of certain products (see below). You will not encounter direct expenses very often, however, and such expenses are likely to be highlighted if they are to be regarded as such.

A **patent** is a method of obtaining legally-enforceable protection for intellectual property such as an invention.

When a business entity invents a new component, product or production process, it may protect its invention by obtaining a patent. A patent is a method of protecting intellectual property by prohibiting its unauthorised use or copying by other business entities. The invention can then be used by the patent owner to improve its products, or reduce its manufacturing costs, which will improve profitability. In effect, the patent owner has an intangible asset from which it expects to receive future economic benefits in the form of increased sales revenues and/or reduced costs.

It is also possible for a patent owner to authorise other business entities to use its patented component, product or production process, subject to specified terms and conditions contained within the licence in exchange for a payment.

A **royalty** is a payment to the patent owner in exchange for use of the patented product, component or production process by another business entity. The royalty is normally directly related to the number of units produced (e.g. $2 per unit produced) during an accounting period. It is therefore a direct cost of production and included in the calculation of prime cost.

The accounting entries for royalties payable to the patent owner are as follows:

Debit:	Royalties expense	$X
Credit:	Payables (or cash paid)	$X

Note that royalties on goods sold would not be included in the direct cost of production calculation, only royalties paid on goods produced.

Prime cost

Prime cost is the total of direct costs, that is, direct materials consumed, plus direct labour and direct expenses (if any). It should be clearly shown as a sub-total in the manufacturing account.

Indirect costs

These include all the other costs of manufacturing that are not part of prime cost. They are also referred to as manufacturing overheads, production overheads or factory overheads. Examples include:

- factory rent
- factory heating, lighting and insurance
- wages and salaries paid to factory supervisors and maintenance engineers (also known as indirect factory labour)
- depreciation of non-current assets used in manufacturing

Note that only costs associated with manufacturing are included. Do not include any post-production costs such as warehousing of finished goods, selling and distribution costs or general administrative costs.

Factory cost of production

Factory cost of production is the total of prime cost and indirect costs consumed in the factory and it is another important subtotal to be shown in the manufacturing account.

The factory cost of production is the total of new costs introduced to the factory. However, there may already be some work in progress in the factory system at the start of the accounting period. Some of this will be completed during the period, but there will probably still be some unfinished, and some new work in progress at the end of the period. We need to adjust the factory cost of production to add in the opening work in progress and deduct the closing work in progress. This is shown in the final section of the manufacturing account.

Factory cost of goods completed

This is the end result of the manufacturing account, and its balance is incorporated into the trading account. In effect, this is equivalent to purchases included in the trading account to calculate gross profit for a trading entity.

4 Layout of the manufacturing account

As stated earlier, the trading account is the place to show the sales revenue earned and the cost of goods sold. In manufacturing business entities, however, the calculation of cost of goods sold will not include purchases and inventory of raw materials, but will instead include the factory cost of goods completed together with opening and closing inventory of finished goods. This part of the statement of profit or loss; in effect the 'factory cost of goods completed' is a substitute for 'purchases' which we have previously used in the trading account of a retailer or trader. It can then be adjusted for opening and closing inventory of finished goods to arrive at cost of goods sold in the accounting period.

The following proforma includes expense headings to enable you to identify how expenses are classified within the manufacturing account.

Manufacturing account for the year ended 31 December 20X1

	$	$
Factory cost of goods completed:		
Opening Inventory of raw materials		12,000
Purchases of raw materials		235,000
		247,000
Closing Inventory of raw materials (include in SOFP)		(14,000)
Raw materials consumed		233,000
Direct manufacturing wages		153,000
Royalty payable		10,000
Other direct factory expenses		5,000
Prime cost		**401,000**
Production overhead:		
Factory supervisors' wages	30,000	
Heating and lighting	16,000	
Factory rent	12,000	
		58,000
Factory costs incurred		**459,000**
Opening work in progress	26,000	
Closing work in progress (include in SOFP)	(21,000)	
		5,000
Factory cost of goods completed (to trading account)		**464,000**

The factory cost of goods completed can then be transferred to the trading account to calculate gross profit.

5 Statement of profit or loss of a manufacturer

These are exactly as for other business entities. The trading account in the statement of profit or loss will deal with finished goods only in order to arrive at gross profit. Other expenses are included in profit or loss as usual.

Trading and profit or loss account for the year ended 31 December 20X1

	$	$
Sales		645,000
Less: Cost of goods sold		
Opening inventory of finished goods	55,000	
Factory cost of goods completed (from manufacturing account)	464,000	
	519,000	
Less: closing inventory of finished goods (include in SOFP)	(35,000)	
Cost of goods sold		(484,000)
Gross profit		161,000
Less: selling and distribution expenses		(67,000)
Less: administration expenses		(55,000)
Net profit before tax		39,000

6 Statement of financial position of a manufacturer

These are also prepared as for other business entities, except that there is likely to be up to four types of inventory:

- bought-in goods for resale
- finished goods
- work in progress
- raw materials.

Based upon the example in the previous sections of this chapter, this would consist of:

Inventories at 31 Dec 20X1	$
Raw materials	14,000
Work in Progress	21,000
Finished goods	35,000
	70,000

The accounting system

The accounting system for a manufacturing entity

Ledger accounts will be prepared in the same way as for other business entities, except that there will be additional ledger accounts for items connected with manufacturing, such as direct factory labour, indirect factory labour, and inventory of work in progress and finished goods. Some items of expense, however, may not be separately established or invoiced. For example, premises insurance might consist of a single invoice covering all the buildings. In such cases, it is necessary to apportion the expenses between manufacturing and other elements (often described as 'factory' and 'office'). In computer-based assessment questions, you will be told what proportions to apply, if appropriate.

The manufacturing account, just as the trading account, and statement of profit or loss as a whole, is part of the double-entry bookkeeping system. Hence it is called the manufacturing 'account' and is a ledger account which can be debited and credited. The items that appear in it will all have an equivalent opposite entry in either the nominal ledger or the trading account. For example, expenses such as direct factory labour will be debited to the direct factory labour ledger account during the year, and then, at the end of the year, the balance will be transferred to the manufacturing account (debit manufacturing account; credit direct factory labour).

The balance on the manufacturing account is transferred to the trading account at the end of the year (debit trading account; credit manufacturing account).

The key to questions in this area is to adopt a methodical approach. Remember that your aim in the manufacturing account is to arrive at the total cost of manufacturing the completed goods in the year. This can be regarded as comprising of three elements:

- the costs directly attributable to the goods produced, such as the raw materials they contain, and the wages of personnel directly involved in manufacturing
- the indirect factory costs, sometimes called factory overheads. These might include the costs of heating and lighting the factory, the rent on factory premises and the wages of factory supervisors
- an adjustment for opening and closing work in progress, similar to the treatment of opening and closing Inventory of finished goods in a trading account.

e.g **Illustration 1**

GCH is a manufacturer of components and the following is an extract of balances from the accounting records of the business entity at 31 December 20X4.

	$
Inventory at 1 January 20X4	
Raw materials	11,000
Work in progress	16,000
Finished goods	20,090
Inventory at 31 December 20X4	
Raw materials	17,000
Work in progress	18,000
Finished goods	18,040
Wages	
Direct manufacturing	203,080
Factory supervisors	13,325
Direct factory fuel and power	91,000
Factory heat and light	4,500
Royalty payable	4,000
Factory rent	3,000
Purchase of raw materials	256,000
Returns inwards	420
Administrative expenses	14,500
Selling and distribution costs	25,286
Sales	800,290

Required:

(a) Prepare the manufacturing account of GCH for the year ended 31 December 20X4

(b) Prepare the statement of profit or loss of GCH for the year ended 31 December 20X4.

Solution

Manufacturing account of GCH for the year ended 31 December 20X4

	$	$
Opening inventory of raw materials		11,000
Purchases of raw materials		256,000
		267,000
Closing inventory of raw materials		(17,000)
Raw materials consumed		250,000
Direct manufacturing wages		203,080
Direct factory fuel and power		91,000
Royalty payable		4,000
Prime cost		548,080
Production overhead:		
Factory supervisors' wages	13,325	
Heat and light	4,500	
Rent	3,000	
		20,825
Factory costs incurred		568,905
Opening work in progress	16,000	
Closing work in progress	(18,000)	
		(2,000)
Factory cost of goods completed		566,905

Note: The closing value of raw materials, work in progress and finished goods at 31 December 20X4 will be included in the statement of financial position at that date.

Statement of profit or loss of GCH for the year ended 31 December 20X4

	$	$
Sales		800,290
Less: Returns inwards		(420)
		799,870
Opening inventory of finished goods	20,090	
Factory cost of goods completed	566,905	
	586,995	
Less: closing inventory of finished goods	(18,040)	
		(568,955)
Gross profit		230,915
Less:		
Selling and distribution costs	25,286	
Administration expenses	14,500	
		(39,786)
Net profit for the year		191,129

Test your understanding 1

What are the component parts of prime cost?

7 Chapter summary

In this chapter we considered the production of a statement of profit or loss, incorporating manufacturing and trading accounts, and a statement of financial position for a manufacturing business entity.

You should appreciate that the only difference in the trading account from that of a non-manufacturing business entity is the substitution of **'factory cost of goods completed' for 'purchases'.**

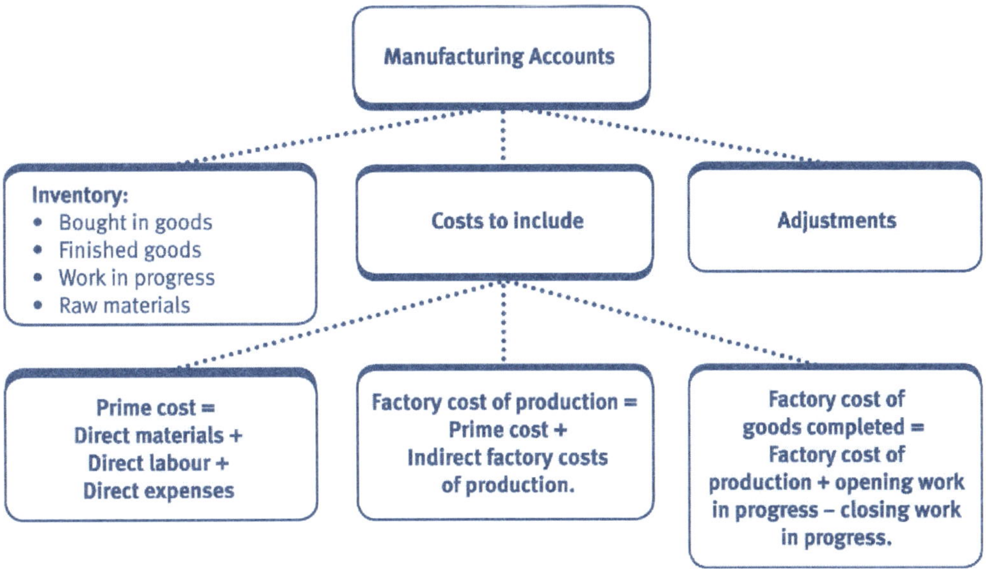

Test your understanding questions

Test your understanding 2

The following information relates to a business entity for the year ended 30 June 20X5:

Inventory at 1 July 20X4	$
Raw materials	10,000
Work in progress	2,000
Finished goods	34,000
Inventory at 30 June 20X5	
Raw materials	11,000
Work in progress	4,000
Finished goods	30,000
Purchases of raw materials	50,000
Direct wages	40,000
Royalties	3,000
Production overheads	60,000
Distribution costs	55,000
Administration expenses	70,000
Sales	300,000

Required:

What was the cost of goods manufactured goods completed for the year ended 30 June 20X5?

$................

Test your understanding 3

If work in progress decreased during an accounting period, then:

A prime cost will decrease

B prime cost will increase

C the factory cost of goods completed will decrease

D the factory cost of goods completed will increase

Test your understanding 4

An increase in the cost of work in progress will:

A increase the prime cost

B decrease the prime cost

C increase the factory cost of goods completed

D decrease the factory cost of goods completed

Test your understanding 5

A business entity has the following manufacturing costs for the year ended 31 March 20X7:

	$
Prime cost	56,000
Factory overheads	4,500
Opening work in progress	6,200
Factory cost of goods completed	57,000

Required:

What was the value of work in progress as at 31 March 20X7?

$.............

Test your understanding 6

The prime cost of goods manufactured is the total of:

A all factory costs before adjusting for work in progress

B all factory costs of goods completed

C all materials and labour

D direct factory costs

Test your understanding 7

The following information relates to MLK as at 30 September:

	20X1	20X0
	$	$
Inventory of raw materials	75,000	45,000
Work in progress inventory	60,000	70,000
Inventory of finished goods	100,000	90,000
For the year ended 30th September 20X1		
Purchases of raw materials	150,000	
Manufacturing wages	50,000	
Factory overheads	40,000	

Required:

What was the prime cost of production in the manufacturing account for the year ended 30 September 20X1?

$.............

The following question is much harder than you would expect to see in your BA3 exam but it is a good question to consolidate your knowledge to date.

Test your understanding 8

MNO makes agricultural machinery, for sale to major suppliers in the industry. The following figures were extracted from its trial balance at 30 September 20X3.

	$000
Sales	2,200
Purchases of parts	650
Carriage inwards	40
Carriage outwards	100
Sales returns	80
Purchases returns	60
Manufacturing labour costs	200
Factory supervisory labour costs	75
Office salaries	108
Other costs	
Heating and lighting (factory $132,000, and admin offices $33,000)	165
Rent and insurance (factory $98,000, and admin offices $24,000)	122
Factory machinery at cost	1,000
Accumulated depreciation of factory machinery	400
Delivery vehicles at cost	300
Accumulated depreciation of vehicles	100
Office machinery at cost	120
Accumulated depreciation of office machinery	80
Opening inventory at 1 October 20X2:	
Raw materials	175
Work in progress	425
Finished goods	115

At 30 September 20X3, the following information was also available:

(a) Inventory, work in progress and finished goods balances as at 30 September 20X3 were as follows:

	$000
Raw materials	147
Work in progress	392
Finished goods	138

(b) Accruals and prepayments at 30 September 20X3 were as follows:

	$000
Heat and light accrued (factory $12,000, and admin offices $3,000)	15
Rent prepaid (factory $18,000, and admin offices $4,000)	22

(c) Depreciation is to be calculated as follows:

- factory machinery, 10 per cent, straight line
- delivery vehicles, 20 per cent, reducing balance
- office machinery, 25 per cent, reducing balance.

(d) Delivery vehicles are used entirely for the delivery of finished goods.

Required:

(a) Prepare the manufacturing account of MNO for the year ended 30 September 20X3.

(b) Prepare the statement of profit or loss of MNO for the year ended 30 September 20X3.

Test your understanding answers

Test your understanding 1

The component parts of prime cost are direct materials, direct labour and direct expenses (overheads).

Test your understanding 2

Cost of goods manufactured is found as follows:

	$
Opening inventory of raw materials	10,000
Purchases of raw materials	50,000
Less: Closing inventory of raw materials	(11,000)
	49,000
Direct wages	40,000
Royalties	3,000
Prime cost	92,000
Production overheads	60,000
	152,000
Less: Increase in work in progress (2,000 – 4,000)	(2,000)
Cost of goods completed	150,000

Test your understanding 3

D

A decrease in work in progress means fewer goods are partly complete, thus the value of completed goods will be higher. A and B are incorrect as work-in-progress has no effect on prime cost.

Test your understanding 4

D

A and B are incorrect as work in progress has no effect on prime cost. An increase in work in progress means that more production is in a partly finished state and therefore less has been completed, therefore C is incorrect.

Test your understanding 5

	$
Prime cost	56,000
Factory overheads	4,500
Opening WIP	6,200
Closing WIP (ß)	(9,700)
Factory cost of goods completed	57,000

The closing WIP must be the balancing item to agree to the factory cost completed of $57,000.

Test your understanding 6

D

Test your understanding 7

The answer is: **$170,000**

Prime cost means the total of direct costs, that is direct materials consumed, direct labour and direct expenses.

	$
Opening inventory of raw materials	45,000
Purchase of raw materials	150,000
Closing inventory of raw materials	(75,000)
Raw materials consumed in production	120,000
Manufacturing wages	50,000
Prime cost	170,000

Test your understanding 8

- Categorise items as applicable to either the manufacturing account or the statement of profit or loss respectively.
- Remember to make any adjustments necessary for accruals and prepayments, and the calculation of depreciation, for items in the manufacturing account and statement of profit or loss respectively.
- Some items in the question might not be required for your answer.

Manufacturing account of MNO for the year ended 30 September 20X3

	$000	$000
Opening inventory of raw materials		175
Purchases	650	
Carriage inwards	40	
	690	
Less: Purchases returns	(60)	
		630
		805
Less: Closing inventory of raw materials		(147)
Direct materials consumed		658
Direct labour		200
Prime cost		858
Factory indirect overheads		
Supervisory labour	75	
Heat and light (132 + 12)	144	
Rent and insurance (98 – 18)	80	

	$000	$000
Depreciation		
Factory machinery (10% × $1,000)	100	
		399
Factory cost of production		1,257
Opening work in progress	425	
Less: Closing work in progress	(392)	
		33
		1,290

- Categorise items before you start the statement of profit or loss.
- Remember to make adjustments for accruals and prepayments, and the calculation of depreciation, before splitting

Statement of profit or loss of MNO for the year ended 30 September 20X3

	$000	$000
Sales		2,200
Less: Sales returns		(80)
		2,120
Opening inventory of finished goods	115	
Factory cost of goods completed	1,290	
	1,405	
Less: closing inventory of finished goods	(138)	
		1,267
Gross profit		853
Expenses:		
Carriage outwards	100	
Office salaries	108	
Admin heat and light ($33,000 + $3,000)	36	
Admin rent and insurance ($24,000 – $4,000)	20	
Depreciation:		
Delivery vehicles		
(20% × ($300,000 –$100,000))	40	
Office machinery		
(25% × ($120,000 –$80,000))	10	
		(314)
Net profit for the year		539

Chapter

18

The statement of cash flows

Chapter learning objectives

When you have completed this chapter, you should be able to:

- prepare a statement of cash flows.

1 Introduction

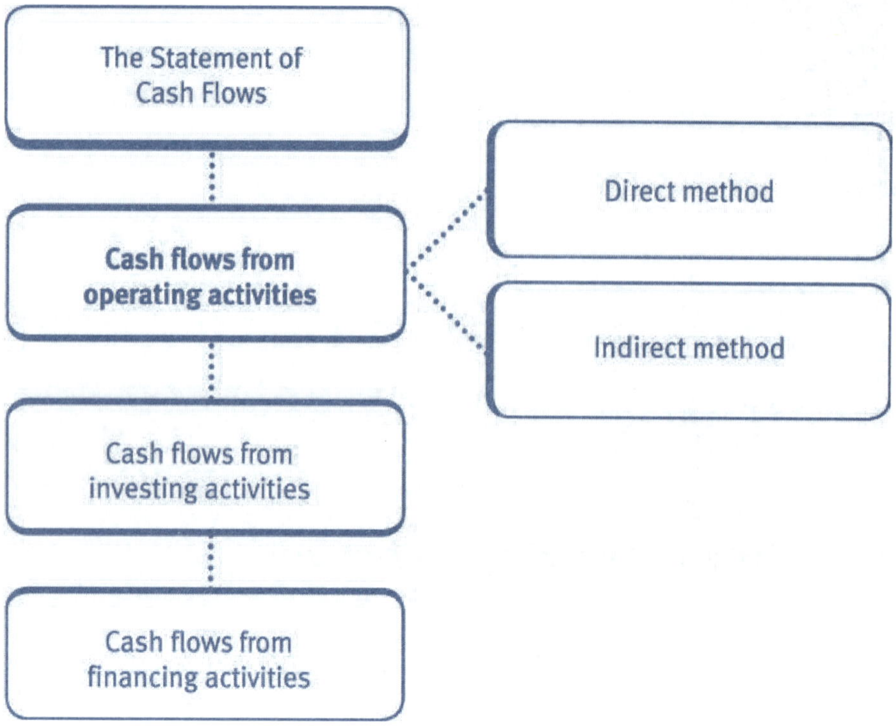

In this chapter, you will learn:

- what a statement of cash flows is
- the format and classification of the statement specified by IAS 7 *Statement of Cash Flows*
- calculation of items for inclusion in the statement of cash flows.

In this chapter we will consider a further financial statement that companies are required to include as part of their annual financial statements – the statement of cash flows.

Although the focus is normally upon preparation of this statement in relation to companies, it may be prepared for any business entity.

2 What is a statement of cash flows?

A statement of cash flows recognises the **importance of liquidity** to a business entity by reporting the effect of the transactions of the entity during the period on the bank, cash and similar liquid assets.

At its simplest, it is a summary of receipts and payments during the period, but this method of presentation does not answer a common question asked by the users of financial statements: 'Why does the profit made during the period not equate to an increase in cash and bank balances?' What is needed, therefore, is a statement that commences with the profit made during the period, and shows how that profit, and other transactions during the same period, have affected the flow of cash into and out of the entity.

The syllabus states that the presentation for a statement of cash flows should be based on IAS 7 *Statement of Cash Flows* and that requirement is followed in this publication.

Why does the profit earned not equal the change in bank and cash balances?

There are three main reasons why this does not occur:

1 Profit is calculated on an accruals basis, which means that revenue is recognised when it is earned, not when it is received, and expenses are deducted on the same basis to match with that revenue. Bank and cash balances change when monies are received and paid out. Thus the bank balance will be different from profit due to items such as the inventory balance, unpaid receivables and payables, accruals and prepayments, both at the start and at the end of the accounting period. For example, an increase in inventory means that there has been an increase in working capital and therefore a net cash outflow during the year. An increase in receivables indicates the same situation. An increase in payables means the business is using credit from supplier to finance its business activities, which represents a net cash inflow to the business.

2 The calculation of profit includes some items that do not affect cash at all or affect it differently. For example, profit for the year is determined after deducting depreciation, which involves no movement in cash. The profit or loss on disposal of a non-current asset will be included in the profit for the year, but it is the **proceeds from the sale** of the asset that will affect the cash and bank balances. In addition, there may be other accrued items in the statement of comprehensive income, taxation for example, where the accruals-based accounting treatment differs from the cash flows to pay the liability. Similarly, the change in allowance for receivables is a non-cash item: any change in the allowance for receivables will affect profit for the year, but will not affect cash flows.

3 Bank and cash balances are affected by some items that do not affect profit, such as the purchase of non-current assets (only depreciation affects profit), the raising of additional capital or the repayment of loans.

The benefits of statements of cash flows

A statement of cash flows is needed as a consequence of the differences between profits and cash, as explained earlier. It helps to assess:

- liquidity and solvency – an adequate cash position is essential in the short term both to ensure the survival of the business entity and to enable debts and dividends to be paid.
- financial adaptability – will the entity be able to take effective action to alter its cash flows in response to any unexpected events?
- future cash flows – an adequate cash position in the longer term is essential to enable asset replacement, repayment of debt and fund further expansion.

The bottom line is: cash flow means survival. An entity may be profitable but, if it does not have an adequate cash flow, it may not be able to pay its debts, purchase goods for resale, pay its staff etc.

The statement of cash flows also highlights where cash is being generated, i.e. either from operating, financing or investing activities. A business entity must be self-sufficient in the long term; in other words it must generate operating cash inflows or it will be reliant on the sale of assets or further finance to keep it afloat.

Cash flows are also objective; they are matters of fact, whereas the calculation of profit is subjective and easy to manipulate.

3 Presentation

IAS 7 *Statement of Cash Flows* requires companies to prepare a statement of cash flows as part of their annual financial statements. The cash flows must be presented using standard headings.

Note: there are two methods of reconciling cash from operating activities, each of which will be discussed later in this chapter.

Statement of cash flows for ABC for the year ended 31 December 20X8

		$
Cash flows from operating activities		
Cash generated from operations		X
Interest paid		(X)
Taxation paid		(X)
Net cash from operating activities		X
Cash flows from investing activities		
Cash paid for purchase of non-current assets	(X)	
Proceeds from the sale of non-current assets	X	
Interest received	X	
Dividends received	X	
Net cash from investing activities		X
		$
Cash flows from financing activities		
Proceeds of share issue	X	
Loan repaid	(X)	
Loan issued	X	
Dividends paid	(X)	
Net cash from financing activities		X
Net increase (decrease) in cash and cash equivalents		X (X)
Cash and cash equivalents b/fwd		X (X)
Cash and cash equivalents c/fwd		X (X)

Key points

- Operating activities are the principal revenue-producing activities of the business entity. This section of the statement begins with cash generated from operations. This figure can be calculated using either the direct or indirect method.
- Investing activities include cash spent on non-current assets, proceeds from the sale of sale of non-current assets and income from investments.
- Financing activities include the proceeds from the issue of shares, dividends paid to shareholders and long-term borrowings made or repaid.

- Net increase or decrease in cash and cash equivalents is the overall increase (or decrease) in cash and cash equivalents during the year. This can be calculated by comparing the level of cash and cash equivalents on the statement of financial position for the current and previous years.
- Cash means cash in hand and bank account balances, less overdrafts.
- Cash equivalents are **'short-term, highly liquid investments that are readily convertible to known amounts of cash and are subject to an insignificant risk of changes in value'** (IAS 7 para 6) (short-term, highly liquid investments, e.g. a 30 day bond).

4 Cash generated from operations

The starting point for a statement of cash flows is the cash flow from operations. 'Operations' are the normal, everyday activities of the entity that earn profit, and that result in cash flow. There are two methods of calculating cash from operations – the direct method and the indirect method.

Direct method

The direct method of presenting cash generated from operations provides more detailed information than the indirect method as it is based upon cash flow information extracted directly from the accounting records. As this method discloses information that would otherwise remain confidential, most companies choose not to use the direct method.

	$
Cash received from customers (W1)	X
Cash payments to suppliers (W2)	(X)
Cash paid to and on behalf of employees (W3)	(X)
Cash inflow from operations	X

The workings referenced above can be calculated as follows:

(W1)

Sales ledger control account

	$		$
Balance b/f	X	Cash receipts (ß)	X
		Contra	X
Sales revenue	X	Balance c/f	X
	X		X

(W2)

Purchases ledger control account

	$		$
Cash payments (ß)	X	Balance b/f	X
Contra	X	Purchases	X
Balance c/f	X		X
	X		X

(W3)

Wages control account

	$		$
Net wages paid (ß)	X	Balance b/f	X
		Statement of profit or loss	X
Balance c/f	X		
	X		X

The direct method could be examined in BA3 to require you to identify or quantify the information required using this method of presentation.

e.g **Illustration 1**

An extract from the statement of profit or loss for ABC for the year ended 31 December 20X2 was as follows:

	$	$
Sales revenue		200,000
Cost of sales		(120,000)
Gross profit		80,000
Less:		
General expenses	(45,000)	
Depreciation of property, plant and equipment	(4,000)	(49,000)
Operating profit		31,000
Less: Finance costs payable		(13,000)
Profit before tax		18,000
Income tax		(5,500)
Profit for the year		12,500

e.g

Illustration 1 (cont'd)

ABC makes all sales on credit. In addition, information relating to inventories, receivables and payables at 31 December 20X2 and 20X1 respectively were as follows:

	20X2	**20X1**
	$	$
Inventories	65,000	50,000
Receivables	50,000	43,000
Payables	60,000	38,000

Required:

Using the direct method calculate ABC's cash generated from operations for year ended 31 December 20X2.

Solution:

	$
Cash received from customers (W1)	193,000
Cash paid to suppliers and on behalf of employees (W2)	(158,000)
Cash generated from operations	35,000

(W1) Sales ledger control account

	$		$
Balance b/f	43,000	Cash receipts (ß)	193,000
Sales revenue	200,000	Balance c/f	50,000
	243,000		243,000

(W2) Expenses and payables control account

	$		$
		Balance b/f	38,000
Cash paid (ß)	158,000	Purchases (W3)	135,000
Balance c/f	60,000	General expenses	45,000
	218,000		218,000

(W3) Cost of sales

	$		$
Op inventory b/f	50,000	Cost of sales	120,000
Purchases (ß)	135,000	Closing inventory c/f	65,000
	185,000		185,000

Note that this method does not require an adjustment for depreciation charges as they are not cash flows. Cash flows relating to finance costs are classified elsewhere in the statement of cash flows.

Indirect method

This method reconciles profit before tax (as reported in the statement of profit or loss) with cash generated from operations as follows:

	$	$
Profit before tax		X
Depreciation charge for the period	X	
(Profit) or loss on disposal of non-current assets	(X)X	
Finance costs payable	X	
Investment income	(X)	
(Increase)/decrease in inventories	(X)X	
(Increase)/decrease in receivables	(X)X	
Increase/(decrease) in payables	X(X)	
		X
Cash generated from operations		X

Adjustments required to profit when preparing cash flows from operations using the indirect method

The following are examples of adjustments which are normally required when preparing cash flows from operating activities using the indirect method:

- Depreciation – added back to profit before tax because it is a non-cash expense
- Loss on disposal of non-current assets – the loss (a non-cash expense) is added back to profit before tax; the cash proceeds on the disposal will be classified as an investing activity cash inflow. Note that a profit on disposal is deducted from profit before tax
- Interest payable expense – this is added back to profit before tax because it is not part of cash generated from operations (the cash payment is deducted elsewhere in the statement of cash flows)
- Increase/decrease in inventories – an increase in inventories indicates that cash has been spent to pay for the increased inventory holding from the start to the end of the year. Therefore, it is deducted from profit before tax as it represents a cash outflow. A decrease in inventories is added to profit before tax as it represents a cash inflow from disposing of inventories.
- Increase/decrease in receivables – an increase in receivables from the start to the end of the year represents sales made on credit but not yet realised in cash received. An increase in receivables is deducted from profit before tax as it represents profit earned by making sales, for which the cash has not yet been received. A decrease in receivables is added to profit before tax as it represents a cash inflow from collecting cash from credit customers.

- Increase/decrease in payables – an increase or in payables from the start to the end of the year represents purchases made on credit which have not yet been paid for. An increase in payables is added to profit before tax as it represents a cash inflow as the business has incurred an expense, but which has not yet been paid. A decrease in payables is deducted from profit before tax which represents a cash outflow as cash is being used to settle liabilities.

e.g

Illustration 2

ABC had the following items included in its statement of financial position as at 31 December 20X2:

	20X2	20X1
	$	$
Inventories	65,000	50,000
Receivables	50,000	43,000
Payables	60,000	38,000

In addition, the statement of comprehensive income for the year ended 31 December 20X2 included the following items:

	$	$
Gross profit		80,000
Less:		
General expenses	(45,000)	
Depreciation of plant	(4,000)	
		(49,000)
Operating profit		31,000
Less: Finance costs payable		(13,000)
Profit before tax		18,000
Income tax		(5,500)
Profit for the year		12,500

Required:

Using the indirect method calculate ABC's cash generated from operations for year ended 31 December 20X2.

Illustration 2 (cont'd)

Solution:

	$
Profit before tax	18,000
Depreciation	4,000
Finance costs payable	13,000
Increase in inventories (65,000 – 50,000)	(15,000)
Increase in receivables (50,000 – 43,000)	(7,000)
Increase in payables (60,000 – 38,000)	22,000
Cash generated from operations	35,000

Whichever method is used to present cash generated from operations, the result will be identical. The remaining elements of the statement of cash flows follow one standard format, which will now be considered.

5 Cash flows from operating activities

We now need to calculate the net cash flow from operating activities by deducting the following items from cash generated from operations:

(a) interest paid

(b) tax paid.

Note that in both cases, **it is the cash paid during the accounting year that is included**. In the case of tax, this will often be payment of the previous year tax liability. In the case of interest payable, this will need to be adjusted for any accruals at the start and end of the accounting period to arrive at interest paid in the year.

Calculation of interest/income taxes paid

The cash flow should be calculated by reference to:

- the charge to profits for the item (shown in the statement of profit or loss) and
- any opening or closing payable balance shown on the statement of financial position

A ledger account working may be useful:

Tax/Interest liability

	$		$
Cash paid **(balancing figure)**	X	Balance b/f	X
Balance c/f	X	Statement of P&L	X
	X		X

6 Cash flows from investing activities

This section of the statement of cash flows deals with payments for the purchase of non-current assets and the proceeds on their disposal. Whilst in practice all the relevant information would be known, in the computer-based assessment it is quite common for a question to give you only part of the information, and you have to calculate the missing information. An example of this is shown below relating to the purchase/sale of a non-current asset.

These amounts are often the trickiest to calculate within a statement of cash flows. It is therefore recommended that ledger account workings are used.

The following ledger accounts will be required for each class of assets.

- asset account
- accumulated depreciation account
- disposals account (where relevant).

A separate asset account working may be required for each class of non-current asset – e.g. land, buildings, plant and equipment in order to identify all movements in the year, such as additions, disposals and revaluations.

Data provided in the source financial statements should then be entered into these ledger accounts and the required cash flows derived – often as a balancing or missing figure.

NB: If there is evidence of a revaluation of property, plant and equipment during the year, remember to include the uplift in value on the debit side of the asset account as this is a non-cash movement.

Non-current assets

	$		$
Balance b/f	X	Disposals at cost	X
Cash paid - additions **(balancing figure)**	X	Balance c/f	X
Revaluation in year	X		
	X		X

Non-current assets – accumulated depreciation

	$		$
Acc dep'n on disposals	X	Balance b/f	X
Balance c/f	X	Dep'n charge	X
	X		X

Any interest and dividends received is straightforward and you can find these figures in the statement of comprehensive income.

7 Cash flows from financing activities

This section of the statement of cash flows includes the proceeds from the issue of shares, along with receipt or repayment of loans during the year. A computer-based assessment question will often not tell you that there have been changes in share capital and/or loans; you have to work this out by looking to see if the ordinary or preference share capital has increased, together with the movement on share premium. Similarly, you will have to look at any loans balances to see if they have increased, in which there has been a cash inflow, or if they have decreased, in which case there has been a cash outflow.

The payment of dividends will be identified in the statement of changes in equity. This figure will normally be the cash paid to shareholders during the accounting year. As dividends are paid out of retained earnings, if information from the statement of changes in equity is not available, it will be necessary to reconcile the opening and closing retained earnings balances to identify dividends paid as a balancing or missing figure as follows:

Retained earnings

	$		$
Dividend paid **(balancing figure)**	X	Balance b/f	X
Balance c/f	X	Profit after tax per SP&L	X
	X		X

If a share issue has been made for cash during the year, the total cash received should be identified for inclusion in the statement of cash flows. The amount to include is the monetary increase in issued share capital plus any increase in the share premium account when comparing the opening and closing statements of financial position.

The receipt of a loan is a cash inflow to the business as this represents additional resources available to the entity. Similarly, repayments of the capital element of a loan during the year is a cash outflow.

e.g

Illustration 3

Continuing with Illustration 2 for ABC, other items in the statements of financial position at 31 December were as follows:

	20X2	20X1
Non-current assets*	$	$
Land at cost	30,000	15,000
Buildings at cost	100,000	60,000
Plant at cost	44,000	28,000
Acc Dep'n - buildings and plant	(18,000)	(14,000)
	156,000	89,000
Current assets		
Bank and cash		3,000
Share capital @$1 shares	50,000	40,000
Share premium	14,000	8,000
Retained earnings	37,500	45,000
Non-current liabilities		
Loan notes	100,000	50,000
Current liabilities		
Taxation	5,500	4,000
Bank overdraft	4,000	

*There were no disposals or revaluations of property, plant and equipment during 20X2.

A dividend of $20,000 was paid in 20X2.

Required:

Complete ABC's statement of cash flows for the year ended 31 December 20X2.

Solution:

Normally a working is required to derive the amount of any tax paid in the year, particularly if the amount paid in the year differs from the opening accrual.

Tax liability

	$		$
Cash paid **(bal fig)**	4,000	Balance b/f	4,000
Balance c/f	5,500	Statement P&L	5,500
	9,500		9,500

As there is no opening or closing accrual for interest payable, the charge in the statement of profit or loss of $13,000 from Illustration 2 must be the amount actually paid in the year.

Notice that the cost of each of non-current asset account has increased. As they are accounted for at cost, the increase represents additions purchased during the year. The increase in accumulated depreciation is the depreciation charge for the year in the statement of profit or loss.

For illustration, the buildings asset account can be prepared as follows:

Buildings - cost

	$		$
Opening balance b/f	60,000	Disposal	N/A
Revaluation in year	N/A		
Cash paid – additions **(bal fig)**	40,000	Closing balance c/f	100,000
	100,000		100,000

From a review of the extracts of the statements of financial position, the total of additions for non-current assets is $71,000 (Land $15,000 + Buildings $40,000 + Plant $16,000 = $71,000). This is an investing activity cash outflow.

For financing activities, there were two cash inflows. There was receipt of a loan of $50,000 (an increase in the liability from $50,000 to $100,000). In addition, there was an issue of shares. The total proceeds received were $16,000 (Issued share capital increased by $10,000 plus the increase in share premium of $6,000).

Payment of the dividend of $20,000 represents a financing activity cash outflow. Although this information was provided in the question content, it would have been possible to derive it by compiling a retained earnings working as follows:

Retained earnings

	$		$
Dividend paid **(balancing figure)**	20,000	Balance b/f	45,000
Balance c/f	37,500	Profit after tax per SP&L	12,500
	57,500		57,500

We can now complete ABC's statement of cash flows for the year ended 31 December 20X2 as follows:

ABC - Statement of cash flows for the year ended 31 December 20X2

	$	$
Cash flow from operating activities		
Cash generated from operations (from Illustration 1 or 2 above)		35,000
Finance costs paid (from Illustration 2 above)		(13,000)
Tax paid		(4,000)
Net cash from operating activities		18,000
Cash flows from investing activities		
Proceeds of sale of non-current assets	N/A	
Cash paid for PPE additions	(71,000)	
Net cash used in investing activities		(71,000)
Cash flows from financing activities		
Equity dividends paid	(20,000)	
Proceeds from issue of shares	16,000	
Receipt of loan	50,000	
Net cash raised in financing activities		46,000
Net increase (decrease) in cash and cash equivalents for the year		(7,000)
Cash and cash equivalents at the beginning of the period		3,000
Cash and cash equivalents at the end of the period		(4,000)

Test your understanding 1

JKL has provided you with the following information in relation to its financial statements for the year ended 30 June 20X4:

	$
Profit before tax, after charging depreciation of $22,300 and interest payable of $10,000	215,500
Purchase of non-current assets during the year	80,000
Repayment of non-current loan	45,000
Issue of shares at nominal value	100,000
Changes in working capital during the year	
Increase in inventories	22,500
Decrease in receivables	18,000
Decrease in payables	14,500
Taxation paid	25,000
Dividends paid	5,000

Note: There was no opening or closing accrual in relation to interest payable.

Required:

Based upon the available information, prepare a statement of cash flows for the year ended 30 June 20X4.

Statement of cash flows for sole traders

The preparation and use of a statement of cash flows is not restricted to companies. Indeed, the statement is a useful source of information for any entity.

For sole traders, dividends would be replaced by cash drawings, and share capital issued would be replaced by cash introduced by the owner. Taxation paid would not appear in the statement of cash flows of a sole trader as this is a personal, rather than business entity, transaction. If the business entity bank account was used to pay a personal tax liability it would be classified as drawings. Otherwise, the preparation of the statement of cash flows would follow the same principles as for a corporate entity.

8 Chapter summary

In this chapter you have studied:

- the reasons for preparing a statement of cash flows
- the standard format and classification specified by IAS 7
- calculation of items for inclusion in the statement of cash flows.

Note that IAS 7 is relevant in subject F1 Financial Reporting in the CIMA Professional Qualification.

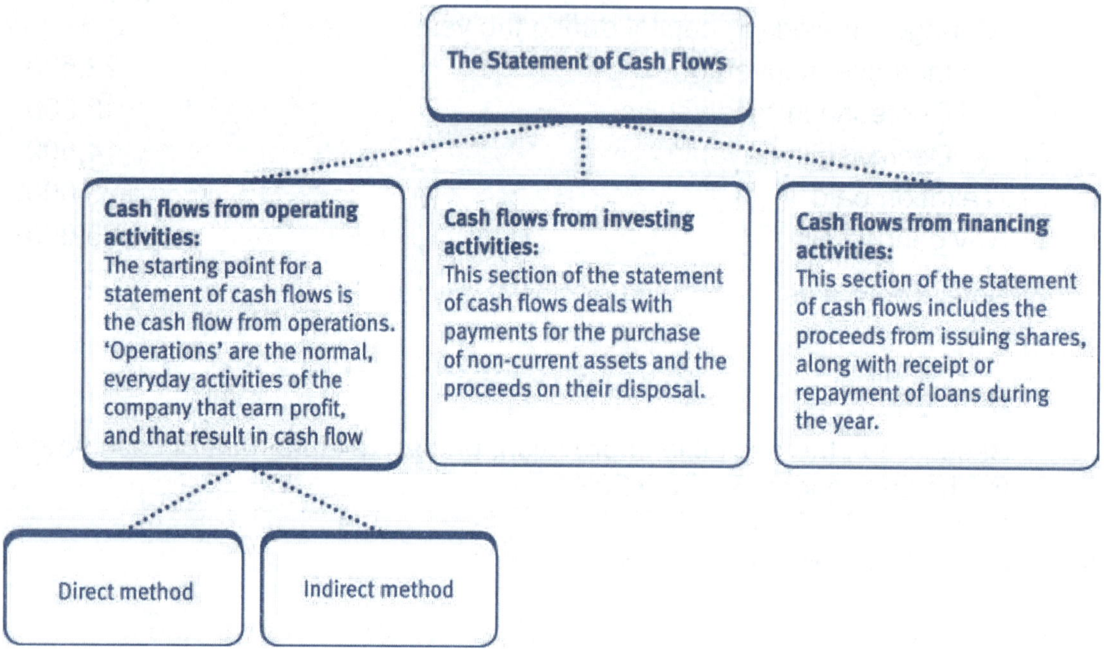

Test your understanding questions

Test your understanding 2

A business entity made a profit before tax of $8,000 but its bank balance has fallen by $5,000.

This could be due to:

A depreciation of $3,000 and an increase in inventories of $10,000

B depreciation of $6,000 and the repayment of a loan of $7,000

C depreciation of $12,000 and the purchase of new non-current assets for $25,000

D the disposal of a non-current asset for $13,000 less than its carrying amount

Test your understanding 3

Extracts from the financial statements of CFS are set out below.

Statement of comprehensive income of CFS for the year ended 31 December 20X8

	$000	$000
Sales revenue		300
Cost of sales		(150)
Gross profit		150
Profit on sale of non-current asset		75
		225
Expenses	(15)	
Depreciation	(30)	
		(45)
Net profit		180

	Balances as at 31 December	
	20X8	20X7
	$000	$000
Inventories, receivables, payables (net)	50	40

Required:

What figure would appear in the statement of cash flows of CFS for the year ended 31 December 20X8 in respect of cash generated from operations?

$...............

Test your understanding 4

The movement on the plant and machinery account of XYZ for the year ended 31 March 20X7 is shown below:

	$
Cost b/f 1 April 20X6	10,000
Additions	2,000
Disposals	(3,000)
Cost c/f 31 March 20X7	9,000
Acc. Depreciation b/d 1 April 20X6	2,000
Charge for the year	1,000
Disposals	(1,500)
Acc. Depreciation c/d 31 March 20X7	1,500
Carrying amount b/d 1 April 20X6	8,000
Carrying amount c/d 31 March 20X7	7,500

The profit on the sale of the machine was $500.

What figures should appear in the statement of cash flows of XYZ for the year ended 31 March 20X7 under the heading of investing activities?

A Movement on plant account $500 and profit on disposal of $500

B Movement on plant account $500 and proceeds on sale of plant $2,000

C Purchase of plant $2,000 and profit on disposal of $500

D Purchase of plant $2,000 and proceeds on sale of plant $2,000

Test your understanding 5

Which of the following will NOT appear in a corporate entity's statement of cash flows?

A Interest paid

B Revaluation gain on a building

C Dividends paid

D Repayment of a loan

Test your understanding 6

The profit before tax for SPA, a corporate entity, was $104,358.

What was the cash generated from operations if:

- the depreciation expense for the year was $9,000
- a non-current asset was sold at a profit of $1,800
- an increase of trade receivables of $10,362, and
- an increase of trade payables of $12,961.

A $134,881

B $117,757

C $88,235

D $114,157

Test your understanding 7

During the year Tree repaid a bank loan of $2m, purchased a new office building for $1m, received dividends of $0.3m and sold an old item of plant and machinery for $0.1m.

What was the total net cash inflow/(outflow) from investing activities in the statement of cash flows?

A $600,000 outflow

B $2,600,000 outflow

C $1,400,000 inflow

D $900,000 outflow

Test your understanding 8

At 31 December 20X5 Topaz had provided $50,000 in respect of income tax. At 31 December 20X6 the corporate entity estimated the tax liability for the year at $57,000. The amount charged as an income tax expense for the year ended 31 December 20X6 was $60,000.

How much will appear in the statement of cash flows for the year ended 31 December 20X6 in respect of income tax paid?

A $50,000

B $53,000

C $57,000

D $60,000

paid 50,000
Cost 57,000
owe 7,000
charge was 60,000

Test your understanding 9

Avtar had the following statement of financial position at 31 March 20X1 and 20X2:

	20X2	20X1
Assets	$000	$000
Non-current assets at cost	1,300	1,000
Accumulated depreciation	(600)	(400)
	700	600
Current assets		
Inventories	1,400	800
Receivables	3,100	2,700
Bank	–	200
	5,200	4,300
Equity and liabilities		
Share capital	1,300	1,000
Share premium	700	500
Retained earnings	1,600	1,500
	3,600	3,000
Current liabilities		
Payables	1,480	1,300
Bank overdraft	120	–
	5,200	4,300

During the year ended 31 March 20X2, non-current assets which cost $50,000 were sold for $40,000 cash. Accumulated depreciation on these assets to 31 March 20X1 was $20,000.

Required:

(a) Insert the missing figures into the ledger accounts below in order to calculate the additions to non-current assets, the profit or loss on sale of non-current assets, and the depreciation charge in the statement of profit or loss for the year ended 31 March 20X2.

Non-current assets at cost

	$		$
Balance b/f		Disposal a/c	
Additions		Balance c/f	
	______		______
	______		______

Non-current asset – accumulated depreciation

	$		$
Disposals a/c		Balance b/f	
Balance c/f		Statement of P&L	
	______		______
	______		______

Non-current assets – disposals

	$		$
Non-current assets at cost		Non-current assets acc. dep'n	
Profit on sale of non-current assets		Disposal proceeds	
	______		______
	______		______

(b) Prepare a statement of cash flows for the year ended 31 March 20X2.

Test your understanding 10

The draft financial statements of BOD are set out below.

Statement of profit or loss of BOD for the year ended 30 September 20X7

	$000
Sales revenue	600
Cost of sales	(410)
Gross profit	190
Profit on sale of non-current asset	10
	200
Operating expenses	(70)
Depreciation	(30)
Operating profit	100
Interest payable	(15)
Profit before tax	85

Statement of financial position of BOD as at 30 September 20X7

	20X7		20X6	
	$000	$000	$000	$000
Assets				
Non-current assets (see note)		450		520
Current assets:				
Inventories	65		50	
Receivables	80		30	
Bank and cash	30		15	
		175		95
		625		615

Equity and liabilities		
Share capital	400	400
Retained earnings	145	95
	545	495
Non-current liability:		
Loan	20	100
Current liabilities:		
Payables	60	20
	625	615

Note: BOD purchased non-current assets for $40,000 during the year ended 30 September 20X7.

Required:

Prepare the statement of cash flows for the year ended 30 September 20X7.

Test your understanding 11

Grange is preparing its statement of cash flows using the direct method and has compiled the following information.

At 1 January 20X5, the bonus accrual was $1,500 and was $2,300 at 31 December 20X5. During 20X5, the wages and salaries expense for the year was $34,600.

What amount will be disclosed by Grange in the statement of cash flows for payments on behalf of employees for the year?

$________

Test your understanding 12

Harvest is preparing its statement of cash flows using the direct method and has compiled the following information.

During the year ended 31 December 20X3, cash purchases were $4,600, and credit purchases were $123,780. Payables at 1 January 20X3 were $12,300, and $14,300 at 31 December 20X3.

What amount will Harvest disclose in the statement of cash flows for payments made to suppliers?

$________

Test your understanding answers

Test your understanding 1

JKL – Statement of cash flows for the year ended 30 June 20X4:

	$	$
Cash flows from operating activities		
Profit before tax		215,500
Add depreciation		22,300
Add: interest payable		10,000
Decrease in receivables	18,000	
Increase in inventories	(22,500)	
Decrease in payables	(14,500)	
Cash generated from operations		228,800
Interest paid		(10,000)
Taxation paid		(25,000)
		193,800
Cash flows from investing activities		
Purchase of non-current assets		(80,000)
Cash flows from financing activities		
Issue of shares	100,000	
Loan repaid	(45,000)	
Dividends paid	(5,000)	
		50,000
Net increase in cash and cash equivalents		163,800

Test your understanding 2

C

	$
Profit before tax	8,000
Add: Depreciation	12,000
Net cash inflow	20,000
Purchase of non-current assets	(25,000)
Decrease	(5,000)

*

Test your understanding 3

	$000
Net profit	180
Add: Depreciation	30
Less: Profit on sale of non-current asset	(75)
Less: Change in working capital	(10)
	125

Test your understanding 4

D

The cash flows are (i) cash paid for additions in the year, and (ii) sale proceeds from the disposal.

Carrying amount of disposal = $1,500 ($3,000 - $1,500), and add back profit on disposal of $500 to give total proceeds of $2,000.

Test your understanding 5

B

A revaluation gain is not a cash entry – debit asset account and credit revaluation reserve. Note that the asset account can no longer be referred to as a cost account as the asset has now been revalued.

Test your understanding 6

D

	$
Profit before tax	104,358
Depreciation	9,000
Profit on sale of asset	(1,800)
Increase in receivables	(10,362)
Increase in payables	12,961
Cash generated from operations	114,157

Test your understanding 7

A

	$
Purchase of new building	(1,000,000)
Proceeds from sale of plant	100,000
Dividends received	300,000
Total outflow from investing activities	(600,000)

The loan repayment is a financing activity item.

Test your understanding 8

B

	$
Estimate for 31 December 20X6	57,000
Under-provision for 31 December 20X5 **(balancing item)**	3,000
Income tax expense 31 December 20X6	60,000

The under-provision means we paid more than we estimated for 20X5, i.e. paid $3,000 + $50,000 estimate = $53,000.

Or:

Tax liability

	$		$
Balance b/f **(balancing figure)**	3,000		
Balance c/f	57,000	Statement of P&L	60,000
	60,000		60,000

Test your understanding 9

(a)

Non-current assets at cost

	$000		$000
Balance b/f	1,000	Disposals a/c	50
Additions (balancing figure)	350	Balance c/f	1,300
	1,350		1,350

Non-current assets – accumulated depreciation

	$		$
Disposals a/c	200	Balance b/f	400
Balance c/f	600	Depreciation expense (charge for the year)	220
	620		620

Non-current assets – disposals

	$		$
Non-current assets at cost	50	Non-current assets acc. dep'n	20
Profit on sale of non-current assets	10	Disposal proceeds	40
	60		60

(b) **Statement of cash flows for the year ended 31 March 20X2**

	$000	$000
Cash flow from operating activities		
Increase in retained earnings (1,600 – 1,500)	100	
Add: Depreciation	220	
Less: Profit on sale of non-current assets	(10)	
	310	
Less: Increase in inventories (1,400 – 800)	(600)	
Less: Increase in receivables (3,100 – 2,700)	(400)	
Add: Increase in payables (1,480 – 1,300)	180	
		(510)
Cash flow from investing activities		
Proceeds of sale of non-current assets	40	
Non-current assets purchased	(350)	
		(310)
Cash flow from financing activities		
Shares issued (1,300 + 700) – (1,000 + 500)	500	
		500
Decrease in cash and Cash and cash equivalents		(320)
at beginning of year cash equivalents during the year		200
Cash and cash equivalents at end of year		(120)

Test your understanding 10

BOD Statement of cash flows for the year ended 30 September 20X7

	$000	$000
Cash flow from operating activities		
Cash generated from operations (see workings)	95	
Interest	15	
	——	80
Cash flows from investing activities		
Sale of non-current assets – see workings	90	
Purchase of non-current asset	(40)	
	——	50
Cash flows from financing activities		
Dividends paid (see workings)	(35)	
Repayment of loan (100 – 20)	(80)	
	——	(115)
Net increase in cash and cash equivalents for the year		15
Cash and cash equivalents at the start of the year		15
Cash and cash equivalents at the end of the year		30

Workings

	$
Operating activities	
Profit before tax	85
Adjustment for non-cash flow items:	
Profit sale of non-current asset	(10)
Depreciation	30
Interest payable	15
	120
Adjustment for working capital:	
Increase in inventories (65 – 50)	(15)
Increase in receivables (80 – 30)	(50)
Increase in payables (60 – 20)	40
	95

Sale of non-current assets	
Carrying amount (520 + 40 – 30 – 450)	80
Profit on sale	10
Proceeds on sale	90
Dividend paid in the year	
Retained earnings brought forward	95
Profit for the year	85
	180
Less: dividend paid in the year (missing figure)	**(35)**
Retained earnings carried forward	145

Test your understanding 11

$33,800

Wages and salaries

	$		$
		Balance b/f	1,500
Cash paid **(β)**	33,800	Statement of P&L	34,600
Balance c/f	2,300		
	36,100		36,100

Test your understanding 12

$126,380

Payments for credit purchases $121,780 + cash purchases $4,600 = $126,380

Payables

	$		$
Cash paid **(β)**	121,780	Balance b/f	12,300
Balance c/f	14,300	Purchases	123,780
	136,080		136,080

Chapter

19

The interpretation of financial statements

Chapter learning objectives

When you have completed this chapter, you should be able to:

- identify information provided by ratios
- identify reasons for the changes in accounting ratios
- calculate basic accounting ratios dealing with profitability, liquidity and risk.

1 Introduction

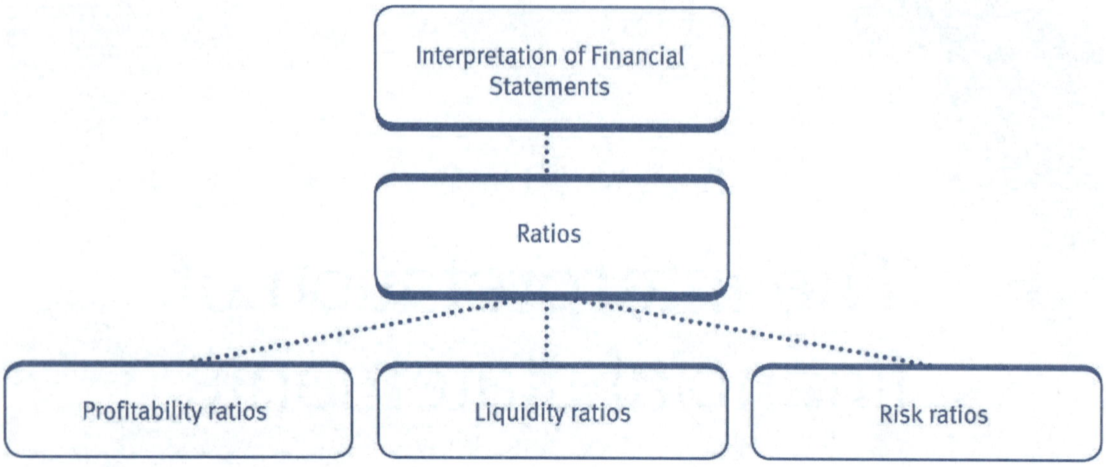

In this chapter, you will learn:

- what is meant by 'interpretation of financial statements'
- to define, calculate and interpret accounting ratios.

You have now reached one of the most important topics in financial accounting – the use and interpretation of accounting information. You now know how to prepare financial statements from various sources of data, but now we return to the content of Chapter 1 and the questions it posed:

- what is accounting?
- who uses financial statements and for what purpose?
- what makes financial statements useful?

The mechanics of the preparation of financial statements form only the start of the accounting process, the end result of which is to provide users with information to enable them to make decisions. The mere presentation of a set of financial statements does not necessarily achieve that objective, and this chapter considers ways of making that information more meaningful.

Understanding the whole of this chapter should be regarded as essential for examination success.

2 What is meant by 'interpretation of financial statements'?

Financial statements provide a great deal of information. However, **one difficulty with these statements is that they show only absolute figures** relating to a particular accounting period. **To enable users to make informed decisions, the statements on their own do not always provide sufficient information, even though they have been prepared in accordance with International Financial Reporting Standards**.

Further detail

Suppose that business entity ABC had a trading account which included sales revenue of $100,000 and profit for the year of $5,000. What does this tell you? It tells you that the sales revenue was $100,000 and the profit was $5,000. Is this good or bad? Is this to be expected? Is this comparable with other businesses? Can a user of the financial statements make decisions on the basis of this information?

The answer is no. That information on its own is not of use. Let us consider two additional business entities as well. DEF had sales revenue of $200,000 and profit for the year of $6,000. GHI had sales revenue of $300,000 and profit for the year of $4,500. Which of the three business entities is best? The answer depends on what the user is looking for.

If the user is looking for the business entity with the highest revenue, that is GHI. If the user is looking for the business entity with the highest profit, that is DEF. Which entity is most successful, in terms of its profit? You might think it is DEF, with its higher profit, but that was achieved from sales of $200,000, whereas ABC had only half that level of sales yet achieved a profit of only $1,000 less than DEF.

We are now embarking on an important area of accounting, that of comparison. We are starting to compare profit with sales revenue, and we are comparing one business entity with another. That is the key technique of the interpretation of financial statements – comparison of one with another.

The following table of information relating to three business entities will be used to illustrate some of the issues involved when interpreting financial information

Entity	Sales revenue	Profit	Capital employed
	$	$	$
ABC	100,000	5,000	50,000
DEF	200,000	6,000	50,000
GHI	300,000	4,500	30,000

Capital employed may be regarded as the amount invested in the business entity. It will be discussed in more detail later in this chapter.

There are comparisons we can make. Although DEF had the highest profit, it was only 3 per cent of its sales revenue. That is identified by applying the following formula:

$$\frac{\text{Profit}}{\text{Sales}} \times 100 = \%$$

ABC achieved a profit of 5 per cent of sales, and GHI achieved a profit of only 1.5 per cent. Therefore, it would appear that GHI performed poorly. However, that takes into account only one year of financial information. It would be useful to look at last year's results and see if any of the business entities have improved their profits.

It might also be useful to compare the profit with other figures, apart from sales. Suppose that the capital employed in ABC was $50,000. A profit of $5,000 is a 10 per cent return on that capital. If DEF had capital employed of $40,000 that would give a return on that capital of 12%. Suppose that GHI's capital employed was only $30,000, its return on that capital would be 15 per cent – so an investor might prefer to choose GHI, whilst a lender might prefer DEF as it has the highest profit figure from which to pay finance costs.

The point is that different users are looking for different information, which a set of financial statements on its own does not necessarily provide. Comparing one set of figures with another set of figures is a useful additional tool to provide information to support decision-making. **These tools are known as the techniques of ratio analysis.**

3 Calculating ratios

A ratio is simply a comparison of one figure with another.

If we have a business entity making a profit of $5,000 on sales revenue of $100,000 we could calculate a ratio to compare the percentage of profit with sales revenue for each year.

This would result in us dividing the profit by the sales revenue as follows

$$\frac{5,000}{100,000} \times 100 = 5\%$$

This ratio means for every $1 of sales revenue we make, 5% of it would result in profit i.e. 5c per $1 of sales revenue.

Ratios use simple calculations based upon the interactions within sets of data. For example, changes in costs of sales are directly linked to changes in sales activity. Changes in sales activity also have an effect upon wages and salaries, receivables, inventory levels etc. Ratios allow us to see those interactions in a simple, concise format.

Ratios are of limited use on their own. Therefore, the following points should serve as a useful checklist if you need to analyse data and comment on it:

- What does the ratio mean?
- What does a change in the ratio mean?
- What is the norm or expected ratio?
- What are the limitations of the ratio?

Using the ratios

Calculating the ratios is only one step in the analysis process. When that is done, the results must be compared with other results. Comparison is commonly made between:

- previous accounting periods
- other business entities (perhaps undertaking the same type of business activities)
- budgets and expectations
- government statistics
- other ratios.

4 Types of ratios

Ratios can be classified into various groupings, according to the type of information they convey. The main groupings are as follows:

- profitability (performance) ratios
- liquidity ratios
- risk ratios
- security ratios.

The last group, security ratios, is not part of your syllabus for this subject. The above list is not exhaustive – a ratio can be compiled from any data if it can be usefully interpreted.

The following statement of profit or loss and statement of financial position will be used to illustrate the calculation and interpretation of accounting ratios.

GHI – Statement of profit or loss for the year ended 31 December 20X8

	$	$
Sales		23,636
Opening inventories	1,225	
Purchases	8,999	
	10,224	
Closing inventories	(1,425)	
Cost of sales		(8,799)
Gross profit		14,837
Expenses		(5,737)
Operating profit		9,100
Interest payable on bank loan		(450)
Profit before tax		8,650
Income tax		(1,000)
Profit for the year		7,650

GHI – Statement of financial position as at 31 December 20X8

Assets	$	$
Non-current assets		14,135
Current assets		
Inventories	1,425	
Receivables	542	
Bank	7,037	
Cash in hand	697	
		9,701
		23,836

Equity and liabilities	
Equity	18,250
Non-current liability	
Bank loan	4,500
Current liability	
Payables	1,086
	23,836

5 Profitability ratios

These are also known as **performance ratios**. They compare the profit figures from the statement of profit or loss with other figures, and are often presented as percentages.

Return on capital employed

People who invest their money in a business entity are interested in the return that business entity is earning on that capital. Expressing this return in the form of a ratio enables comparison with other possible investment opportunities.

This ratio is a key measure of return. It measures the amount of earnings generated per $1 of capital, and is usually stated as a percentage. The ratio can be calculated in several different ways, according to the information required of it, and depending on what is meant by the two terms 'capital employed' and 'return'. In this Learning System, one method of calculating the return on capital is discussed – the return on total capital employed (ROCE).

- **Capital employed** can consist of total capital employed (equity + non-current liabilities) or just equity. In using total capital employed we include long-term loans as well as equity, and this is used when calculating ROCE. You should remember that equity is share capital plus all reserves. Furthermore, it is more correct to use the average of capital employed during the year, as the profit has been earned throughout the year. The capital at the start of the year would have been different, having been affected by share issues, loan issues or repayments, and the addition of profit for the year. However, in many computer-based assessments, the question may just require you to use the capital at the end of the year.
- **Return** is another way of describing profit. The profit figure to be taken will depend on which figure is taken for capital employed. If capital employed is taken as being total capital employed, then it is the operating profit figure (i.e. profit before interest and before tax) that is required to be used as the 'return', as this is the profit available to finance the total investment in the business entity.

The **ROCE** is defined, and calculated for GHI, as follows:

$$\frac{\text{Operating profit}}{\text{Average capital employed}} \times 100 = \frac{9,100}{18,925} \times 100 = 48\%$$

Average total capital employed is arrived at by taking the average of:

	$	
Closing total capital employed (18,250 + 4,500)	22,750	
Opening total capital employed (22,750 – 7,650 retained profit)	15,100	
	37,850	÷ 2 = $18,925

In simple terms ROCE measures how much operating profit is generated for every $1 capital invested in the business entity. In this example 48c generated for every $1 invested.

Don't forget total capital employed means equity + non-current liabilities

Further detail

Note that the profit figure used when calculating opening capital is 'retained' profit. This would normally be the profit after the payment of dividends and would be found in the statement of changes in equity. However, in this example no dividends were paid and therefore the figure is taken from the statement of profit or loss.

Overdrafts less cash balances (i.e. net overdrafts) are normally excluded from capital employed. This assumes that overdrafts are temporary and are not considered to be a source of permanent finance for the entity.

If it is not possible to calculate the average capital employed, then use the closing capital figure, but bear in mind that it may not be representative of the capital employed throughout the year.

What does this mean?

The return on capital employed (ROCE) is a key ratio for interpretation of profitability and performance. It is often used to compare the performance of business entities in the same industry, or one business entity can compare its current ROCE with either a target or prior year ROCE.

In principle, a higher ROCE indicates that a business entity has made better use of its resources to generate operating profit. However, this may be affected by the choice of accounting policies and business practices applied by an individual business entity as follows:

- if a business entity revalued its land and buildings, the value of capital employed will increase, with no increase in productive or operational activity to increase operating profit. In this situation, ROCE is likely to fall.
- if a business entity has property, plant and equipment which is coming to the end of its expected useful lives, it will have a relatively low net carrying value. This will reduce capital employed, with the consequence that it will increase ROCE.
- if a business entity invests in new property, plant and equipment, this will increase capital employed immediately (therefore reduce ROCE in the short-term), and it may be some time before this is reflected by an increase in operating profits in future years.

Test your understanding 1

Which one of the following statements taken in isolation would be a plausible explanation for an increase in the return on capital employed from 9% to 12%?

A The business entity managed to reduce finance costs during the year

B The business entity changed the mix of products sold, with the consequence that a greater quantity of more profitable products were sold during the year

C The business entity revalued its land and buildings during the year

D The business entity changed the mix of products sold, with the consequence that a greater quantity of less profitable products were sold during the year

Test your understanding 2

Which of the following transactions taken in isolation would result in an increase in capital employed?

A Selling inventory at a profit

B Writing off an irrecoverable debt

C Paying a payable in cash

D Increasing the bank overdraft to purchase a non-current asset

Gross profit margin

On a unit basis the gross profit represents the difference between the unit sales price and the direct cost per unit. The margin works this out on an average basis across all sales for the year. Similarly, the gross profit achieved by a business entity will be the difference between total sales revenue and the direct costs of purchase or manufacture of the goods sold.

This ratio (also known as the gross profit to sales revenue ratio) is defined as, and calculated for GHI, as follows:

$$\frac{\text{Gross profit}}{\text{Sales revenue}} \times 100 = \frac{14{,}837}{23{,}636} \times 100 = 62.8\%$$

It shows us that for every $1 in sales revenue 62.8% of it will be gross profit, i.e. approximately 63c. It also indicates that the cost of the goods sold represents 37.2% of their sales value.

What does this mean?

It is normally expressed as a percentage, but do try to understand the meaning of the percentage. The calculation shows that for every $1 of sales revenue, 62.8c was available to support payment of the remaining expenses, the possible payment of dividends and the retention of profits for the future. Whilst its value is useful for comparing the results of similar business entities, the trend of gross profit margin over time is a more appropriate use of the ratio.

Suppose the ratio in the previous year had been 64.3 per cent. How can we interpret the decline over the year?

There are several possibilities:

- sales revenue remained the same, but costs have increased
- sales revenue increased, but costs increased by a greater proportion
- it was necessary to keep sales prices steady, despite rising costs, in order to retain market share
- suppliers increased their prices, or perhaps the business entity lost the advantage of trade discounts
- the sales mix changed: if several different products are sold they will not all be equally profitable. It is possible that in the current year a higher proportion of the less profitable products were sold.

You can perhaps see that the above changes can be classified as either volume changes or price changes.

The gross profit margin could be a measure of the effectiveness of the sales team, pricing policies, purchasing methods and (in a manufacturing entity) the production processes.

The decline will not be as a result of holding inventory, as this is adjusted for in the cost of sales calculation.

Test your understanding 3

Which of the following statements taken in isolation would be a plausible explanation for an increase in the gross profit margin of a business entity from 18% to 20%?

A The business entity reduced administration expenses during the year

B The business entity repaid loans during the year

C The business entity purchased goods for resale from a new supplier at a reduced cost per unit during the year

D The business entity made a bonus issue of shares during the year

Gross profit mark-up

This ratio is an alternative measure of profitability. It is defined as, and calculated for GHI as follows

$$\frac{\text{Gross profit}}{\text{Cost of sales}} \times 100 = \frac{14{,}837}{8{,}799} \times 100 = 168.6\%$$

This ratio shows us that the selling price of the goods was equal to the cost of those goods, plus 168.6 per cent of the cost. In other words, for every $1 we spent on the cost of goods, we added $1.69 (approximately) to arrive at sales revenue generated of $2.69.

Test your understanding 4

If an item had a selling price of $350 and a gross profit mark-up of 40 per cent, what was its cost?

$...............

Operating profit margin

This ratio is defined, and calculated for GHI, as follows:

$$\frac{\text{Operating profit}}{\text{Sales revenue}} \times 100 = \frac{9{,}100}{23{,}636} \times 100 = 38.5\%$$

It shows us that for every $1 in sales revenue 38.5% of it will be operating profit, i.e. approximately 39c.

The operating margin is an expansion of the gross margin and includes all of the items that come after gross profit but before finance charges and taxation, such as selling and distribution costs and administration costs in the statement of profit or loss.

If the gross margin is a measure of how profitably a business entity can produce and sell its products and services, the operating margin also measures how effectively the business entity manages/administers that process. Therefore, if a business entity can minimise its distribution costs and administrative expenses, this will improve the operating margin. Note that minimising distribution costs and administrative expenses will have no impact upon the gross profit margin.

What does this mean?

The value of this ratio lies in its comparison over time and with other business entities and the industry average. In this example the operating profit percentage was 38.5c. In itself, this has no meaning – only by comparing it is it possible to derive any benefit from the calculation. To interpret this percentage fully would involve an examination of its components. Given that operating profit is equal to gross profit less expenses, a change in this percentage could arise either from a change in gross profit or from a change in one or more of the expenses deducted from gross profit. Further analysis would be needed.

By the time you have reached operating profit, there are many more factors to consider. If you are provided with a breakdown of expenses you can use this for further line-by-line comparisons. Bear in mind that:

- some costs are fixed or semi-fixed (e.g. property costs) and therefore not expected to change in line with revenue
- other costs are variable (e.g. packing and distribution, and commission) and will therefore change in line with business activity levels

Test your understanding 5

A business entity operates on a gross profit margin of 33 1/3 per cent. Gross profit on a sale was $800, and operating expenses were $680.

Required:

What was the operating profit margin?

.... per cent.

Net profit margin

This ratio is defined, and calculated for GHI, as follows

$$\frac{\text{Net profit after tax}}{\text{Sales revenue}} \times 100 = \frac{7,650}{23,636} \times 100 = 3.2\%$$

One important point to note is that the statement of profit or loss for a sole trader excludes income tax which is regarded as a personal, rather than business, expense. Therefore, the profit after tax figure will, in effect, be the profit for the year. For a corporate business, income tax is regarded as a business expense and this is deducted in arriving at the net profit for the year.

This ratio shows that for every $1 in sales revenue 3.2% of it will be net profit, i.e. approximately 3.2c.

This ratio will be affected by all of the factors that affect the earlier ratios calculated for gross profit margin and operating profit margin. In addition, net profit margin will also affected by the following:

- any increase or decrease in finance costs
- any increase or decrease in tax paid by a corporate business entity.

Test your understanding 6

Which of the following statements taken in isolation would be a plausible explanation for a decrease in the net profit margin of a sole trader from 7% to 5%?

A The sole trader paid more personal tax during the year

B The sole trader paid more finance costs during the year

C The sole trader paid less personal tax during the year

D The sole trader withdrew more cash for personal use during the year

Test your understanding 7

Which of the following statements taken in isolation would be a plausible explanation for an increase in the net profit margin of UVW, a corporate business entity, from 9% to 11%?

A UVW purchased property, plant and equipment during the year

B UVW made an issue of shares during the year

C UVW paid more income tax during the year

D UVW paid less income tax during the year

Non-current asset turnover

The non-current asset turnover is defined, and calculated for GHI, as follows:

$$\frac{\text{Sales revenue}}{\text{Non-current assets}} = \text{times p.a.} \quad \frac{23{,}636}{14{,}135} = 1.67 \text{ times}$$

This ratio measures how efficiently a business entity can generate sales revenue from the use of its non-current assets. This is similar to ROCE but in this case we measure the sales revenue generated for every $1 capital invested in non-current assets in the business entity. Generally speaking, the higher the ratio the more efficient the entity has been in using its non-current assets to generate sales revenue.

This means for every $1 invested in non-current assets, sales revenue of $1.67 was generated.

What does this mean?

This ratio can be used to compare the performance of a business entity over time.

Factors which may lead to a fall in the ratio include:

- additions to non-current assets during the year which have not yet been fully utilised to generate increased sales during the year
- revaluation of land and buildings during the year, which will increase the carrying amount of non-current assets, but without leading to any increase in sales revenue.

Note that any additions to non-current assets would be expected to lead to increased sales revenues in future years and therefore improve the ratio over a number of years, even though the ratio would fall initially.

6 Liquidity ratios

These ratios refer to the ability of a business entity to pay its liabilities in the short term.

There are two main liquidity ratios.

The current ratio

This is also known as the working capital ratio, as it is based on working capital or net current assets. It is a measure of the liquidity of a business entity that compares its current assets with those liabilities due to be paid within 1 year of the statement of financial position date (otherwise known as current liabilities).

It is defined, and calculated for GHI, as follows:

$$\frac{\text{Current assets}}{\text{Current liabilities}} = \frac{9{,}701}{1{,}086} = 8.9 : 1$$

This means for every $1 owed by the business entity and classified as a current liability, it has $8.90 in current assets to pay those liabilities. On the assumption that inventory will be sold and that trade receivables will pay amounts outstanding, this should be more than sufficient to generate cash to pay those liabilities as they fall due.

Notice how the ratio is expressed, as a comparison of current assets with current liabilities. The ratio can also be stated as:

Current assets : current liabilities

What does it mean?

The importance of this ratio is the information it gives about the liquidity of a business entity. Current liabilities are expected to be settled in cash within a reasonably short space of time, typically within twelve months of the statement of financial position date. Does the business entity have sufficient liquid resources to do this? Clearly, its cash and bank balances are liquid; trade receivables should convert into cash quite soon (perhaps during the next month or so), and inventory should presumably be sold in the normal course of day-to-day trading activities, eventually generating cash inflows. The calculation tells us that the business entity has $8.90 in current assets with which to pay every $1 of its current liabilities.

A high ratio, such as the one in our example, means that current assets are easily sufficient to cover current liabilities. A ratio of below one – meaning that current liabilities exceed current assets – could imply danger of illiquidity and inability to pay current liabilities as they fall due. It used to be thought that a ratio of 2:1 was ideal, but this depends on the type of business activities, the extent of its reliance upon credit, rather than cash, transactions and the industry it operates in. Therefore, such an explicit statement of an ideal or target current ratio is no longer appropriate.

Although a high ratio gives comfort to payables, it may mean that the business entity is holding considerably more in current assets than it requires in the short term. This is wasteful, as current assets rarely earn income – inventories needs to be sold in order to produce profits, receivables will not pay more than the amount outstanding, and bank balances may earn only very small amounts of interest. Indeed, a business entity with a high level of inventories might indicate difficulty in selling it, whilst a high level of receivables might indicate poor credit control or poor cash collection from receivables.

The current ratio should, however, be considered in the light of what is normal for the business entity. For example, supermarkets tend to have low current ratios in comparison with other types of business activity, such as manufacturing entities, because:

- there are few trade receivables
- there is a high level of trade payables
- there is usually very tight cash control, to fund investment in developing new sites and improving sites.

It is also worth considering:

- availability of further finance e.g. is there an overdraft facility available and to what extent is it currently used? Very often this information is relevant but is not disclosed in the financial statements. If additional borrowing facilities are available, a business entity will be able to continue trading with the support of the bank, even though its current ratio may indicate that there could be liquidity problems

- seasonal nature of the business activities – one way of doing this is to compare the interest charges in the statement of profit or loss with the overdraft and other loans in the statement of financial position; if the interest rate appears unusually high, this is probably because the business entity has had higher levels of borrowings during the year
- long-term liabilities, when they do fall due and how will they be financed or repaid?
- nature of the inventories – when inventories are slow moving, the quick ratio probably provides a better indicator of short-term liquidity.

The quick ratio

This ratio is defined, and calculated for GHI, as follows:

$$\frac{\text{Current assets excluding inventories}}{\text{Current liabilities}} = \frac{8,276}{1,086} = 7.6 : 1$$

Alternatively, it can be expressed as:

Current assets excluding inventory : current liabilities

The quick ratio is also known as the acid test ratio because by eliminating inventories from current assets it provides the acid test of whether the business entity has sufficient liquid resources (receivables and cash) to settle its short-term liabilities,

Note that, a supermarket which maintains high levels of inventories, this ratio will be particularly low. The supermarket will be dependent upon a fast turnover of inventories to generate cash so that it has sufficient liquidity to sustain its activities.

What does it mean?

This is similar to the current ratio, but takes the more prudent view that inventory may take some time to convert into cash, and therefore the true liquidity position is measured by the relationship of receivables and cash only to current liabilities. The calculation tells us that the business entity has $7.60 in 'quick' assets with which to pay each $1 in its current liabilities. Again, a very high ratio is very comforting, but may be wasteful as mentioned above. It is not easy to give an indication of an 'ideal' quick ratio, other than to suggest that it should perhaps be more than 1:1. However, note that many retail business entities with substantial and regular cash sales can operate with a very low quick ratio, due to a rapid rate of inventory turnover and a very few, if any, receivables.

A low ratio may need further investigation before conclusions can be drawn. For example, if current liabilities includes payables not due for payment for nine or ten months (rather than within the next month e.g. corporate income tax), the ratio may be distorted.

Test your understanding 8

Which one of the following statements is true of a company who hold closing inventory?

A A business entity will always have an acid test ratio lower than its current ratio

B A business entity will always have an acid test ratio higher than its current ratio

C It is not possible to state whether the acid test ratio will always be higher or lower than the current ratio

D If a business entity has a current ratio of less than 1:1, this means that it must be in financial difficulties

Test your understanding 9

Which of the following would be a plausible explanation for an increase in the current ratio of a business entity from 1.10: 1 to 1.15: 1, in the absence of any other information?

A The business entity purchased new premises which was financed by a long-term bank loan

B The business entity made a bonus issue of shares during the year

C The business entity repaid a bank loan during the year

D The business entity made a rights issue of shares during the year

Inventory turnover

Inventory turnover calculates how many times that level of inventory has been turned over, or sold, during the year.

This ratio is defined, and calculated for GHI, as follows:

$$\frac{\text{Cost of sales}}{\text{Inventory}} \text{ inventory turnover times per annum} = \frac{8{,}799}{1{,}425} = 6.17 \text{ times per annum}$$

In principle, it is better to have a higher inventory turnover as it indicates that inventory is being sold at a faster, rather than slower, rate. A supermarket, for example, is likely to have a very high inventory turnover rate as goods are sold very soon after they have been received in store. In contrast, a manufacturing business is likely to have a slower inventory turnover rate. That said, if the inventory turnover level is too high it could be an indication of possible cash flow problems.

This can be developed further by considering the inventory turnover rate for different products within a supermarket. Some items, such as canned foods and drinks may have a relatively long shelf-life and their inventory turnover rate may be lower than, for example, fresh fruit and salad which may be sold in full each day.

Another way of expressing this is to calculate the average inventory holding period as follows:

$$\frac{\text{Inventory}}{\text{Cost of sales}} \times 365 = \text{inventory days} \quad \frac{1{,}425}{8{,}799} \times 365 = 59 \text{ days}$$

This figure gives the number of days that, on average, an item is held in inventory before it is sold. It can also be calculated using the inventory turnover rate as follows:

$$\frac{365}{6.17} = 59 \text{ days}$$

This could also be calculated using average inventory. This is calculated by taking the opening and closing inventory for the period and dividing by 2, i.e. \$1,225 + \$1,425 = \$2,650/2 = \$1,325. Use of the average inventory figure would eliminate the impact of fluctuations in the inventory level upon the calculation.

This would result in an average inventory holding period of:

$$\frac{1{,}325}{8{,}799} \times 365 = 55 \text{ days}$$

What does it mean?

Whether inventory turnover or inventory holding period is calculated, both measures provide information to help evaluate how efficient inventory management has been in the business entity for the accounting period under review. It can then be compared with the equivalent figure for previous accounting periods, or against budget, to assess performance.

The higher the inventory turnover rate, the lower will be the inventory holding period. The number of inventory days is relevant to the context of the trading entity whereas in a manufacturing entity, it will approximate to the production cycle and in a cream cake shop perhaps as low as 1 day!

If inventory days are relatively high, this may indicate that inventory levels are too high and there is additional finance tied up in inventory which could perhaps be used more effectively elsewhere. If cash is paid out when inventory is purchased, that cash outlay will not be recovered by the business until the inventory is sold and the customer pays the amount outstanding, which may be after a period of credit is taken, perhaps one month or even longer.

If the inventory level is too low, this may show an overzealous application of the 'just-in-time' concept and consequential risks of running out of inventory. It may also indicate a business heading towards a cash flow crisis by running down inventory levels. Inventory days need to be compared to that of other business entities and compared to previous years for the same entity. Increasing inventory days may be investigated further by separately analysing raw materials (RM), work in progress (WIP) and finished goods (FG) to cost of goods sold. An increase in RM days may indicate mismanagement in the buying department; an increase in WIP may indicate production delays. If FG days increase, this may be a sign of decline in demand for the product and an increase in obsolete items.

Test your understanding 10

MRB prepared the following trading account for the year ended 31 May 20X8:

	$	$
Sales		45,000
Opening inventories	4,000	
Purchases	26,500	
	30,500	
Less: Closing inventories	(6,000)	
		(24,500)
Gross profit		20,500

Required:

What was MRB's average inventory holding period for the year (calculated to the nearest full day)?

.... days.

Test your understanding 11

Which of the following would be a plausible explanation for an increase in the average inventory days of a business entity from 30 days to 35 days, in the absence of any other information?

A The business entity stock-piled inventory in preparation for a sales campaign early in the following year

B The business entity introduced more efficient inventory management procedures

C The business entity employed more staff in the warehouse

D The business entity made more sales in the year

Trade receivables collection period

This is a measure of the average time taken by customers to settle their debts.

It is defined, and calculated for GHI, as follows

$$\frac{\text{Trade receivables}}{\text{Credit sales}} \times 365 = \frac{542}{23{,}636} \times 365 = 8 \text{ days}$$

Where details are available, only credit sales should be considered as cash sales do not involve customers taking credit. In the absence of specific information relating to cash and credit sales, total sales can be used as the best available information.

The sales figure will exclude sales tax but receivables will include sales tax, and so strictly speaking the figure is not comparing like-with-like. This sales tax on sales or receivables is not usually known and so this is inevitable. However, if the sales tax is known, then the figures should be adjusted so that both either include, or exclude, sales tax.

The result of this calculation should be compared with the number of days credit is normally allowed by the business entity to its customers. If it appears that customers are taking longer to pay than they should do, it may be necessary to take remedial action.

Remember that this is the average credit period taken by credit customers. There may be some receivables which have been outstanding for only two weeks, whilst other receivables have been outstanding for several months.

The calculated collection period can then be compared with the standard credit terms or policy of the business entity. Are credit customers complying with the credit terms? Is the business entity applying or enforcing its terms of business effectively?

As with inventory days, a slowing down in the speed of collecting debts will have a detrimental effect on cash flow. On the other hand, it may be that the business entity has deliberately offered extended credit in order to increase sales.

Test your understanding 12

The annual sales of EFG were $235,000. Half of the sales were made on credit terms, with the remainder on a cash basis. The trade receivables in the statement of financial position were $23,500.

Required:

What was the trade receivables collection period (to the nearest day)?

.... days

Test your understanding 13

Which of the following would be a plausible explanation for a reduction in the trade receivables collection period of a business entity from 45 days to 35 days, in the absence of any other information?

A The business entity took advantage of early settlement discount offered by suppliers

B Credit customers took advantage of early settlement discount offered by the business entity

C The business entity made more credit sales during the year

D The business entity made more sales for cash during the year

Trade payables payment period

This is a measure of the average time taken to pay suppliers. Although it is not strictly a measure of asset efficiency on its own, it is part of the overall management of net current assets.

It is defined, and calculated for GHI, as follows:

$$\frac{\text{Trade payables}}{\text{Credit purchases}} \times 365 = \frac{1,086}{8,999} \times 365 = 44 \text{ days}$$

As with the calculation of the average credit period taken by credit customers, the purchases figure should exclude any cash purchases. If there is no purchases figure available the best alternative is to use cost of sales as the denominator. Similarly, payables should ideally include only trade payables and exclude payables for expenses or non-current assets. Consequently, the calculation of this ratio may be distorted by the use of the cost of sales figure, rather than the credit purchases figure.

The purchases figure will exclude sales tax but payables will include sales tax, and so strictly speaking the figure is not comparing like-with-like. The sales tax on purchases or payables is not usually known and so this is inevitable. However, if the sales tax is known, then the figures should be adjusted so that both either include, or exclude, sales tax.

What does it mean?

The result of this ratio can also be compared with the receivables days. A business entity does not normally want to offer its customers more time to pay than it receives from its own suppliers, otherwise this could adversely affect cash flow. Generally, the longer the payables payment period, the better, as the business entity holds on to its cash for longer, but care must be taken not to upset suppliers by delaying payment unduly, which could result in the loss of discounts or a supplier refusing to supply goods on credit.

It is important to recognise when using these ratios that it is the trend of ratios that is important, not the individual values. Payment periods are longer in some types of business entity than in others.

Test your understanding 14

NOP purchased goods from suppliers during the year at a total cost of $800,000, of which $50,000 were purchased for cash. The trade payables outstanding at the end of the year amounted to $125,650.

Required:

What was the average trade payables payment period for the year (to the nearest day)?

.... days

Test your understanding 15

Which of the following would be a plausible explanation for a reduction in the trade payables payment period of a business entity from 41 days to 35 days, in the absence of any other information?

A The business entity took advantage of early settlement discount offered by suppliers

B Credit customers took advantage of early settlement discount offered by the business

C The business entity made more credit purchases during the year

D The business entity made more cash purchases during the year

A note on the total working capital period

Total working capital period

This measures the total length of time for which working capital is tied up in inventory, receivables and payables, before becoming available for use. It is the total of the number of inventory days, receivables days, less payables days. Using the calculations for GHI from the earlier section of this chapter, you can see that this is:

Number of days – inventory	59
Number of days – receivables	8
Less number of days – payables	(44)
Total working capital days	23

This tells us that it takes, on average, 23 days in which to sell the inventory, receive payment from receivables and pay the payables. The total of 23 days may not seem too lengthy for a manufacturing entity, but it does indicate the level of working capital needed in order to finance the ordinary activities of the business entity, which may result in the need for an overdraft or other sources of finance.

7 Risk ratios

Different business entities have different methods of financing their activities. Some rely mainly on the issue of share capital and the retention of profits; others rely heavily on loan finance; most have a combination of the two.

The gearing ratio (or leverage ratio)

Gearing is a measure of the relationship between the amounts of finance provided by external parties (e.g. loan finance) to the total capital employed.

It is defined, and calculated for GHI, as follows:

$$\frac{\text{Debt}}{\text{Total capital employed}} \times 100 = \frac{4{,}500}{22{,}750} \times 100 = 20\%$$

You should recall from the discussion above regarding the return on total capital employed (ROCE), that total capital employed is equity plus debt ($18,250 + 4,500). This ratio has been calculated based on the capital employed at the date of the statement of financial position. An alternative would be to use the average capital employed and average loan capital during the year.

This ratio indicates that, for every $1 of capital financing the business entity, 20c is provided in the form of loan finance. Providers of loan capital to the entity are creditors and they have a prior claim to return of their capital ahead of providers of equity capital should the business entity get into financial difficulty. Therefore, from the perspective of a provider of equity capital, loan capital is considered to be a source of financial risk. There is the risk that providers of loan finance will not have their loan repaid; in which case, they will have a claim over the assets of the entity for repayment of the amount due to them. There is also the risk that providers of loan finance will not be paid interest and finance charges due to them. This will be considered in more detail when interest cover is defined and explained.

Most business entities are financed by a combination of equity and debt capital and, therefore, have some element of gearing risk. One benefit of an entity having some element of debt finance is that interest and finance charges are normally tax-deductible expenses. Hopefully, it can be appreciated that, if the gearing ratio was considerably higher than 20% just calculated, this would increase the financial risk borne by the providers of equity finance. If, for example, the gearing ratio was 80%, it would indicate that a significant proportion of the long-term finance of the entity was provided by external loan finance. Therefore, should the entity get into financial difficulty, loan providers would have first claim on available assets to recover the amount due to them. This would leave very little (if anything) available for the equity holders. Similarly, the entity would need to generate profits sufficient to meet interest and finance payments before a return (dividend) could be paid to equity holders.

Test your understanding 16

The draft statement of financial position of BAD at 31 March 20X0 is set out below.

Assets	$	$
Non-current assets		450
Current assets		
Inventories	65	
Receivables	110	
Prepayments	30	
		205
		655

	$	$
Equity and liabilities		
Ordinary share capital		400
Retained earnings		100
		500
Non-current liability		
Loan		75
Current liabilities		
Payables	30	
Bank overdraft	50	
		80
		655

Required:

What is the gearing percentage of BAD at 31 March 20X0 (calculated to the nearest full percentage point)?

.... per cent

Test your understanding 17

Which of the following would be a plausible explanation for a reduction in the gearing ratio of a business entity from 22% to 20%, in the absence of any other information?

A The business entity negotiated with the bank and agreed to convert its overdraft into a five-year loan during the year.

B The business entity accounted for an upward revaluation of its land and buildings during the year

C The business entity made a bonus issue of shares during the year

D The business entity paid a dividend to its shareholders during the year

Interest cover

Interest cover is normally considered at the same time as gearing. Like the gearing ratio, interest cover helps users of financial statements to assess financial risk. Interest cover is a measure of the number of times that operating profit is able to 'cover' the interest payments due on long-term loans. It provides lenders with an idea of the level of security for payments due to them.

It is defined, and calculated for GHI, as follows:

$$\frac{\text{Operating profit}}{\text{Interest payable}} = \frac{9{,}100}{450} = 20 \text{ times}$$

This shows lenders that the interest charge in the statement of profit or loss is covered 20 times by the current level of operating profit (i.e. profit before accounting for interest and tax charges). Therefore, the level of operating profit would need to fall significantly before they were unable to cover interest and finance costs. An alternative view is that the level of interest and finance charges would need to rise significantly (e.g. from additional loan finance raised or increases in interest rates and charges) before they fully absorbed operating profit and left no profit for providers of equity capital.

The figure calculated of 20 times would normally be regarded as a fairly comfortable level of interest cover but, of course, it is future profits that will determine the actual level of interest cover. The lower the level of interest cover, the greater the financial risk is presumed to be.

Ratio analysis for sole traders

All of the above ratios can be calculated for sole traders, as well as for limited companies.

Test your understanding 18

For the year ended 30 June 20X6, interest cover of KLM was 7 times, which was a decrease from 10 times for the year ended 30 June 20X5.

Based upon the available information, which two of the following statements taken in isolation would be plausible reasons to explain this change?

A The business entity raised additional loan finance during 20X5-X6

B The business entity generated increased sales revenues by increasing selling prices during 20X5-X6

C The business entity made increased tax payments during 20X5-X6

D The business entity incurred increased operating expenses during 20X5-X6

E The business entity raised additional equity capital during 20X5-X6

Test your understanding 19

For the year ended 31 December 20X8, interest cover of TUY was 12 times, which was an increase from 8 times for the year ended 31 December 20X7.

Based upon the available information, which two of the following statements taken in isolation would be plausible reasons to explain this change?

A The business entity reduced its loan liabilities by making significant loan repayments in January 20X8

B The business entity raised additional equity capital in January 20X8

C The business entity launched a successful marketing campaign during 20X8 in which it reduced unit selling prices slightly, but managed to increase sales revenues significantly

D The business entity incurred increased production costs during 20X8 and was not able to increase selling prices of its products to customers

E The business entity renegotiated its bank loans so that the loan term was extended at the same rate of interest

Illustration 1

Note: The following illustration is not in the form or style that you would expect to face in the real examination. However, it is a good learning exercise and should help you to understand how to interpret a basic set of financial statements. The solution includes comments on interpretation that should help you to understand how the business entity has performed over the two years in question.

NEV manufactures and retails office products. Its summarised financial statements for the years ended 30 June 20X4 and 20X5 were as follows:

Statements of profit or loss for the year ended 30 June

	20X4	**20X5**
	$000	$000
Revenue	1,159,850	1,391,820
Cost of Sales	(753,450)	(1,050,825)
Gross profit	406,400	340,995
Operating expenses	(170,950)	(161,450)
Profit from operations	235,450	179,545
Finance costs	(14,000)	(10,000)
Profits before tax	221,450	169,545
Tax	(66,300)	(50,800)
Net profit	155,150	118,745

Statements of financial position as at 30 June

		20X4		20X5
	$000	$000	$000	$000
Non-current assets		341,400		509,590
Current Assets				
Inventory	88,760		109,400	
Receivables	206,550		419,455	
Bank	95,400		–	
		390,710		528,855
		732,110		1,038,445
Equity and reserves				
Share capital	100,000		100,000	
Share premium	20,000		20,000	
Revaluation reserve	–		50,000	
Retained earnings	287,420		376,165	
		407,420		546,165
Non-current liabilities				
Loans		83,100		61,600
Current liabilities				
Payables	179,590		345,480	
Overdraft	–		30,200	
Tax	62,000		55,000	
		241,590		430,680
		732,110		1,038,445

The directors of NEV concluded that sales revenue for the year ended 30 June 20X4 fell below budget and introduced measures during the year end 30 June 20X5 to improve the situation. These included:

- cutting prices
- extending credit facilities to customers
- leasing additional machinery in order to be able to manufacture more products.

The directors are now reviewing the results for the year ended 30 June 20X5.

Calculate the following ratios for NEV based upon the information available and comment upon its profitability, liquidity and financial position:

(a) gross profit margin

(b) operating profit margin

(c) return on capital employed

(d) current ratio

(e) quick ratio

(f) inventory holding period

(g) receivables collection period

(h) payables payment period

(i) gearing ratio

(j) interest cover

Solution

Profitability

	20X4		20X5	
GP%	$\frac{406,400}{1,159,850}$	35.0%	$\frac{340,995}{1,391,820}$	24.5%
OP%	$\frac{235,450}{1,159,850}$	20.3%	$\frac{179,545}{1,391,765}$	12.9%
ROCE	$\frac{235,450}{490,520}$	48.0%	$\frac{179,545}{607,765}$	29.5%

The revenue of the entity has increased by 20% on last year. It would therefore appear that the strategy of cutting prices and extending credit facilities has attracted customers and generated an increase in revenue.

Despite this increase, the operating profit margin has declined from 20.3% to 12.9%.

There are several possible reasons behind this deterioration:

- the reduction in sales prices
- increased asset hire or rental costs
- increased depreciation due to the revaluation and additional purchases of non-current assets
- increased irrecoverable debt due to the extended credit facilities.

The return on capital employed has dropped significantly from 48% to 29.5%. The possible reasons for this decline include:

- the reduction in operating profit margins
- the revaluation of non-current assets, which would increase capital employed.

Liquidity

	20X4		20X5	
Inventory days	$\frac{88,760 \times 365}{753,480}$	43 days	$\frac{109,400 \times 365}{1,050,825}$	38 days
Receivables days	$\frac{206,550 \times 365}{1,159,850}$	65 days	$\frac{419,455 \times 365}{1,391,820}$	110 days
Payables days	$\frac{179,590 \times 365}{753,450}$	87 days	$\frac{345,480 \times 365}{1,050,825}$	120 days
Current ratio	$\frac{390,710}{241,590}$	1.6:1	$\frac{528,855}{430,680}$	1.2:1
Quick ratio	$\frac{301,950}{241,590}$	1.2:1	$\frac{419,455}{430,680}$	1:1

NEV's results show a deteriorating liquidity position; both the current and quick ratios have worsened. The main reasons for this appear to be:

- the reduction in cash and consequent increase in overdrafts
- the increase in trade payables.

The overall cause could be the extension of credit facilities to customers. Credit customers are taking an extra 45 days to pay on average. As a result, NEV appears to have less cash to pay its suppliers and it is therefore using up its cash resources and overdraft facilities.

Receivables days have increased from an appropriate level of 65 days to 110 days. Although the benefits of this strategy have been shown by the increase in revenue, it would seem that NEV is now allowed customers too much credit. It would be recommended that receivables days should be reduced to closer to 90 days.

The large increase in payables days could lead to problems, unless suppliers have specifically agreed to offer NEV extended repayment deadlines. If not, then they may refuse to sell goods to NEV on a credit basis.

Financial position

	20X4		**20X5**	
Interest cover	235,450 / 14,000	16.8	179,545 / 10,000	17.9
Gearing*	83,100 / 490,520	16.9%	61,600 / 607,765	10.1%

* Gearing has been calculated using the 'debt/debt + equity' formula.

Both the gearing level and the interest cover have fallen. The key reason appears to be the reduction in loans during the year.

It appears as though NEV has used cash to repay their loan finance. This does not appear to be a sensible decision because the reduction in cash within the entity has led to an increase in expensive overdrafts and an increase in payables days, which may upset suppliers.

Both the gearing and the interest cover were strong in 20X4 (i.e. the interest cover was more than adequate and the gearing level appeared to be low). This indicated that NEV could afford to sustain its loans without significant penalty. It is now using an overdraft facility which will carry a much higher interest charge than long-term loans.

To improve its position NEV could seek further long terms loans. It is not a risky business from a gearing position and it has plenty of assets to use as security for any lenders.

8 Chapter summary

This very important chapter is one worth spending time over. In a computer-based assessment, not only will you be expected to calculate ratios, but you may need to be able to do any or all of the following:

- explain what the ratio attempts to show
- discuss the results of your calculations
- suggest possible reasons for good/poor results or differences from previous years, other companies or expectations.

The accounting requirements is relevant in subject F1 Financial Reporting and also subject F3 Advanced Financial Reporting in the CIMA Professional Qualification.

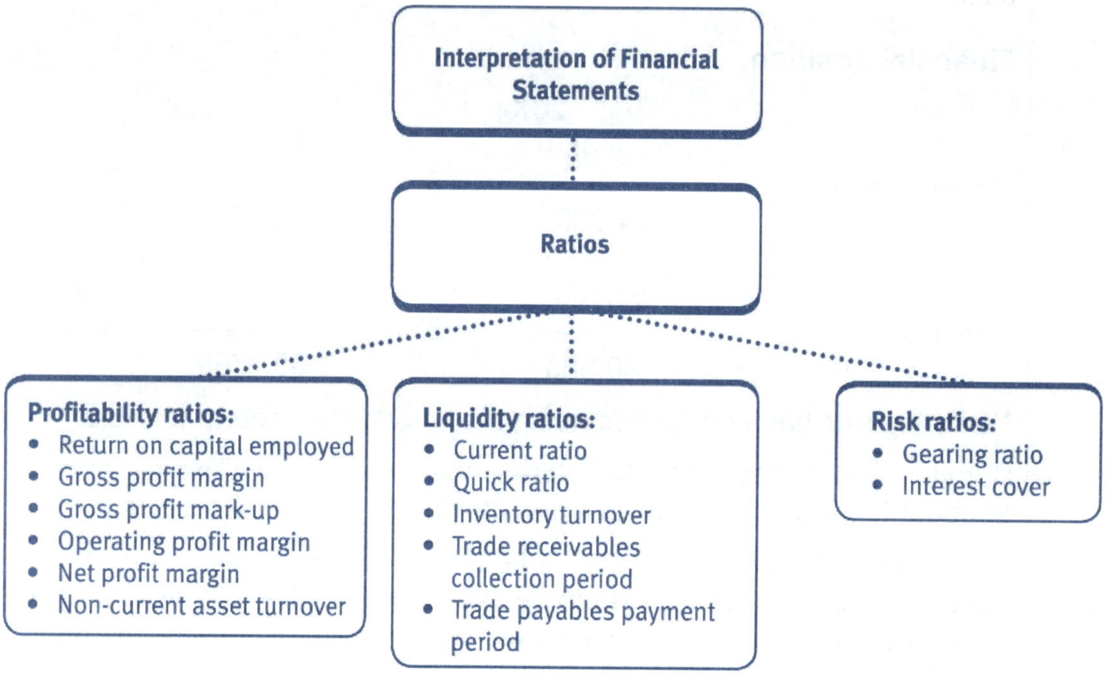

Test your understanding questions

Test your understanding 20

A business entity had sales of $110,000 and purchases of $80,000 for an accounting period. Inventory valuation at the start of the accounting period was $12,000 and the closing inventory valuation was $10,000.

Required:

What was the inventory holding period using average inventory?
.... days

Test your understanding 21

At the start of an accounting period, a business entity had a bank balance of $3,250. It subsequently purchased goods on credit for $10,000 and goods are normally sold at a gross profit mark-up of 120%. Half of the goods purchased were sold, less discount allowed of 5 per cent for early settlement of the amount due which was taken up by customers as expected. All takings were banked.

Required:

Based upon the available information, what was the operating profit?
$...............

Test your understanding 22

The following information was extracted from the statement of financial position of STU:

	$000
Inventories	1,900
Receivables	1,000
Bank overdraft	100
Payables	1,000

The industry norm for this type of business entity is 1.8

Its liquidity position could be said to be:

A very well controlled, because its current assets far outweigh its current liabilities

B poorly controlled, because its quick assets are less than its current liabilities

C poorly controlled, because its current ratio is significantly higher than the industry norm of 1.8

D poorly controlled, because it has a bank overdraft

Test your understanding 23

The gross profit mark-up is 40 per cent where:

A sales are $120,000 and gross profit is $48,000

B sales are $120,000 and cost of sales is $72,000

C sales are $100,800 and cost of sales is $72,000

D sales are $100,800 and cost of sales is $60,480

Test your understanding 24

The statement of profit or loss of BCD for the year ended 30 September 20X8 included the following:

	$000
Operating profit	1,200
Interest	(200)
Profit before tax	1,000
Income tax	(400)
Profit for the period	600

Its statement of financial position at 30 September 20X7 included the following

	$000
Share capital	8,000
Retained earnings	1,200
	9,200
10% Loan	2,000
	11,200

Required:

What was the return on average capital employed (ROCE) for the year ended 30 September 20X8?

.... per cent

Test your understanding 25

A sole trader made a loss during his financial year, but has more cash at the end of the year than he did at the beginning.

Which of the following statements taken in isolation could be a reason for this?

A The sole trader took more out in drawings this year than last

B Some non-current assets were sold during the year

C Receivables took longer to pay this year than last

D Prepayments were higher at the end of this year

Test your understanding 26

The inventory turnover ratio is six times when:

A sales revenue is $120,000 and the average inventory level at selling price is $20,000

B purchases are $240,000 and the average inventory level at cost is $40,000

C cost of goods sold is $180,000 and the average inventory level at cost is $30,000

D net purchases are $90,000 and closing inventory at cost is $15,000.

Test your understanding 27

An increase in inventories of $250, a decrease in the bank balance of $400 and an increase in trade payables of $1,200 would result in which of the following:

A a decrease in working capital of £1,350

B an increase in working capital of £1,350

C a decrease in working capital of £1,050

D an increase in working capital of £1,050

Test your understanding 28

BRT made a return on capital employed of 25.5%. Its profit before interest and taxation amounted to $60,000. The asset turnover ratio (calculated as sales/capital employed) was 85%.

What was the value of sales revenue?

A $70,588

B $100,840

C $200,000

D $276,817

Test your understanding 29

You are considering the purchase of a small business entity, IJK, and have managed to obtain a copy of its financial statements for the last accounting year to 30 September 20X3 as follows:

IJK – Statement of profit or loss for the year to 30 September 20X3

	$	$
Sales revenue		385,200
Less: Cost of goods sold		
Opening inventory	93,250	
Purchases	174,340	
Less: Closing inventory	(84,630)	
		(182,960)
Gross profit		202,240
Less: Expenses		
Selling and delivery costs	83,500	
Administration costs	51,420	
Depreciation	36,760	
		(171,680)
Net profit		30,560

IJK – Statement of financial position as at 30 September 20X3

	$	$
Assets		
Non-current assets		
Assets at cost	235,070	
Less accumulated depreciation	(88,030)	
		147,040
Current assets		
Inventory	84,630	
Receivables and prepayments	36,825	
Bank and cash	9,120	
		130,575
		277,615
Capital and liabilities		
Capital at 1 October 20X2		197,075
Net profit for the year		30,560
Proprietor's drawings		(12,405)
		215,230
Current liabilities		
Payables and accruals		62,385
		277,615

You have also obtained information relating to another entity, RZT, in the same industry as IJK as follows:

(i)	Net profit percentage	10.4%
(ii)	Return on capital employed	14.2%
(iii)	Current ratio	2.09: 1
(iv)	Quick ratio	0.74: 1

Required:

(a) Calculate the equivalent accounting ratios for IJK from the financial statements presented above. You should base capital employed upon the year end capital employed:

(i) Net profit percentage

(ii) Return on capital employed

(iii) Current ratio

(iv) Quick (acid test) ratio

(b) For each ratio calculated, state one possible reason why RZT could have a different ratio to IJK.

Test your understanding answers

Test your understanding 1

B

Finance costs will not affect operating profit (profit before interest and before tax), so this will not affect ROCE. Revaluation of land and buildings will increase capital employed, but without impacting upon operating profit. Therefore it is plausible that ROCE would decrease, rather than increase, as a result. If more units of less profitable products were sold during the year, this would reduce operating profit and, ROCE would fall as a result.

Test your understanding 2

A

Capital employed is increased by making a profit, or by adding more capital. Writing off an irrecoverable debt is clearly the opposite of making a profit; transactions such as B and C merely adjust the split of assets and liabilities but do not add anything overall.

Test your understanding 3

C

A reduction in administration expenses will improve operating profit, but not gross profit. An issue of bonus shares and repayment of loans will not affect gross profit.

Test your understanding 4

$250

Mark-up is gross profit as a percentage of cost of sales, so a mark-up of 40 per cent will result in a selling price of 140 per cent of cost of sales. Thus, if the selling price is $350, this represents 140 per cent of the cost of sales, therefore 100 per cent would be 350/140 × 100 = $250 cost price.

This can be confirmed by checking that 40 per cent of $250 gives a mark-up of $100, and hence a selling price of $350.

A common mistake is candidates simply calculate 40 per cent of $350 to arrive at $140 as the mark-up (and hence $210 as the cost of sales); this is obviously incorrect as the mark-up is not 40 per cent of sales, but 40 per cent of cost of sales.

Test your understanding 5

5%

Reconstruction of statement of profit or loss:

	$	
Sales	2,400	(100%)
Cost of sales	(1,600)	(66%)
Gross profit	800	(33%)
Operating expenses	(680)	
Operating profit (120/2,400) × 100	120	(i.e. 5%)

Test your understanding 6

B

Remember that personal tax paid by a sole trader is not a business expense and should not be in the statement of profit or loss. Similarly, any cash withdrawn from the business for personal use should be accounted for as drawings and are a reduction in the proprietor's capital account.

Test your understanding 7

D

The purchase of property, plant and equipment is capital expenditure and will not affect profit for the year. Similarly, an issue of shares will not affect profit for the year. If UVW paid more income tax in the year, this will reduce profit for the year, and consequently also reduce the net profit margin. Remember that, for a corporate business, the net profit margin is calculated using profit after tax for the year.

Test your understanding 8

A

The current ratio includes inventory, whereas the acid test ratio excludes inventory. Consequently, the acid test ratio will always be lower than the current ratio. A business may have a current ratio of less than 1:1 and it may be able to continue operating as normal. A supermarket is a good example of a business which can operate with a current ratio of less than 1:1.

Test your understanding 9

D

A bonus issue affects only share capital and share premium/retained earnings. The purchase of non-current assets financed by a long-term loan does not affect current assets or current liabilities. Repayment of a bank loan will reduce cash and bank balances and will reduce the current ratio. A rights issue will raise cash for the business and this will improve the current ratio.

Test your understanding 10

Inventory days are:

$$\frac{\text{Average inventory}}{\text{Purchases}} \times 365 \quad \frac{[(4000 + 6000)/2]}{24,500} \quad 365 = 74 \text{ days}$$

Test your understanding 11

A

More efficient inventory management would be expected to lead to a reduction in the average inventory holding period. The employment of more warehouse staff may (but not necessarily) lead to reduced holdings of inventory, rather than increased holdings of inventory. Selling more goods may lead to an increase or decrease in the average inventory holding period, depending upon how inventory is managed or controlled in the business. An increase in inventory in advance of a sales campaign will increase the average inventory holding period.

Test your understanding 12

73 days

Receivables including sales tax/Credit sales including sales tax = $23,500/$117,500 × 365 days = 73 days.

Test your understanding 13

B

Early settlement discount offered by suppliers will reduce the trade payables payment period. Making more sales for cash will not affect the trade receivables collection period. Making more credit sales may or may not change the average collection period, depending upon how effective the business is collecting cash from customers. If credit customers take advantage of early settlement discount offered by the business, this will reduce the trade receivables collection period.

Test your understanding 14

61 days

Trade payables payment period = Trade payables/credit purchases × 365

125,650/(800,000 – 50,000) × 365 = 61 days

Remember to exclude cash purchases from the calculation of the ratio.

Test your understanding 15

A

Early settlement discount offered by suppliers will reduce the trade payables payment period. Making more purchases for cash will not affect the trade payables payment period. Making more credit purchases may or may not change the average payment period, depending upon how effective the business is paying its suppliers. If credit customers take advantage of early settlement discount offered by the business, this will reduce the trade receivables collection period.

Test your understanding 16

13%

Gearing = Debt/Debt + equity = 75/(75 + 500) = 13%

Test your understanding 17

B

Accounting for revaluation of land and building during the year would increase revaluation reserve within equity in the statement of financial position and consequently reduce the gearing ratio. The payment of a dividend would reduce equity, and therefore increase the gearing ratio. Conversion of an overdraft (in current liabilities) to a long-term loan (in non-current liabilities) would increase the gearing ratio. A bonus issue of shares would increase share capital and reduce either share premium and/or retained earnings within equity only. It would not affect the gearing ratio.

Test your understanding 18

A and D

If additional loan finance was raised during 20X5-X6, KLM would expect to make increased finance payments, which would reduce interest cover. If additional operating expenses were incurred, this would reduce operating profit, and consequently also reduce interest cover.

If KLM generated additional sales revenues, this would be expected to increase operating profit and therefore also increase interest cover. Tax payments made in the year do not affect operating profit, so this would have no impact upon interest cover.

Test your understanding 19

A and C

A reduction in loan liabilities would lead to reduced interest and finance charges which, in turn, would lead to an increase in interest cover. A significant increase in sales revenues would lead to increased operating profits which, in turn, would lead to an increase in interest cover.

Raising additional equity finance, will not, in itself, lead directly to changes in profit and/or finance payments. Increased production costs would reduce operating profit which, in turn, would lead to a reduction in interest cover. An extension of the loan term would not change interest cover.

Test your understanding 20

Inventory days are found by dividing cost of goods sold by average inventory and multiplying by 365. Average inventory is:

$$\left(\frac{12{,}000 + 10{,}000}{2}\right) = £11{,}000$$

Cost of goods sold is found as follows:

	$
Opening inventory	12,000
Purchases	80,000
	92,000
Less: Closing inventory	(10,000)
Cost of goods sold	82,000

Rate of inventory turnover is therefore:

$$\frac{\$\,11{,}000}{\$\,82{,}000} \times 365 = 49 \text{ days}$$

Test your understanding 21

Operating profit $5,450

The answer can be calculated as follows:

	$
Cost of goods purchased	10,000
Cost of the goods that have been sold	5,000
Gross profit mark-up on these goods = 5,000 × 120%	6,000
Therefore, selling price =	11,000
Cash discount given = 5% of $11,000	550
Therefore, operating profit = gross profit less discount ($11,000 – $5,000 – $550)	5,450

Test your understanding 22

C

The current ratio is current assets: current liabilities, that is 2,900:1,100 = 2.6:1. The quick ratio is current assets minus inventories: current liabilities, that is 1,000:1,100 = 0.9:1. The current ratio is high compared with the industry standard of 1.8:1, whilst the quick ratio is within acceptable limits of the 'norm' of 1:1. Without any evidence of the reason for the high inventory levels, its current ratio would appear to be higher than is required, and hence liquidity is poorly controlled.

Test your understanding 23

C

	$
Sales were	100,800
Cost of sales was	(72,000)
Gross profit	28,800

Gross profit mark-up = Gross profit/Cost of sales × 100 = 28,800/72,00 × 100 = 40%

Test your understanding 24

ROCE = Profit before interest and tax/Average capital employed × 100

Average capital employed	= Opening capital + closing capital/2
Closing capital employed	= Opening capital plus profit for the year
	= 11,200 + 600 = $11,800
Average capital employed	= 11,200 + 11,800/2 = $11,500

Thus ROCE = 1,200/11,500 × 100 = 10.43%

Test your understanding 25

B

An increase in receivables (answer C) and prepayments (answer D) would result in a reduction in cash flow, not an increase. Drawings also reduce cash flow (answer A).

The sale of non-current assets, whether at a profit or a loss, will bring cash into the enterprise and could explain an increase in cash despite making a loss.

Test your understanding 26

C

The rate of inventory turnover is the number of times that inventory is used up during a year, and is measured as the ratio of the cost of sales to average inventory (at cost) during the year. The turnover ratio is 6 times when the cost of goods sold is $180,000 and average inventory is $30,000.

Test your understanding 27

A

	$
Increase in inventory	250
Decrease in cash	(400)
Increase in payables	(1,200)
Change in working capital	(1,350)

Test your understanding 28

C

Profit before interest and taxation = $60,000

Return on capital employed = 25.5%

Capital employed = $60,000/25.5% = £235,294

Asset turnover ratio = Revenue/capital employed = 85%

Revenue = 85% × $235,294 = $200,000.

Test your understanding 29

	Ratio:	Calculation	Comment:
(i)	Net profit/Sales × 100	30,560 / 385,200 × 100 = 7.93%	IJK has a lower net profit percentage – this could be due to it being less efficient in purchasing goods for resale, or being less efficient in controlling selling and administration costs.
(ii)	Net profit/closing Capital employed × 100	30,560/215,230 × 100 = 14.20%	
(iii)	Current assets/current liabilities	130,575/62,385 = 2.09	
(iv)	Quick assets/current liabilities	45,945/62,385 = 0.74	

One reason for two businesses having a different ROCE is that, if RZT had invested in new non-current assets during the latter part of the year, that would increase capital employed, but without necessarily generating profit, thereby reducing ROCE.

One reason for two businesses having a different current ratio could be the credit terms granted to each set of customers. For example, if one business introduced an extended credit policy and gave their credit customers three months credit, that would increase its current assets significantly, and hence, lead to an increase in the current ratio.

The quick ratio is a measure of liquidity that focusses upon cash and receivables. If two businesses held the same total value of current assets and current liabilities, they would have the same current ratio. If, however, one business held a significant proportion of its current assets in the form of inventory, this would lead to a very low quick ratio. In contrast, if the other business held only a small proportion of its current assets in the form of inventory, this lead to a higher quick ratio than its competitor.

Chapter

20

Case study questions

Note: The following questions are harder than you will be expected to attempt for your BA3 exam and are not in exam style or format. However, they are excellent learning exercises to develop your knowledge and understanding of recording transactions in ledger accounts, and then progressing towards preparation of the trial balance and completion of financial statements. Each of the questions deals with several syllabus areas, but will not necessarily deal with all aspects of the syllabus.

Test your understanding 1

On 1 January, PRO started a business with $2,500 in the bank and $500 cash. The following transactions occurred:

2 Jan	He bought raw materials on credit for $700 from JMA.
3 Jan	He sold goods for $300 on credit to GGO.
7 Jan	He sold goods for $1,100 to KLE on credit.
12 Jan	He bought equipment for $3,000, paying by cheque.
18 Jan	He paid wages of $50 by cheque.
20 Jan	He bought raw materials for $350, paying by cheque.
	He took $80 from the cash box for himself.
28 Jan	He paid JMA $250 by cheque
30 Jan	He transferred $200 cash into the bank from his cash box.

Required:

(a) Record the above transactions in the ledger accounts provided below.

Capital

		$			$
31 Jan	Drawings		1 Jan	Bank	
				Cash	

Bank

		$			$
1 Jan	Capital		12 Jan	Equipment	
30 Jan	Cash		18 Jan	Wages	
			20 Jan	Purchases	
			28 Jan	JMA	

Cash

		$			$
1 Jan	Capital		20 Jan	Drawings	
			30 Jan	Bank	

Purchases

		$			$
2 Jan	JMA				
20 Jan	Bank				

JMA

		$			$
28 Jan	Bank		2 Jan	Purchases	

Sales

		$			$
			3 Jan	GGO	
			7 Jan	KLE	

GGO

		$			$
3 Jan	Sales				

		$			$
7 Jan	Sales				

Equipment

		$			$
12 Jan	Bank				

Wages

		$			$
18 Jan	Bank				

Drawings

		$			$
20 Jan	Cash				

(b) Balance off the ledger accounts and prepare a trial balance.

Trial balance of PRO as at 31 January

	Debit	Credit
	$	$
Capital		
Bank		
Cash		
Purchases		
Payables		
Sales		
Receivables		
Equipment		
Wages		
Drawings		
	____	____
	____	____

Test your understanding 2

SMA commenced business as a decorator on 1 January.

1 Jan	Commenced business by paying $1,000 into a business bank account
3 Jan	Bought a motor van on credit from ABG for $3,000
4 Jan	Bought decorating tools and equipment on credit from BAP for $650.
8 Jan	Bought paint for $250, paying by cheque.
10 Jan	Received $400 cash from a customer for work done.
12 Jan	Bought paint for $150, paying in cash.
14 Jan	Issued an invoice to a customer, KOR, for $750 for work done.
18 Jan	Returned some of the decorating tools, value $80, to BAP.
23 Jan	Took $50 of the cash to buy a birthday present for his son.
28 Jan	KOR paid $250 by cheque towards his bill.

Required:

(a) Calculate the balance on each account at 31 January, by completing the ledger accounts provided below

Capital

	$		$

Bank

	$		$

Motor van

	$		$

ABG

$	$

Tools and equipment

$	$

BAP

$	$

Purchases

$	$

Sales

$	$

Cash

$	$

KOR

$	$

Drawing

$	$

(b) **Prepare the trial balance at 31 January**

	Debit – $	Credit – $
Capital		
Bank		
Motor van		
ABG		
Tools and equipment		
BAP		
Purchases		
Sales		
Cash		
KOR		
Drawings		

Test your understanding 3

After calculating net profit for the year ended 31 March 20X8, WLS has the following trial balance:

	Debit ($)	Credit ($)
Land and buildings – cost	10,000	
Land and buildings – acc. depreciation at 31 March 20X8		2,000
Plant – cost	12,000	
Plant – acc. depreciation at 31 March 20X8		3,000
Inventory	2,500	
Receivables control account	1,500	
Bank	8,250	
Payables control account		1,700
Rent prepaid	400	
Wages accrued		300
Capital account		19,400
Profit for the year ended 31 March 20X8		9,750
	34,650	36,150

A suspense account was opened for the difference in the trial balance.

Immediately after production of the above, the following errors were discovered:

(i) A sale of $300 to RAM had been debited to MAM, a payable, in the individual list of balances (memorandum accounts). However, it had been correctly recorded in the sales account.

(ii) The heat and light account had been credited with gas paid $150.

(iii) GGO had been credited with a cheque received from GRO for $800 in the individual list of receivable balances (memorandum accounts).

(iv) The insurance account contained a credit entry for insurance prepaid of $500, but the balance had not been carried down and hence had been omitted from the above trial balance.

(v) Purchase returns had been overcast by $700.

Required:

(a) Complete the table below to indicate the journal entries necessary to correct each of the above errors.

Item	Name of account	Debit amount ($)	Credit amount ($)
(i)			
(ii)			
(iii)			
(iv)			
(v)			

(b) the missing items into the suspense account given below, in respect of any errors that you have identified in (a), and total the account:

Suspense account

	$	Description	Item no	$
Balance as per trial balance				

(c) Name the type of error that has occurred in each of items (i) and (iii) above (max. five words each).

(i)

(ii)

(d) Insert the missing items into the boxes below to show the recalculated net profit for the year to 31 March 20X8:

		$
First draft profit		9,750
Adjustment re: heat and light		
Adjustment re: purchase returns		
Revised net profit		

(e) Insert the missing figures into the statement of financial position of WLS at 31 March 20X8, given below:

	Cost	**Acc. dep'n.**	**Carrying amount**
Assets	$	$	$
Non-current assets			
Land and buildings	10,000	(2,000)	
Plant	12,000	(3,000)	
	22,000	(5,000)	

Current assets		
Inventory		
Receivables		
Prepayments		
Bank		
Capital and liabilities		
Capital		
Add: Profit for the year		
Current liabilities		
Payables		
Accrual		

Test your understanding 4

The assistant accountant of BCL has prepared a sales ledger control account at 30 September 20X5 for you to reconcile with the list of sales ledger balances at that date. The control account balances are:

Debit balances	$225,015
Credit	$1,250

The list of balances extracted from the sales ledger totals $225,890. You discover the following:

(i) The credit balances have been included in the list of receivables as debit balances.

(ii) A sales invoice for $6,400 plus sales tax at 17.5 per cent has been recorded in the sales daybook as $4,600 plus sales tax at 17.5 per cent. It has been entered correctly in the sales ledger.

(iii) A dishonoured cheque for $450 from a customer has been recorded correctly in the control account, but no entry has been made in the receivable's personal account.

(iv) A contra entry between the sales and purchase ledgers of $750 has been omitted from the control account.

(v) The control account contains receipts from cash sales of $860 but does not contain the invoices to which these receipts refer; no entries have been made in the sales ledger for these invoices or receipts.

(vi) No entries have been made in the control account for irrecoverable debts written off ($2,150) and allowance for receivables ($2,400). Ignore sales tax for item (vii).

Required:

(a) Complete the table below to show the entries needed in the sales ledger control account to correct the present balance; consider each of the seven items mentioned if no entry is required in the control account, write N/E' in the 'Description' column and ignore the other columns.

	Description (max. 4 words each)	**Debit/ Credit?**	**Amount $**
(i)			
(ii)			
(iii)			
(iv)			
(v)			
(vi)			
(vii)			

(b) Complete the missing figures given below to calculate the revised sales ledger control account balance:

	$
Original balance (226,415 – 1,250)	225,165
Add: Debit entries required	
Less: Credit entries required	
Revised balance	

(c) **Two** of the seven items noted above required adjustment to the list of sales ledger balances. Insert the missing entries into the statement given below

	$
Original total of sales ledger balances	225,890

Items requiring adjustment

Item no.	**Description (max. two words each)**	**Adjustment $**
Total adjustment		
Corrected total		

Test your understanding 5

ABC does not maintain full accounting records. For the year ended 31 December 20X5 ABC was able to provide you with the following information:

	At 1 January	**At 31 December**
	$	$
Inventory	2,950	3,271
Receivables	325	501
Payables for purchases	736	1,014
Accrued wages payable	74	83

You were able to prepare the following summary of ABC's cash and bank transactions for the year:

Cash	$	**Bank**	$
Opening balance	49	Opening balance	920
Receipts		Receipts	
Shop takings	5,360	Cheques from customers	1,733
Cheques cashed	260	Shop takings paid in	3,995
	5,669		6,648
Payments		Payments	
Purchases	(340)	Purchases	(2,950)
Wages	(102)	Wages	(371)
Other expenses	(226)	Other expenses	(770)
Drawings	(820)	Purchase of van	(1,250)
Paid into bank	(3,995)	Cash withdrawn	(260)
Closing balance	186	Closing balance	1,047

ABC believes that one customer owing $27 will definitely not pay. On the basis of past experience, ABC believes that an allowance for receivables of $19 is also required. The van is to be depreciated at the rate of 20 per cent per annum, straight line, and assuming no residual value.

Required:

(a) Calculate ABC's opening capital balance as at 1 January 20X5.

(b) Calculate the total sales for the year ended 31 December 20X5.

(c) Calculate the total purchases for the year ended 31 December 20X5.

(d) Calculate the gross profit for the year ended 31 December 20X5.

(e) Calculate the wages expense for the year ended 31 December 20X5.

(f) Calculate the depreciation charge for the year ended 31 December 20X5.

(g) Calculate the total expenses for the year ended 31 December 20X5.

(h) Calculate the net profit for the year ended 31 December 20X5.

(i) Calculate ABC's closing capital balance as at 31 December 20X5.

(j) Calculate the total of current assets included in the statement of financial position at 31 December 20X5.

(k) Calculate the total of current liabilities included in the statement of financial position at 31 December 20X5.

Test your understanding 6

DWS prepares its financial statements to 30 September each year. On 30 September 20X4 its trial balance was as follows:

	Debit ($)	Credit ($)
Plant and machinery:		
Cost	125,000	
Acc. depreciation at 1 October 20X3		28,000
Office equipment		
Cost	45,000	
Acc. depreciation at 1 October 20X3		15,000
Inventory at 1 October 20X3	31,000	
Purchases and sales	115,000	188,000
Returns inwards and outwards	8,000	6,000
Selling expenses	12,000	
Heat and light	8,000	
Wages and salaries	14,000	
Directors' fees	5,000	
Printing and stationery	6,000	
Telephone and fax	6,000	
Rent and insurance	4,000	
Trade receivables and payables	35,000	33,000
Allowance for receivables at 1 October 20X3		4,000
Bank	3,000	
Petty cash	1,000	
Dividend paid	2,000	
Ordinary shares of 50¢ each		100,000
Share premium account		8,000
General reserve		7,000
Retained earnings balance at 1 October 20X3		34,000
Suspense account	3,000	
	423,000	423,000

The following additional information at 30 September 20X4 is available:

(i) Closing inventory of goods for resale amount to $53,000.

(ii) Prepayments

Telephone and fax rental	$1,000
Insurance	$1,000

(iii) Accruals:

Wages and salaries	$1,500
Directors' fees	2% of net turnover
Auditor's fees	$3,500

(iv) Irrecoverable debts to be written off amount to $3,000.

(v) Allowance for receivables is to be amended to $1,600.

(vi) The following bookkeeping errors are discovered:

- The purchase of an item of inventory has been debited to the office equipment account, cost $1,200.
- The payment of $1,300 to a payable has been recorded by debiting the bank account and crediting the payable's account. Any remaining balance on the suspense account is to be added to prepayments or accruals, as appropriate, on the statement of financial position.

(vii) The figure in the trial balance for the bank balance is the balance appearing in the cash book, prior to the reconciliation with the bank statement. Upon reconciliation, it is discovered that

- unpresented cheques amount to $3,000
- bank charges not entered in the ledgers amount to $4,000.

(viii) Depreciation of non-current assets is to be calculated as follows:

Plant and machinery	10% on cost
Office equipment	33.33% on the reducing balance at the end of the year

(ix) A final dividend of 1.5¢ per share was declared before the year end, but not paid until after the year end.

(x) $10,000 is to be transferred to general reserves.

(xi) An accrual of $1,000 for income tax is required.

Required:

(a) Prepare the statement of profit or loss for the year ended 30 September 20X4.

(b) Prepare the statement of changes in equity for the year ended 30 September 20X4.

(c) Prepare the statement of financial position at 30 September 20X4.

Test your understanding answers

Test your understanding 1

(a)

Capital

		$			$
31 Jan	Drawings		1 Jan	Bank	
31 Jan	Drawings	80		Cash	
	Balance c/d	3,420	31 Jan	Net profit	500
		3,500			3,500
			1 Feb	Balance b/d	3,420

Bank

		$			$
1 Jan	Capital		12 Jan	Equipment	
30 Jan	Cash		18 Jan	Wages	
			20 Jan	Purchases	
			28 Jan	JMA	
		3,650			3,650
			1 Feb	Balance b/d	950

Cash

		$			$
1 Jan	Capital		20 Jan	Drawings	
			30 Jan	Bank	
			31 Jan	Balance c/d	220
		500			500
1 Feb	Balance b/d	220			

Purchases

		$			$
2 Jan	JMA	700	31 Jan	Trading a/c	1,050
20 Jan	Bank	350			
		1,050			1,050

JMA

		$			$
28 Jan	Bank	250	2 Jan	Purchases	700
31 Jan	Balance c/d	450			
		700			700
			1 Feb	Balance b/d	450

Sales

		$			$
31 Jan	Trading a/c	1,400	3 Jan	GGO	300
			7 Jan	KLE	1,100
		1,400			1,400

GGO

		$			$
3 Jan	Sales	300			

KLE

		$			$
7 Jan	Sales	1,100			

Equipment

		$			$
12 Jan	Bank	3,000			

Wages

		$			$
18 Jan	Bank	50	31 Jan	Statement of profit or loss	50
		50			50

Drawings

		$			$
28 Jan	Cash	80	31 Jan	Capital account	80
		80			80

(b) **Trial balance of PRO as at 31 January**

	Debit	**Credit**
	$	$
Capital		3,000
Bank		950
Cash	220	
Purchases	1,050	
Payables		450
Sales		1,400
Receivables (300 + 1,100)	1,400	
Equipment	3,000	
Wages	50	
Drawings	80	
	5,800	5,800

Test your understanding 2

Note: All account balances have been brought down and dated 1 February as this activity requires only the preparation of ledger accounts and extraction of a trial balance, not preparation of financial statements.

(a)

Capital

		$			$
			1 Jan	Bank	1,000

Bank

		$			$
1 Jan	Capital	1,000	8 Jan	Purchase	250
28 Jan	KOR	250	31 Jan	Balance c/d	1,000
		1,250			1,250

Motor van

		$			$
3 Jan	ARG	3,000			

ARG

		$			$
			3 Jan	Motor van	3,000

Tools and equipment

		$			$
4 Jan	BAP	650	18 Jan	BAP	80
			3 Jan	Balance c/d	570
		650			650
1 Feb	Balance b/d	570			

BAP

		$			$
18 Jan	Tools	80	4 Jan	Tools	650
31 Jan	Balance c/d	570			
		650			650
			1 Feb	Balance b/d	570

Purchases

		$			$
8 Jan	Bank	250			
12 Jan	Cash	150	31 Jan	Balance c/d	400
		400			400
1 Feb	Balance b/d	400			

Sales

		$			$
			10 Jan	Cash	400
31 Jan	Balance c/d	1,150	14 Jan	KOR	750
		1,150			1,150
			1 Feb	Balance c/d	1,150

Cash

		$			$
10 Jan	Sales	400	12 Jan	Purchases	150
			23 Jan	Drawings	50
			31 Jan	Balance c/d	200
		400			400
1 Feb	Balance b/d	200			

KOR

		$			$
14 Jan	Tools	750	28 Jan	Bank	250
			31 Jan	Balance c/d	500
		750			750
1 Feb	Balance b/d	500			

Drawings

		$			$
23 Jan	Cash	50			

(b) The balances on the accounts are as follows:

	Debit – $	Credit – $
Capital		1,000
Bank	1,000	
Motor van	3,000	
ABG		3,000
Tools and equipment	570	
BAP		570
Purchases	400	
Sales		1,150
Cash	200	
KOR	500	
Drawings	50	
	5,720	5,720

Test your understanding 3

- Part (a) is straightforward, but take care to identify those corrections that involve the suspense account.
- To assist with Part (d), examine the journal entries; identify those that affect profit (i.e. revenue or expense accounts); if they are being debited, this will reduce profit; if they are being credited this will increase profit.

(a) **Journal entries**

		Debit $	Credit $
(i)	RAM	300	
	MAM		300
(ii)	Heat and light	300	
	Suspense account		300
(iii)	GGO	800	
	GRO		800
(iv)	Insurance prepaid	500	
	Suspense account		500
(v)	Purchase returns	700	
	Suspense account		700

(b)

Suspense account

	$		$
Balance as per trial balance	1,500	Heat and light (ii)	300
		Insurance (iv)	500
		Purchase return (v)	700
	1,500		1,500

(c) (i) Error of principle

(ii) Error of commission

(d) **Adjustment of profit**

	$
First draft profit	9,750
Adjustment re: heat and light	(300)
Adjustment re: purchase returns	(700)
Revised net profit	8,750

(e) **Statement of financial position of WLS as at 31 March 20X8**

	Cost	Acc. dep'n.	Carrying	Amount
	$	$	$	$
Assets				
Non-current assets				
Land and buildings	10,000	(2,000)		8,000
Plant	12,000	(3,000)		9,000
	22,000	(5,000)		17,000
Current assets				
Inventory		2,500		
Receivables (1,500 + 300)		1,800		
Prepayments (400 + 500)		900		
Bank		8,250		
				13,450
				30,450

	Cost	Acc. dep'n.	Carrying	Amount
Capital and liabilities				
Capital				19,400
Capital 19,400 Add				8,750
				28,150
Current liabilities				
Payables (1,700 + 300)			2,000	
Accrual			300	
				2,300
				30,450

Test your understanding 4

- Remember to include the sales tax element in the incorrect sales invoice.
- The allowance for receivables is never included the control account, nor is it adjusted for in the individual sales ledger account.

(a)

	Description	Debit/ Credit?	Amount $
(i)	N/E		
(ii)	Error in daybook	Debit	2,115
(Iv)	Contra	Credit	750
(v)	Cash sales	Debit	860
(vi)	Irrecoverable debts written off	Credit	2,150

(b)

	$
Original balance (225,015 – 1,250)	223,765
Add: Debit entries required	2,975
Less: Credit entries required	(2,900)
Revised balance	223,840

(c)

	$
Original total of sales ledger balances	225,890
(i) Credit balances*	(2,500)
(iii) Dishonoured cheque	450
Revised balance	223,840

* This is a reversal – therefore require (2 × $1,250) = $2,500.

Test your understanding 5

(a) **Capital balance at 1 January 20X5**

	$
Inventory	2,950
Receivables	325
Bank	920
Cash	49
	4,244
Less: Liabilities ($736 + $74)	(810)
	3,434

(b) **Total sales**

Receivables account

	$		$
Balance b/d	325	Bank	1,733
Credit sales (bal fig)	**1,909**	Irrecoverable debt	27
		Balance c/d (501 – 27)	474
	2,234		2,234

Total sales = credit sales + cash sales = $1,909 + $5,360 = $7,269

(c) **Total purchases**

Payables account

	$		$
Bank	2,950	Balance b/d	736
Balance c/d	1,014	**Credit purchases (bal fig)**	**3,228**
	3,964		3,964

Total purchases = credit purchases + cash purchases = $3,228 + $340 = $3,568.

(d) **Gross profit for the year**

		$
Sales (answer (b))		7,269
Opening inventory	2,950	
Purchases (answer (c))	(3,568)	
	6,518	
Less: Closing inventory	(3,271)	
Cost of goods sold		(3,247)
Gross profit		4,022

(e) **Wages expense**

Wages account

	$		$
Cash	102	Balance b/d	74
Credit sales (bal figure)	371	**Statement of profit or loss**	**482**
Balance c/d	83		
	556		556

(f) **Depreciation charge**

Depreciation (20% × $1,250) = $250

(g) **Total expenses for the year**

	$
Wages (answer (e))	482
Other expenses (226 + 770)	996
Irrecoverable debts	27
Allowance for receivables	19
Depreciation (answer (f))	250
Gross profit	1,774

(h) **Gross profit for the year**

		$
Gross profit (answer (d))		4,022
Wages (answer (e))	482	
Other expenses (226 + 770)	996	
Irrecoverable debts	27	
Allowance for receivables	19	
Depreciation (answer (f))	250	
		(1,174)
Net profit for the year		2,248

(i) Closing capital balance

	$
Balance at 1 January 20X5 (answer (a))	3,434
Net profit for the year (answer (h))	2,248
Less: Drawings for the year	(820)
Net profit for the year	4,862

(j) Total current assets

Current assets	$
Inventory	3,271
Receivables less allowance (474 – 19)	455
Bank	1,047
Cash	186
	4,959

(k) Total current liabilities

Current liabilities	$
Payables	1,014
Accrued wages	83
	1,097

The completed statement of profit or loss and statement of financial position are provided for reference.

Statement of profit or loss for the year ended 31 December 20X5		
	$	$
Gross profit (answer (d))		7,269
Wages (answer (e))	2,950	
Other expenses (226 + 770)	(3,568)	
Irrecoverable debts		
Allowance for receivables	6,518	
Depreciation (answer (f))	(3,271)	
		(3,247)
Net profit for the year		4,022
Wages (answer (e))	482	
Other expenses (226 + 770)	996	
Irrecoverable debts	27	
Allowance for receivables	19	
Depreciation (answer (f))	250	
		(1,774)
Net profit for the year		2,248

Statement of financial position as at 31 December 20X5

Assets	Cost	Acc. dep'n	Carrying amount
	$	$	$
Non-current assets			
Van	1,250	(250)	1,000
Current assets			
Inventory		3,271	
Receivables less allowance (474 – 19)		455	
Bank		1,047	
Cash		186	
(answer (j))			4,959
			5,959

Assets	Cost	Acc. dep'n	Carrying amount
Capital and liabilities			
Balance at 1 January 20X5 (answer (a))			3,434
Net profit for the year		2,248	
Less: Drawings		(820)	
Retained profit for the year			1,428
			4,862
Balance at 31 December 20X5 (answer (i))			
Current liabilities			
Payables		1,014	
Accrued wages		83	
(answer (k))			1,097
			5,959

Test your understanding 6

(a) **Statement of profit or loss of DWS for the year ended 30 September 20X4**

	$	$
Sales		188,000
Less: Returns inwards		(8,000)
		180,000
Opening inventory	31,000	
Purchases (115,000 + 1,200)	116,200	
Returns outward	(6,000)	
Closing inventory	(53,000)	
Cost of goods sold		(88,200)
Gross profit		91,800

	$	$
Selling expenses	12,000	
Heat and light	8,000	
Wages and salaries (14,000 + 1,500)	15,500	
Directors' fees (5,000 + 3,600)	8,600	
Printing and stationery	6,000	
Telephone and fax (6,000 – 1,000)	5,000	
Rent insurance (4,000 – 1,000)	3,000	
Auditor's fees	3,500	
Irrecoverable debts written off	3,000	
Change in allowance for receivables (see workings)	(2,400)	
Bank charges accrued	4,000	
Depreciation of plant and machinery	12,500	
Depreciation of office equipment	9,600	
		(88,300)
Operating profit		3,500
Income tax		(1,000)
Profit for the period		2,500

Statement of changes in equity of DWS for year ended 30 September 20X4

	Share capital $	Share premium $	General reserve $	Retained earnings $	Total $
Balance at the start of the period	100,000	8,000	7,000	34,000	149,000
Profit for the period				2,500	2,500
Dividends (2,000 + 3,000)				(5,000)	(5,000)
Transfer to general reserve			10,000	(10,000)	–
Balance at the end of the period	100,000	8,000	17,000	21,500	146,500

(b) **Statement of financial position of DWS at 30 September 20X4**

	Cost ($)	Acc. depreciation ($)	Carrying amount ($)
Non-current assets			
Plant and machinery	125,000	(40,500)	84,500
Office equipment	43,800	(24,600)	19,200
	168,800	(65,100)	103,700
Current assets			
Inventory	53,000		
Receivables (32,000 – 1,600)	30,400		
Prepayments (3,000 + 1,000 + 1,000)	5,000		
Petty cash	1,000		
			89,400
			193,100
Equity and liabilities			
Ordinary shares of 50c each			100,000
Share premium account			8,000
General reserve account (7,000 + 10,000)			17,000
Retained earnings			21,500
			146,500
Current liabilities			
Payables (33,000 – 2,600)		30,400	
Accruals (1,500 + 3,600 + 3,500)		8,600	
Overdraft (3,000 – 2,600 – 4,000)		3,600	
Income tax		1,000	
Declared final dividend		3,000	
			46,600
			193,100

Workings

Re note (vi)

	$
Increase purchases by	1,200
Decrease office equipment by	1,200
Decrease bank by (2 × 1,300)	2,600
Decrease payables by	2,600

This leaves the $3,000 suspense account balance 'untouched'. Therefore, increase prepayments by $3,000 as instructed.

Re notes (iv) and (v)

	$
Receivables in trial balance	35,000
Irrecoverable debt written off	(3,000)
	32,000

New allowance for receivables is $1,600; therefore decrease allowance by $2,400.

Depreciation calculations

Plant and machinery: (10% of $125,000) = $12,500

Office equipment: (($45,000 – $1,200) – $15,000) × 33.33% = $9,600

Director's fee accrual = 2% × 180,000 = $3,600

Dividend accrual = $100,000/0.5 = 200,000 shares × 0.015 = 3,000

Chapter

21

Mock Assessment 1

Chapter learning objectives

This section is intended for use when you have completed your study and initial revision. It contains a complete mock assessment.

This should be attempted as an exam conditions, timed mock. This will give you valuable experience that will assist you with your time management and examination strategy.

CIMA Cert BA

Fundamentals of Financial Accounting – BA3

Illustrative computer-based assessment

Instructions: attempt all 60 questions

Time allowed: 2 hours

Do not look at or attempt this illustrative computer-based assessment until you have fully completed your revision and are about to sit your computer-based assessment.

Illustrative computer-based assessment 1: Questions

Test your understanding 1

Which one of the following statements is true in relation to integrated reports?

A An integrated report should contain only historical financial information

B An integrated report should contain a combination of financial and non-financial information which is historical only

C An integrated report should contain a combination of financial and non-financial information which is forward-looking only

D An integrated report should contain a combination of financial and non-financial information, which is both historical and forward-looking

Test your understanding 2

ABC receives goods from DEF on credit terms and ABC subsequently pays by cheque. ABC then discovers that the goods are faulty and cancels the cheque before it is cashed by DEF.

Required:

How should ABC record the cancellation of the cheque in his books?

A Debit payables, and credit returns outwards

B Credit bank, and debit payables

C Debit bank, and credit payables

D Credit payables, and debit returns outwards

Test your understanding 3

The profit of an entity may be calculated by using which of the following formulae?

A Opening capital – drawings - capital introduced – closing capital

B Closing capital + drawings – capital introduced – opening capital

C Opening capital – drawings – capital introduced – closing capital

D Closing capital + capital introduced – opening capital

Test your understanding 4

An entity had sales revenue for the year of $3 million and receivables at the end of the year of $600,000. At the start of the year, it had an allowance for receivables of $25,000. The entity has assessed that it requires an allowance for receivables of $23,000 at the end of the year. In addition, irrecoverable debts of $4,250 were written off during the year.

Required:

(a) What was the total charge to profit or loss for the year in relation to irrecoverable debts and allowance for receivables?

$ ....

(b) What was the net amount included in the statement of financial position at the end of the year for receivables?

$ ....

Test your understanding 5

Which of the following should be accounted for as capital expenditure?

A The cost of painting a building

B The replacement of windows in a building

C The purchase of a car by a garage for resale

D Legal fees on the purchase of a building

Test your understanding 6

A business entity purchased a machine on credit terms for $18,000 plus sales tax at 15 per cent. The business is registered to account for sales tax.

Required:

Select the accounting entries required to record this transaction by the business entity.

		Dr	Cr
		$	$
A	Machinery	18,000	
B	Payables		18,000
C	Machinery	20,700	
D	Payables		20,700
E	Sales tax	2,700	
F	Sales tax		2,700

Test your understanding 7

IJK purchased land and buildings at a cost of $5 million (land element $1 million) on 1 January 20X2. At that date, the buildings had an estimated useful life of fifty years. On 31 December 20X5, the land and buildings were revalued to $6 million (land element $1.5 million).

Required:

Which of the items noted below should be used to record this transaction in the accounting records of IJK?

		Dr	Cr
		$000	$000
A	Non-current assets	1,000	
B	Non-current assets		1,000
C	Accumulated depreciation	320	
D	Accumulated depreciation		320
E	Revaluation surplus	1,320	
F	Revaluation surplus		1,320

Test your understanding 8

On 1 May 20X0, AVC paid rent in advance for the year to 30 April 20X1 of $2,280. On 1 May 20X1, AVC paid rent of $2,400 for the year to 30 April 20X2.

Required:

(a) What was the charge to the statement of profit or loss for the year ended 30 November 20X1?

$ ....

(b) What was the entry required in the statement of financial position as at 30 November 20X1?

$ .... accrual/prepayment (delete which does not apply)

Test your understanding 9

At the year end, ALB had items in closing inventory which had been purchased for $12,000, and which are expected to be sold for $13,000, less selling costs of $1,500.

Required:

At what value should ALB include these items of inventory in the financial statements?

$ ....

Test your understanding 10

At 31 December 20X3, the balance on XYZ's bank statement was $1,650 overdrawn. The bank statement included bank charges of $100 which have not been entered in the cash book. There were unpresented cheques totalling $950 and deposits not yet credited of $1,200. The bank statement also included a direct debit payment of $320 which related to another account holder ZYX.

Required:

What was the cash book balance to include in the financial statements as at 31 December 20X3?

$...............debit/credit (delete which does not apply)

Test your understanding 11

FGH had a cash balance of $200 in the till at 30 June 20X5. At 1 July 20X4 there was a cash balance of $100 in the till and receivables of $2,000. Total sales for the year ended 30 June 20X5 were $230,000. The value of trade receivables at 30 June 20X5 were $3,000. Cheques banked from credit sales during the year were $160,000 and cash sales of $50,000 had been banked.

Required:

What was the amount of missing cash presumed to be stolen during the year?

$.................

Test your understanding 12

RST has an accounting year end of 31 December. RST purchased a car for $10,000 on 1 April 20X5. At that date it was estimated to have no residual value at the end of its useful life. The car was subject to depreciation at 20% using the straight-line basis, charging a full year in the year of purchase and none in the year of disposal. The car was traded in for a replacement vehicle in August 20X8 at a part-exchange value of $1,800.

Required:

(a) What was the profit or loss on disposal?

$...............profit/loss (delete which does not apply)

(b) What was the amount (if any) disclosed under 'Investing Activities' in the statement of cash flows for the year ended 31 December 20X8 in relation to the vehicle traded in?

$..............inflow/outflow (delete which does not apply)

Test your understanding 13

A business entity included in inventory any goods received before the year end but for which invoices were not received until after the year end.

Required:

Which concept is this in accordance with?

A Historical cost

B Accruals

C Consistency

D Materiality

Test your understanding 14

ING operates the imprest system for petty cash. On 1 July there was a float of $250. During July the petty cashier received $50 from staff for using the photocopier and a cheque for $100 was cashed for an employee. The cheque was paid directly into ING's bank account. During July, cheques were drawn for $600 for petty cash. It was decided to reduce the cash float to $180 from 1 August.

Required:

How much cash was paid out by the petty cashier in July?

$.................

Test your understanding 15

Which one of the following statements does not explain the distinction between financial statements and management accounts?

A Financial statements are primarily for external users and management accounts are primarily for internal users

B Financial statements are normally produced annually and management accounts are normally produced more frequently, e.g. monthly

C Financial statements are more accurate than management accounts

D Financial statements are normally subject to an external audit whereas management accounts are not subject to an external audit

Test your understanding 16

Which one of the following errors would be identified by extraction of a trial balance

A The sales returns daybook had been totalled as $3,450.19, instead of $3,540.19

B The debit entry relating to the part-exchange value received upon disposal of a motor vehicle had been debited to the repairs and maintenance expense account.

C The closing balance on the trade receivables' ledger control account had been miscalculated as $13,742.50, instead of $17.342.50

D The journal entry relating to accounting for the value of closing inventory had not yet been posted.

Test your understanding 17

When reconciling the trade payables' ledger control account with the list of individual payables' ledger balances at the end of the month, it was identified that the total of the purchases day book had been overstated by $600.

Required:

Select the accounting entries required to correct this error by the business entity.

			$
A	Debit	Trade payables' ledger control account	600
B	Credit	Trade payables' ledger control account	600
C	Debit	Purchases	600
D	Credit	Purchases	600

Test your understanding 18

RSJ is a builder with ten employees. In April 20X0, it paid the following amounts:

Net salaries after deduction of employees' income tax and social security tax	$16,000
Employees' income tax and employees' social security tax for March 20X0	$7,000
Employer's social security tax for March 20X0	$3,000

At 30 April 20X0, RSJ owed $8,000 for April's employees' income tax and employees' social security tax and $3,500 for April's employer's social security tax.

Required:

What was RSJ's total expense for payroll costs for the month of April 20X0?

$.................

Test your understanding 19

The following information relates to EFG:

	At 30th September 20X1	At 30th September 20X0
	$000	$000
Inventory of raw materials	70	50
Work in progress	60	70
Inventory of finished goods	100	90

For the year ended 30th September 20X1

Purchases of raw materials	$165,000
Manufacturing wages	$30,000
Factory overheads	$40,000

Required:

What was the prime cost of production in the manufacturing account for the year ended 30th September 20X1?

$ ....

Test your understanding 20

State whether each of the following statements are TRUE or FALSE:

		TRUE/FALSE
A	When valuing inventory at cost, inward transport costs should be excluded	
B	When valuing inventory at cost, production overheads should be included	
C	When valuing inventory at cost, carriage outward costs should be excluded	

Test your understanding 21

At 30 June 20X0 the electricity ledger account had an accrual of $400 and a credit balance was brought down on 1 July 20X0. During the year ended 30 June 20X1, electricity invoices totalling $5,000 were paid. In July 20X1 an invoice for $900 was paid for the quarter ended 31 August 20X1.

Required:

(a) What was the electricity expense in the statement of profit or loss for the year ended 30 June 20X1?

$.................

(b) What was the amount of the accrual or prepayment included in the statement of financial position as at 30 June 20X1?

$................. accrual/prepayment (delete which does not apply)

Test your understanding 22

The allowance for receivables in the nominal ledger of BCD at 31 October 20X0 was $11,000. During the year ended 31 October 20X1 irrecoverable debts of $7,000 were written off. At 31 October 20X1, it was determined that an allowance for receivables of $7,000 was required.

Required:

What was BCD's total expense in the statement of profit or loss for the year ended 31 October 20X1 relating to irrecoverable debts and the allowance for receivables?

$.................

Electricity Expense

5000	400
300 accrual	4900 to SOPL

5400

Test your understanding 23

The following is an extract from the statement of financial position of BYZ for the years ended 31 July 20X1 and 20X0.

	20X1	**20X0**
	$000	$000
Inventory	40	90
Receivables	55	10
Payables	45	30
Accruals	15	20

Required:

Based upon the available information, what total amount should be included within cash generated from operations in the statement of cash flows of BYZ for the year ended 31 July 20X0?

$................. inflow/outflow (delete which does not apply)

Test your understanding 24

At 30 June 20X4, STU had inventory valued at $14,000. This excluded goods returned by a customer on the last day of the month as the wrong product was supplied. The goods had been purchased by STU for $4,000 and were invoiced to the customer at a mark-up of 25 per cent.

Required:

What was the value of STU's inventory at 30 June 20X4?

$.................

Test your understanding 25

If the totals of debit and credit balances extracted from the nominal ledger of an entity to produce a trial balance did not agree, which one of the following errors could be the cause of this failure to balance?

A The cost of a machine had been debited to the machine repairs account, with the other part of the transaction correctly accounted for

B A cheque received from a customer was banked but no ledger account entries were made for this transaction

C A sale of goods on credit was credited to the receivables' ledger control account with the other part of the transaction correctly accounted for

D The increase in the accumulated depreciation provision on machinery had been credited to the cost of machinery account

Test your understanding 26

TRE has several employees and provided the following information from its payroll for the months of January and February:

January	Gross Salary	Tax	Social security	Net pay
	$2,200	$500	$100	$1,600
February	Gross Salary	Tax	Social security	Net pay
	$2,500	$550	$110	$1,840

Tax and social security are payable to the government one month after they are deducted from employees' salaries.

Required:

What was the total cash paid in February by TRE in relation to payroll costs?

$..................

Test your understanding 27

When a business entity produces a statement of profit or loss and other comprehensive income, which one of the following items is included in 'other comprehensive income'?

A Profit on sale of a non-current asset

B Interest received

C Government grant received

D Revaluation surplus on property revaluation

Test your understanding 28

NER purchased a machine for $18,000. In addition, NER incurred transportation costs of $1,700 and installation costs of $500. The machine broke down at the end of the first month in use and cost $400 to repair. NER depreciates machinery at 10% per annum on cost, assuming no residual value.

Required:

What was the carrying amount of the machine after one year?

$..................

Test your understanding 29

Which of the following might explain the debit balance on a purchase ledger account?

A The business entity accounted for a discount received which it was not entitled and paid less than the amount due

B The business entity mistakenly paid too much to the supplier

C The bookkeeper failed to enter a contra with the sales ledger

D The bookkeeper failed to post a cheque paid to the account

Test your understanding 30

The following information relates to Questions 30 and 31.

QRS purchased an item of plant and equipment on 1 July 20X6for $50,000. In addition, QRS spent $5,000 to get the plant installed and operational, and $3,000 for a three-year warranty. At the date of purchase, it was estimated that the item of plant had an estimated useful life of five years, and a residual value of $3,000. Depreciation is charged on a straight-line basis, with a proportionate charge in the year of purchase and disposal as appropriate. QRS has an annual accounting year end of 31 December.

The item of plant and equipment was disposed of on 1 October 20X9 for cash proceeds of $20,000.

Required:

What as the depreciation charge included in the financial statements for the year ended 31 December 20X6?

$..................

Test your understanding 31

Required:

Based upon the information available, what was the gain or loss on disposal of the item of plant in 20X9?

$.................. gain/loss (delete which does not apply)

Test your understanding 32

The following information relates to HGF for the year ended 31 December 20X8.

	$
Cost of property plant and equipment at 1 January 20X8	444,000
Accumulated depreciation of property plant and equipment at 1 January 20X8	130,000
Revaluation surplus arising on property during the year	15,000
Carrying amount property, plant and equipment disposals during the year	17,000
Proceeds from disposals of property, plant and equipment during the year	35,000
Property, plant and equipment at cost or valuation at 31 December 20X8	467,000
Accumulated depreciation on property, plant and equipment at 31 December 20X8	138,000
Depreciation charge on property, plant and equipment for the year	8,500

Required:

What was the cash paid for additions to property, plant and equipment made during the year ended 31 December 20X8 as disclosed in the statement of cash flows?

$.................

Test your understanding 33

Extracts from the financial statements of ASB are set out below.

Statement of profit or loss for the year ended 31 December 20X1

		$000
Revenue		400
Cost of sales		(175)
Gross profit		225
Profit on sale of non-current asset		80
		305
Expenses	35	
Depreciation	40	(75)
Operating profit		230

	31st December 20X1	31st December 20X0
	$000	$000
Net current assets	65	50

Required:

What figure should appear in the statement of cash flows of ASB for the year ended 31 December 20X1 for cash generated from operations?

$..................

Test your understanding 34

SPA made an issue of shares during the year comprising 200,000 $1 ordinary shares at a premium of 20c per share which were paid for in cash.

Required:

Identify the correct ledger account entries required to record the issue of shares from the following list.

		Dr	Cr
		$	$
A	Bank	240,000	
B	Share capital		200,000
C	Share premium		40,000
D	Share premium		240,000
E	Share capital		240,000
F	Bank	200,000	
G	Share capital		160,000

Test your understanding 35

EMP's trial balance did not balance at 31 May 20X1 and a suspense account was opened. The following errors were subsequently discovered:

- insurance of $700 prepaid at 1 June 20X0 had not been brought down as an opening balance on the insurance account
- wages expense of $6,000 had been incorrectly debited to the purchases account
- the bookkeeper had failed to accrue for the telephone invoice owing at 31 May 20X1 of $400.

After these errors had been corrected, the trial balance was in agreement.

Required:

What was the initial difference on the trial balance at 31 May 20X1 before the errors were corrected?

$.................debit/credit (delete which does not apply)

Test your understanding 36

SAQ is a builder with numerous small items of equipment. SAQ calculates depreciation using the reducing balance method of 20%. At 1 May 20X3 the equipment had a carrying amount of $11,475. During the year ended 30 April 20X4, SAQ purchased equipment at a cost of $4,362 and sold equipment with a carrying amount of $3,257 for $4,000.

Required:

What was SAQ's depreciation charge on equipment for the year ended 30 April 20X4?

$.................

Test your understanding 37

If the return on capital of a business entity changed from 14% to 16%, which one of the following, taken in isolation, could be a plausible reason for that change?

A The business entity changed the sales mix of products sold during the year

B The business entity revalued its land and buildings during the year

C The business entity reduced its finance charges during the year

D The business entity paid less income tax on its profit for the year

Test your understanding 38

The following information relates to Questions 38 – 40:

The financial statement of SPA are set out below.

Statement of profit or loss for the year ended 30 November 20X2

	$000	$000
Turnover		6,000
Opening inventory	200	
Purchases	3,100	
Closing inventory	(400)	
		(2,900)
Gross profit		3,100
Operating expenses		(400)
Operating profit		2,700
Interest		(200)
Profit for the period		2,500

Statement of financial position of SPA as at 30 November 20X2

	$000	$000
Assets		
Non-current assets		3,500
Current assets		
Inventory	300	
Receivables	900	
Bank	50	1,250
		4,750
Equity and liabilities		
Share capital		2,200
Retained earnings		2,100
		4,300
Current liabilities - Trade payables		450
		4,750

Test your understanding 38

Required:

What was the return on capital employed for SPA?

.... :%

Test your understanding 39

Required:

What was the asset turnover ratio of SPA using the total capital employed at the year end?

.... :1

Test your understanding 40

Required:

(a) What was the 'quick' or 'acid test' ratio for SPA?

.... :1

(b) If an entity had a current ratio of 0.8:1 what would this mean?

A The entity has more current assets than current liabilities

B The entity has more current liabilities than current assets

C The entity has no inventory

D The entity would definitely have short-term liquidity problems

Test your understanding 41

A credit balance of $800 brought down on X's account in the books of YZA means that:

A X owes YZA $800

B YZA owes X $800

C YZA has paid X $800

D YZA has overpaid X by $800

Test your understanding 42

Match the following groups who make use of financial information with their responsibilities

A	The government	1	Appointing directors
B	The shareholders	2	Ensuring that all accounting transactions are properly recorded and summarised in the accounts
C	Suppliers	3	Collecting statistical information useful to help manage the economy
D	The directors	4	Ensuring that amounts outstanding are collected when due

Test your understanding 43

NBV provided you with the following information as at 31 July 20X7:

	$
Inventory at 1 August 20X6:	
Raw materials	22,000
Work in progress	4,000
Finished goods	63,000
Inventory at 31 July 20X7	
Raw materials	25,000
Work in progress	1,000
Finished goods	72,000
Purchases of raw materials	220,000
Dircct wages	300,000
Royalties on goods sold	45,000
Production overheads	360,000
Distribution costs	70,000
Administration expenses	290,000
Sales	1,400,000

Required:

What was NBV's cost of goods manufactured for the year ended 31 July 20X7?

$..............

Test your understanding 44

The sales ledger control account of DSA had a balance at 1 November 20X1 of $30,000. During November 20X1, credit sales were $67,000, cash sales were $15,000 and receipts from customers, excluding cash sales, and after deducting cash discounts of $1,400 were $60,000. Sales returns during November 20X1 were $4,000.

Required:

What was DSA's sales ledger control account balance at 30 November 20X1?

$...............

Test your understanding 45

State the single journal adjustment required to account for the net effect of irrecoverable debts of $2,100 written off and also a decrease in the allowance for receivables of $350.

Delete as appropriate	Account title	$
Debit/Credit		
Debit/Credit		
Debit/Credit		

Choose from the following list of account titles:

Allowance for receivables

Irrecoverable debt expense account

Sales ledger control account

Test your understanding 46

The bank statement of MNB at 31 July 20X1 showed a credit balance of $10,300. You subsequently discover that the bank had dishonoured a customer's cheque for $500 and had charged bank charges of $150, neither of which is recorded in the cash book. At 31 July 20X1, there were unpresented cheques totalling $1,700. You also identified that a receipt from a customer of $400 had been recorded as a credit in your cash book.

Required:

State the cash book balance of MNB that reconciles to the bank statements at 31 July 20X1:

$...............debit/credit (delete whichever does not apply)

Test your understanding 47

A business entity valued its inventory using the 'first in, first out' method to determine cost. At the start of the accounting period, inventory consisted of 12 units at a cost of $4 each. During the accounting period, 60 units were purchased at a cost of $5 per unit, and this was followed by a sale of 18 units, along with a further sale of 23 units. All sales were made at a price of $15 per unit.

Required:

What was the value of inventory at the end of the accounting period?

$...............

Test your understanding 48

Which one of the following statements best defines a book of prime entry?

A A book of prime entry is one in which transactions are entered prior to being recorded in ledger accounts

B A book of prime entry is one in which ledger accounts are maintained

C A book of prime entry is one in which the principles of double-entry bookkeeping must be applied

D A book of prime entry is one in which memorandum accounts are kept

Test your understanding 49

You have been provided with the following information in relation JGH:

Sales and purchases for the year ended 30 September 20X4 were $310,000 and $165,000 respectively. The inventory valuation at 1 October 20X3 was $21,000 and $18,000 at 30 September 20X4.

Required:

Calculate the average inventory holding period of JGH for the year ended 30 September 20X4. State your answer to the nearest whole day.

.... days

Test your understanding 50

Which two of the following statements are correct?

A Sales less factory cost of goods completed equals gross profit

B Prime cost is recorded in the trading account

C Factory cost of goods completed is recorded in the trading account

D Closing work in progress is not included in the statement of financial position

E Royalty payments on goods manufactured are included in prime cost

Test your understanding 51

The following information relates to NBV for the year ended 31 July 20X5.

	$000
Prime cost	370
Carriage outwards	90
Depreciation delivery vehicles	50
Factory indirect overheads	560
Increase in WIP	65
Decrease in inventory of finished goods	40

Required:

What was the factory cost of goods completed for the year ended 31 July 20X5?

$ ....

Test your understanding 52

The following information relates to CTA for the year ended 31 December 20X4.

Machinery	$000
Cost at 1 January 20X4	90
Additions	30
Disposal	(20)
Cost at 31 December 20X4	100
Accumulated depreciation at 1 January 20X4	20
Depreciation charge for the year	5
Disposal during the year	(3)
Accumulated depreciation at 31 December 20X4	22

The profit on disposal of a machine was $3,000.

Required:

Based upon the available information, what was the net cash flow from investing activities of CTA for the year ended 31 December 20X4?

$ .... inflow/outflow (delete as appropriate)

Test your understanding 53

ITC has a policy that all items of equipment which cost less than $1,000 are charged to an expense account rather than accounted for as a capitalised item of property, plant and equipment.

Required:

Which accounting concept is this an example of?

A Money measurement

B Prudence

C Going concern

D Materiality

Test your understanding 54

KPT is preparing financial statements for the year ended 30 June 20X3. Rent is payable on 1 February, 1 May, 1 August and 1 November quarterly in advance. The quarterly charge for rent was $900 and, from 1 February, this was increased to $1,200.

Required:

What amounts should be included in the financial statement of KPT relating to rent for the year ended 30 June 20X3?

Rent expense = $ ....

$ .... accrual/prepayment (delete as appropriate)

Test your understanding 55

The following information is an extract from the financial statements of FWD for the two years ended 31 August 20X2 and 20X3.

	20X3	**20X2**
	$000	$000
Inventory	22	16
Receivables	18	20
Bank	14	12
	54	48
Payables	(14)	(18)
	40	30

Required:

What net amount should the statement of cash flows of FWD include in arriving at cash flow from operations for the year ended 31 August 20X3?

$ .... inflow/outflow (delete as appropriate)

Test your understanding 56

ACO has a quick (acid) test ratio of 2:1 as at 30 September 20X8. Current assets included inventory of $12,000 and trade receivables of $4,000. Trade payables were $8,000.

Required:

What was the bank balance of ACO as at 30 September 20X8?

$ ....debit/credit (delete as appropriate)

Test your understanding 57

The warehouse manager of GHI has produced the following schedule of the values of three items (X1, X2 and X3) included in inventory as at 30 April 20X3:

	Cost	**Net realisable value**
	$000	$000
X1	15	25
X2	10	6
X3	14	18
	39	47

Required:

In accordance with IAS 2 *Inventories*, at what value should these items of inventory be included in the financial statements of GHI for the year ended 30 April 20X3?

$ ....

Test your understanding 58

At 1 June 20X5, the sales ledger control account of BCD had a balance of $20,000. During June 20X5, sales were $180,000, comprising credit sales of $170,000 and cash sales of $10,000. Total receipts from cash and credit customers during June 20X5 were $165,000. During June 20X5, it was recognised that $3,000 of receivables were irrecoverable and that a further $5,000 may not be paid. On 30 June 20X5, a contra entry of $2,000 was made between the sales and purchase ledger control accounts and credit customers returned goods at a value of $6,000.

Required:

What was the balance on BCD's sales ledger control account at 30 June 20X5?

$..................

Test your understanding 59

Which of the following items would you expect to see in a statement of changes in equity?

	Yes	No
Dividends paid		
Profit for the year		
Directors' salaries		
Revaluation of property		
Taxation		

Test your understanding 60

The following information relates to EFG for the year ended 31 August 20X7.

	$
Retained profit for the year	25,000
Cash generated from operations	23,000
Dividend paid	2,000
Profit on sale of non-current assets	500
Proceeds from sale of non-current assets	6,000
Taxation paid	1,000
Interest paid	3,500
Payments for non-current assets	7,000
Issue of loan notes	4,000

Required:

What was the net cash inflow or outflow of EFG for the year ended 31 August 20X7 based upon the available information?

S .... inflow/outflow (delete as applicable)

Test your understanding answers

Test your understanding 1

D

Test your understanding 2

C

There would also need to be additional accounting entries to record return of the goods as follows: Dr Payables and Cr Returns outwards.

Test your understanding 3

B

Test your understanding 4

(a) Irrecoverable debts $4,250 less reduction in allowance for receivables $2,000 = $2,250

(b) Net amount for receivables = $600,000 – $23,000 = $577,000. Note that the irrecoverable debts have already been written off and do not need to be removed from receivables.

Test your understanding 5

D

Test your understanding 6

A, D and E

Test your understanding 7

			$000	$000
A	Debit	Non-current assets	1,000	
C	Debit	Accumulated depreciation	320	
F	Credit	Revaluation surplus		1,320

		Land	Building	Surplus
		$000	$000	$000
Initial cost		1,000	4,000	
Depreciation to date of revaluation	4/50 × 4,000		(320)	
Carrying amount at date of revaluation		1,000	3,680	
Revaluation surplus (bal fig)		500	820	1,320
Revalued carrying amount		1,500	4,500	

Test your understanding 8

(a) Charge to statement of profit or loss
(5/12 × $2,280) + (7/12 × $2,400) = $2,350

(b) Prepayment in statement of financial position
(5/12 × $2,400) = $1,000

Test your understanding 9

$11,500

Inventory is always valued at lower of either cost ($12,000) or fair value less costs to sell ($13,000 – $1,500 = $11,500).

Test your understanding 10

		$
Bank statement balance	overdrawn	(1,650)
Unpresented cheques		(950)
Outstanding deposits		1,200
Bank error		320
Cash book – credit balance		(1,080)

Test your understanding 11

Sales ledger control

	$		$
Opening receivables	2,000	Cheques banked credit sales	160,000
Credit sales (balancing figure)	161,000	Closing receivables	3,000
	163,000		163,000

Cash account

	$		$
Opening balance	100	Cash banked	50,000
Cash sales ($230,000 – $161,000 credit sales)	69,000	Cash missing	18,900
		Closing balance	200
	69,100		69,100

Cash missing is $18,900.

Test your understanding 12

(a) Loss on disposal = $2,200

Carrying amount at date of disposal: $10,000 × 40% = $4,000 (i.e. after depreciation has been charged for each of the years ended 31 December 20X5, 20X6 and 20X7.

(b) Nil cash inflow/outflow

For the vehicle traded in, there would be no accounting entry within 'Investing activities' in the statement of cash flows in the year of disposal. The disposal value received is its part-exchange value, and not cash received. The loss on disposal is an adjustment to profit before tax within 'operating activities'.

Test your understanding 13

B

Test your understanding 14

Cash account

	$		$
1 July bal b/d	250	Cash cheque	100
Photocopying	50	**Cash paid out (balancing figure)**	**620**
		31 July bal c/d	180
Cash from bank	600		
	900		900

Test your understanding 15

C

Test your understanding 16

C

This is the only error which affects the trial balance. For item A, an equal value of debits and credits has been posed, and for item D a journal entry has been omitted completely. For item B, there has been a debit entry, although to the wrong ledger account.

Test your understanding 17

			$
A	Debit	Trade payables' ledger control account	600
D	Credit	Purchases	600

Test your understanding 18

	$
Net salaries for April	16,000
Employees' social security and tax for April	8,000
Employer's social security	3,500
	27,500

Test your understanding 19

	$
Prime cost is direct materials and direct labour	
Opening inventory of raw materials	50,000
Purchases	165,000
Closing inventory of raw materials	(70,000)
Raw materials consumed	145,000
Manufacturing wages	30,000
	175,000

Test your understanding 20

		TRUE/FALSE
A	When valuing inventory at cost, inward transport costs should be excluded	False
B	When valuing inventory at cost, production overheads should be included	True
C	When valuing inventory at cost, carriage outward costs should be excluded	True

Test your understanding 21

Electricity account

		$			$
30 June 20X1	Cash paid	5,000	1 July 20X0	bal b/d	400
30 June 20X1	**Accrual bal c/d – $900 × 1/3**	300	30 June 20X1	**Statement of profit or loss**	**4,900**
		5,300			5,300

Test your understanding 22

	$
Allowance for receivables at 31 October 20X1	7,000
Allowance for receivables at 31 October 20X0	(11,000)
Reduction in allowance	(4,000)
Irrecoverable debts written off	7,000
Statement of profit or loss expense	3,000

Test your understanding 23

	$000
Inventory	50
Receivables	(45)
Payables	15
Accruals	(5)
Cash inflow	15

Test your understanding 24

	$
Inventory at valuation	14,000
Goods on sale or return accounted for at cost	4,000
Inventory valuation	18,000

Test your understanding 25

C

The entry to the receivables' ledger control account should be a debit, not a credit as stated.

Test your understanding 26

	$
Net pay February	1,840
Tax deducted in January – paid in February	500
Social security deducted in January – paid in February	100
	2,440

Test your understanding 27

D

Items A, B and C would be recorded in the 'statement of profit or loss' in arriving at profit after tax for the year, rather than 'other comprehensive income'.

Test your understanding 28

	$
Cost of machine	18,000
Transportation	1,700
Installation	500
	20,200
Depreciation at 10%	(2,020)
Carrying amount	18,180

Note that the repair cost is an expense charged to profit or loss.

Test your understanding 29

B

Test your understanding 30

$5,200

Amount capitalised: Cost $50,000 + $5,000 installation = $55,000. The warranty cost is expensed to profit or loss over the three-year warranty period.

Depreciable amount: Capitalised cost $55,000 – $3,000 estimated residual value = $52,000.

Pro-rata charge in the year of purchase 6/12 × 1/5 × $52,000 = $5,200.

Test your understanding 31

Loss on disposal $1,200

Proceeds = $20,000

Annual depreciation = $55,000 – $3,000 = $52,000/5 years = $10,400

Proceeds = $20,000

Carrying amount at disposal date = $55,000 – $5,200 – $10,400 – $10,400 – $7,800 = $21,200

Loss on disposal = 20,000 – $21,200 = $1,200

Test your understanding 32

$25,000

	$	$
Cost at 1 January 20X8	444,000	
Accumulated depreciation at 1 January 20X8		130,000
Revaluation surplus in year	15,000	
Carrying amount of disposals in year		17,000
Depreciation charge for the year		8,500
Cash paid – missing figure	25,000	
Property plant and equipment at 31 December 20X8 c/d		467,000
Accumulated depreciation at 31 December 20X8 c/d	138,500	
	622,500	622,500

Test your understanding 33

	$000
Operating profit	230
Add: Depreciation	40
Less: Profit on sale	(80)
	190
Increase in working capital	(15)
Cash generated from operations	175

Test your understanding 34

A, B and C

Test your understanding 35

$700 debit	$700
Insurance balance omitted	
Wages misposted – does not affect trial balance	Nil
Accrual omitted – does not affect trial balance	Nil

The accounting entries required to clear the suspense account and correct the trial balance are:

		$
Debit	Insurance	700
Credit	Suspense	700

Test your understanding 36

	$
Carrying amount at the beginning of the year	11,475
Purchases	4,362
Disposals at carrying amount	(3,257)
	12,580
Depreciation at 20%	2,516

Test your understanding 37

A

If proportionately more units of the more profitable products were sold, this would increase operating profit, and also return on capital employed. A reduction in income tax paid, a reduction in administration expenses or a reduction in finance charges are not relevant as they do not affect operating profit. Revaluation of land and buildings will increase capital employed, and lead to a reduction in return on capital employed.

Test your understanding 38

$$\frac{\text{Operating profit}}{\text{Total capital employed}} = \frac{\$2,700,000}{\$4,300,000} \times 100 = 63\%$$

Test your understanding 39

$$\frac{\text{Turnover}}{\text{Total capital employed}} = \frac{\$6{,}000{,}000}{\$4{,}300{,}000} = 1.39:1$$

Test your understanding 40

(a)

$$\frac{\text{Receivables + Bank}}{\text{Current liabilities}} = \frac{\$900{,}000 + \$50{,}000}{\$450{,}000} = 2.11 : 1$$

(b) **B**

If an entity had more current liabilities than current assets, it could be an indicator of liquidity problems, but not necessarily so. Many retail entities continue to operate effectively with a current ratio of less than 1:1.

Test your understanding 41

B

Test your understanding 42

(A3) (B1) (C4) (D2)

Test your understanding 43

	$
Inventory at beginning of year – raw materials	22,000
Purchases	220,000
Inventory at end of year – raw materials	(25,000)
Direct wages	300,000
Royalty on goods sold	45,000
Production overheads	360,000
Inventory at beginning of year – work in progress	4,000
Inventory at end of year – work in progress	(1,000)
	925,000

Test your understanding 44

Sales ledger control account

		$			$
1 Nov 20X1	Balance b/d	30,000		Bank	60,000
	Credit sales	67,000		Cash discounts	1,400
				Sales returns	4,000
			30 Nov 20X1	Bal c/d	31,600
		97,000			97,000

Test your understanding 45

		$
Debit	Irrecoverable debt expense account	1,750
Debit	Allowance for receivables	350
Credit	Sales ledger control account	2,100

Note that the reduction in the allowance is credited to the statement of profit or loss by offsetting it against the expense for irrecoverable debts.

Test your understanding 46

Bank reconciliation:	$
Balance at bank 31 July 20X1 (credit balance = cash in the bank for MNB)	10,300
Unpresented cheques	(1,700)
	8,600
Opening balance in cash book – balancing figure	8,450
Dishonoured cheque	(500)
Bank charges	(150)
Error ($400 × 2)	800
Cash book - debit balance	**8,600**

Test your understanding 47

	Units	Unit	Total
		$	$
Opening inventory	12	4	48
Purchases	60	5	300
Issue	(12)	4	(48)
Issue	(6)	5	(30)
Issue	(23)	5	(115)
Closing inventory	**31**	**5**	**155**

Test your understanding 48

A

Test your understanding 49

42 days

Average inventory is opening inventory $21,000 + closing inventory $18,000 = $39,000/2 = $19,500

Cost of goods sold is opening inventory $21,000 + purchases $165,000 – closing inventory $18,000 = $168,000

Inventory days is ($19,500 / $168,000 × 365 = 42 days

Test your understanding 50

C and E

Test your understanding 51

	$000
Prime cost	370
Factory indirect overheads	560
Increase in WIP	(65)
Factory cost of goods completed	865

Test your understanding 52

		$000
Additions		(30)
Asset disposal – cost	20	
– depreciation	(3)	
– carrying amount	17	
Profit on disposal	3	
Proceeds on disposal		20
Net cash outflow on investing activities		(10)

Test your understanding 53

D

Test your understanding 54

Rent account

		Dr	Cr
		$	$
1 Jul 20X2	Bal b/d ($900 × 1/3)	300	
1 Aug 20X2	Bank	900	
1 Nov 20X2	Bank	900	
1 Feb 20X3	Bank	1,200	
1 May 20X3	Bank	1,200	
30 Jun 20X3	Statement of profit or loss		4,100
30 Jun 20X3	Bal c/d ($1200 × 1/3)		400
		4,500	4,500

Rent expense = $4,100. Prepayment = $400.

Test your understanding 55

	$
Inventory	(6,000)
Receivables	2,000
Payables	(4,000)
Cash outflow	(8,000)

Test your understanding 56

		$
Receivables	4,000	
Bank (missing figure – debit balance)	12,000	16,000
Payables		8,000
Quick (acid) test		2:1

Note that inventory is excluded from the quick (acid) test ratio calculation.

Test your understanding 57

	$000
X1 – cost	15
X2 – net realisable value	6
X3 – cost	14
	35

Inventory is valued at the lower of cost and net realisable value for each separate item or product.

Test your understanding 58

Sales ledger control account

	$		$
Opening balance	20,000	Receipts from credit customers	155,000
Credit sales	170,000	Irrecoverable debts	3,000
		Contra	2,000
		Returns	6,000
		Closing balance	24,000
	190,000		190,000

Notes:

Cash sales are excluded from the ledger control accounts.

Any allowance for receivables is excluded from the sales ledger control account.

Test your understanding 59

	Yes	No
Dividends paid	✓	
Profit for the year	✓	
Directors' salaries		✓
Revaluation of property	✓	
Taxation		✓

Test your understanding 60

	$
Cash generated from operations	23,000
Interest paid	(3,500)
Taxation paid	(1,000)
Proceeds from sale of non-current assets	6,000
Payments for non-current assets	(7,000)
Dividend paid	(2,000)
Issue of loan notes	4,000
Net cash inflow	19,500

Chapter

22

References

The Board (2020) *IAS 1 Presentation of Financial Statements*. London: IFRS Foundation

The Board (2020) *IAS 2 Inventories*. London: IFRS Foundation.

The Board (2020) *IAS 7 Statement of Cashflows*. London: IFRS Foundation

The Board (2020) *IAS 16 Property, Plant and Equipment*. London: IFRS Foundation.

The Board (2020) *IAS 38 Intangible Assets*. London: IFRS Foundation.

The Board (2020) *IFRS 15 Revenue from Contracts with Customers*. London: IFRS Foundation.

The Board (2020) *The Conceptual Framework for Financial Reporting*. London: IFRS Foundation.

A

B

C

D

E

F

G

H

I

J

L

M

N

O

P

Q

R